CAN THE PUBLIC BE TRUSTED?

When do citizens voluntarily comply with regulations rather than act out of fear of sanctions? *Can the Public Be Trusted?* challenges prevailing regulatory paradigms by examining when democratic states can rely on voluntary compliance. Drawing on behavioral science, law, and public policy research, Yuval Feldman explores why voluntary compliance, despite often yielding superior and more sustainable outcomes, remains underutilized by policymakers. Through empirical analysis of policy implementation in COVID-19 response, tax compliance, and environmental regulation, Feldman examines trust-based governance's potential and limitations. The book presents a comprehensive framework for understanding how cultural diversity, technological change, and institutional trust shape voluntary cooperation. By offering evidence-based insights, Feldman provides practical recommendations for balancing trust, accountability, and enforcement in regulatory design. This book is essential reading for scholars, policymakers, and practitioners seeking to optimize regulatory outcomes through enhanced voluntary compliance. This title is also available as open access on Cambridge Core.

Yuval Feldman directs the Voluntary Compliance (VComp) Lab at Bar-Ilan University, integrating behavioral science, legal theory, and regulatory compliance. He has published over eighty articles in leading law and social science journals and received numerous honors, including a European Research Council (ERC) Advanced Grant and the Bruno Award. His book *The Law of Good People* (Cambridge, 2018) develops a framework for understanding the interaction between behavioral ethics, compliance, and regulation.

Can the Public Be Trusted?

ON THE PROMISE AND PERILS OF VOLUNTARY COMPLIANCE

YUVAL FELDMAN
Bar-Ilan University

CAMBRIDGE
UNIVERSITY PRESS

CAMBRIDGE
UNIVERSITY PRESS

Shaftesbury Road, Cambridge CB2 8EA, United Kingdom

One Liberty Plaza, 20th Floor, New York, NY 10006, USA

477 Williamstown Road, Port Melbourne, VIC 3207, Australia

314–321, 3rd Floor, Plot 3, Splendor Forum, Jasola District Centre, New Delhi – 110025, India

103 Penang Road, #05–06/07, Visioncrest Commercial, Singapore 238467

Cambridge University Press is part of Cambridge University Press & Assessment, a department of the University of Cambridge.

We share the University's mission to contribute to society through the pursuit of education, learning and research at the highest international levels of excellence.

www.cambridge.org
Information on this title: www.cambridge.org/9781009060943

DOI: 10.1017/9781009057998

When citing this work, please include a reference to the DOI 10.1017/9781009057998

First published 2025

A catalogue record for this publication is available from the British Library

A Cataloging-in-Publication data record for this book is available from the Library of Congress

ISBN 978-1-316-51221-0 Hardback
ISBN 978-1-009-06094-3 Paperback

Contents

Figures and Tables

FIGURES

TABLES

Preface

Consider the following real-life example from the COVID pandemic to illustrate the central dilemma this book addresses:

During a pandemic, a state must decide how to admit children to schools safely. There are two options:

1. Install thermometers at school entrances, operated by staff, to check each child's temperature.
2. Implement a system where parents sign daily pledges, affirming they've checked their child's temperature at home and the child is fever-free.

Each approach has its merits and drawbacks. The first method, reminiscent of classical command-and-control regulation, is highly effective but has several disadvantages: First, it may slow down the entry process; second, it could potentially intimidate children; and lastly, it's costly to staff each school daily with an inspector! Furthermore, it might prevent the ability of the parent and the child to develop any sense of autonomy in fulfilling their civic duties. In areas where no such enforcement exists, relying on some external regulator or enforcer might prove problematic (see discussion in Chapter 3 regarding the different crowding-out processes).

The second – trust-based – approach, relying on parental responsibility, seems appealing in terms of the costs being saved and the positive effects on society but presents its challenges:

- It requires trusting parents to conduct and report accurate checks.
- It necessitates a system to ensure pledges are consistently submitted.
- It ignores the possibility of false reports despite the pledges, especially by those parents whose kids have a fever, but who might have to work and hence will send their children to school.
- If parents are negligent or dishonest this might allow the pandemic to spread.

This scenario encapsulates the book's core exploration: the trade-offs between direct command and control regulation and trust-based systems in achieving public health and safety goals. It raises questions about the balance between effectiveness, cost, personal responsibility, and social trust in regulatory approaches.

This example illuminates a crucial question: To what extent should policymakers design their strategies based on the fear of those who might exploit the state's trust? We must consider the threshold of cooperation necessary for policymakers to shift from command-and-control regulatory approaches to trust-based policies.

The dilemma lies in whether to focus on worst-case scenarios, preparing for those who will only comply under coercion and monitoring, or to design policies such as self-regulation that can absorb a certain level of noncompliance, assuming such lack of cooperation will not escalate beyond manageable levels. This balance is critical in determining the overall effectiveness and sustainability of regulatory regimes.[1]

To what extent can states trust their citizens to cooperate with laws and regulations with the least possible use of coercive measures? What insights can the state and the public gain from adopting a legitimacy-based approach and to what extent is achieving legitimacy itself a desirable goal from a liberal democratic perspective? Our interest is not just theoretical but also related to an applied interest in the reliance on voluntary compliance:

Scalability: Can interventions that promote voluntary compliance, often tested in controlled settings, be effectively implemented on a larger scale among a heterogeneous population? This question reflects a wider discussion in behavioral economics about the challenges of scaling-up interventions from laboratory or small-scale field experiments to large-scale policy implementations.

External validity: Do the findings observed in laboratory settings also apply to real-world contexts with genuine stakes and complex motivational structures? Can voluntary compliance strategies be applied universally across diverse cultural, economic, and regulatory contexts?

Long-term effects: We lack robust longitudinal data to confirm whether the positive outcomes of voluntary compliance initiatives persist over a long period of time. What are the situations in which voluntary compliance proves to be more effective, cost-efficient, and expedient than traditional regulatory approaches?

THE INABILITY TO DEFINE **VOLUNTARY** COMPLIANCE

It should be stated upfront that "voluntary" is one of the most complex concepts to define. Part of the problem with voluntary compliance is related to understanding what exactly "voluntary" means in this context. Part of the discussion needed to advance our understanding of voluntary compliance involves distinguishing between various optional dichotomies. These distinctions can help clarify several aspects of compliance. They shed light on whether compliance is spontaneous or induced and reveal the regulatee's awareness of their decision to comply, as seen

[1] Coglianese, Cary, and Evan Mendelson. "Meta-regulation and self-regulation." In *The Oxford handbook on regulation,* edited by Martin Cave et al., Oxford University Press, 2010: 146–168.

in many nudge scenarios. Furthermore, they illuminate the interplay between voluntary actions and extrinsic measures, such as optional positive incentives. Lastly, these distinctions help us evaluate the true extent of the coercion-free nature of voluntary compliance measures. By examining these aspects, we can gain a more nuanced understanding of the complex dynamics involved in compliance behavior.

These discussions could lead to a much more nuanced and meaningful understanding of the antecedents of cross-sectional variation in levels and types of voluntary compliance. Such understanding may be promoted by focusing on dependent variables beyond the classical regulatory and compliance measures of impact (e.g., proportion and typology of cooperators, wide-ranging impact of regulatory tools, quality of cooperation, beyond-compliance measures of cooperation, and the likelihood of internalization processes following the regulatory intervention). Additionally, it is important to focus on the long-term effect of regulation (by measuring attitudes repeatedly on the same panel).

Chapters 1–3, and to some extent Chapter 4, explore the degree to which voluntary actions are truly free from coercion. Can we truly determine when people's actions are independent of indirect state coercion through mechanisms like market reputation? We examine various interpretations of voluntary compliance, considering whether it stems from intention, intrinsic motivation, morality, or noninstrumental factors. Our working definition is: behavior primarily motivated by factors other than state deterrence, such as reciprocity, trust, morality, or belief in the law's content.

This represents an ideal form of compliance achievable in certain contexts. The book examines the advantages and disadvantages of pursuing this ideal and whether regulators can effectively build upon it, or if some degree of monitoring will always be necessary, potentially preventing this ideal from being fully realized.

Returning to our COVID-19 example, we must weigh the long-term implications of trust-based approaches (such as parent pledges) against more stringent measures (like mandatory temperature checks). The key question becomes: Under which regulatory regime will the overall welfare of society, encompassing both public health and social capital, be maximized both in the short term and in the long term?

This consideration extends beyond immediate compliance rates to include broader societal impacts. Trust-based approaches may foster a sense of civic responsibility and strengthen social cohesion, potentially leading to more sustainable long-term compliance. Conversely, strict enforcement might ensure higher immediate compliance but could crowd out trustworthiness and diminish voluntary cooperation over time.[2] Some recent studies around this topic have come up with mixed results depending on punitive expectations of the public, the dimensions of strict enforcement, and the culture of a given country.[3]

2 Bohnet, Iris, Bruno S. Frey, and Steffen Huck. "More order with less law: On contract enforcement, trust, and crowding." *American Political Science Review* 95.1 (2001): 131–144.

3 Grimmelikhuijsen, Stephan, et al. "Does enforcement style influence citizen trust in regulatory agencies? An experiment in six countries." *Journal of Public Administration Research and Theory* 35.1 (2024): muae018.

Moreover, we must consider the adaptability of these approaches. As societal norms and circumstances evolve, how well can each regulatory strategy adjust to maintain effectiveness? The optimal approach may involve a nuanced combination of trust-based and enforcement-oriented policies, calibrated to the specific context and adaptable to changing conditions.[4]

This book addresses a crucial debate within the behavioral legal policy literature: Should we focus on changing people's intrinsic motivations toward law and regulation, or should we concentrate on altering situations through regulatory instruments such as corporate pollution controls or tax incentives? Or maybe in light of the booming concept of nudges – which are not coercive on one hand but don't focus on intrinsic motivation on the other – this research provides important insights into the limitations and potential of behavioral interventions.[5] While situational changes often yield more immediate and measurable success, we argue that fostering intrinsic motivation remains vital for long-term policy effectiveness.[6] We recognize that achieving and verifying intrinsic motivation may be unrealistic, which necessitates adopting a broader definition of voluntary compliance as noncoercive or nondeterrent regulatory approaches. However, even these approaches have limitations, as some form of monitoring will inevitably be necessary.

The fundamental tension in regulatory policy lies between traditional command-and-control approaches and more cooperative, trust-based regulatory strategies. While command-and-control regulation relies primarily on monitoring and sanctions to ensure compliance, trust-based approaches attempt to achieve compliance through less coercive means, such as pledges, self-regulation, and appeals to intrinsic motivation. This distinction raises important questions about how regulators should approach their mandate: Should they maintain strict oversight and enforcement, or can they effectively rely on cooperative approaches that foster voluntary compliance?

While ideally, compliance would be intrinsically motivated – what John Braithwaite calls "commitment" rather than "capitulation"[7] – the relationship between regulatory approach and compliance motivation is complex and context-dependent.

This book adopts an inclusive working definition of voluntary compliance that extends beyond purely intrinsic motivation to encompass all noncoerced compliance. While this broader definition presents certain theoretical challenges (discussed in Chapter 2), it offers practical advantages over focusing solely on intrinsic motivation. By examining compliance with noncoercive regulatory initiatives, we

4 Gunningham, Neil, and Darren Sinclair. "Smart regulation." In *Regulatory theory: Foundations and applications*, edited by Peter Drahos, Australian National University Press, 2017: 133–148.

5 Chater, Nick, and George Loewenstein. "The i-frame and the s-frame: How focusing on individual-level solutions has led behavioral public policy astray." *Behavioral and Brain Sciences* 46 (2023): e147.

6 Feldman, Yuval, and Oren Perez. "How law changes the environmental mind: An experimental study of the effect of legal norms on moral perceptions and civic enforcement." *Journal of Law and Society* 36.4 (2009): 501–535.

7 Braithwaite, John. "The essence of responsive regulation." *UBC Law Review* 44 (2011): 475–520.

can more objectively identify and analyze voluntary compliance without determining individual psychological motivations, which are inherently difficult to verify. Nevertheless, much of our discussion centers on fostering intrinsic motivation, as this represents the most desirable form of voluntary compliance.

This analysis suggests that rather than viewing command-and-control and trust-based regulation as mutually exclusive alternatives, regulators might benefit from understanding when and how to deploy different regulatory tools to achieve optimal compliance outcomes. The goal should be to identify conditions under which trust-based approaches can effectively foster voluntary compliance while maintaining sufficient oversight to protect public interests. The difficulty is in understanding whether voluntary compliance is related to intrinsic motivation, awareness, or simply having some discretion whether to comply or not.

Our thesis posits that encouraging individuals to adopt and believe in environmentally friendly behaviors is crucial not only for direct impact but also for creating a societal ecosystem that supports broader environmental initiatives. For instance, individuals with strong environmental values are more likely to demand corporate environmental responsibility through mechanisms like ESG (environmental, social, and governance) criteria. Moreover, they are more inclined to support government policies that incentivize environmentally friendly behavior, such as increased environmental taxes.[8]

Thus, the shift in people's environmental beliefs is significant beyond their immediate personal behaviors. It cultivates a sense of personal responsibility to effect change in the world around them, creating a more robust foundation for environmental policy.[9] Relying solely on nudges,[10] while ignoring the role of reflection and autonomy, may, in the long term, lead to a precarious situation where policies lack sustained public backing.[11]

In essence, while immediate behavioral changes are valuable, nurturing intrinsic motivations creates a more resilient and adaptable framework for environmental protection. Ultimately, policymakers must carefully assess the trade-offs between short-term compliance and long-term societal welfare, considering not only the immediate policy goals but also the broader implications for social trust, institutional legitimacy, and civic engagement.

This approach carries multiple risks that require careful consideration. First, it's difficult to predict how many people will cooperate with softer regulatory

8 Harring, Niklas, and Sverker C. Jagers. "Should we trust in values? Explaining public support for pro-environmental taxes." *Sustainability* 5.1 (2013): 210–227.

9 Schultz, P. Wesley, et al. "Values and their relationship to environmental concern and conservation behavior." *Journal of Cross-Cultural Psychology* 36.4 (2005): 457–475.

10 Sunstein, Cass R., and Lucia A. Reisch. *Trusting nudges: Toward a bill of rights for nudging*. Routledge, 2019.

11 Hertwig, Ralph, and Till Grüne-Yanoff. "Nudging and boosting: Steering or empowering good decisions." *Perspectives on Psychological Science* 12.6 (2017): 973–986.

approaches. Second, we must evaluate whether high-quality compliance is always necessary. In some contexts, like vaccination, the prevalence of compliance might be more important than its quality. Finally, we must consider the challenges of influencing not just public behavior, but also intrinsic motivation. Are we prepared to address these potential pitfalls?

This book will address these fundamental questions that arise in nearly every aspect of legal and social policymaking. These questions affect a wide range of issues, including compliance with tax laws, environmental regulations, traffic and driving laws, commercial ethics, and, more recently, COVID-19 regulations.

SHORT DESCRIPTION OF THE CHAPTERS IN THE BOOK

To better understand the flow of chapters in the book, please see the following list with their descriptions:

Chapter 1: Introduces the challenges of trusting public cooperation without monitoring and coercion, considering current research on the relationship between concepts such as cooperation and honesty, and examines the effectiveness of voluntary compliance.

Chapter 2: Analyses compliance motivations and their alignment with existing taxonomies: extrinsic vs. intrinsic motivations, cooperation vs. coercion, and trust-based vs. monitoring-based approaches. Explores the advantages of voluntary compliance over coerced compliance both in the short term and in the long term.

Chapter 3: Compares the impact of different regulatory tools (command and control, mandates, and incentives relative to reasoning, honesty oath, and nudge) on the crowding out of different types of intrinsic compliance motivations.

Chapter 4: Investigates moderating factors such as trust-related mechanisms, norms, and institutions, and their ability to explain the relationship between intrinsic motivation and compliance which is free of regulatory coercion.

Chapter 5: Discusses the perils of voluntary compliance, including variation between individuals in the likelihood of voluntary compliance, costs and risks of changing intrinsic motivation by states, and potential risks to the cooperating public. The chapter examines a crucial paradox: when governments shift from monitoring to seeking public collaboration, they may inadvertently create more problematic regulatory approaches. While appearing gentler on the surface, these strategies could prove more manipulative from a democratic standpoint and more intrusive from a liberal perspective.

Chapter 6: Explores the role of culture (e.g., trust, solidarity, rule of law) in predicting the success of voluntary compliance and its malleability toward trust-based rather than coercion-based regulation.

Chapter 7: Assesses the potential of technological tools to ensure voluntary compliance without coercion and improve predictability of trustworthiness, focusing on the ethical challenges such differentiation might create.
Chapter 8: Examines the likelihood of voluntary compliance in public health contexts, with emphasis on lessons learned during COVID-19 regarding trust in mask-wearing, social distancing, and vaccine uptake.
Chapter 9: Analyzes voluntary compliance in tax contexts, focusing on the importance of procedural justice and tax morale. Explores conditions under which governments can achieve optimal revenue levels.
Chapter 10: Investigates factors influencing voluntary compliance with environmental regulations, exploring the role of environmental motivation in shaping behavior and analyzing various types of pro-environmental actions.
Chapter 11: Concludes with normative messages on contexts where states can trust public cooperation without coercion, addressing jurisprudential and normative aspects of governments attempting to gain public cooperation without reliance on coercion

To help map the richness and the challenges of the book the following series of figures will be presented:

Figure 0.1 illustrates the rich tapestry of literature on voluntary compliance and its competing predictions regarding compliance motivations and drivers. At its center, the figure maps the parallel relationship between regulatory approaches (from coercive to cooperative) and motivational factors (from extrinsic to intrinsic). The right side presents contextual examples explored throughout the book, including cultural variations, and specific domains such as COVID-19 responses, environmental behavior, taxation, and ethical compliance (detailed in Chapters 6 and 8–10).

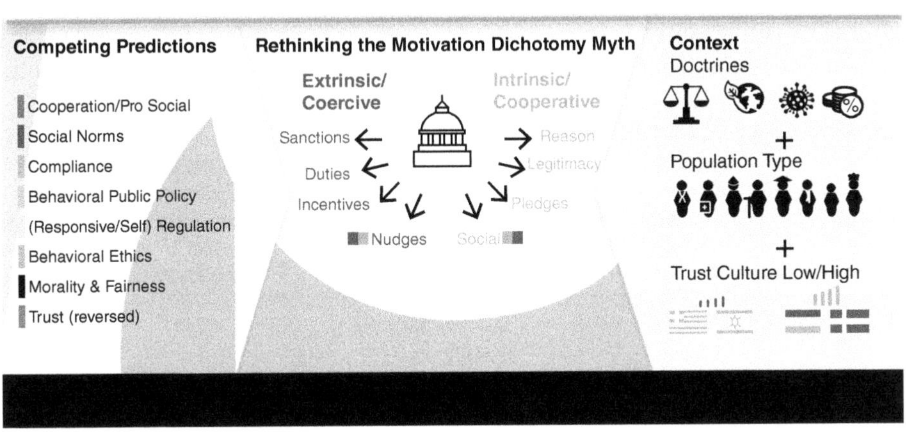

FIGURE 0.1 High variance in the likelihood of voluntary compliance generation and efficacy.

Figure 0.2 unpacks the concept of *effective* voluntary compliance across three dimensions. The left section addresses descriptive challenges, highlighting the limitations and contradictions in current data regarding the effectiveness of different regulatory interventions (explored in Chapters 2 and 4). The center examines the multidimensional impact of *effective* voluntary compliance across temporal, societal, and doctrinal contexts, arguing that its social and behavioral benefits extend beyond immediate compliance outcomes. The right section confronts normative challenges, including the role of governmental influence in fostering internalization and trust (Chapter 5) and the emerging reliance on technology in trust-based compliance systems (Chapter 7).

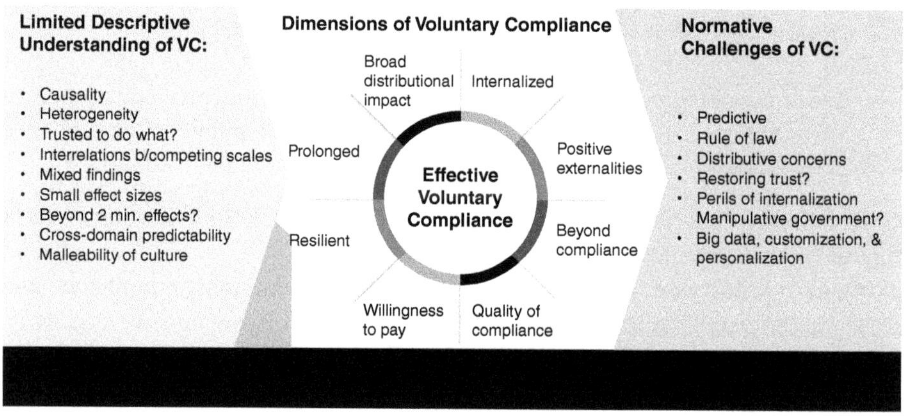

FIGURE 0.2 The challenges of effective voluntary compliance.

Figure 0.3 organizes diverse regulatory and compliance motivation approaches into paired dichotomies, revealing the relationship between regulatory strategies and compliance outcomes. As detailed in Chapters 3 and 4, this framework demonstrates that the voluntary compliance dilemma extends beyond the simple coercion–cooperation divide, encompassing broader questions about achieving public cooperation with laws and regulations.

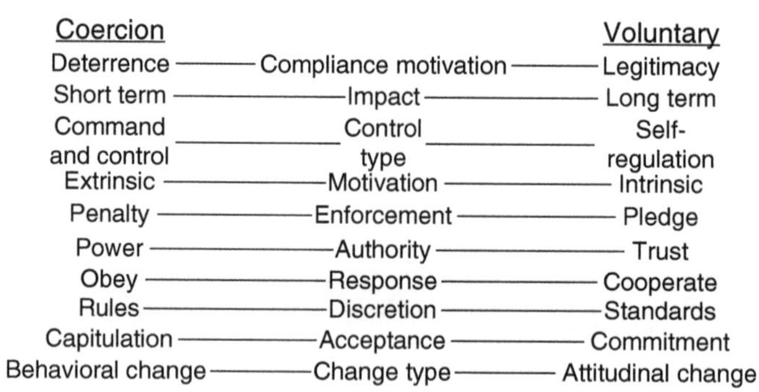

FIGURE 0.3 Regulatory style and compliance.

Figure 0.4 maps the multiple interpretations of "voluntary compliance," underscoring the concept's complexity and its relationship with the regulatory strategy. Chapter 1 examines how different theoretical traditions contribute distinct layers to our understanding of voluntary compliance, creating a multifaceted framework for analyzing compliance behavior.

Nature of Voluntariness	Regulatory Approach
Spontaneous	Order without law
Not coerced	No Sanction / monitoring?
Market like decision	Positive / negative incentives
Intrinsically motivation	Reasoning
Lack of Awareness	Habit / Nudge
Mandated	Duty
Reputation	Social norms
Citizenship	Legitimacy / trust
Moralistic	Guilt

FIGURE 0.4 The many accounts of voluntary compliance.

Acknowledgments

For their insightful comments, I wish to thank Tom Tyler, Robert MacCoun, Yotam Kaplan, Assaf Hamdani, Doreen Lustig, Alon Klement, Michael Simkovic, Hajin Kim, Lior Strahilevitz, Omri Ben-Shachar, Jacob Goldin, Jonathan Masur, Richard McAdams, Koen Verhoest, Nicola Riva, Flaminio Squazzoni, Fabio Franchino, Alessia Damonte, Benjamin van Rooij, Clair Hill, Lucia Reisch, Peter John, Anne-Lise Sibony, Shaun Marcom, David Levi-Faur, David Zarrin, and Neysun Mahboubi. I am also grateful to the participants in workshops at Michigan Law School, Penn Law School, Cambridge Sustainability, Cambridge Law, University of Chicago Law and Economics Workshop, Boston College, Yale Law School, Northeastern Business School, Cambridge Law School, National University of Singapore, Rotterdam University, Hebrew University Law Faculty Workshop, LSE Law School, Erasmus Law School, and the Safra Center for Ethics.

I want to thank the postdoctoral fellows who have worked with me in the VComp Lab: Dr. Libby Maman, Dr. Michaela Assouline, Dr. Liran Maimoni, Dr. Rinat Markovitch, and Dr. Yoni Slater. For their excellent research assistance, I thank Michael Goldboim, Shira Gelb, Mari Aharony, Inbal Moussafir, Shachar Ankori, Daniell Ben Arie, Itay Faust, Sammey Green, Ayala Sela, Daniel Janeli, Stav Gershon, Raz Halperin, Arie Balaban, Shoshana Ben-David, and Gaia Sarfati. Special thanks to Shachar Ankori for also overseeing the production processes and her handling of the index. I am also thankful to Gily Keidar and Danielle Ben Arie for their help with the graphic design and to Sigal Doron for her excellent linguistic editing.

Finally, I would like to express my deepest gratitude to my siblings and their spouses – Ronen, Hedva, Amir, and Hava Feldman – for their unwavering love and support. I am also grateful to my parents-in-law, Menachem and Zippi Finkelstein, for welcoming me into their family with open arms. To my beautiful and compassionate children – Liav, Yaara, Adva, Ori, and Daniel – you bring immeasurable joy and meaning to my life. Finally, to my spouse Michal, my best friend, partner, and the love of my life – your presence makes everything possible.

This book is dedicated to the memory of my mother, Rachel Feldman, who, despite numerous health challenges, showed remarkable strength in raising us single-handedly after the untimely passing of my father. Her unwavering dedication and resilience inspired my work and will continue to guide me always.

This research was supported by ERC AdG VComp 101054656.

Author's Note

Most discussions about regulation and trust focus on a familiar problem: the public's declining trust in government institutions. This book takes a different approach by examining a crucial but overlooked challenge: democratic governments' struggle to understand when, why, and to what extent citizens willingly cooperate with policies. At its heart, this book explores a paradox: While voluntary compliance – where people follow rules because they want to rather than because they're forced to – produces better results, regulators rarely truly rely on it.

Current research in psychology and related fields suggests that when people comply voluntarily, the results are better across multiple dimensions: compliance lasts longer, spreads to other areas of behavior, and produces higher quality outcomes than when people comply out of fear of punishment or desire for rewards. However, it remains unclear which regulatory tools and methods are likely to foster this sense of voluntariness and even less clear how to determine whether softer regulatory approaches genuinely lead to more voluntary responses. In the last decade, we've seen a significant shift toward "softer" regulatory approaches that try to build on trust and cooperation rather than force. These include self-regulation, nudges, public pledges, voluntary compliance programs by corporations, and new types of regulatory bodies that work alongside traditional enforcement agencies. Yet despite these changes and the clear benefits of voluntary compliance, most regulators remain reluctant to trust the public's willingness to cooperate.

Drawing on diverse fields – including regulation theory, behavioral ethics, public policy, and research on social cooperation – this book examines both the promise and challenges of voluntary compliance in modern governance. It asks fundamental questions: How can we identify which regulatory approaches best encourage lasting, high-quality compliance? Why do regulators keep falling back on traditional tools like monitoring, incentives, and punishments, even when these methods often undermine people's natural motivation to comply and can lead to worse outcomes over time? As the book develops, it becomes clear that regulators' hesitation is not without merit, given the limits of current empirical evidence on voluntary compliance and the challenges of government attempting to achieve compliance without coercion.

The book's first three chapters build a new framework for understanding three interconnected concepts: voluntary compliance, intrinsic motivation, and crowding out (how external pressures can weaken internal motivation). They examine how softer regulatory approaches, which are based on trust, legitimacy, and reasoning, can work together to create effective voluntary compliance across different personal, situational, regulatory, and cultural settings. Currently, two major gaps limit our understanding: We don't fully grasp how intrinsic motivation works or how exactly crowding out affects compliance behavior. These gaps make it difficult to see how different regulatory approaches might complement rather than conflict with each other.

Chapters 4–7 work to precisely define "effective voluntary compliance" and distinguish it from similar concepts. The book brings together diverse research to evaluate trust-based regulatory approaches through specific measurable indicators: compliance duration, positive societal ripple effects, rule internalization, and impacts on trust and social connections. This analysis helps identify which regulatory tools best encourage willing cooperation while protecting people's internal motivation to do the right thing.

The book then tackles several critical challenges to voluntary compliance's effectiveness. One major concern is distributive fairness: What happens when some people cooperate while others take advantage of regulators' trust? Another challenge emerges when governments try to influence people's internal motivations rather than just their behavior – potentially crossing into problematic territory from a liberal perspective. Chapter 7 explores how modern technology might help protect cooperation and enable regulators to treat cooperators and noncooperators differently, while Chapter 6 examines how cultural differences affect voluntary compliance outcomes.

To ground these theoretical insights, the book examines voluntary compliance in three regulatory areas: tax collection, healthcare policy (primarily COVID-related), and environmental protection. These case studies compare approaches based on legitimacy, moral appeal, and reputation. The research reveals important limitations in our current understanding, including inconsistent findings and relatively small effects of intrinsic motivation on compliance.

The concluding chapters of this book wrestle with the complex implications of voluntary compliance for democratic societies while offering practical guidance for regulatory implementation. While the research strongly advocates for trust-based regulation and procedural justice as long-term drivers of societal improvement and social capital development, it also acknowledges significant limitations. A key constraint emerges from the book's emphasis on ensuring rather than merely enhancing compliance – the persistent reality of substantial noncompliance challenges widespread implementation of purely trust-based approaches. Though research consistently demonstrates that procedural justice and legitimacy reliably predict compliance, they cannot guarantee universal adherence and, in some contexts, the cost of misplaced trust may prove too high. Nevertheless, the book maintains its fundamental commitment to public trust as a long-term regulatory strategy, even while recognizing the short-term risks this approach may entail.

Chapter 11 provides a practical taxonomy for navigating this tension, offering regulators a framework to assess when trust-based approaches are most appropriate based on factors such as required compliance quality, necessary proportion of adherence, and potential costs of excessive trust. The conclusion presents actionable recommendations for governments seeking to foster citizen cooperation across varied cultural and regulatory contexts, advocating for a balanced approach that builds trust with proven reliable actors while maintaining appropriate oversight where needed. Throughout, the book argues that while voluntary compliance holds tremendous potential, its successful implementation requires sophisticated understanding of the interplay between rules, incentives, and human motivation. This understanding becomes crucial in avoiding the paradox where attempts to create a more trusting regulatory environment inadvertently result in more intrusive and discriminatory practices. Only by comprehending these nuanced dynamics can regulators design approaches that enhance rather than suppress people's natural cooperative tendencies.

Conceptual Glossary

In this glossary, I will outline the main concepts this book advances and their meanings. Similar terms appear across different literatures. This makes it crucial to clarify the specific meanings of the concepts we focus on.

Differentiated Trust: Chapter 7 examines how trust can be calibrated based on past behavior and public response across regulatory domains. This differentiation creates potential risks: gaps between actual and perceived trustworthiness may undermine state credibility and correlations between past behavior and protected group membership require careful consideration.

Effective Voluntary Compliance: As detailed in Figure 0.2, this describes voluntary compliance that is sustainable over time, demonstrates higher willingness to pay, and resists external disruption. To be considered effective, voluntary compliance must reach sufficient participation rates relative to regulatory requirements and generate positive externalities for other societal factors.

Intrinsic Voluntary Compliance: This represents compliance driven by intrinsic motivation – a subset of voluntary compliance particularly relevant for regulatory tools like honesty oaths and reasoning approaches. Given the difficulty of objectively determining intrinsic motivation, our taxonomies generally use the broader definition of voluntary compliance (absence of regulatory coercion).

Subjective Crowding Out: Chapter 3 analyzes how people perceive their voluntary compliance being displaced by other regulatory tools. We examine the psychological mechanisms of motivation crowding out, focusing on individuals' experiences when regulatory interventions supersede their personal motivations to comply.

(Subjective) Trustworthiness: While we use an objective regulatory definition for voluntary compliance, our analysis of trustworthiness focuses on citizens' subjective feelings of being trusted by the state. This perceived trustworthiness plays a crucial role in building social capital among compliant citizens.

Voluntary Compliance: Chapter 2 explores various interpretations of "voluntary" compliance. While individual motivations for voluntary compliance can be difficult to assess externally, we adopt a regulatory-focused definition: compliance that occurs without regulatory coercion, distinguishing it from traditional command-and-control approaches.

1

Introduction

The idea of citizens' voluntary compliance and cooperative behavior is discussed from different perspectives in nearly all the social sciences (psychology, sociology economics, political science, criminology, and more) as well as in the literature of law and even philosophy.[1] From the outset, it seems safe to argue that obtaining voluntary compliance from citizens, especially if it is intrinsically motivated, is the most desirable and utopic method of governance.[2] However, to a large extent, policymakers feel that in order to trust the public to comply, thereby helping them uphold their commitment to protect the public interest, policymakers need strong assurances that those regulated will indeed behave according to the law. Without clear evidence about the effectiveness of voluntary compliance, policymakers fear they might harm rather than protect the public, potentially achieving worse outcomes and eroding their authority. This creates a prisoner's dilemma between states and their citizens,[3] where regulators adopt suboptimal policies and citizens view regulators as untrustworthy – all because regulators cannot reliably predict when and how the public will cooperate. By and large, much of this deficit is a function of the relatively weak and limited empirical basis of our understanding of when and to what extent people can be trusted in a given situation. As a result, risk-averse policymakers resort to monitoring and coercive measures, simply because it is very challenging to identify in advance the proportion of the public who will engage in

1 Kirchler, Erich, and Ingrid Wahl. "Tax compliance inventory TAX-I: Designing an inventory for surveys of tax compliance." *Journal of Economic Psychology* 31.3 (2010): 331–346. Tyler, Tom R., and Steven L. Blader. "Identity and cooperative behavior in groups." *Group Processes & Intergroup Relations* 4.3 (2001): 207–226.

2 Underhill, Kristen. "When extrinsic incentives displace intrinsic motivation: Designing legal carrots and sticks to confront the challenge of motivational crowding-out." *Yale Journal on Regulation* 33 (2016): 213–280.

3 The prisoner's dilemma demonstrates how self-interest, absent communication, leads individuals to choose betrayal over cooperation despite producing worse outcomes for everyone. For an elaboration see Axelrod, Robert. "Effective choice in the prisoner's dilemma." *Journal of Conflict Resolution* 24.1 (1980): 3–25.

more voluntary forms of cooperation in a given situation.[4] The recent COVID-19 pandemic crisis led some countries to resort to sanctions and fear-based rhetoric to ensure public cooperation and offers an excellent example of the mechanisms and effects of the more coercive process.[5] These coercive measures were employed despite the overwhelming and recognized evidence of the short and long-term advantages of more lenient, less coercive regulatory measures.[6] These have been shown to motivate people to engage in better quality compliance even in areas and contexts in which monitoring is impossible.[7] However, despite these clear advantages of relying on voluntary compliance, regulators across most regulatory domains resort to traditional approaches in more contexts than previously assumed because of what they perceive as the constant risk and lack of precise knowledge regarding the likelihood of cooperation.

Deeper insights into the likelihood and quality of voluntary compliance can help advance the theoretical understanding of the nature of the interaction between democratic governments and their residents. This can also improve policymaking in cases where voluntary cooperation produces better results than coerced compliance or when the tools makers could employ to coerce cooperation are limited, disruptive, or too costly. As an alternative approach, much of the discussion in this book will demonstrate the extent to which voluntary cooperation could and should be sought and the optimal ways to achieve it. The different costs of voluntary compliance in terms of equality, communication, uncertainty, and increased risk to the public will also be explored here. Additionally, the benefits of voluntary compliance in terms of its effect on autonomy, resilience, quality of compliance, and enhanced trust relationships will be discussed as well.[8]

The voluntary compliance paradigm developed here will enable researchers and policymakers to make better informed decisions about when, how, and to what extent states *could* resort to softer regulatory approaches and less coercive measures when trying to change the short and long-term behavior of the public. Since part of the discussion of voluntary compliance is related to intrinsic motivation, where people

4 Gächter, Simon, Benedikt Herrmann, and Christian Thöni. "Trust, voluntary cooperation, and socio-economic background: Survey and experimental evidence." *Journal of Economic Behavior & Organization* 55.4 (2004): 505–531.

5 Jørgensen, Frederik, Alexander Bor, and Michael Bang Petersen. "Compliance without fear: Individual-level protective behaviour during the first wave of the COVID-19 pandemic." *British Journal of Health Psychology* 26.2 (2021): 679–696.

6 Scholz, John T. "Cooperation, deterrence, and the ecology of regulatory enforcement." *Law and Society Review* 18.2 (1984): 179–224.

7 Krarup, Signe. "Can voluntary approaches ever be efficient?" *Journal of Cleaner Production* 9.2 (2001): 135–144.

8 Vaughan, Diane. "Autonomy, interdependence, and social control: NASA and the space shuttle challenger." *Administrative Science Quarterly* (1990): 225–257. Findings show that noncompliance with EU Emissions Trading Systems regulations correlates with low levels of trust. See: Jo, Ara. *Trust and compliance: Evidence from the EU emissions trading scheme*. Grantham Research Institute on Climate Change and the Environment, 2019.

believe in the purpose of the relevant law or regulation, we must examine if states are even allowed to engage in practices that could potentially shift people's intrinsic motivation toward the "desirable" direction. The behavioral analysis of when states can trust members of the public will be accompanied by a normative discussion on when, and to what extent, states *should* do so, given the potential broader effects of such an approach on the public and other players. Clearly, to evaluate these effects, it is important to identify who will cooperate voluntarily and to what extent.[9]

The different chapters of the book will address issues such as what regulatory approach is more likely to elicit voluntary compliance, what could undermine such compliance, and what needs to be done to understand how the individual, situational, regulatory, and cultural dimensions of the behavioral regulatory policy paradigm interact. In addition, we will review and analyze methods balancing the risk to the public of reduced regulatory coercion and monitoring with the potential long-term advantages to the public arising from a cooperative regulatory approach in which deserving regulatees feel trusted. The nature of this analysis is inevitably flexible, as it must adapt to the distinct types of behaviorally based regulatory tools and target different populations with diverse backgrounds and ethical preferences.

REVERSING THE TRUST PARADIGM

In research and policy analysis, "trust" is typically studied in the context of the trust of the public in institutions.[10] This book seeks to reverse the trust paradigm and examine how we can identify ex ante when governments can trust the public and to what extent, and how trust should affect the regulatory style and governments' efforts to foster the public's voluntary cooperation. The apparently unambiguous goal of governments to have their citizens engage in voluntary compliance is examined from different social science perspectives (psychology, social economics, political science, criminology, law, and philosophy).[11]

9 Compare with Chapter 6 on technological enforcement.

10 Cook, Timothy E., and Paul Gronke. "The skeptical American: Revisiting the meanings of trust in government and confidence in institutions." *Journal of Politics* 67.3 (2005): 784–803.

11 For psychology see: Clark, Cory, et al. "Predictors of COVID-19 voluntary compliance behaviors: An international investigation." *Global Transitions* 2 (2020): 76–82; Alm, James, Erich Kirchler, and Stephan Muehlbacher. "Combining psychology and economics in the analysis of compliance: From enforcement to cooperation." *Economic Analysis and Policy* 42.2 (2012): 133–151. For social economics see: Tyler, Tom R. *Why people obey the law*. Princeton University Press, 2006; Kirchler, Erich, Erik Hoelzl, and Ingrid Wahl. "Enforced versus voluntary tax compliance: The 'slippery slope' framework." *Journal of Economic Psychology* 29.2 (2008): 210–225; McKendall, Marie, Beverly DeMarr, and Catherine Jones-Rikkers. "Ethical compliance programs and corporate illegality: Testing the assumptions of the corporate sentencing guidelines." *Journal of Business Ethics* 37 (2002): 367–383. For political science see: Bodea, Cristina, and Adrienne LeBas. "The origins of voluntary compliance: Attitudes toward taxation in urban Nigeria." *British Journal of Political Science* 46.1 (2016): 215–238; Sjöstedt, Martin, and Amanda Linell. "Cooperation and coercion: The quest for quasi-voluntary compliance in the governance of African commons." *World Development* 139 (2021): 105333. For criminology

To date, the empirical basis of our understanding of when and to what extent the public can be trusted in a given situation is weak both theoretically and normatively. Theoretically, since most of the relevant literature (compliance, ethics cooperation, and more) rarely intersects. Most studies focus narrowly on single behaviors (e.g., recycling) in specific regulatory contexts, failing to examine broader questions about distributive effects across heterogeneous populations or the long-term sustainability of behavioral changes driven by regulation. While meta-analyses suggest that most people are generally honest, this narrow focus limits our understanding of how compliance patterns vary across different contexts and time frames and how regulatory interventions affect different population segments over time.[12] While we now know how to identify the contexts in which self-perceived "good" people can cheat,[13] we still do not know how to accurately predict ex ante in what regulatory contexts such unethicality will dominate.[14] The behavioral public policy literature typically evaluates interventions like nudges and incentives based on their immediate effectiveness.[15] However, it often overlooks crucial dimensions such as population heterogeneity, long-term effects on trust, and variations in compliance quality across different regulatory tools. As a result, risk-averse policymakers resort to monitoring and to coercive measures due to insufficient information about the benefits of voluntary compliance. The costs associated with such approaches include resulting inequality, communication challenges, uncertainty, and increased risk to the public.[16] For example, the recent COVID-19 pandemic led many countries to resort to sanctions and fear-based rhetoric to gain public cooperation following the first signs of noncompliance.[17] These governments had limited ability to understand whether fear-based rhetoric

see: Jackson, Jonathan, et al. "Why do people comply with the law? Legitimacy and the influence of legal institutions." *British Journal of Criminology* 52.6 (2012): 1051–1071; Jackson, Jonathan, and Jacinta M. Gau. *Carving up concepts? Differentiating between trust and legitimacy in public attitudes towards legal authority*. Springer International Publishing, 2016. For law see: Tyler, Tom R., and Jonathan Jackson. "Popular legitimacy and the exercise of legal authority: Motivating compliance, cooperation, and engagement." *Psychology, Public Policy, and Law* 20.1 (2014): 78; Scholz, John T. "Voluntary compliance and regulatory enforcement." *Law & Policy* 6.4 (1984): 385–404; Murphy, Kristina. "Procedural justice and its role in promoting voluntary compliance." *Regulatory Theory: Foundations and Applications* (2017): 43–58. For philosophy see: Gribnau, Hans. "Voluntary compliance beyond the letter of the law: Reciprocity and fair play." In *Building trust in taxation*, edited by B. Peeters, H. Gribnau, and J. Badisco, Intersentia, 2017: 17–49. See also Figure 0.1.

12 Köbis, Nils C., et al. "Intuitive honesty versus dishonesty: Meta-analytic evidence." *Perspectives on Psychological Science* 14.5 (2019): 778–796.

13 Feldman, Yuval. *The law of good people: Challenging states' ability to regulate human behavior*. Cambridge University Press, 2018.

14 Feldman, Yuval, and Yotam Kaplan. "Preference change and behavioral ethics: Can states create ethical people?" *Theoretical Inquiries in Law* 22.2 (2021): 85–110.

15 Oliver, Adam, ed. *Behavioural public policy*. Cambridge University Press, 2013.

16 Vaughan. "Autonomy, interdependence, and social control."

17 Stolow, Jeni A., et al. "How fear appeal approaches in COVID-19 health communication may be harming the global community." *Health Education & Behavior* 47.4 (2020): 531–535.

actually improved any aspects of compliance, not to mention a lack of knowledge on the possible negative effect on intrinsic motivation.

CURRENT RESEARCH ON VOLUNTARY COMPLIANCE

The existing literature on voluntary cooperation lacks any discussion about how its analysis interacts with regulatory policy or whether it can contribute to a systematic shift in governments' regulatory policies. Much of the compliance literature provides only limited insights into fundamental theoretical questions. While studies explore various concepts – ranging from trust and incentives to behavioral ethics and nudges – they rarely examine how different regulatory interventions affect trust or solidarity over time. In contrast, this book combines regulatory policy theory and behavioral theories to answer the most fundamental question of compliance – when and to what extent should states trust the public to cooperate and what regulatory policies are most likely to foster voluntary compliance? This book's premise is that the motivation to cooperate voluntarily with a regulatory requirement cannot be understood by using only a single perspective (see Figure 0.4). Therefore, behavioral, institutional, and cultural contexts must be combined across many types of doctrines, cultures, and behaviors to help create a regulatory balance that can offer insights into the advantages and disadvantages of striving for voluntary compliance.

As described, one of the hardest challenges in discussing voluntary compliance is spelling out the relevant notion of voluntariness. Another related challenge is to explicate the effect of motivation on the scope of voluntariness. For instance, should we count situations where people are deterred to comply as mere compliance rather than voluntary compliance? What about cases where an individual motivation to comply is instrumental – in that it pays to behave according to what the state wants, or simply harder not to comply?

In this chapter, we will examine the concept of voluntary compliance from multiple perspectives and will briefly review some of the main parts of the existing literature. While some of these bodies of literature will receive more attention in later chapters, our focus at this stage is to provide a broad overview and establish a working definition of the voluntary compliance dilemma.

DIVERSE COMPLIANCE MOTIVATIONS

In the last decade, the regulation literature (compare with Figure 0.3) has been studying softer approaches aimed at reducing the excessive regulatory burden and eliciting voluntary compliance.[18] Two especially relevant paradigms are responsive regulation

[18] Attari, Shahzeen Z., et al. "Preferences for change: Do individuals prefer voluntary actions, soft regulations, or hard regulations to decrease fossil fuel consumption?" *Ecological Economics* 68.6 (2009): 1701–1710.

and self-regulation. The widely discussed *responsive regulation* paradigm advances a more flexible and customized approach whereby smarter, less coercive regulatory measures are targeted at those parts of the population for whom coercive measures are not needed.[19] The emerging *self-regulation* paradigm focuses on transferring responsibility for the creation of standards and their enforcement to the regulated parties or businesses.[20]

Some of the complexity of the issues around compliance is reflected in the growing research on compliance motivation,[21] in which scholars differ in their perceptions of what can be considered the leading motivation for compliance, whether procedural legitimacy, costs of compliance, deterrence, obligation to obey the law, or political orientation.[22] As part of our conceptual work regarding regulatory theory, we will present an original taxonomy which will examine to what extent voluntary compliance and regulatory tools can be considered *cooperative*. This includes defining, for example, large incentives or System 1 nudges,[23] with a special focus on trust-based and behavioral-based regulation.

[19] Ayres, Ian. *Responsive regulation: Transcending the deregulation debate*. Vol. 35. Oxford University Press, 1992.

[20] Bartle, Ian, and Peter Vass. "Self-regulation within the regulatory state: Towards a new regulatory paradigm?" *Public Administration* 85.4 (2007): 885–905.

[21] Feldman, Yuval. "Five models of regulatory compliance motivation: Empirical findings and normative implications." *Handbook on the Politics of Regulation* 1 (2011): 335–346.

[22] For procedural legitimacy see: Tyler, Tom R. "The psychology of legitimacy: A relational perspective on voluntary deference to authorities." *Personality and Social Psychology Review* 1.4 (1997): 323–345; Tyler, Tom R. "Psychological perspectives on legitimacy and legitimation." *Annual Review of Psychology* 57.1 (2006): 375–400. For costs of compliance see: Botchkovar, Ekaterina V., Charles R. Tittle, and Olena Antonaccio. "General strain theory: Additional evidence using cross-cultural data." *Criminology* 47.1 (2009): 131–176; Donovan, Jenny L., and David R. Blake. "Patient non-compliance: Deviance or reasoned decision-making?" *Social Science & Medicine* 34.5 (1992): 507–513; Paternoster, Raymond, and Sally Simpson. "A rational choice theory of corporate crime." In *Routine activity and rational choice*, edited by Roland V. Clarke and Marcus Felson, Routledge, 2017: 37–58. For deterrence see: Apel, Robert. "Sanctions, perceptions, and crime: Implications for criminal deterrence." *Journal of Quantitative Criminology* 29 (2013): 67–101; Nagin, Daniel S. "Deterrence in the twenty-first century." *Crime and Justice* 42.1 (2013): 199–263. For obligation to obey the law see: Fine, Adam, et al. "Rule orientation and behavior: Development and validation of a scale measuring individual acceptance of rule violation." *Psychology, Public Policy, and Law* 22.3 (2016): 314–329; Posch, Krisztian, et al. "'Truly free consent'? Clarifying the nature of police legitimacy using causal mediation analysis." *Journal of Experimental Criminology* 17 (2021): 563–595; Tyler, Tom. "Procedural justice and policing: A rush to judgment?" *Annual Review of Law and Social Science* 13.1 (2017): 29–53. For political orientation see: Prior, Markus. "Media and political polarization." *Annual Review of Political Science* 16.1 (2013): 101–127; Spohr, Dominic. "Fake news and ideological polarization: Filter bubbles and selective exposure on social media." *Business Information Review* 34.3 (2017): 150–160.

[23] That is, nudges that influence behavior in an implicit manner – such as defaults, which may go entirely unnoticed, as will be explored in Chapter 4. For elaboration see, for example, Van Gestel, L. C., M. A. Adriaanse, and D. T. D. De Ridder. "Do nudges make use of automatic processing? Unraveling the effects of a default nudge under type 1 and type 2 processing." *Comprehensive Results in Social Psychology* 5.1–3 (2021): 4–24.

Defining regulatory tools based on their level of cooperativeness becomes more complicated because the incorporation of behavioral approaches into regulation has led to a dramatic increase in the variety of regulatory tools available to policymakers (e.g., nudges, framing, pledges, and so on). While the greater number of tools available makes the instrument choice dilemma more complex, this variety also offers concrete, quantitative means to measure and compare their efficacy.[24] The nudge approach for example,[25] based on the influential work of Richard Thaler and Cass Sunstein,[26] represents an important addition to the regulatory choice dilemma, and has led numerous scholars to examine when nudges can be relied upon to replace more compulsory rules.[27]

SOME ADVANTAGES OF VOLUNTARY COMPLIANCE

As suggested (compare with Figures 0.3 and 0.4), and as will be developed in more detail in the next few chapters, the advantages of voluntary compliance and its importance have been recognized across a number of dimensions.[28] Voluntary compliance, especially when driven by intrinsic motivation,[29] is usually considered more sustainable and of higher quality than coerced compliance. In contrast, when governments rely on coercive measures due to lack of trust in public cooperation, compliance tends to be short term and heavily dependent on the presence of sanctions.[30] In addition, reliance on intrinsic voluntary compliance is more likely to increase feelings of trust and trustworthiness among regulated entities,[31] entail lower enforcement costs,[32] and result in a higher quality of cooperation.[33] Compliance that is more voluntary is also more likely to lead to greater

24 Feldman, Yuval, and Orly Lobel. "The incentives matrix: The comparative effectiveness of rewards, liabilities, duties, and protections for reporting illegality." *Texas Law Review* 88 (2009): 1151–1212.

25 See Chapter 4, which focuses on regulatory approaches that attempt to explain nudges.

26 Thaler, R., and Cass Sunstein. "Nudge: Improving decisions about health, wealth and happiness." *Amsterdam Law Forum; HeinOnline: Online*, 2008.

27 E.g., Feldman, Yuval, and Orly Lobel. "Behavioral trade-offs: Beyond the land of nudges spans the world of law and psychology." *San Diego Legal Studies Paper* 14–158 (2014).

28 Winter, Søren C., and Peter J. May. "Motivation for compliance with environmental regulations." *Journal of the Association for Public Policy Analysis and Management* 20.4 (2001): 675–698.

29 Cooter, Robert. "Do good laws make good citizens? An economic analysis of internalized norms." *Virginia Law Review* 86 (2000): 1577–1602.

30 Gunningham, Neil, Robert A. Kagan, and Dorothy Thornton. "Social license and environmental protection: Why businesses go beyond compliance." *Law & Social Inquiry* 29.2 (2004): 307–341.

31 Feldman, Yuval. "The complexity of disentangling intrinsic and extrinsic compliance motivations: Theoretical and empirical insights from the behavioral analysis of law." *Washington University Journal of Law and Policy* 35 (2011): 11–52.

32 Frey, Bruno S. "Does monitoring increase work effort? The rivalry with trust and loyalty." *Economic Inquiry* 31.4 (1993): 663–670.

33 Feldman, Yuval, and Henry E. Smith. "Behavioral equity." *Journal of Institutional and Theoretical Economics: JITE* (2014): 137–159.

resilience, as evidenced in findings from research on therapeutic jurisprudence and on happiness.[34]

Efforts to understand how to stimulate and encourage voluntary compliance have acknowledged that factors related to fairness, morality, duty to obey, and trust play an important role in compliance in areas from environmental and health regulations (including COVID-19 measures) to traffic and tax laws.[35]

VOLUNTARY COMPLIANCE AND INTRINSIC MOTIVATION

Chapter 2 will explore the complex nature of intrinsic motivation and its relationship to voluntary compliance. While intrinsic motivation is often seen as a key component of voluntary compliance – driving people to want to comply rather than merely following rules – this relationship warrants closer examination.[36] First, intrinsic motivations may sometimes work against truly voluntary compliance, particularly when they operate through self-imposed constraints like guilt rather than genuine willingness to comply.[37] In contrast, a normative perspective on a rule of law would arguably want normative members of society to have strong instincts about engaging in wrongful behavior.

Indeed, there is a growing recognition of the importance of intrinsic compliance motivations,[38] which supports the preference for tailoring the focus of compliance

34 For greater resilience see: Patall, Erika A., Harris Cooper, and Jorgianne Civey Robinson. "The effects of choice on intrinsic motivation and related outcomes: A meta-analysis of research findings." *Psychological Bulletin* 134.2 (2008): 270. For therapeutic jurisprudence see: Winick, Bruce J. "The jurisprudence of therapeutic jurisprudence." *Psychology, Public Policy, and Law* 3.1 (1997): 184–206; Wexler, David. "Therapeutic jurisprudence: An overview." *Thomas M. Cooley Law Review* 17 (2000): 125–134. For happiness see: Posner, Eric A., and Cass R. Sunstein, eds. *Law and happiness*. University of Chicago Press, 2010; Bronsteen, John, Christopher Buccafusco, and Jonathan S. Masur. *Happiness and the law*. University of Chicago Press, 2014.

35 Dana, Jason, Roberto A. Weber, and Jason Xi Kuang. "Exploiting moral wiggle room: Experiments demonstrating an illusory preference for fairness." *Economic Theory* 33 (2007): 67–80. Fine, Adam D., and Benjamin van Rooij. "Legal socialization: Understanding the obligation to obey the law." *Journal of Social Issues* 77.2 (2021): 367–391. Torgler, Benno. "Tax morale, rule-governed behaviour and trust." *Constitutional Political Economy* 14 (2003): 119–140. Van Rooij, Benjamin, et al. "Compliance with COVID-19 mitigation measures in the United States." *Amsterdam Law School Research Paper* 2020–21 (2020).

36 See the discussion of my work with Barak-Corren and Robinson on the ultra-orthodox enlistment, where the focus is on having them want to be in the military not just complying with the regulation against their will. Barak-Corren, Netta, Shelley Robinson, and Yuval Feldman. "Haredi draft from the Haredi perspective: Attitudes, motivations, and social perceptions." Available at SSRN, March 25, 2024, https://ssrn.com/abstract=4776500.

37 O'Keefe, Daniel J. "Guilt as a mechanism of persuasion." In *The persuasion handbook: Developments in theory and practice*, edited by James Price Dillard and Michael Pfau, SAGE Publications, 2002: 329–344; Massi Lindsey, Lisa L. "Anticipated guilt as behavioral motivation: An examination of appeals to help unknown others through bone marrow donation." *Human Communication Research* 31.4 (2005): 453–481.

38 Gächter, Simon, and Jonathan F. Schulz. "Intrinsic honesty and the prevalence of rule violations across societies." *Nature* 531.7595 (2016): 496–499; Dai, Zhixin, Fabio Galeotti, and Marie Claire

measures to individuals' motivations.[39] Generally, it has been shown that extrinsic motivators, such as deterrence, are not only less effective than was once assumed, but that they also undermine the ability of intrinsic motivation to enhance compliance with regulatory efforts.[40]

WHY INTRINSIC VOLUNTARY COMPLIANCE CAN'T BE OUR WORKING DEFINITION

As suggested, despite the importance of intrinsic motivation to voluntary compliance, it will be unrealistic to limit our discussion of voluntary compliance only to such behaviors for the following reasons: First, in most cases behavior is not motivated by just one factor and hence it will be impossible to isolate what actually affected people. Second, there is some limitation in basing the definition of voluntary on the subjective feeling of the individual what motivates them. Third, as will be discussed in more detail in Chapters 2 and 3, which focus on crowding-out motivation, it is not fully clear from the literature what counts as intrinsic and what counts as extrinsic motivation. Insights from the social norms literature also have great importance because this approach, too, weakens the dichotomy between external versus internal measures, as people's reactions to their surrounding communities reflect a combination of intrinsic and extrinsic motivations.[41]

Furthermore, intrinsic voluntary compliance is not just an unrealistic ideal, it also raises hard challenges for compliance research, for example, in circumstances that do not present a clear moral violation, not *malum in se* but rather *malum prohibitum*.[42] In such cases, where the violation is a legal but not a moral one, adding an explanation for why it is important to obey the law might intensify guilt, which would prevent people from making fully free choices. From many perspectives, the fact that someone makes a choice because they want to, and not because of any

Villeval. "Cheating in the lab predicts fraud in the field: An experiment in public transportation." *Management Science* 64.3 (2018): 1081–1100; Luttmer, Erzo FP, and Monica Singhal. "Tax morale." *Journal of Economic Perspectives* 28.4 (2014): 149–168; Tyler, Tom R., and Steven L. Blader. "Can businesses effectively regulate employee conduct? The antecedents of rule following in work settings." *Academy of Management Journal* 48.6 (2005): 1143–1158.

39 Cooter. "Do good laws make good citizens?" 1577; Porat, Ariel. "Changing people's preferences by the state and the law." *Theoretical Inquiries in Law* 22.2 (2021): 215–246; Feldman, Yuval, and Yotam Kaplan. "Ethical blind spots and regulatory traps: On distorted regulatory incentives, behavioral ethics and legal design." In *Law and economics of regulation: Economic analysis of law in European legal scholarship*. Vol. 11, edited by K. Mathis and A. Tor, Springer International Publishing, 2021: 37–54.

40 See generally Frey, Bruno S., and Felix Oberholzer-Gee. "The cost of price incentives: An empirical analysis of motivation crowding-out." *American Economic Review* 87.4 (1997): 746–755; Underhill. "When extrinsic incentives displace intrinsic motivation," 213.

41 Feldman, Yuval. "The expressive function of trade secret law: Legality, cost, intrinsic motivation, and consensus." *Journal of Empirical Legal Studies* 6.1 (2009): 177–212.

42 Travers, Michael L. "Mistake of law in mala prohibita crimes." *University of Chicago Law Review* 62.3 (1995): 1301–1331.

external measure, positive or negative, seems like the most complete representation of voluntary compliance. However, there are many examples in which being intrinsically motivated might actually reduce your freedom to choose a specific behavior. For example, if someone wants to improve their social image by complying with a certain rule, is it plausible to argue that their compliance is not voluntary only because it is done for extrinsic reasons? A similar question arises about the nonvoluntary nature of the compliance in the opposite context, where, for example, an individual's compliance is driven by guilt.

BEHAVIORAL ETHICS AND COMPLIANCE

Behavioral ethics is another relatively new field exploring people's ethical decision-making processes.[43] My previous book, *The Law of Good People*, examines the challenges faced by governments that need to regulate people who do not view themselves as needing regulation in view of their ethical and legal perceptions or, more accurately, misperceptions, of their own behavior.[44] Scientific research on honesty and dishonesty has spiked in recent years,[45] with most studies mentioning "dishonesty" in the context of rule following or rule violation.[46] Laboratory studies of dishonesty have shown dishonesty in games to be related to various types of unethical behaviors outside the laboratory. For example, dishonesty in dice-roll and coin-toss tasks has been associated with free-riding on buses and not returning undeserved pay.[47] This line of study could presumably lead to some pessimism about the advisability of the government trusting the public. However, because the opposite phenomenon – a connection between honesty and compliance to rules that are not solely related to honesty – has not been studied, it is not clear to what extent honest people differ from cooperators or compliers. For example, are honest people more likely to care for the environment?

In addition, current dishonesty research, while focusing on the notion of the proportion of dishonest people,[48] nonetheless fails to predict the distributive effect of the situational factors that might undermine honesty.[49] The recognition that

[43] Treviño, Linda K., Gary R. Weaver, and Scott J. Reynolds. "Behavioral ethics in organizations: A review." *Journal of Management* 32.6 (2006): 951–990.

[44] Feldman, Yuval, Benjamin van Rooij, and Melissa Rorie. "Rule-breaking without crime: Insights from behavioral ethics for the study of everyday deviancy." *The Criminologist* 44.2 (2019): 8–11.

[45] Bazerman, Max H., and Francesca Gino. "Behavioral ethics: Toward a deeper understanding of moral judgment and dishonesty." *Annual Review of Law and Social Science* 8.1 (2012): 85–104; Feldman. *The law of good people*.

[46] Pascual-Ezama, David, et al. "Cheaters, liars, or both? A new classification of dishonesty profiles." *Psychological Science* 31.9 (2020): 1097–1106.

[47] Dai, Galeotti, and Villeval. "Cheating in the lab predicts fraud in the field." Potters, Jan, and Jan Stoop. "Do cheaters in the lab also cheat in the field?" *European Economic Review* 87 (2016): 26–33.

[48] Gibson, Rajna, Carmen Tanner, and Alexander F. Wagner. "Preferences for truthfulness: Heterogeneity among and within individuals." *American Economic Review* 103.1 (2013): 532–548.

[49] Feldman. *The law of good people*.

different people engage in misconduct on different levels of awareness and intentionality is an important contribution to understanding the likelihood of coercive versus cooperative regulatory styles succeeding in creating voluntary compliance in different segments of the population. Reviewing this literature is also important to help discern the proportion of "good" people in a given population, who might be more likely to react to trust-enhancing cooperative regulatory measures.

According to this approach, if even moral people cannot be completely trusted, given their ability to misperceive their own behavior, how can states trust the entirety of the public? Along that line, in related works I have endeavored to create a taxonomy of the situations in which government should be more concerned about the likelihood of nondeliberative and unintended unethicality.[50] In addition, in collaboration with others, I have also examined various ways in which a design aimed at inducing people to self-deceive themselves might work,[51] as might the "self-imposed red lines" that people adopt for their self-serving interpretations of the law.[52]

The connection between behavioral ethics and compliance is especially relevant to Chapter 9 on taxation morals, where we concentrate primarily on the resemblance of the literature on this issue with research about honesty and examine to what extent the predictions from honesty research are relevant to compliance. In contrast, in Chapter 10 on environmental compliance, our examination focuses mostly on cooperation and prosocial behavioral research to understand when compliance is likely to occur. While these distinctions are not mutually exclusive, it is possible to recognize that there are systematic differences between these three regulatory domains. Thus, for example, we can explore several questions when discussing taxation. Can people be trusted to declare their donations without attaching the receipts? Extending beyond the issue of taxation to traffic laws why can't Israelis for example, be trusted to turn right on red?[53]

HOW MANY COOPERATORS DO WE NEED?

The connection between honesty and compliance discussed in this chapter becomes especially important regarding the question of governments' ability to trust the public. The roles of institutions and external regulatory contexts vary significantly when examining compliance, cooperation, and honesty as distinct behavioral phenomena.

50 Feldman, Yuval, and Yotam Kaplan. "Big data and bounded ethicality." *Cornell Journal of Law and Public Policy* 29 (2019): 39–94.

51 Pe'er, Eyal, and Yuval Feldman. "Honesty pledges for the behaviorally-based regulation of dishonesty." *Journal of European Public Policy* 28.5 (2021): 761–781.

52 Feldman, Yuval, and Eliran Halali. "Regulating 'good' people in subtle conflicts of interest situations." *Journal of Business Ethics* 154 (2019): 65–83.

53 Barak-Corren, Netta. "Regulating for integration by behavioral design: An evidence-based approach for culturally responsive regulation." *Regulation & Governance* 16.4 (2022): 1079–1100.

However, since there are possible correlations between honesty and compliance, it is important to examine current research to understand how many people we know are lying and to gain at least some preliminary accounts of how many people cheat. In that context, the conclusions from the broad research seems to be mixed. On the one hand, an extensive meta-analysis suggested that,[54] on average, 50 percent of people are dishonest.[55] On the other hand, a highly influential economics paper found the number of liars appears to be much smaller.[56] This inconsistency, which appears in honesty studies as well, raises important questions about whether enough people will comply voluntarily without coercion. The research emphasizes the need to gather empirical data about compliance patterns before determining the appropriate level of regulatory coercion. In Chapter 11, we will present a taxonomy of legal situations more conducive to voluntary compliance, along with an analysis of the proportion of compliers needed for different regulatory contexts.

VOLUNTARY COMPLIANCE AND TRUST

An additional important body of literature involves the growing recognition of the importance of trust and legitimacy in achieving voluntary compliance. Numerous studies across almost all the social sciences have sought to understand what builds trust and how trust contributes to the creation of a just and functioning society.[57] However, most of this literature focuses on how people can trust public and legal institutions and overlooks the mechanisms state institutions need in order to trust the public.[58] As will be discussed in more detail in Chapter 4, in the context of commercial translations, a prime example of the importance of trust and reputation can be found in classic studies of the diamond industry, which has long relied on the extralegal enforcement of its business norms and the order without law mentioned

54 Gerlach, Philipp, Kinneret Teodorescu, and Ralph Hertwig. "The truth about lies: A meta-analysis on dishonest behavior." *Psychological Bulletin* 145.1 (2019): 1–44.

55 As we discuss in later chapters, another area which also focused on proportion of cooperators, defectors, and conditional cooperators is behavioral game theory, where, in many studies, the majority, or at least the largest group in society, is of conditional cooperators. Chaudhuri, Ananish, and Tirnud Paichayontvijit. "Conditional cooperation and voluntary contributions to a public good." *Economics Bulletin* 3.8 (2006): 1–14.

56 In that regard, see a quote from Abeler, Johannes, Daniele Nosenzo, and Collin Raymond. "Preferences for truth-telling." *Econometrica* 87.4 (2019): 1115–1153. "Three key insights follow from our study. First, our meta-analysis shows that the data are not in line with the assumption of payoff-maximizing reporting but rather with some preference for truth-telling. Second, our results suggest that a preference for being seen as honest and a preference for being honest are the main motivations for truth-telling. Finally, policy interventions that rely on voluntary truth-telling by some participants could be very successful, in particular if it is made hard to lie while keeping a good reputation" (1120).

57 Glaeser, Edward L., et al. "Measuring trust." *Quarterly Journal of Economics* 115.3 (2000): 811–846; Hardin, Russell. "Trust and trustworthiness." *Russell Sage Foundation* (2002).

58 Hibbing, John R., and Elizabeth Theiss-Morse. *Congress as public enemy: Public attitudes toward American political institutions*. Cambridge University Press, 1995.

in the next paragraph.[59] Similar dynamics can be found in the cotton industry and among farmers in Shasta County, California.[60] While clearly there are some reciprocal relationships between parties in places, many of the mechanisms related to the ability of governments to trust its own citizens,[61] drawing on concepts such as social capital and interpersonal trust.[62]

VOLUNTARY COMPLIANCE WITHOUT LAW?

As mentioned in the early parts of the chapter, it is possible to consider voluntary compliance in situations where it is social norms and not any particular laws that need to be observed. The order without law literature offers an additional theoretical perspective on voluntary compliance, indicating that behavioral change can be achieved even with the limited involvement of the state.[63] This type of literature usually emphasizes that in many situations, people can find alternative arrangements to those imposed by the law. This book goes beyond this insight; our approach aims to understand how people could interact to build sufficient confidence with the government, while enabling the government to take a step back and trust in the public's reactions. Ideally, these prevailing public responses would be stable and effective enough over time to reduce the need for alternative regulatory mechanisms. Such an approach by the state could be taken in the context of public responses to regulation (as in cases such as using children's car seats, where voluntary compliance was achieved by applying reason and science),[64] or even in the absence of

59 Bernstein, Lisa. "Opting out of the legal system: Extralegal contractual relations in the diamond industry." In *Contract-freedom and restraint*, edited by Richard A. Epstein, Routledge, 2013: 359–403.

60 Bernstein, Lisa. "Private commercial law in the cotton industry: Creating cooperation through rules, norms, and institutions." *Michigan Law Review* 99.7 (2001): 1724–1790; Ellickson, Robert C. *Order without law: How neighbors settle disputes*. Harvard University Press, 1991.

61 Monitoring technology is deployed for multiple purposes in universities, in contexts from learning analytics to attendance tracking, as a replacement for placing trust in students. See Ross, Jen, and Hamish Macleod. "Surveillance, (dis)trust and teaching with plagiarism detection technology." Proceedings of the 11th International Conference on Networked Learning, 2018.

62 Putnam, Robert. "Social capital: Measurement and consequences." *Canadian Journal of Policy Research* 2.1 (2001): 41–51. See, for example, Luria, Gil, Ram A. Cnaan, and Amnon Boehm. "National culture and prosocial behaviors: Results from 66 countries." *Nonprofit and Voluntary Sector Quarterly* 44.5 (2015): 1041–1065. Other explanations have been given for prosocial behavior, such as: religious participation (see Putnam, Robert D., and David E. Campbell. *American grace: How religion divides and unites us*. Simon & Schuster, 2012). Changes in patterns of prosocial motivation between Grades 2 and 12 were examined in five samples from four countries: West Germany, Poland, Italy, and the United States. See Boehnke, Klaus, et al. "Developmental pattern of prosocial motivation: A cross-national study." *Journal of Cross-Cultural Psychology* 20.3 (1989): 219–243.

63 Ellickson. *Order without law*.

64 Zaza, Stephanie, et al. "Reviews of evidence regarding interventions to increase use of child safety seats." *American Journal of Preventive Medicine* 21.4 (2001): 31–47; Rivara, Frederick P., et al. "Booster seats for child passengers: Lessons for increasing their use." *Injury Prevention* 7.3 (2001): 210–213; Stasson, Mark, and Martin Fishbein. "The relation between perceived risk and preventive action: A

regulation, such as where the social and community norms emerged without any state involvement (as in the case of allocating fencing costs among the farmers in Shasta County).[65] Nonetheless, it is unclear whether one can even define compliance with social and community norms as voluntary.

While these studies demonstrate how social norms can shift around smoking in public spaces and sexual harassment for example, caution is needed in generalizing these examples to other behavioral contexts, as the mechanisms driving norm change may be context-specific.[66] These few cases do not enable us to build a comprehensive account of when monitoring and sanctioning are not needed. Nor do they help us understand the mechanisms of why voluntary compliance succeeded in these cases. In fact, these few cases have provided a very limited view of the social norms involved in voluntary compliance.

For example, as will be discussed in more detail in Chapter 4, Lisa Bernstein conducted studies in the diamond and the cotton industries,[67] and found that close social groups with shared values are able to function and maintain order and rules with only limited formal legal intervention. One last important point in the context of nonformal controls begs the question, is compliance also voluntary when people are not being coerced formally, but, rather, motivated to act in a certain way directly through incentives, or indirectly through community norms or reputational mechanisms?

BEHAVIORAL PUBLIC POLICY AND VOLUNTARY COMPLIANCE

The literature on behavioral public policy and voluntary compliance, emphasizing the recognition that people cannot comply solely by reacting to prices, as classical economics suggests, serves as one of the basic foundations of this book.[68] Behavioral

within-subject analysis of perceived driving risk and intentions to wear seatbelts." *Journal of Applied Social Psychology* 20.19 (1990): 1541–1557; Şimşekoğlu, Özlem, and Timo Lajunen. "Social psychology of seat belt use: A comparison of theory of planned behavior and health belief model." *Transportation Research Part F: Traffic Psychology and Behaviour* 11.3 (2008): 181–191.

65 Ellickson. *Order without law*.

66 Existing evidence indicates an overall significant post-legislative positive effect regarding voluntary home-smoking restrictions. See Monson, Eva, and Nicole Arsenault. "Effects of enactment of legislative (public) smoking bans on voluntary home smoking restrictions: A review." *Nicotine & Tobacco Research* 19.2 (2017): 141–148; Wakefield, Melanie A., et al. "Effect of restrictions on smoking at home, at school, and in public places on teenage smoking: Cross sectional study." *BMJ* 321.7257 (2000): 333–337. How #MeToo did what laws did not. See more: Leopold, Joy, et al. "The hashtag heard round the world: How# MeToo did what laws did not." *Equality, Diversity and Inclusion: An International Journal* 40.4 (2021): 461–476; Parker, Christine. "How to win hearts and minds: Corporate compliance policies for sexual harassment." *Law & Policy* 21.1 (1999): 21–48.

67 Bernstein. "Opting out of the legal system"; Bernstein. "Private commercial law in the cotton industry."

68 Chetty, Raj. "Behavioral economics and public policy: A pragmatic perspective." *American Economic Review* 105.5 (2015): 1–33.

public policy has contributed to the greater variety of regulatory tools available to policymakers (e.g., nudges, framing, pledges, and so on) aimed at changing people's behavior through means other than coercion. However, behavioral public policy suffers from the absence of any normative perspective.

Nudges, as discussed earlier in this chapter,[69] are situated somewhere in the middle between the more intrinsically oriented interventions, such as morality and reason, and the more extrinsically oriented measures, such as incentives and sanctions. Nudges themselves can, of course, range from educating people to reminding them of their morality and the likelihood of getting sanctioned. They can also lie somewhere in the middle where they simply change the choice of architecture of legal decisions.[70]

As suggested, there has been a growth in the number of interventions in the behavioral regulatory era, with some comparative studies conducted.[71] However, most of these intervention studies do not involve concrete, quantitative measurements and thus do not allow for comparisons of the efficacy of the interventions,[72] leading numerous scholars to examine when nudges can be relied upon to replace more compulsory rules.[73] The seminal work of Katy Milkman, for example, shows the negative correlation between expert predictions of which regulatory intervention is better at changing behavior.[74] An important goal of Milkman's important comparative project was distinguishing between the various long-term impacts of the vast array of behavioral regulatory tools, which lie somewhere on the spectrum between intrinsic and extrinsic measures, as discussed earlier in this chapter.

THE IMPORTANCE OF CULTURE IN VOLUNTARY COMPLIANCE

To better understand the issue of compliance, it is critical to clarify how trust, social diversity, social inclusiveness, solidarity, and helpfulness affect the different levels of social cohesion across different countries. Generally, countries with a higher value of social cohesion are more likely to have also higher level of innovation and social progress.[75] In Chapter 6 of the book, focusing on culture and

69 Thaler, Richard H., and Cass R. Sunstein. *Nudge: The final edition.* Yale University Press, 2021.

70 Münscher, Robert, Max Vetter, and Thomas Scheuerle. "A review and taxonomy of choice architecture techniques." *Journal of Behavioral Decision Making* 29.5 (2016): 511–524.

71 Mertens, Stephanie, et al. "The effectiveness of nudging: A meta-analysis of choice architecture interventions across behavioral domains." *Proceedings of the National Academy of Sciences* 119.1 (2022): e2107346118.

72 Feldman and Lobel. "The incentives matrix," 1151.

73 Feldman and Lobel. "Behavioral trade-offs."

74 Milkman, Katherine L., et al. "A 680,000-person megastudy of nudges to encourage vaccination in pharmacies." *Proceedings of the National Academy of Sciences* 119.6 (2022): e2115126119.

75 Borisov, I. V., and Szergej Vinogradov. "The role of social cohesion in social and economic processes." In *Business and management sciences: New challenges in theory and practice.* Szent István University,2018: 521–539.

voluntary compliance, we examine the huge variation that exists between the different countries with regard to trust, power, collectivist versus individualistic culture, solidarity, and other values that appear to predict the likelihood of voluntary compliance.[76]

NONVOLUNTARY COMPLIANCE

As described, important literature has emerged that identifies voluntary compliance and self-regulation as the optimal guiding principles of regulatory governance. However, these concepts can be elusive and thus difficult to fully understand conceptually and practically on both the individual level and the aggregate level, which is of interest to the regulatory state. In this book, we show that many of these studies on voluntary compliance were carried out in very contextualized circumstances, thus limiting the possibility of generalizing them to the realm of broader policies.

Fully understanding the effect of sanctions on voluntariness becomes even more complicated when we move from a behavioral perspective to the less direct, sociological one, according to which punishment is viewed as a solidarity-producing mechanism.[77] Generally speaking, the literature lacks clarity on whether voluntary compliance encompasses situations involving positive incentives or behavioral nudges – a crucial distinction since the relationship between coercion and voluntary compliance isn't always straightforward. For example, if a reputational mechanism is put in place that increases the reputational cost people will pay for not upholding a certain norm, can their ensuing compliance be considered voluntary because people want to belong to a certain community in which certain behavior is considered desirable? In essence, as we will examine Chapter 2 (discussing intrinsic motivation), our question is whether compliance can be considered voluntary only when people autonomously *want* to cooperate. Or is compliance voluntary also when people are not being coerced, but, rather, incentivized to act in a certain way directly through incentives, or indirectly, through reputational mechanisms? Similarly, when nonvoluntary interventions induce voluntary compliance, how long do they successfully affect people's choices to cooperate? Some of these questions will be examined in Chapter 3, which examines the connection between regulatory tools used and the likelihood that voluntary compliance will emerge from them.

76 Elahee, Mohammad N., Susan L. Kirby, and Ercan Nasif. "National culture, trust, and perceptions about ethical behavior in intra-and cross-cultural negotiations: An analysis of NAFTA countries." *Thunderbird International Business Review* 44.6 (2002): 799–818; Oh, Se Hyung. "Do collectivists conform more than individualists? Cross-cultural differences in compliance and internalization." *Social Behavior and Personality: An International Journal* 41.6 (2013): 981–994.

77 Garland, David. *Punishment and modern society: A study in social theory*. University of Chicago Press, 1993.

SPONTANEOUS COMPLIANCE

The first approach of spontaneous compliance could differentiate between induced and spontaneous, where the focus on the definitions is related to the process whereby people choose to comply. Under this approach, any time an individual chooses to comply without any external intervention, the compliance should be considered voluntary. Examples of such an approach include various social and commercial practices that have evolved in relational contracts; for instance, certain personal behaviors affecting the environment, such as not eating meat or buying recycled products.[78] Behavior that arises naturally from a person's own desires, without any external inducement, can also be classified as voluntary. Such a definition of voluntary limits the contexts in which voluntary compliance is possible. For example, in the area of taxation, there is no expectation that people will freely want to pay a tax that does not exist.

SHOULD VOLUNTARY COMPLIANCE BE AN AWARE CHOICE?

A second approach, following our previous discussion regarding nudges, might focus on conscious awareness that a decision is voluntary and people are fully aware of their behavior and its impact. It is possible to argue that when people unreflectively engage in compliance because it is a default in their behavior, the voluntary element of it is absent. Embedded in this approach is some criticism of nudge approaches, which are considered noncoercive. However, as discussed in Chapter 4 in more detail, nudges do take advantage of some automatic behavioral processes, much like engaging in binge watching on Netflix and other streaming services may be induced because of the default created by the next episode in a ten-second feature.[79]

VOLUNTARY COMPLIANCE AS AN AUTONOMOUS CHOICE

Another related approach to voluntary compliance involves the question of whether the regulatee's feeling is a subjective or an objective one.[80] Arguably, if people subjectively feel that they have the freedom not to comply, their compliance is voluntary, even if this is not the case objectively.[81] Alternatively, if people in a certain group make similar compliance choices, it may be reasonable to conclude that

[78] Moser, Andrea K. "Consumers' purchasing decisions regarding environmentally friendly products: An empirical analysis of German consumers." *Journal of Retailing and Consumer Services* 31 (2016): 389–397.

[79] http://persuasion-and-influence.blogspot.com/2018/03/next-episode-in-10seconds-default.html.

[80] Nelson, Robert M., et al. "The concept of voluntary consent." *American Journal of Bioethics* 11.8 (2011): 6–16.

[81] Ryan, Richard M., and Edward L. Deci. "Autonomy is no illusion." In *Handbook of experimental existential psychology*, edited by Jeff Greenberg, Sander L. Koole, and Tom Pyszczynski, The Guilford Press, 2004: 449–479.

there may be some social mechanism that causes people to comply, even if they subjectively think that this is their voluntary choice.

VOLUNTARY COMPLIANCE AS DISCRETION

Another way to understand the meaning of voluntary compliance is related to the amount of discretion that states give people. The more discretion people have, the more they can apply their own interpretations of what is expected from them.[82] While it is generally understood that giving people discretion cannot be considered voluntary compliance, it is true that when people have multiple behaviors to choose from within certain requirements, it can have an effect on their actions.[83] People can decide: Should I always wear a mask, or only when I'm near people? Never turn on red, or turn on red when traffic allows for it?

Much of the inspiration for writing this book came from the COVID crisis, during which states came to understand the classical limits of compliance. One prominent dilemma faced by many countries involved whether to trust people with the decision to wear a mask all the time or only when there were people near them.[84] Since the definition of what it means to be near people is flexible, people have some leverage to define terms like crowded or near people and decide their level of compliance and how careful they wanted to be. In Israel for example, in the early days of COVID, everybody had to wear masks all the time, as if their discretion could not be trusted. This nondiscretionary approach reflects certain assumptions in Israeli culture. For example, unlike most other countries in the world, some countries, including Israel don't allow cars to turn right on red lights, not trusting drivers' discretion.[85] There is a similar debate between safe sex and abstention in the literature regarding sex education for adolescents.[86]

VOLUNTARY COMPLIANCE AND ENFORCEMENT

A third approach, and probably the easiest to work with, focuses on whether the motivation behind compliance is coerced by state sanctions or by other barriers

[82] Schlag, Pierre. "Rules and standards." *UCLA Law Review* 33 (1985): 379–430; Kaplow, Louis. "Rules versus standards: An economic analysis." In *Scientific models of legal reasoning*, edited by Scott Brewer, Routledge, 2013: 11–84.

[83] Feldman, Yuval, and Doron Teichman. "Are all legal probabilities created equal?" *New York University Law Review* 84 (2009): 980–1022.

[84] As, for example, was the situation in the US. See DeJonckheere, Melissa, et al. "Views on COVID-19 and use of face coverings among US youth." *Journal of Adolescent Health* 68.5 (2021): 873–881.

[85] Zador, Paul, Jack Moshman, and Leo Marcus. "Adoption of right turn on red: Effects on crashes at signalized intersections." *Accident Analysis & Prevention* 14.3 (1982): 219–234.

[86] Kohler, Pamela K., Lisa E. Manhart, and William E. Lafferty. "Abstinence-only and comprehensive sex education and the initiation of sexual activity and teen pregnancy." *Journal of Adolescent Health* 42.4 (2008): 344–351.

which makes noncompliance impossible. An example of the latter can be found in the context of public transportation. There are some places where there is simply no way to travel without a ticket. In such places, people are likely to be complying with at least some public transportation rules.

In some cases, administrative tools, such as fines, are used to enforce fare payment, for example. There are several enforcement strategies such as: increasing the fine amount; improving the fine collection procedure; changing the offence from civil to criminal; improving the ability to identify the identity of the passengers; and adopting a joint fast-track justice procedure for paying fines.[87]

In other public transportation systems, where enforcement is accomplished using inspectors,[88] the compliance is voluntary but there is some risk of being caught not complying that people take into account.[89] Although current research distinguishes between totally voluntary and coerced voluntary behavior, it is not entirely clear what level of expected sanction could be seen as reducing or even eliminating the individual's perceived or actual voluntarism.

TECHNOLOGY AND VOLUNTARY COMPLIANCE

The relationship between voluntary compliance and enforcement is closely linked to another concept that is already significantly impacting compliance: the use of monitoring technology and algorithmic predictions. These advancements enhance the ability of states to "trust" certain individuals in specific contexts that were previously difficult to predict or verify.

Chapter 7 will examine the contribution of technology to the emergence of voluntary compliance in light of technology's capacity to improve monitoring and to make the monitoring mechanism less noticeable. The goal of technology in our context is to make it easier for people to trust each other. This is not because they actually do trust each other, but because an algorithm suggests that they can be more relaxed about the risks they take when trusting people. Technology enables

[87] Hansen, Stephen, Brian Whitelaw, and Janis D. Leong. "Tackling fare evasion on Calgary transit's CTrain system." *Sustaining the Metropolis* 84 (2012): 84–95. https://onlinepubs.trb.org/onlinepubs/circulars/ec177.pdf#page=94; Larwin, Thomas F. "Off-board fare payment using proof-of-payment verification." Vol. 96. Transportation Research Board, 2012. https://ssti.us/wp-content/uploads/sites/1303/2012/03/Proof-of-payment-TRB.pdf; Torres-Montoya, Mariana. "Tackling fare evasion in Transantiago: An integrated approach." Transportation Research Board 93rd Annual Meeting, No. 14-4641. 2014; Reddy, Alla V., Jacqueline Kuhls, and Alex Lu. "Measuring and controlling subway fare evasion: Improving safety and security at New York City Transit Authority." *Transportation Research Record* 2216.1 (2011): 85–99.

[88] Bijleveld, Catrien. "Fare dodging and the strong arm of the law: An experimental evaluation of two different penalty schemes for fare evasion." *Journal of Experimental Criminology* 3 (2007): 183–199; Barabino, Benedetto, Cristian Lai, and Alessandro Olivo. "Fare evasion in public transport systems: A review of the literature." *Public Transport* 12 (2020): 27–88.

[89] Dai, Galeotti, and Villeval. "Cheating in the lab predicts fraud in the field." Barabino, Lai, and Olivo. "Fare evasion in public transport systems."

less intrusive forms of surveillance that could reduce behavioral resistance. While this suggests a need to minimize surveillance's negative effects, we must also consider whether increased technological monitoring should be accompanied by greater tolerance for minor infractions. The cashless economy illustrates this tension – while it reduces the need for trust-based tax compliance through technological solutions, public resistance to COVID contact-tracing apps demonstrates that technological surveillance, even for clear public benefit, often faces significant opposition.[90] Chapter 7 will also look at what types of apps and technological monitoring people are more likely to resist.

INCENTIVES AND VOLUNTARY COMPLIANCE

An additional regulatory approach, which is based on incentives and will be discussed in more detail in Chapter 2 (which focuses on intrinsic motivation), Chapter 3 (which focuses on crowding out), and Chapter 10 (which focuses on environmental compliance), is related to increasing the use of incentives.[91] Incentives such as subsidies and tax breaks have various advantages over sanctions since they are seen as being better suited for fostering cooperation, encouraging innovation, and reducing enforcement costs. Part of the advantage of incentives seems to be in the fact that they cause people to want to comply even when they do it for extrinsic financial reasons. However, especially with higher incentives and when environments are competitive, people may not really have a real choice other than to behave in a way that will maximize the regulatory incentives they receive for compliance. In such situations, one might question whether incentivized compliance, which could be viewed as voluntary, is indeed truly voluntary. This is especially true if we remember that part of the attempt to clarify what voluntary compliance is related to examining when it might be enduring, lead to positive externalities, and cause people to engage in behavior beyond compliance.

VOLUNTARY COMPLIANCE AND SELF-REGULATION

As described, relevant literature has emerged that identifies voluntary compliance and self-regulation as the optimal guiding principles of regulatory governance. Both processes are heavily conditioned upon the creation of trust both between people and between people and their governments. However, these concepts can be elusive. As a result, it is difficult to fully capture important behavioral and institutional factors that moderate the behavioral effect of different regulatory governance

[90] Rowe, Frantz. "Contact tracing apps and values dilemmas: A privacy paradox in a neo-liberal world." *International Journal of Information Management* 55 (2020): 102178.

[91] Laffont, Jean-Jacques, and Jean Tirole. *A theory of incentives in procurement and regulation*. MIT Press, 1993.

measures.[92] Considering the range of situations in which there is public interest in promoting honest and ethical behavior, this lacuna is especially significant for legal and public policy, as such behavior goes beyond mere compliance with the rules.[93] While a liberal democratic state may only be able to expect and demand compliance concerning what is required by the law, it is invaluable to understand what underlies questions of compliance as well as behavior that goes beyond compliance with explicit rules. Our ability to accurately predict such behavior influences policy regarding how to best encourage both accounts of honesty regarding compliance and other aspects of ethicality, which can contribute to better theoretical predictions about voluntary cooperation with different regulatory measures.

Thus, the main purpose of this book is to create a new conceptual framework from voluntary compliance that will combine concepts from different literatures, such as being honest, trustworthy, moral, compliant, and cooperative. It will also examine to what extent findings from the different literatures can help explain and accurately predict voluntary compliance and in what contexts. Clearly, there are many situations in life where one is required to comply. These include contexts where, for example, honesty does not play an important part (e.g., environmental compliance), some contexts within which compliance and honesty are far more tightly intertwined (e.g., misreporting income on tax forms), and still more contexts within which the relevant behavior appears to be linked primarily to rule-surpassing honesty. Other contexts involve some other aspect of substantive ethicality, as distinct from mere compliance (e.g., reporting problems in the sale of property, withholding information that could help a customer find a less costly solution, or information about an imminent price drop).[94]

THE DESIRED PROPORTION OF VOLUNTARY COOPERATORS AND REGULATORS' DILEMMA

In light of these dilemmas about nonvoluntary interventions, other issues to be examined at the group level are the proportion of people who are likely to cooperate and their characteristics relative to the group; that is, whether they belong to the weaker or stronger parts of the group.[95] Other questions include: How can

92 Barak-Corren, Netta, and Yael Kariv-Teitelbaum. "Behavioral responsive regulation: Bringing together responsive regulation and behavioral public policy." *Regulation & Governance* 15 (2021): S163–S182.

93 Bicchieri, Cristina. *The grammar of society: The nature and dynamics of social norms*. Cambridge University Press, 2005.

94 In the relevant chapters, I will discuss some of the working papers in which cross-domain predictability of human misconduct is examined normatively (with Aronson and Lobel) and behaviorally (with Assoulin, Slater, and Gilad).

95 For the proportion of people in the group in the context of honesty, see Gneezy, Uri, Bettina Rockenbach, and Marta Serra-Garcia. "Measuring lying aversion." *Journal of Economic Behavior &*

regulators determine in advance whether or not the advantages from voluntary compliance will be outperformed by a complete lack of compliance? How likely it is that people will hold moral views that reflect those of the state? Are there people who are more likely to engage in voluntary compliance across all disciplines? These issues become important at the level of the regulatory toolbox available to policymakers. Here, there are many barriers to relying on regulatory tools aimed at enhancing voluntary compliance in order to create a culture of compliance and trust within states. Indeed, many models have attempted to offer various taxonomies of compliance. For example, Valerie Braithwaite's motivational postures of commitment differentiates between the following modes of compliance: capitulation, resistance, disengagement, and game playing, which are helpful for thinking about such variation.[96]

SITUATIONAL ANALYSIS OF VOLUNTARY COMPLIANCE

The variation in compliance motivation discussed in this chapter with regard to the likelihood of voluntary compliance may not depend on just who the particular individual is, but also on the environment in which that individual is operating.[97] Behavioral ethics research indicates that most people are capable of engaging in ordinary unethicality if they are able to deceive themselves, either deliberately, by finding a justification for noncompliance, or with limited deliberateness, by engaging in motivated reasoning in ambiguous situations.[98] Thus, according to this approach, when policymakers are interested in determining when they can trust people to exhibit a greater likelihood of cooperation, they need to pay special attention to the situational characteristics that might enhance the likelihood that more people will cooperate voluntarily with the government's approach. These characteristics include lack of ambiguity, clear victims, the logic behind the regulation, and visible compliance behavior.[99]

LACK OF RESEARCH ON CONTEXTUAL FACTORS

While, as suggested, the literature on voluntary compliance is vast and multifaceted, it nevertheless is unable to generalize beyond the specific context being studied.

Organization 93 (2013): 293–300; Brewer, Marilynn B., and Roderick M. Kramer. "Choice behavior in social dilemmas: Effects of social identity, group size, and decision framing." *Journal of Personality and Social Psychology* 50.3 (1986): 543–549.

96 Braithwaite, Valerie, Kristina Murphy, and Monika Reinhart. "Taxation threat, motivational postures, and responsive regulation." *Law & Policy* 29.1 (2007): 137–158.

97 Feldman, Yuval, and Yotam Kaplan. "Big data and bounded ethicality." *Cornell Journal of Law and Public Policy* 29 (2020): 39–93.

98 Dana, Weber, and Xi Kuang. "Exploiting moral wiggle room."

99 Feldman and Kaplan, "Big data and bounded ethicality."

There are indeed several predictors indicating that, in a given regulatory context, more lenient regulatory measures are likely to be at least as effective as more coercive ones. However, one can never suggest that voluntary compliance is always better as its efficacy is based upon numerous indicators, such as cultural and social norms, personality, institutions, characteristics of the regulatory environment, and more. That said, there is limited data about how these factors interact, which thus constrains the ability of regulators to identify the situations in which less coercive measures are more likely to be effective. For example, it is known that, in certain countries, people can be trusted to pay their public transportation fares without coercion.[100] The problem is that these anecdotal findings are not consistent and therefore offer little to no evidence about what mechanisms drive the success of this voluntary compliance. Nor do they offer any guidance as to how similar trust-based systems might work in other countries or contexts.

ARE NUDGES VOLUNTARY COMPLIANCE?

Another regulatory approach, which will be discussed more extensively in Chapters 2 and 3, relates to the role of nudges in shifting people's behavior. This approach is distinct from the previous discussion but complements our understanding of behavioral regulation.

Much of the original research on nudges focused on demonstrating that they are not paternalistic, despite their early applications in areas such as nutrition, consumerism, and long-term savings. These studies aimed to demonstrate that nudges can influence behavior while preserving individual autonomy. As Thaler and Benartzi's research shows,[101] nudges are designed to guide choices without imposing restrictions. However, the fact that they are employed with limited awareness by the public could potentially lead to them being perceived as a more sophisticated form of coercion.[102] This literature is important in the context of compliance research because

[100] Sohail, Muhammad, D. A. C. Maunder, and Sue Cavill. "Effective regulation for sustainable public transport in developing countries." *Transport Policy* 13.3 (2006): 177–190; see also Uslaner, Eric M., Barabino Benedetto, Sara Salis, and Bruno Useli. "Fare evasion in proof-of-payment transit systems: Deriving the optimum inspection level." *Transportation Research Part B: Methodological* 70 (2014): 1–17; Barabino, Benedetto, Sara Salis, and Bruno Useli. "What are the determinants in making people free riders in proof-of-payment transit systems? Evidence from Italy." *Transportation Research Part A: Policy and Practice* 80 (2015): 184–196; Guarda, Pablo, et al. "Decreasing fare evasion without fines? A microeconomic analysis." *Research in Transportation Economics* 59 (2016): 151–158.

[101] Thaler, Richard H., and Shlomo Benartzi. "Save more tomorrow™: Using behavioral economics to increase employee saving." *Journal of Political Economy* 112.S1 (2004): S164–S187.

[102] Hausman, Daniel M., and Brynn Welch. "Debate: To nudge or not to nudge." *Journal of Political Philosophy* 18.1 (2010): 123–136; Rebonato, Riccardo. "A critical assessment of libertarian paternalism." *Journal of Consumer Policy* 37 (2014): 357–396; Hansen, Pelle Guldborg, and Andreas Maaløe Jespersen. "Nudge and the manipulation of choice: A framework for the responsible use of the nudge approach to behaviour change in public policy." *European Journal of Risk Regulation* 4.1 (2013):

it unravels many of the dichotomies that frequently appear in the regulation literature. In these cases, governments either attempt to focus on external factors, such as prices, or on internal factors, such as morality.[103]

On one hand, the whole of the debate around liberal paternalism is based on the argument that people are free to choose and that nudges do not force them to make any particular choice or to choose at all.[104] On the other hand, much of the research on nudges focuses on the lack of self-reflection and transparency associated with them and on the fact that many nudges, even the basic ones, focus on biases such as the status quo.[105] As a result, it is possible to argue that nudges could be viewed as supporting a regime with limited individual deliberation.

Clearly, when people are being "gently pushed" to behave in a certain way by some default-rule choice architecture, it is very hard to define whether their compliance motivation is voluntary. When voluntary is defined as noncoerced, then clearly behaving in a certain way due to the default rule does not involve coercion. However, if people do not know why they behave in a certain way, their self-perception of voluntary choice is inevitably missing.[106]

At the same time, it is impossible to ignore the importance of nudges in the process of sanctions and monitoring-free regulation. Nudges are used in many cases where laws cannot be used, such as to boost vaccination and to encourage organ donation, healthier diets, and long-term savings. These are cases where the preservation of choice is crucial and thus laws are naturally less likely to be successful.[107] Nonetheless, nudges are increasingly being used in contexts such as employment discrimination and tax compliance,[108] where laws could otherwise be used.

In such situations, it is important to also discuss the expressive value of the mechanisms that are used. For example, through some choice architecture modifications,

3–28; White, Mark D. "Why nudges are unethical." In *The manipulation of choice: Ethics and libertarian paternalism*, edited by Mark D. White, Palgrave Macmillan US, 2013: 81–102; Bovens, Luc. "The ethics of nudge." In *Preference change: Approaches from philosophy, economics and psychology*, edited by Till Grüne-Yanoff and Sven Ove Hansson, Springer Netherlands, 2009: 207–219; Science and Technology Committee. "Behaviour change." House of Lords report, 2011. https://publications.parliament.uk/pa/ld201012/ldselect/ldsctech/179/17902.htm.

[103] Parker, Christine. *Reducing the risk of policy failure: Challenges for regulatory compliance: Final version*. OECD, 2000.

[104] Loewenstein, George, and Nick Chater. "Putting nudges in perspective." *Behavioural Public Policy* 1.1 (2017): 26–53; Sunstein, Cass R. "Do people like nudges?" *Administrative Law Review* 68 (2016): 177–232.

[105] Bruns, Hendrik, et al. "Can nudges be transparent and yet effective?" *Journal of Economic Psychology* 65 (2018): 41–59.

[106] Sunstein, Cass R. "People prefer System 2 nudges (kind of)." *Duke Law Journal* 66 (2016): 121–169.

[107] Grüne-Yanoff, Till, and Ralph Hertwig. "Nudge versus boost: How coherent are policy and theory?" *Minds and Machines* 26.1 (2016): 149–183.

[108] Bohnet, Iris, Alexandra Van Geen, and Max Bazerman. "When performance trumps gender bias: Joint vs. separate evaluation." *Management Science* 62.5 (2016): 1225–1234; Fonseca, Miguel A., and Shaun B. Grimshaw. "Do behavioral nudges in prepopulated tax forms affect compliance? Experimental evidence with real taxpayers." *Journal of Public Policy & Marketing* 36.2 (2017): 213–226.

it may be possible to encourage people to avoid discriminating and not just to hire minorities.[109] Consequently, in areas where we have no alternative, nudges are clearly preferable to simply asking the public nicely to behave in a certain way. However, it should be acknowledged that from the perspective of the book, which is interested in long-term effects on compliance, the short-term compliance achieved thorough nudges has its limitations.[110]

Recent behavioral public policy scholarship has explored agency-preserving nudges, particularly the "nudge-plus" approach, which enhances policy effectiveness by incorporating opportunities for personal reflection.[111] Such nudges might enhance our ability to combine the efficacy of nudges with some advantages, regarding a process of reflection and internalization.

RESPONSIVE REGULATION AND THE CHALLENGE OF MOTIVATIONAL HETEROGENEITY

A key concept in behavioral approaches is responsive regulation, which involves predicting behavior and adapting regulatory strategies to the characteristics of people and organizations requiring oversight. This comprehensive framework acknowledges that effective regulation requires a mix of incentives and deterrence, calibrated to different contexts and compliance motivations. By analyzing how different groups respond to various regulatory tools,[112] policymakers can better understand when noncoercive approaches work best and recognize that a one-size-fits-all regulatory approach is unlikely to succeed across diverse populations.[113] According to this analysis, states must instead rely on a sequential approach where more lenient means precede increasingly harsher measures against those who refuse to engage in voluntary cooperation. This book will examine some of the aspects of responsive and flexible regulation paradigms. It seeks to identify and classify the factors that need to be addressed when determining how to reach a level of voluntary compliance that will be sensitive to the risks to the public associated with different regulatory settings.

109 Bohnet, Van Geen, and Bazerman. "When performance trumps gender bias."

110 Feldman, Yuval, and Orly Lobel. "Behavioral trade-offs: Beyond the land of nudge spans." In *Nudge and the law: A European perspective*, edited by Alberto Alemanno and Anne-Lise Sibony, Bloomsbury, 2015: 301–323.

111 Banerjee, Sanchayan, and Peter John. "Nudge plus: Incorporating reflection into behavioral public policy." *Behavioural Public Policy* 8.1 (2021): 1–16.

112 E.g., compare with Figure 0.1.

113 See: Braithwaite, Valerie. "Responsive regulation and taxation: Introduction." *Law & Policy* 29.1 (2007): 3–10; Job, Jenny, Andrew Stout, and Rachael Smith. "Culture change in three taxation administrations: From command-and-control to responsive regulation." *Law & Policy* 29.1 (2007): 84–101; Ivec, Mary, and Valerie Braithwaite. "Applications of responsive regulatory theory in Australia and overseas: Update." *RegNet Occasional Paper* 23 (2015); Hill, Linda, and Liz Stewart. "'Responsive regulation' theory and the Sale of Liquor Act." *Social Policy Journal of New Zealand* 11 (1998): 49–66.

VOLUNTARY COMPLIANCE AND THERAPEUTIC JURISPRUDENCE

Part of the potential advantage of voluntary compliance involves people's well-being in addition to their increased personal commitment and perception of better compliance. If people are given the choice to comply, they will enjoy better cognitive and emotional capacities for dealing with uncertainties, adapting, and demonstrating greater resilience.[114] This aspect of the book's examination of voluntary compliance will draw on the classical literature about therapeutic jurisprudence,[115] as well on the data accumulated in research on happiness,[116] in an effort to improve our understanding of the advantages of having people comply voluntarily and not as a response to external pressure. Understanding the causal relationships is highly complicated. The government's ability to rely upon noncoercive mechanisms is strongly connected to the type of society in which such mechanisms are likely to work. In addition, policymakers rely heavily on expectations that people are more likely to benefit from being able to cooperate voluntarily.

CAN CORPORATIONS BE TRUSTED?

Another important issue of great significance from a regulatory standpoint is whether corporations can be trusted by regulators and policymakers. As discussed in Chapter 10, with much of the debate today on self-regulation involving businesses and corporations, considerable research emphasizes the importance of understanding corporations' impact on the environment rather than focusing on individual behavior.[117] Corporations and businesses' ethical behavior has come to be viewed as an aspect of their performance and, as a result, has been subject to increasing interest.[118] Although some aspects of my research indicate that corporations might be hotbeds for unethicality,[119] there are many reasons to believe that the bureaucratic and transparent nature of corporate operations, as well as their greater sensitivity to reputational mechanisms,[120] might make them more likely than individuals to

[114] Patall, Cooper, and Civey Robinson. "The effects of choice on intrinsic motivation and related outcomes," 270.

[115] Winick. "The jurisprudence of therapeutic jurisprudence," 184; Wexler. "Therapeutic jurisprudence," 125.

[116] Posner and Sunstein, eds. *Law and happiness*; Bronsteen, Buccafusco, and Masur. *Happiness and the law*.

[117] Chater, Nick, and George Loewenstein. "The i-frame and the s-frame: How focusing on individual-level solutions has led behavioral public policy astray." *Behavioral and Brain Sciences* 46 (2023): e147.

[118] McGuire, Jean B., Alison Sundgren, and Thomas Schneeweis. "Corporate social responsibility and firm financial performance." *Academy of Management Journal* 31.4 (1988): 854–872.

[119] Feldman, Yuval, Adi Libson, and Gideon Parchomovsky. "Corporate law for good people." *Northwestern University Law Review* 115 (2020): 1125.

[120] Swift, Tracey. "Trust, reputation and corporate accountability to stakeholders." *Business Ethics: A European Review* 10.1 (2001): 16–26.

consistently adhere to self-regulation. Another aspect of the focus on the corporate culture involves examining data about corporate behavior about trust in their employees and customers.[121] Part of what the book aims to examine is whether organizational practices can be applied to the state context. While many corporations engage in various strategies to enhance the feeling of trust by their customers and employees,[122] states rarely demonstrate similar motivation, perhaps because of their size and limited ability to know how their citizens will behave.

VOLUNTARY COMPLIANCE: THE NORMATIVE DILEMMA

As this book unfolds, we will develop a new conceptual paradigm that will explore the benefits of voluntary compliance for democratic states across a few regulatory domains. Our analysis includes an examination of the factors that can undermine the attempt of states to achieve voluntary compliance. We will also discuss what needs to be done to better understand the interaction between individual, situational, regulatory, and cultural dimensions in order to maintain voluntary compliance. In addition, the book will suggest methods for considering how to balance the risk to the public of reduced monitoring with the advantages to the public of regulated entities that feel they are trusted by the state. The nature of this analysis inevitably changes when discussing more extensive types of regulations where the target population includes broad layers of the public. Chapter 5 examines a crucial paradox: When governments shift from monitoring to seeking public collaboration, they may inadvertently create more problematic regulatory approaches. While appearing gentler on the surface, these strategies could prove more manipulative from a democratic standpoint and more intrusive from a liberal perspective. Some of the questions that need to be asked include: What contextual factors should regulators and experts consider when deciding which approach to take? What factors can they take into account when assessing what proportion of the public can be trusted? In particular, what individual and group related factors can be considered when trying to assess the likelihood that individuals or segments of the population can be trusted to cooperate with more trusting regulatory approaches?[123] How do these factors influence the responsive regulation approach? In addition, how might the current empirical data and theories on how voluntary compliance enhances people's mental well-being intersect with the therapeutic jurisprudence literature?

[121] Garland, *Punishment and modern society*.

[122] Keh, Hean Tat, and Yi Xie. "Corporate reputation and customer behavioral intentions: The roles of trust, identification and commitment." *Industrial Marketing Management* 38.7 (2009): 732–742.

[123] See work in progress by Ori Aronson, Yuval Feldman, and Orly Lobel. "The behavioral challenges of trust-based regulation: Navigating the complexities of past behavior as a predictor." Working paper available at SSRN 5117987 (2025). https://papers.ssrn.com/sol3/papers.cfm?abstract_id=5117987.

WHICH REGULATIONS DRIVE VOLUNTARY COMPLIANCE?

Throughout the chapters exploring the association between regulation and trust, we will address the question of which regulatory interventions are more likely to lead to voluntary compliance. As explained in the beginning of the chapter, it is not completely clear whether indeed focusing on intrinsic motivation is more likely to lead to voluntary compliance. First, the distinction between the different instruments is not distinct enough. Furthermore, in many cases, nudges are designed in such a way that an approach we perceive as having one effect is actually working through a different mechanism. Is it always the case that market mechanisms are unlikely to lead to voluntary compliance in the long run? For example, consider Milkman's work on habit formation.[124] She found that people tend to adopt behaviors in a consistent, almost mechanistic way, basically without relying on factors that we discuss such as trust or reflecting on knowledge or other types of moral reasoning. Chapter 3 argues that it is not clear at all which legal instrument leads to more coercion and that the boundaries between the different instruments are vague. Additionally, Chapter 5 will address the limitations of voluntary compliance. It is possible that voluntary compliance could lead states to engage in manipulative practices to influence attitudes, which may ultimately limit people's voluntary choices.

Furthermore, it is possible that by imposing guilt on people through the use of moral-reasoning mechanisms, we might ensure voluntary compliance, but we might also cause damage by imposing mental costs on them. This is because situations where noncompliance might cause them to feel worse about themselves can be mentally and emotionally taxing.[125] Guilt-based motivation has many advantages from the state's perspective, as it affects people's behavior in much the same way that religion does.[126] However, as we know from studies in education,[127] for example, it is not entirely clear that such an approach should be adopted by a liberal state in the context of the overall welfare of the people, even if doing so can reduce monitoring costs and enhance trustworthiness and social capital in society.

WHAT ARE WE INTERESTED IN CHANGING?

Another important topic, examined in Chapter 3, relates to the question of what we are trying to change when we talk about voluntary compliance. Are we trying

[124] Milkman, Katherine L., Julia A. Minson, and Kevin G. M. Volpp. "Holding the hunger games hostage at the gym: An evaluation of temptation bundling." *Management Science* 60.2 (2014): 283–299.

[125] Carlsmith, J. Merrill, and Alan E. Gross. "Some effects of guilt on compliance." *Journal of Personality and Social Psychology* 11.3 (1969): 232–239.

[126] London, Perry, Robert E. Schulman, and Michael S. Black. "Religion, guilt, and ethical standards." *Journal of Social Psychology* 63.1 (1964): 145–159.

[127] Baumeister, Roy F. "Inducing guilt." In *Guilt and children*, edited by Jane Bybee, Academic Press, 1998: 127–138.

to change people's motivation, which basically means also their preferences, attitudes, and habits? As suggested, while intrinsic motivation and voluntary compliance might be viewed as related, they are in fact quite distinct concepts. Hence, we do not necessarily need to change people's intrinsic motivations in order to achieve voluntary compliance. The various perspectives on voluntary compliance outlined in this chapter indicate that the relationships between its elements are not necessarily mutually exclusive. Furthermore, when discussing intrinsically motivated voluntary compliance, we are not necessarily talking about changing people's intrinsic motivation. Nonetheless, it may certainly be possible to prime or stimulate people's preexisting intrinsic motivation by telling them, for example, that doing the moral thing in a given context means complying with the law.[128] Such an approach is common in many field studies conducted in a tax context.[129] Here, we do not suggest changing people's morality, but rather building on an existing moral sentiment to improve compliance. However, even with this distinction, many problems remain with such an approach, as will be discussed in Chapter 5.

IS CULTURE MALLEABLE?

A similar question arises with regard to culture. If we want to examine the ability of governments to trust the public, do we need to change the culture, or is it enough to simply understand the culture? This will enable us to determine whether voluntary compliance is a viable option. A third option might be to make small modifications to a culture to allow for certain voluntary practices to work. Improving voluntary tax compliance may require targeted interventions rather than comprehensive changes to all known compliance factors. Chapter 6 is dedicated to a discussion about the interaction between culture and voluntary compliance. It also reviews the debate among scholars about whether policymakers can lead cultural change.[130] This can be done either directly, by focusing on policies related to solidarity (as was done in the Nordic counties), or indirectly, by addressing immigration (as related to the research by Putnam on diversity and social capital).[131]

SUMMARY

This first chapter introduces the central dilemma facing governments in their approach to regulatory compliance. While voluntary compliance is often viewed as

[128] Feldman. "The expressive function of trade secret law."

[129] Luttmer and Singhal. "Tax morale"; Bott, Kristina M., et al. "You've got mail: A randomized field experiment on tax evasion." *Management Science* 66.7 (2020): 2801–2819.

[130] Please see our discussion of both the work of Gelfand and of Hofstade in Chapter 6 discussing culture and compliance.

[131] Putnam, Robert D. "E pluribus unum: Diversity and community in the twenty-first century: The 2006 Johan Skytte Prize Lecture." *Scandinavian Political Studies* 30.2 (2007): 137–174.

the ideal, sustainable, and most beneficial form of cooperation between states and citizens, policymakers frequently resort to more coercive measures due to uncertainty about public response. This chapter explores the complexities of voluntary compliance, examining various perspectives from different social sciences and highlighting the challenges in predicting when and to what extent the public can be trusted to comply willingly with laws and regulations. It examines the nuances of what constitutes "voluntary" compliance, discussing concepts such as intrinsic motivation, nudges, and the role of culture in shaping compliance behaviors.

The chapter also outlines key issues that will be addressed throughout the book, including the balance between coercive and cooperative regulatory approaches, the impact of different regulatory tools on compliance motivation, and the potential long-term effects of various compliance strategies on trust and social capital. By introducing these themes, the chapter sets the stage for a comprehensive exploration of voluntary compliance across different regulatory domains. The subsequent chapters will build on this foundation, examining specific areas such as tax compliance, environmental regulations, and public health measures, while also considering the roles of technology, culture, and behavioral insights in shaping effective and ethical regulatory policies.

2

What Is Intrinsic Compliance Motivation?

INTRODUCTION

While intrinsically motivated compliance might seem like the clearest approach to defining voluntary compliance – *where people will want to comply, not just comply* – relying solely on this definition presents several challenges. First, it sets an unrealistic ideal that few people could achieve. Second, individuals often comply for multiple reasons, making it difficult to identify the dominant motivation. Third, basing a definition on subjective factors that are hard to observe externally is problematic from a practical standpoint.

For these reasons, this book adopts a broader definition: compliance that occurs without state coercion. Although this approach might include some forms of compliance that are not truly voluntary, it offers a more practical framework since it focuses on regulatory approaches rather than individual motivations. Nevertheless, within this broader framework, understanding which intrinsically motivated approaches are more likely to result in voluntary compliance remains critically important.

Presumably, certain motivations are more likely to enhance trustworthiness in people. For example, an action motivated by external circumstances, such as monitoring and incentives, seems less stable or sustainable than actions resulting from intrinsic motivations that reflect an individual's personality traits and beliefs. The stability of such intrinsic motivations is supported by both law and economics accounts. For example, according to Robert Cooter's equilibrium perspective, internalization of legal norms is likely to produce stable civic acts in the public.[1]

It should, of course, be borne in mind that voluntary compliance is not contingent on changing individual motivation. As discussed in Chapter 1, the term voluntary compliance can have multiple meanings. Moreover, motivation theories do not presume to suggest that changing individuals' motivation is a solution to all societal problems.[2]

1 Cooter, Robert. "Do good laws make good citizens? An economic analysis of internalized norms." *Virginia Law Review* 86 (2000): 1577–1602.

2 This qualification was recently suggested in Chater, Nick, and George Loewenstein. "The i-frame and the s-frame: How focusing on individual-level solutions has led behavioral public policy astray."

However, in many ways, compliance motivation is the driving force behind the change which this book seeks to effect in both regulation and compliance literatures. Motivation theories challenge dominant accounts, such as the nudge theory, which attempts to change individuals' behavior while ignoring their underlying motivations. Hence, the aim of this chapter is to examine whether motivation analysis could reduce and limit the role of the state in monitoring individual behaviors.

WHY IS INTRINSIC MOTIVATION IMPORTANT FOR COMPLIANCE?

As discussed, the literature on compliance has advocated the advantage of intrinsic motivation regarding voluntary compliance.[3] This advantage is based on three significant characteristics. First, when people are intrinsically motivated to accomplish a given task, there is less needed to monitor their compliance with the task's instructions. In addition, their compliance is more resilient. Finally, their performance is more likely to exceed the required behavior.[4] Therefore, it is possible to appreciate that intrinsically motivated behavior is advantageous in the context of legal compliance.[5] To better clarify this advantage in the context of the scholarship on legal compliance, further scrutiny of the three characteristics of intrinsically motivated behavior mentioned is needed. This is the goal of the next sections.

WHAT IS INTRINSIC MOTIVATION?

The book's skeptical stance toward intrinsic motivation as a reliable predictor of compliance stems from two key factors. First, empirical findings cast doubt on its predictive power. Second, and perhaps more fundamentally, the concept itself suffers from definitional ambiguity (see Figure 0.3). This lack of conceptual clarity makes intrinsic motivation both difficult to measure behaviorally and challenging to apply as a normative framework. In psychology, intrinsic motivation is defined as the desire to engage in an activity for its own sake rather than for external rewards.[6] This

Behavioral and Brain Sciences 46 (2023): e147. Chater and Lowenstein argue that focusing on individuals' behaviors essentially lets organizations and states off the hook for their responsibilities to global and social challenges (such as climate change, for instance). However, it should be noted that the view suggested in this book is not to reduce the responsibilities of the state by empowering the role of individuals, but rather examine the possibility of limiting the role of the state in monitoring individual behavior.

3 Dwenger, Nadja, et al. "Extrinsic and intrinsic motivations for tax compliance: Evidence from a field experiment in Germany." *American Economic Journal: Economic Policy* 8.3 (2016): 203–232.

4 Feldman, Yuval. "The complexity of disentangling intrinsic and extrinsic compliance motivations: Theoretical and empirical insights from the behavioral analysis of law." *Washington University Journal of Law and Policy* 35 (2011): 11–52.

5 Boussalis, Constantine, Yuval Feldman, and Henry E. Smith. "Experimental analysis of the effect of standards on compliance and performance." *Regulation & Governance* 12.2 (2018): 277–298.

6 Halla, Martin. "The link between the intrinsic motivation to comply and compliance behaviour: A critical appraisal of existing evidence." In *Handbook on the shadow economy*, edited by Friedrich Schneider, Edward Elgar Publishing, 2011: 375–408.

is related to self-determination and to behaviors that increase people's autonomy, enjoyment, and competence.[7] When an individual finds a behavior rewarding, they benefit from it and are more likely to continue engaging in it.[8] That said, extrinsic motivation is involved when an individual is motivated to engage in behavior for reasons unrelated to the action itself.

The difference between these two perspectives of intrinsic and extrinsic motivation may be related to the question of how to treat factors such as fairness, legitimacy, and morality.[9] In the legal literature, these factors are viewed as elements of intrinsic motivation. However, when applying the pure psychological definition of scholars like Edward Deci,[10] these factors may not actually be considered intrinsic, as they are not related to the activity itself but to questions such as whether the social institutions that require it are just and accepted by others. Some of the differences might be related to the fact that, regarding compliance, the behavior itself is often not driven by individual choice but is imposed upon the individual. In some cases, the individual may internalize the behavior, although it was not originally their choice.

INTRINSIC MOTIVATION: REASON, TRUST, MORALITY, AND PROCEDURAL JUSTICE

A notable trend across various disciplines is the growing recognition of the significance of intrinsic motivation. However, the concept of intrinsic motivation itself is subject to diverse interpretations. Broadly speaking, three distinct approaches have emerged in understanding this phenomenon. One approach to intrinsic motivation focuses on persuasion in the logic or science behind the law.[11] This approach could even be attributed to Plato, for whom the mechanisms of intrinsic motivation extended beyond morality.[12] As argued in Stalley's paper on Plato's laws, people are more likely to obey of their own free will if they are persuaded and understand

7 Ryan, Richard M., and Edward L. Deci. "Self-determination theory and the facilitation of intrinsic motivation, social development, and well-being." *American Psychologist* 55.1 (2000): 68–78.

8 Reeve, Johnmarshall, Steven G. Cole, and Bradley C. Olson. "Adding excitement to intrinsic motivation research." *Journal of Social Behavior and Personality* 1.3 (1986): 349–363.

9 Tyler, Tom R. "Legitimacy and rule adherence: A psychological perspective on the antecedents and consequences of legitimacy." In *The psychology of justice and legitimacy*, edited by D. Ramona Bobocel, Aaron C. Kay, Mark P. Zanna and James M. Olson, Psychology Press, 2011: 251–271; see also Figure 0.1.

10 Ryan, Richard M., and Edward L. Deci. "Intrinsic and extrinsic motivations: Classic definitions and new directions." *Contemporary Educational Psychology* 25.1 (2000): 54–67.

11 Ariel, Barak. "Deterrence and moral persuasion effects on corporate tax compliance: Findings from a randomized controlled trial." *Criminology* 50.1 (2012): 27–69.

12 Bobonich, Christopher. "Persuasion, compulsion and freedom in Plato's Laws." *The Classical Quarterly* 41.2 (1991): 365–388; Stalley, Richard F. "Persuasion in Plato's 'Laws.'" *History of Political Thought* 15.2 (1994): 157–177.

the logic behind the law.[13] This approach is also consistent with the work of Eyal Zamir and colleagues,[14] which examines why giving reasons as a potential nudge can enhance compliance. Their focus is on showing how providing clear and convincing explanations for the request and explaining the logic behind it can increase the level of compliance.

Another approach, related to the content of the law but from a different perspective, argues that obeying the law is the moral thing to do,[15] due to the potential harm caused by the violation of the law.[16] Nonetheless, the notion of morality, while always viewed as part of intrinsic motivation, is not necessarily tied to the law. For example, morality could be perceived as related to the general feeling of guilt people might have (see Figure 0.4). This feeling is more related to the personality of the individual than to the content of the law.[17] However, there can be a possible connection between persuasion and morality in the sense that it is more immoral to violate laws that do make sense than laws that do not.

Finally, a third "intrinsic motivation" mechanism is related to procedural justice and legitimacy.[18] As discussed in more detail later in this chapter, numerous studies have highlighted the importance of legitimacy and procedural justice, which underlie the functioning of the legal system and the laws that people are expected to obey.[19] Accordingly, it has been found that when police and criminal justice officials treat citizens fairly and respectfully, people are more likely to follow the law.[20] Citizens' perceptions of receiving procedurally just treatment are closely tied to perceptions of police legitimacy, which are strongly associated with legal compliance. Interestingly, while perceptions of morality are considered important in experimental studies, no advantage of morality was found in experimental field studies (see Figure 0.1). For example, looking at randomized field experiments, Barak Ariel found that using warning letters with moral arguments or threats of penalties did not significantly improve tax-reporting compliance.[21]

13 Bobonich. "Persuasion, compulsion and freedom in Plato's Laws."

14 Lewinsohn-Zamir, Daphna, Eyal Zamir, and Ori Katz. "Giving reasons as a means to enhance compliance with legal norms." *University of Toronto Law Journal* 72.3 (2022): 316–355.

15 Friedman, Lawrence M. *Impact: How law affects behavior*. Harvard University Press, 2016.

16 Wasieleski, David M., and Sefa Hayibor. "Breaking the rules: Examining the facilitation effects of moral intensity characteristics on the recognition of rule violations." *Journal of Business Ethics* 78 (2008): 275–289.

17 Frey, Bruno S., and Benno Torgler. "Tax morale and conditional cooperation." *Journal of Comparative Economics* 35.1 (2007): 136–159.

18 Jackson, Jonathan, et al. "Why do people comply with the law? Legitimacy and the influence of legal institutions." *British Journal of Criminology* 52.6 (2012): 1051–1071. Compare with Figure 0.3.

19 Jackson et al. "Why do people comply with the law?"

20 Sunshine, Jason, and Tom R. Tyler. "The role of procedural justice and legitimacy in shaping public support for policing." *Law & Society Review* 37.3 (2003): 513–547. For a different approach see Nagin, Daniel S., and Cody W. Telep. "Procedural justice and legal compliance." *Annual Review of Law and Social Science* 13.1 (2017): 5–28.

21 Ariel. "Deterrence and moral persuasion effects on corporate tax compliance."

DISTINGUISHING BETWEEN INTRINSIC AND EXTRINSIC MOTIVATIONS

Distinguishing between intrinsic and extrinsic motivations is a major challenge for researchers and even more so for policymakers. These motivations are not necessarily as mutually exclusive as some might assume.[22]

Defining internalized compliance for regulatory and compliance research requires careful consideration. While compliance research typically takes a broad view of internalization, regulatory contexts may need a more specific and targeted definition. For example, if the goal is to have people internalize the law, it might be unrealistic and even problematic for an individual to become a 100 percent true believer in the law (see Figure 0.2). That is, it may not be desirable to have people become wholehearted believers in any law while lacking any doubts, which are considered legitimate in democratic regimes.

Therefore, a broader definition of internalized compliance, which might be more suitable for our book's argument, is that it occurs when no monitoring exists. For our purposes, even if people are not true believers, this level of compliance could be considered intrinsic.

IDENTIFYING COMPLIANCE MOTIVATIONS

The classical argument for the importance of understanding motivation in compliance in general, and voluntary compliance in particular, is related to the assumed advantage of intrinsic motivation over extrinsic motivation. This argument suggests that when people are motivated by intrinsic motivation, enforcement is not only less expensive but also might lead people to behaviors that could not be achieved by mere deterrence.[23] In many situations, it is desirable to encourage behavior beyond simply compliance. In such cases, noninstrumental motivation is often the most effective means of attaining the sought-after changes in human behavior.[24] This effectiveness seems to be the main justification for using a legal design, which can be aligned with the most likely dominant motivation in any given situation. It is believed that such a legal design is likely to produce a general acceptance of the policy as just, reasonable, or legitimate. This, in turn, is likely to cause people to rely on their intrinsic motivation when complying with it.

22 Feldman. "The complexity of disentangling intrinsic and extrinsic motivation."

23 A well-known demonstration of this claim is given in Gneezy, Uri, and Aldo Rustichini. "A fine is a price." *Journal of Legal Studies* 29.1 (2000): 1–17. Gneezy and Rustichini investigate whether imposing a fine on certain misconduct functions as a "price-tag" over that behavior. Using an experimental setting, they impose a monetary fine on parents who were late picking up their children from daycare. They observed that, contrary to traditional accounts on deterrence, once the fines were introduced, the number of parents arriving late increased steadily rather than decreased;

24 Tyler, Tom, John Dienhart, and Terry Thomas. "The ethical commitment to compliance: Building value-based cultures." *California Management Review* 50.2 (2008): 31–51.

However, the main shortcoming of this approach is clear. It is difficult to predict, identify, and clarify which intrinsic motivation will be superior to an extrinsic one without collecting data for every given situation. Nonetheless, this complexity of determination or prediction could be moderated in some "victimless" areas of legal behavior, such as corporate contexts. However, as we shall see in the remainder of this chapter, even if the indeterminacy is mitigated in these victimless contexts, a host of related questions arise. For example, are we likely to see higher levels of voluntary compliance in these contexts? Could the proportion of people engaging in voluntary compliance be determined in advance? What is the sustainability or erosion of voluntary compliance over time? Is there a difference between different types of intrinsic motivations? Are there behaviors which are more likely to be positively affected by intrinsic motivation? In this chapter and later on, we will also examine the risks of attempting to change people's intrinsic motivation.

DEFINING WHAT TYPES OF MOTIVATIONS CAN BE CONSIDERED VOLUNTARY

As described in Chapter 1, when discussing subjective voluntary compliance, one of the greatest challenges is clarifying the relevant notion of voluntariness. Another related challenge is understanding how motivation affects the scope of voluntariness. For example, how voluntary is compliance when deterrence is achieved through basic compliance rather than voluntary compliance? What about cases where an individual's motivation to comply is instrumental to their own goals? In these cases, is it advantageous to behave by the state's demands, or simply harder not to comply? What kinds of compliance motivation can still be considered voluntary?

There may be a few distinctions regarding what is meant by voluntary compliance, which we will outline in brief to allow for a meaningful comparison. In terms of intrinsic motivation to comply, it is possible to make a distinction between what the individual feels and the objective reality. For example, when a given monetary benefit seems excessively high they may interpret it as diminishing their ability to exercise free choice, thereby affecting their motivation. Naturally, voluntary compliance is not related just to the perception of motivation, some people view things like perceived capacity to comply and finding the opportunity to comply as being related to voluntary compliance. However, as discussed in Chapter 1, at this stage of the argument's development, the focus is primarily on the motivational framework rather than on various contextual factors.

PRICE MOTIVATION

The literature that discusses the price motivation approach is a very extensive one, given the centrality of both deterrence and incentives within legal scholarship.[25] Many scholars have argued that perceptions of the severity and certainty of punishment do not affect delinquent behavior.[26] This argument limits the ability of deterrence to explain both self-reported and actual compliance,[27] particularly if individuals have little awareness of the law in the books.[28] A common argument in the literature is that people are not very sensitive to the severity of a punishment, but are sensitive to the probability of being detected.[29] Other analyses that reviewed the literature for and against deterrence concluded that deterrence is an important policy tool when using the appropriate measurements.[30] Kinneret Teodorescu and colleagues have demonstrated that detection likelihood is more important than its severity. They argue that a policy combining a high probability of inspection with low severity of fines is more effective than an economically equivalent policy.[31]

In pursuing this book's goal to better understand the balance between compliance and voluntary compliance, the price model seems to offer the clearest accommodation between the two approaches. Sanctions are perceived as the most typical approach to compliance,[32] while rewards are one of the most typical approaches to cooperation.[33] However, as discussed in Chapter 1, the meaning of voluntary is key to understanding this issue. It is possible that incentives could be seen as limiting people's ability to choose freely. Furthermore, the most straightforward research in this context is related to crowding out and the effect of incentives on intrinsic motivation.[34]

25 Zimring, Franklin E., Gordon Hawkins, and James Vorenberg. *Deterrence: The legal threat in crime control*. University of Chicago Press, 1973: 345–369. Also see Tittle, Charles R. *Sanctions and social deviance: The question of deterrence*. Praeger Publishers, 1980: 45–60; Feldman, Yuval. *The law of good people: Challenging states' ability to regulate human behavior*. Cambridge University Press, 2018.

26 Paternoster, Raymond, and Leeann Iovanni. "The deterrent effect of perceived severity: A reexamination." *Social Forces* 64.3 (1986): 751–777.

27 Braithwaite, John, and Toni Makkai. "Testing an expected utility model of corporate deterrence." *Law & Society Review* 25 (1991): 7–40.

28 Robinson, Paul H., and John M. Darley. "Does criminal law deter? A behavioral science investigation." *Oxford Journal of Legal Studies* 24.2 (2004): 173–205.

29 Doob, Anthony N., and Cheryl Marie Webster. "Sentence severity and crime: Accepting the null hypothesis." *Crime and Justice* 30 (2003): 143–195.

30 Nagin, Daniel S. "Criminal deterrence research at the outset of the twenty-first century." *Crime and Justice* 23 (1998): 1–42; Fine, Adam, and Benjamin van Rooij. "For whom does deterrence affect behavior? Identifying key individual differences." *Law and Human Behavior* 41.4 (2017): 354–360.

31 Teodorescu, Kinneret, et al. "Frequency of enforcement is more important than the severity of punishment in reducing violation behaviors." *Proceedings of the National Academy of Sciences* 118.42 (2021): e2108507118.

32 Some of the arguments here are based on my paper Feldman. "The complexity of disentangling intrinsic and extrinsic compliance motivations," 11–52. For classic discussion of deterrence theory (e.g., Becker, G. S. "Crime and punishment: An economic approach." In *The economic dimensions of crime*, edited by N. G. Fielding, A. Clarke, and R. Witt, Palgrave Macmillan, 1968).

33 Balliet, Daniel, Laetitia B. Mulder, and Paul A. M. Van Lange. "Reward, punishment, and cooperation: A meta-analysis." *Psychological Bulletin* 137.4 (2011): 594–615.

34 Weibel, Antoinette, Meike Wiemann, and Margit Osterloh. "A behavioral economics perspective on the over justification effect: Crowding-in and crowding-out of intrinsic motivation." In *The Oxford*

NEGATIVE VS. POSITIVE INCENTIVES

Prospect theory, developed by Daniel Kahneman and Amos Tversky, is a fundamental paradigm in behavioral economics. It describes how people choose between probable alternatives involving risk where the probabilities of outcomes are known.[35]

The concept of loss aversion, a key component of prospect theory, has been extensively discussed in the legal field.[36] Many experts have examined various contexts in which losses are perceived as more impactful than equivalent gains.[37] In a study with Doron Teichman and Amos Schurr,[38] we demonstrated that people interpret their contractual obligations more aggressively and with greater self-motivation when trying to avoid a loss.

Building on this understanding of loss aversion, we can examine the differences between fines and incentives in regulatory contexts. While this comparison might seem to align with the loss–gain dichotomy of prospect theory, it extends beyond it due to additional social and normative components associated with fines.[39] For instance, receiving a fine can lead to social stigmatization, stemming from the expressive function of laws and punishments.[40] It can also result in reputational damage and in some cases, a criminal record.[41] In contrast, not receiving an incentive typically has minimal social consequences, as it's less likely to become public knowledge.

Despite attempts to equate fines and prices through the "fine-is-a-price paradigm," this approach doesn't fully capture the complexity of all fines. There remain significant aspects of fines that distinguish them from mere financial losses or foregone gains.[42] This distinction underscores the need for a more nuanced approach when designing regulatory strategies, considering not just the economic impact but also the social and psychological effects of different policy tools.

handbook of work engagement, motivation, and self-determination theory, edited by Marylene Gange, Oxford University Press, 2014: 72–84.

35 Tversky, Amos, and Daniel Kahneman. "Loss aversion in riskless choice: A reference-dependent model." *Quarterly Journal of Economics* 106.4 (1991): 1039–1061.

36 Zamir, Eyal. "Loss aversion and the law." *Vanderbilt Law Review* 65 (2012): 829.

37 Ariely, Dan, Joel Huber, and Klaus Wertenbroch. "When do losses loom larger than gains?" *Journal of Marketing Research* 42.2 (2005): 134–138.

38 Feldman, Yuval, Amos Schurr, and Doron Teichman. "Reference points and contractual choices: An experimental examination." *Journal of Empirical Legal Studies* 10.3 (2013): 512–541.

39 Balliet, Mulder, and Van Lange. "Reward, punishment, and cooperation," 594; Bansal, Sangeeta, and Shubhashis Gangopadhyay. "Tax/subsidy policies in the presence of environmentally aware consumers." *Journal of Environmental Economics and Management* 45.2 (2003): 333–355.

40 Feinberg, Joel. "The expressive function of punishment." In *Shame punishment*, edited by Thom Brooks, Routledge, 2019: 3–26.

41 Cohen, Mark A. "Corporate crime and punishment: An update on sentencing practice in the federal courts, 1988–1990." *Boston University Law Review* 71 (1991): 247–280.

42 See Feldman, Yuval, and Doron Teichman. "Are all legal dollars created equal?" *Northwestern University Law Review* 102 (2008): 223–262.

Despite the economic perspective that negative and positive incentives are similar, negative incentives might be more likely to undermine voluntarism while positive incentives may not.[43] As we will outline in the following paragraphs, is it the case that people can choose not to receive a positive incentive, or are they more likely to be sanctioned? For the most part, economists tend to argue for some symmetry between being sanctioned to not being rewarded.[44] But due to the contributions that followed that the introduction of Kahneman and Tversky's prospect theory, we better understand the difference between not getting positive rewards and getting negative rewards. This is because even simply paying a fine seems to carry with it a moral and social price that is not associated with merely not winning the reward. Rewards here refer to positive incentives that reward citizens or companies for compliant behavior.[45]

Within the body of research on rewards, we can focus on various types of rewards. These include economic rewards, such as lottery prizes, monetary payments or restitutions, government benefits, subsidies, nonmonetary rewards, and social rewards, such as praise.[46] Other studies focus on rewards in the form of collective goods or benefits.[47] Rewards have been studied in a variety of contexts, including taxation and the environment,[48] both of which will be discussed in more detail in the

43 Underhill, Kristen. "When extrinsic incentives displace intrinsic motivation: Designing legal carrots and sticks to confront the challenge of motivational crowding-out." *Yale Journal on Regulation* 33 (2016): 213–280.

44 See Grabosky, Peter N. "Regulation by reward: On the use of incentives as regulatory instruments." *Law & Policy* 17.3 (1995): 257–282.

45 Becker. "Crime and punishment"; Feldman. "The complexity of disentangling intrinsic and extrinsic compliance motivations," 11–52; Feldman, Yuval, and Orly Lobel. "The incentives matrix: The comparative effectiveness of rewards, liabilities, duties, and protections for reporting illegality." *Texas Law Review* 88 (2009): 1151–1212; also see Feld, Lars P., and Bruno S. Frey. "Tax compliance as the result of a psychological tax contract: The role of incentives and responsive regulation." *Law & Policy* 29.1 (2007): 102–120; also see Grabosky, Peter N. "Fear of crime, and fear reduction strategies." *Current Issues in Criminal Justice* 7.1 (1995): 7–19.

46 See Torgler, Benno. "Tax morale: Theory and empirical analysis of tax compliance." Dissertation, University of Basel, 2003; also see Fabbri, Marco, Paolo Nicola Barbieri, and Maria Bigoni. "Ride your luck! A field experiment on lottery-based incentives for compliance." *Management Science* 65.9 (2019): 4336–4348; Nosenzo, Daniele, et al. "Encouraging compliance: Bonuses versus fines in inspection games." *Journal of Law, Economics, & Organization* 30.3 (2014): 623–648; Alm, James. "Measuring, explaining, and controlling tax evasion: Lessons from theory, experiments, and field studies." *International Tax and Public Finance* 19 (2012): 54–77; Bansal and Gangopadhyay. "Tax/subsidy policies in the presence of environmentally aware consumers"; Koessler, Ann-Kathrin, et al. "Commitment to pay taxes: Results from field and laboratory experiments." *European Economic Review* 115 (2019): 78–98; Handgraaf, Michel J. J., Margriet A. Van Lidth De Jeude, and Kirstin C. Appelt. "Public praise vs. private pay: Effects of rewards on energy conservation in the workplace." *Ecological Economics* 86 (2013): 86–92.

47 Alm, James, Gary H. McClelland, and William D. Schulze. "Changing the social norm of tax compliance by voting." *Kyklos* 52.2 (1999): 141–171. Also see Becker, Winfried, Heinz-Jürgen Büchner, and Simon Sleeking. "The impact of public transfer expenditures on tax evasion: An experimental approach." *Journal of Public Economics* 34.2 (1987): 243–252.

48 For taxation see: Alm, James, Gary H. McClelland, and William D. Schulze. "Why do people pay taxes?" *Journal of Public Economics* 48.1 (1992): 21–38; also see Dwenger, et al. "Extrinsic and intrinsic

following chapters. Other studies have focused on the efficacy of rewards in a more specific context such as fare dodging and voter registration.[49] The total available evidence on the effect of rewards is somewhat limited, with some studies conducted in the laboratory and others in the field.[50] Even this limited evidence on the scope of the effect of rewards leads us to believe that incentives are only partially influencing people's ability to choose to abstain from certain behaviors.

OBLIGATION TO OBEY THE LAW

In a study conducted with Adam Fine and colleagues, we examined the obligation to obey the law (OOL) as a concept independent of other motivations for compliance.[51] We developed and validated the "rule orientation" scale to investigate individual differences in the perceived acceptability of legal rule violations. This new measure assesses how individuals perceive rules, it determines whether individuals view rules as rigid and inflexible or if they acknowledge exceptions. In that paper, we reviewed various literature, including research on neutralization, moral flexibility, and moral disengagement, to identify the key circumstances under which individuals may find it justifiable to violate the law. These circumstances encompass a lack of law knowledge, a cost-benefit analysis favoring violation, social norms supporting rule-breaking, conflicts between laws and personal morals, and a perceived lack of procedural justice in lawmaking and enforcement. In essence, the rule orientation scale measures the degree to which individuals accept justifications for illegal behavior.

In the paper, we systematically compared the scale to existing measures of legal and moral reasoning, finding that a person's orientation to rules significantly predicted their intention to engage in various low-level crimes. This was true even after controlling for the effects of deterrent threats, subjective perceptions of punishment severity, and perceived social norms. In a second study in that paper, we examined the

motivations for tax compliance," 203–232. For the environment see: Julian, Erik Gómez-Baggethun, and Torsten Krause. "Motivation crowding by economic incentives in conservation policy: A review of the empirical evidence." *Ecological Economics* 117 (2015): 270–282. Also see Maki, Alexander, et al. "Paying people to protect the environment: A meta-analysis of financial incentive interventions to promote pro-environmental behaviors." *Journal of Environmental Psychology* 47 (2016): 242–255; and Bansal and Gangopadhyay. "Tax/subsidy policies in the presence of environmentally aware consumers."

49 For fare dodging see: Fabbri, Barbieri, and Bigoni. "Ride your luck!" For voter registration see: Kölle, Felix, et al. "Low-cost interventions to promote voter registration: What works and why?" No. 2017-16. CeDEx Discussion Paper Series, 2017; John, Peter, Elizabeth MacDonald, and Michael Sanders. "Targeting voter registration with incentives: A randomized controlled trial of a lottery in a London borough." *Electoral Studies* 40 (2015): 170–175. Also see Panagopoulos, Costas. "Extrinsic rewards, intrinsic motivation and voting." *Journal of Politics* 75.1 (2013): 266–280.

50 Alm, James. "What motivates tax compliance?" *Journal of Economic Surveys* 33.2 (2019): 353–388, but see Brockmann, Hilke, Philipp Genschel, and Laura Seelkopf. "Happy taxation: Increasing tax compliance through positive rewards?" *Journal of Public Policy* 36.3 (2016): 381–406.

51 Fine, Adam, et al. "Rule orientation and behavior: Development and validation of a scale measuring individual acceptance of rule violation." *Psychology, Public Policy, and Law* 22.3 (2016): 314.

relationship between rule orientation and offending digital behavior across different enforcement contexts. Our findings suggest that individuals with low rule orientation may be able to justify such offending behavior, regardless of the presence of an explicit enforcement campaign, their perceptions of sanction severity, or their beliefs about the social acceptability of violating the law. These studies highlight the importance of individual differences in rule orientation regarding understanding ethical decision-making, criminal decision-making, and other aspects of legal decision-making.

In a follow-up paper,[52] we focused on national differences in the rule orientation scale. To explore national differences in the OOL, we analyzed data from a survey conducted among a convenience sample (n = 716) of law students in the Netherlands, the United States, Israel, and China. Despite existing research on procedural justice and OOL suggesting potential differences, our data did not reveal significant variations in OOL across these markedly different national populations. This unexpected result prompted us to delve deeper into understanding why no such differences were found and what implications these findings have for our understanding of OOL and compliance more broadly.

Several potential explanations can account for these findings. It's possible that the sense of OOL is more universal than previously thought, transcending national and cultural boundaries. Alternatively, our measures of OOL might not have been sensitive enough to capture subtle cross-cultural differences. The influence of national and cultural factors on OOL might also be counterbalanced by other, more individual-level factors, creating a complex interplay that obscures clear patterns. Furthermore, in an increasingly interconnected world, there might be a convergence of values related to law-abiding behavior across different societies, leading to shared global values that minimize national differences. These various explanations highlight the complexity of understanding OOL in a global context and suggest avenues for further research to disentangle these potential factors. Our joint study contributes to the growing body of research on OOL, which has recently begun to examine the concept as distinct from legitimacy. This renewed interest has led to the development of new measures to capture OOL, with studies examining various influences on OOL, such as procedural justice, impulsivity, morality, values, teacher legitimacy, and parental influence.[53]

CONTENT-RELATED COMPLIANCE MOTIVATIONS

In this section, we outline compliance motivations that are related to the specific content of the law rather than to perceptions of the institution enforcing it.

52 Van Rooij, Benjamin, et al. "The obligation to obey the law: Exploring national differences." *Crime, Law and Social Change* 82.2 (2024): 415–432.

53 Fine, et al. "Rule orientation and behavior," 314; Wang, Hongyu, and Yanyan Zhang. "The effects of personality traits and attitudes towards the rule on academic dishonesty among university students." *Scientific Reports* 12.1 (2022): 1–7.

Science and Reason-Based Motivations and Intrinsic Voluntary Compliance

In the context of COVID-19, for example, it became clear that at some levels compliance was related to people's understanding that the regulations were based on epidemiological science.[54] People's trust in the science behind the law was crucial to their decision to comply. This is a pure example of intrinsic compliance, where the law is being obeyed because it is the right thing to do (see Figure 0.3).

The second regulatory approach in this context refers to a reason-driven individual. According to this approach, the main assumption about human motivation is that individuals look to regulators to convince them of the wisdom of engaging in constructive and efficient behavior while abstaining from destructive behavior. According to this rational, informational account of the law, the legislative process aggregates information to produce a decision that is superior to the opinion of any individual legislator. As a result, if a legislative body prohibits public smoking, people might be less likely to smoke publicly because the process of enacting the legislation leads people to update their beliefs.[55] Kagan and colleagues have taken a somewhat different view of informative functioning in the context of the environment, where the law clarifies the boundary between activities that are harmful to the environment and activities that should be tolerated.[56] Another context where policymakers have focused on individual information processing is in the creation of traffic laws. In this area, it is common to find informative campaigns that attempt to use scientific knowledge to increase people's positive response to these laws.[57] This model is similar to the 2011 taxonomy of Garry Gray and Susan Silbey regarding how regulators are perceived in various organizations.[58] One of the models, "The regulator as an ally," is based on the perceived expertise and knowledge of regulators by the people they regulate. Recent work by Daphna Lewinsohn-Zamir and colleagues,[59] which was mentioned earlier in this chapter, demonstrates the potential of this idea. They have experimentally examined the effect of nudges, which are basically

[54] Plohl, Nejc, and Bojan Musil. "Modeling compliance with COVID-19 prevention guidelines: The critical role of trust in science." *Psychology, Health & Medicine* 26.1 (2021): 1–12.

[55] Dharmapala, Dhammika, and Richard H. McAdams. "The Condorcet jury theorem and the expressive function of law: A theory of informative law." *American Law and Economics Review* 5.1 (2003): 1–31.

[56] Kagan, Robert A., Neil Gunningham, and Dorothy Thornton. "Explaining corporate environmental performance: How does regulation matter?" *Law & Society Review* 37.1 (2003): 51–90.

[57] Latour, Michael S., and Shaker A. Zahra. "Fear appeals as advertising strategy: Should they be used?." *Journal of Services Marketing* 2.4 (1988): 5–14; also see Tay, Richard. "General and specific deterrent effects of traffic enforcement: Do we have to catch offenders to reduce crashes?" *Journal of Transport Economics and Policy (JTEP)* 39.2 (2005): 209–224.

[58] Gray, Garry C., and Susan S. Silbey. "The other side of the compliance relationship." In *Explaining compliance: Business responses to regulation*, edited by Christine Parker and Vibeke Lehmann Nielsen, Edward Elgar Publishing, 2011: 123–138.

[59] Lewinsohn-Zamir, Zamir, and Katz. "Giving reasons as a means to enhance compliance with legal norms."

explanations about why one should obey certain requests, such as why one should not park in certain areas or why one should not throw paper towels down the toilet. Using vignette-based studies, they show that people are more likely to obey when given reasons to do so, compared to situations where no explanations are given.

Social Motivation

Social motivation can be divided into distinct subcategories that have different implications for their ability to maintain voluntary compliance. The rich literature on social norms focuses on the prevailing norms and the effect of both their descriptive and injunctive components on how people behave.[60] When examining the distinction between intrinsic and extrinsic motivation, it is important to note that intrinsic motivation is related to behavioral and social concepts such as solidarity and social identity. Extrinsic motivation, on the other hand, is related to factors such as reputation and social approval. Intrinsic motivation is also related to concepts such as solidarity and social identity.

Intrinsic versus Extrinsic Social Compliance Motivation

As suggested, social norms are among the strongest motivators for behavior. This can be seen as either related to the procedure – in the sense that if most others obey, you should obey too – or as related to the content of the law, where in some contexts the law aligns with the social values people believe in. In these contexts, the law is not related to either correctness or justness, but it does cause people to feel that their social identity will be enhanced if they comply with it.

In this regard, social motivation is a hybrid creature that combines the procedure, which involves how many others are complying, with the content, which involves how similar the social and legal values are. In this case, we seek to examine whether social norms can be viewed as coercive or voluntary and we recognize that laws carry both extrinsic and intrinsic motivational attributes, which can be difficult to distinguish. While extrinsic motivation through social conformity (following laws because others do) plays a role in expressive law, its effectiveness may be limited. This limitation becomes particularly problematic when people underestimate how many others actually comply with the law.[61]

Viewing social norms as external motivators with costs, it is important to consider the concept of altruistic punishment for deviance. This is especially important, as it examines the consequences of deviating from prevailing social norms and how others may punish those who do so. Ernst Fehr and Simon Gachter have argued that people are far less altruistic when they perceive that they are unlikely to receive

60 See discussion in chapter 3 of Feldman, *The law of good people*.

61 Cooter, Robert D., Michal Feldman, and Yuval Feldman. "The misperception of norms: The psychology of bias and the economics of equilibrium." *Review of Law & Economics* 4.3 (2008): 889–911.

the approval of others for their actions.[62] At the same time, social norms in the legal context have also an intrinsic component related to expressive law, socialization, and internalization, as will be shown in the next section, focusing on understanding social norms in law and economics.

INFORMATIVE EFFECTS OF LAW

Law and economics scholars have applied the informative approach to study social norms and various models of signaling and reputation. These models are mostly captured under the notion of expressive law.[63] Richard McAdams' attitudinal theory of expressive law suggests that enacting laws can solve a pluralistic ignorance problem by clarifying the underlying attitudes of the majority of people in a community or society.[64] According to this approach, people are primarily motivated to obey the law due to their desire to gain the approval of others.

Now looking at Posner's famous model of signaling,[65] we can see that individuals signal to their surroundings by, for example, paying taxes, that they belong to a good group of people.[66] However, even if the law signals to people what the prevailing norms are or what is the right thing to do going forward, it is still necessary for these norms to be seen as representing the majority view. Also, many laws are simply not that popular, at least not at first. This makes relying on social norms in all cases where the law is not popular highly problematic.

In diverse societies, some communities may prioritize their own internal norms over formal laws. Yet many scholarly discussions of social norms overlook this heterogeneity, instead assuming a homogeneous society where norms affect everyone similarly. For example, the underlying message of the works of Robert Scott,[67] Richard McAdams, and Janice Nadler,[68] assumes that there are unified norms. For them,

62 Fehr, Ernst, and Simon Gächter. "Altruistic punishment in humans." *Nature* 415.6868 (2002): 137–140. For critique on this model Pedersen, Eric J., Robert Kurzban, and Michael E. McCullough. "Do humans really punish altruistically? A closer look." *Proceedings of the Royal Society B: Biological Sciences* 280.1758 (2013): 1–8.

63 Sunstein, Cass R. "Social norms and social roles." *Columbia Law Review* 96 (1996): 903–968; also see Cooter. "Do good laws make good citizens?," 1577–1601, and McAdams, Richard H. "The focal point theory of expressive law." In *Encyclopedia of law and economics*. Edward Elgar Publishing, 2000: 1650–1701.

64 McAdams, Richard H. "An attitudinal theory of expressive law." *Oregon Law Review* 79 (2000): 339–390.

65 Posner, Richard A. "Rational choice, behavioral economics, and the law." *Stanford Law Review* 50 (1997): 1551–1576.

66 Posner, Eric A. "Law and social norms: The case of tax compliance." *Virginia Law Review* 86 (2000): 1781–1820.

67 Scott, Robert E. "The limits of behavioral theories of law and social norms." *Virginia Law Review* 86 (2000): 1603–1648.

68 McAdams, Richard H., and Janice Nadler. "Coordinating in the shadow of the law: Two contextualized tests of the focal point theory of legal compliance." *Law & Society Review* 42.4 (2008): 865–898.

the main problem is that people are not always aware of them and only the expressive function of the law reveals to them what the majority of people are thinking.

While discussions of law often focus on social identity and values, not all laws connect directly to people's core beliefs and the role of intrinsic motivation can vary significantly depending on the type of law in question. It could be that intrinsic motivation is even more important for laws that affect people's daily lives than for laws that are obeyed less frequently, where the interaction with the state is on a more legal footing and thus easier to monitor.

As we will show in further discussion, many working in this field assume that social norms are operative only when they are the prevailing norms. One notable example of this is Cristina Bicchieri's philosophical analysis of the function and importance of social norms.[69]

SOCIAL NORMS AS INTRINSIC MOTIVATION?

In examining how laws can influence social norms, we need to explore whether these norms operate through intrinsic motivation – such as group identity and the need to belong – or through extrinsic factors like the fear of shaming and social disapproval.

Social norms are often viewed as an important contributor to compliance in many studies. However, they are not necessarily part of intrinsic motivation, which is often driven by internal factors. In contrast, social norms are far more related to external forces, such as social punishment and shame.[70]

Prevailing social norms have been shown to be highly important in the context of normative messages. For example, a field study examining the effectiveness of signs requesting that guests participate in an environmental conservation program found that it was possible to encourage hotel guests to care more about their environmental footprints. This field experiment, alternating different signs in a hotel regarding towel usage, found that people are more likely to comply with appeals that use descriptive norms rather than with traditional appeals.[71] However, when communicating to people what the norms are, especially in field experiments, it becomes unclear what leads to the change, especially with respect to norms. People often internalize social norms, transforming what is considered acceptable behavior into personal preferences and desires. This process of internalization means that

[69] Bicchieri, Cristina. *Norms in the wild: How to diagnose, measure, and change social norms.* Oxford University Press, 2016.

[70] Kahan, Dan M. "The secret ambition of deterrence." In *Deterrence*, edited by Thom Brooks, Routledge, 2019: 409–496.

[71] Goldstein, Noah J., Robert B. Cialdini, and Vladas Griskevicius. "A room with a viewpoint: Using social norms to motivate environmental conservation in hotels." *Journal of Consumer Research* 35.3 (2008): 472–482.

individuals may come to genuinely want to engage in behaviors that align with societal expectations, rather than merely complying out of external pressure. Along these lines, some studies have examined whether social norms continue to influence behavior even under conditions of complete anonymity.[72]

At the same time, it is important to recognize studies on socialization,[73] which show that social norms become part of an individual's identity.[74] If people behave as they think people in their social role and status need to behave, does this mean that are doing so for intrinsic reasons? Is their behavior related to the action itself? Clearly, theories of signaling indicate that such motivation can be considered extrinsic.[75] But can a situation in which the behavior is seen as socially expected of someone in a certain position, but where they receives no reward from the behavior itself, be explained?

Among the researchers studying social norms, Cristina Bicchieri, mentioned earlier, is one of the leading scholars.[76] In her influential book,[77] *The Grammar of Society*, she argues that for a norm to exist, a sufficient number of people must believe that it pertains to a given type of situation and enough people must behave according to that norm. According to Bicchieri, norm compliance depends on a conditional preference to cooperate, depending on whether others will cooperate as well.

In a later book,[78] she takes a more behavioral and experimental approach and attempts to examine how it is possible to change people's expectations of the behavior of others. In this book too, she finds that the most important factor influencing the likelihood of change is the expectation of others' behavior.

What is important in her work is the notion of conditional preferences, which breaks down the intrinsic extrinsic divide upon which much of this book is built.[79]

72 Cooter, Robert D. "Three effects of social norms on law: Expression, deterrence, and internalization." *Oregon Law Review* 79 (2000): 1–22; also see Gavrilets, Sergey, and Peter J. Richerson. "Collective action and the evolution of social norm internalization." *Proceedings of the National Academy of Sciences* 114.23 (2017): 6068–6073; Etzioni, Amitai. "Social norms: Internalization, persuasion, and history." *Law & Society Review* 34.1 (2000): 157–178; and Crandall, Christian S., Amy Eshleman, and Laurie O'Brien. "Social norms and the expression and suppression of prejudice: The struggle for internalization." *Journal of Personality and Social Psychology* 82.3 (2002): 349–378.

73 Robert B. Cialdini and Melanie R. Trost. "Social influence: Social norms, conformity, and compliance." In *The handbook of social psychology*, edited by D. T. Gilbert, S. T. Fiske, and G. Lindzey, McGraw-Hill, 1998: 151–192.

74 Bicchieri, Cristina, Ryan Muldoon, and Alessandro Sontuoso. "Social norms." In *The Stanford encyclopedia of philosophy*, edited by Edward N. Zalta and Uri Nodelman, Stanford University Press, 2018.

75 Posner. "Law and social norms," 1781.

76 E.g., see Hansson, Sven Ove. *The dynamics of norms*, edited by Cristina Bicchieri, Richard Jeffrey, and Brain Skyrms, Cambridge University Press, 1997; see also Kelly, Daniel, and Taylor Davis. "Social norms and human normative psychology." *Social Philosophy and Policy* 35.1 (2018): 54–76.

77 Bicchieri, Cristina. *The grammar of society: The nature and dynamics of social norms*. Cambridge University Press, 2005.

78 Bicchieri. *Norms in the wild*.

79 Bicchieri, Cristina. "Norms, preferences, and conditional behavior." *Politics, Philosophy & Economics* 9.3 (2010): 297–313.

According to her analysis, people's desires and behaviors are influenced by their expectations of others' actions. This suggests that intrinsic motivation is not static, but rather dynamic and socially influenced. In other words, what people "want" to do is shaped by their perceptions of social norms and expectations.

SOCIAL NORMS AS A BEHAVIORAL INTERVENTION

Many studies have been conducted to determine the effectiveness of using social norms to increase compliance. For example, Shahar Ayal and his coauthors conducted a field experiment to test cues to encourage people to pay for public transportation, a prevailing social norm.[80] Two experiments were conducted in two railroad stations in France to study the impact of watching eye cues and descriptive social norm messages on fare evasion. The results from both studies suggest that watching eye cues alone is not effective in a crowded train station. However, exposing passengers to watching eye cues together with a descriptive social norm messaging campaign reduced the fare evasion rates observed by standard inspection operations. This approach also eliminated lying behavior measured by the die-under-cup paradigm, which enables researchers to investigate how people behave in situations where they can cheat without any associated risk.[81]

Competing Intrinsic Accounts of Social Motivation

A more intrinsic view of social norms, which is distinct from the research associated with Robert Cooter and other law and economics scholars, is related to group effects.[82] Behaving as others do is not related to the information or costs.[83] The importance of group identity and the individual's need to belong is beyond debate in psychology.[84] Group identity motivation is widely recognized in the social dilemma context as a way to counteract the self-interest of the individual.[85] In the context of

80 Ayal, Shahar, Jérémy Celse, and Guy Hochman. "Crafting messages to fight dishonesty: A field investigation of the effects of social norms and watching eye cues on fare evasion." *Organizational Behavior and Human Decision Processes* 166 (2021): 9–19.

81 Shalvi, Shaul, et al. "Justified ethicality: Observing desired counterfactuals modifies ethical perceptions and behavior." *Organizational Behavior and Human Decision Processes* 115.2 (2011): 181–190.

82 See, for example, Cooter. "Three effects of social norms on law," 1.

83 Jackson, Jay W. "Reactions to social dilemmas are influenced by group identification motives." *Advances in Psychology Research* 16 (2002): 167–183.

84 Baumeister, Roy F., and Mark R. Leary. "The need to belong: Desire for interpersonal attachments as a fundamental human motivation." *Psychological Bulletin* 117.3 (1995): 497–529.

85 Brewer, Marilynn B., and Roderick M. Kramer. "Choice behavior in social dilemmas: Effects of social identity, group size, and decision framing." *Journal of Personality and Social Psychology* 50.3 (1986): 543–549. Also see Jackson, Ronald L. "Cultural contracts theory: Toward an understanding of identity negotiation." *Communication Quarterly* 50.3–4 (2002): 359–367.

public goods, Jean-Robert Tyran and Lars Feld have demonstrated through experiments that people are conditional cooperators and want to engage in legal compliance when they have a reason to believe that others will do the same.[86] Dan Kahan has suggested a different nonidentity view for why people care about what others are doing. According to his approach, the individual needs to believe that other members of society share their commitment to the law to maintain their commitment to society and its rules.[87] The focus is not on reputation or identity but rather on the fear of being the only "sucker" who obeys the law.

When considering various accounts of social norms, it's crucial to remember that even the most noninstrumental interpretations may not align with the original concept of intrinsic motivation. These norms might not be considered intrinsic to the act itself. With this understanding, we now turn our attention to exploring justice motivation

JUSTICE-BASED MOTIVATIONS

In addition to social motivation, there is another type of motivation that assumes that an individual is mainly motivated by morality and fairness. Given the assumed care for morality by the individual, legal policymakers should design laws in a way that emphasizes their moral virtue, namely the potential harm to others that would be prevented by compliance.[88]

Distributive Justice

A motivation for justice is one of the most fundamental intrinsic motivations for compliance.[89] Within the concept of fairness, several subconcepts have received considerable attention in the literature. One of the well-known distinctions in this context is between procedural and distributive justice. Distributive justice focuses on the substance of the law. People are more likely to comply with the law when they believe that, under the law, individuals get what they are entitled to or the punishment that they deserve.[90] While distributive justice is a highly studied concept

[86] Tyran, Jean-Robert, and Lars P. Feld. "Why people obey the law: Experimental evidence from the provision of public goods." Available at SSRN 290231 (2002). https://papers.ssrn.com/sol3/papers.cfm?abstract_id=290231.

[87] Kahan, Dan M. "Trust, collective action, and law." *Boston University Law Review* 81 (2001): 333–348.

[88] Tapp, June L., and Felice J. Levine. "Persuasion to virtue: A preliminary statement." *Law and Society Review* (1970): 565–582. Also see Robinson, Paul H., and John M. Darley. "Testing competing theories of justification." *North Carolina Law Review* 76 (1997): 1095–1144.

[89] Fehr, Ernst, and Klaus M. Schmidt. "A theory of fairness, competition, and cooperation." *Quarterly Journal of Economics* 114.3 (1999): 817–868; also see Kahneman, Daniel, Jack L. Knetsch, and Richard Thaler. "Fairness as a constraint on profit seeking: Entitlements in the market." *American Economic Review* (1986): 728–741.

[90] See generally, Darley, John M., Paul H. Robinson, and Kevin M. Carlsmith. "The ex-ante function of the criminal law." *Law & Society Review* 35 (2001): 165–189.

in law, philosophy, and related topics, it has not been very central to the study of compliance. This may be because many compliance decisions do not involve real distributive justice issues. However, there are certainly issues of distributive justice in many contexts such as taxes, torts, and contracts. In addition, there is a significant similarity between the impact of morality, which is widely studied, and distributive justice on an individual's motivation to comply.

MORALITY AS INTRINSIC MOTIVATION?

Another limitation of current research on intrinsic motivation is related to the question of how the type of motivation interacts with the likelihood of internalization. In many ways, morality is seen as a type of motivation that comes from within the individual. Once the moral norm is in place, there is no need to look for external motivation. It is also considered a more effective and sustainable form of compliance.[91] In an online field experimental study conducted on a large sample, moral framing was found to be the most effective way to encourage people to perform an undesirable task following previous commitment, while the legal frame was found to be the least effective.[92] Lawrence Friedman's 2016 book, *Impact: How Law Affects Behavior*, emphasizes three key factors that influence law's effect on behavior. He distinguishes between extrinsic factors, such as rewards and peer pressure, and factors related to intrinsic motivation, which operate through communication and include elements like conscience, legitimacy, and morality.[93] However, the main problem with looking at morality as intrinsic motivation is that it does not necessarily relate to the actual behavior that one needs to comply with. For instance, people may feel a moral obligation to behave in a particular manner, not because of anything related to the behavior itself, but rather to maintain their self-image as compliant individuals or to avoid being free riders. Additionally, morality is highly connected to guilt and people might comply not because of the action, but because of the fear of feeling guilty for not complying.[94] It is not clear whether, under the classical account of intrinsic motivation, behaving to avoid feeling guilty could be seen as internal or external to the self.

Procedural Justice

Procedural justice is a concept that focuses on the impact of how decisions are made and its effect on compliance as intrinsic motivation rather than the content of the

91 Frey and Torgler. "Tax morale and conditional cooperation."

92 Eigen, Zev J. "When and why individuals obey contracts: Experimental evidence of consent, compliance, promise, and performance." *Journal of Legal Studies* 41.1 (2012): 67–93.

93 Friedman. *Impact: How law affects behavior.*

94 Boster, Franklin J., et al. "A meta-analytic review of the effect of guilt on compliance." *Social Influence* 11.1 (2016): 54–67.

decision or the law itself.[95] It considers the importance of neutrality and voice in the decision-making process. This concept has been extensively studied in the field of psycho-legal scholarship. Starting with the work of scholars such as John Thibaut and Laurens Walker, E. Allan Lind and Tom Tyler, and G. S. Leventhal and colleagues,[96] a list of requirements has been suggested that need to be satisfied for people to experience procedural justice. These include consistency, accuracy, and representativeness. The concept of procedural justice has both instrumental and intrinsic value, even without considering its effect on legitimacy. One of the leading scholars who has explored the contribution of procedural justice legal compliance is Tom Tyler.[97] In his widely cited book, *Why People Obey the Law*, Tyler suggests that procedural fairness – the way people are treated by authorities – is the main motivation for legal compliance.[98] The unique contribution of morality to legal compliance has been demonstrated in various legal contexts, even in areas that are usually viewed as economic ones, such as taxation.[99] The view that procedural justice is extrinsic to the decision to comply may be related not only to the fact that it is associated with the system behind the law, rather than the content of the law, but also to the mechanism it employs.

The information heuristics approach is a paradigm that could mostly supports the instrumental view.[100] This approach suggests that procedural justice enhances compliance by helping people understand the law's true content. Rather than valuing procedural fairness for its own sake, people use it as a proxy to assess whether the law itself will be fair. While this view of procedural justice is instrumental in relation to outcomes, it can still generate intrinsic motivation to obey the law – a motivation that exists independently of monitoring or external incentives. The group-based approach to procedural justice emphasizes the importance of feeling a sense of belonging and being treated with dignity as a valued member of the group,

[95] Walters, Glenn D., and P. Colin Bolger. "Procedural justice perceptions, legitimacy beliefs, and compliance with the law: A meta-analysis." *Journal of Experimental Criminology* 15 (2019): 341–372.

[96] Thibaut, John W., and Laurens Walker. *Procedural justice: A psychological analysis*. L. Erlbaum Associates, 1975; Lind, E. Allan, and Tom R. Tyler. *The social psychology of procedural justice*. Springer Science & Business Media, 1988; Leventhal, Gerald S., J. Karuza and W. R. Fry. "Beyond fairness: A theory of allocation preferences." In *Justice and social interaction*, edited by Gerold Mikula, Springer-Verlag, 1980: 167–218.

[97] Tyler, Tom R. "Justice, self-interest, and the legitimacy of legal and political authority." In *Beyond self-interest*, edited by J. J. Mansbridge, University of Chicago Press, 1990: 171–179; also see Brockner, Joel, Tom R. Tyler, and Rochelle Cooper-Schneider. "The influence of prior commitment to an institution on reactions to perceived unfairness: The higher they are, the harder they fall." *Administrative Science Quarterly* 37.2 (1992): 241–261.

[98] Tyler, Tom R. *Why people obey the law*. Princeton University Press, 2006.

[99] Wenzel, Michael. "Motivation or rationalisation? Causal relations between ethics, norms and tax compliance." *Journal of Economic Psychology* 26.4 (2005): 491–508.

[100] Lind, E. A., K. Van den Bos, and H. A. Wilke. "The psychology of procedural and distributive justice viewed from the perspective of fairness heuristic theory." In *Justice in the workplace: From theory to practice*, edited by R. Cropanzano, Psychology Press, 2001: 49–66.

whether at the organizational or state level.[101] This focus on group membership and respect shifts the concept of procedural justice in law from a purely instrumental view to one that incorporates social and psychological elements.

While this approach is not strictly instrumental, it does introduce an element that could be seen as extrinsic to the law itself. The content of the law, which is usually what will be seen as intrinsic compliance motivation when speaking, for example, on tax morale and environmental motivation, is no longer the sole issue; instead, the focus is on how the law and its procedures make people feel about their place in the group. People are more likely to obey procedurally just laws not only because of the laws' content, for example, taxes are low or the environment should be protected, but because the process makes them feel respected and included in the community, rather than alienated from it.[102]

This perspective suggests that procedural justice in law operates on both intrinsic and extrinsic levels: intrinsic in its concern with fair processes and extrinsic in its consideration of group dynamics and individual feelings of belonging. The result is a more nuanced understanding of why people comply with the law, one that bridges legal, psychological, and sociological perspectives.

LEVI'S APPROACH TO VOLUNTARY COMPLIANCE

Margaret Levi and her coauthors have proposed an important approach to procedural justice in the context of compliance that focuses on legitimacy and voluntary compliance.[103] In their work, they focus on an important aspect related to the book – "quasi-voluntary" compliance. This type of compliance is related to a combination of coercion and consent and is conditional upon the government behaving in a trustworthy way. Generally speaking, Levi and her colleagues have made several important contributions to our understanding of how trust influences public cooperation.[104] Of particular relevance to this book is their nuanced analysis of the complex relationship between trust and various forms of social and political cooperation.[105] Their work explores how trust not only encourages cooperation but also how cooperative behaviors can, in turn, build and reinforce trust, creating a dynamic feedback loop in social and political interactions.

101 Sunshine, Jason, and Tom Tyler. "Moral solidarity, identification with the community, and the importance of procedural justice: The police as prototypical representatives of a group's moral values." *Social Psychology Quarterly* 66.2 (2003): 153–165.

102 Tyler, Tom R., and Steven L. Blader. "The group engagement model: Procedural justice, social identity, and cooperative behavior." *Personality and Social Psychology Review* 7.4 (2003): 349–361.

103 Levi, Margaret, and Audrey Sacks. "Legitimating beliefs: Sources and indicators." *Regulation & Governance* 3.4 (2009): 311–333.

104 Levi, Margaret, and Laura Stoker. "Political trust and trustworthiness." *Annual Review of Political Science* 3.1 (2000): 475–507.

105 Levi, Margaret. *Consent, dissent, and patriotism*. Cambridge University Press, 1997.

Levi discusses two strands in the research: One strand includes political trust, trustworthy government, and citizen compliance; while the other strand includes political trust, social trust, and cooperation, which in her work, usually means working with others. However, as this book endeavors to emphasize, cooperation might also be related to how people behave regarding the requirements of the state, as in the case of environmental regulation, where some of the requirements are really a matter of cooperation, rather than compliance. For example, when the government tries to encourage people to cooperate in contexts such as using public transportation or buying electric cars, it is not possible to talk about compliance, let alone force them to comply. When analyzing the value of voluntary compliance, we need to consider the importance of cooperation. If we recognize that cooperation is more common than compliance, as is the case in some aspects of environmental cooperation, then we might have a greater need for cooperation (see Figure 0.2).

In a different study Margaret Levi and colleagues,[106] focus on "willing compliance"; they suggest that this is mostly related to factors of legitimacy and procedural justice.[107] Another study in which Levi was involved relied on two datasets (one from the United States and one from sub-Saharan Africa).[108] It indicated that legitimacy affects compliance and that it's influenced by perceived trustworthiness, which in itself is built upon factors such as perception of leadership motivations, administrative competence, and government performance. The authors analyzed the extent to which citizens perceive that the government upholds procedural justice. While conducting cross-sectional analyses, they found that citizens' judgments about the government are strongly influenced by procedural justice. This finding is important because it suggests that procedural justice is a significant predictor of both types of legitimacy, value-based and behavior-based, which are connected to compliance. This work suggests that the way governments exercise their authority influences their legitimacy and their shape. However, this work has been mostly criticized for the lack of experimental evidence actually showing that procedural justice has indeed improved the quality of compliance.[109]

There is an impressive body of research supporting the importance of procedural justice in various contexts.[110] As reviewed so far, numerous studies have demonstrated

[106] Levi, Margaret, Audrey Sacks, and Tom Tyler. "Conceptualizing legitimacy, measuring legitimating beliefs." *American Behavioral Scientist* 53.3 (2009): 354–375.

[107] For further discussion of the relationship between procedural justice, legitimacy and compliance see Levi, Margaret, Tom R. Tyler, and Audrey Sacks. "The reasons for compliance with law." In *Understanding social action, promoting human rights*, edited by Ryan Goodman, Derek Jinks and Andrew K. Woods, Oxford University Press, 2012: 70–99.

[108] Levi, Tyler, and Sacks. "The reasons for compliance with law."

[109] Nagin, Daniel S., and Cody W. Telep. "Procedural justice and legal compliance: A revisionist perspective." *Criminology & Public Policy* 19.3 (2020): 761–786.

[110] Folger, Robert, and Jerald Greenberg. "Procedural justice: An interpretive analysis of personnel systems." In *Research in personnel and human resources management*. Vol. 3, edited by K. Rowland and G. Ferris, JAI Press, 1985: 141–183.

strong links between perceptions of procedural fairness and compliance with laws and regulations. However, some recent research has challenged the extent of this relationship, suggesting that the connection between procedural justice and compliance may not be as straightforward as previously thought.[111]

While these studies provide valuable insights into the role of procedural justice in shaping behavior, they offer limited understanding of voluntary compliance beyond self-reported intentions to obey the law. This gap highlights the need for further research to explore the mechanisms underlying voluntary compliance and how it relates to perceptions of procedural justice.

The assumption that people's compliance will be better if they have legitimate reasons for complying is very plausible, but for the most part, it has not been proven experimentally, thus limiting inferring causality.[112] As suggested in Chapter 1, the main advantage of such compliance is that it is less dependent on extrinsic reasons, making it more likely to be long term and sustainable. However, it is important to note that research into organizational context and performance has usually associated intrinsic motivation with quality of performance and extrinsic motivation with quantity of performance.[113] Based on this distinction, it is possible to speculate that a similar effect will happen with regard to compliance. Naturally, when people comply only to avoid punishment, they may focus only on behaviors that can be monitored. These usually emphasize quantitative aspects of compliance rather than its qualitative aspects.[114]

THE ADVANTAGE OF PROCEDURAL JUSTICE IN GENERATING INTRINSIC VOLUNTARY COMPLIANCE

Procedural justice is more likely to be related to the next model, which focuses not on the content of the law but on the institution. Procedural justice focuses on how laws are created rather than their content, representing one of two key pathways to achieving voluntary compliance. One is through the morality of the action and the other is through trust in the state. The second option is clearly easier and may be more appealing to a broader consensus of the population. It is difficult to imagine a situation where everyone agrees on a particular law. In that regard, even the effect of reason giving, which is seen as part of allowing people to feel that they

[111] Walters and Bolger. "Procedural justice perceptions, legitimacy beliefs, and compliance with the law."

[112] Murphy, Kristina, Lorraine Mazerolle, and Sarah Bennett. "Promoting trust in police: Findings from a randomised experimental field trial of procedural justice policing." *Policing and Society* 24.4 (2014): 405–424.

[113] Cerasoli, Christopher P., Jessica M. Nicklin, and Michael T. Ford. "Intrinsic motivation and extrinsic incentives jointly predict performance: A 40-year meta-analysis." *Psychological Bulletin* 140.4 (2014): 980–1008.

[114] Compare with the argument made in Feldman, Yuval, and Doron Teichman. "Are all legal probabilities created equal?" *New York University Law Review* 84 (2009): 980–1022.

understand the law, might also be perceived as some sort of procedural fairness. By simply explaining what it is doing, the authorities manage to show the public that they care about them. The state need not create laws where the content is approved by the public.

LEGITIMATE LAWS AND MORAL MOTIVATION

Legislation must be responsive to human motivation and its legitimacy is the main feature that ensures this. Legitimacy is often defined as the perception that the law was formulated and executed with full authority and it is more important than the content of the law itself.[115] The distinction between moral individual and immoral rule models becomes problematic since rules that violate people's moral principles are inherently unlikely to be viewed as legitimate. However, there appears to be a real difference between obeying the law because the government has the power to force people to do so. Indeed, within the concept of legitimacy, some scholars focus more on the legalistic and institutional perspectives, while others give more weight to the content of the law. Jeffrey Fagan and Tom Tyler discuss the gap between the various perspectives of legitimacy, demonstrating the differences between legitimacy's sociological, legal, and moral aspects.[116]

Along the same lines, it seems that the discussion of citizenship as a mutually exclusive model lies at the heart of the ability to speak about legitimacy as a distinctive concept within the moral nature of the law's content. In many cases, when an individual is obeying the law due to an obligation, rather than due to a belief in the morality of the law, there is a greater chance that that the individual will obey the law, even when they do not fully agree with its content.[117] Another study demonstrated how institutional actions can result in conflict and resistance when institutions prioritize perpetuating their authority and technical expertise over meeting the social and developmental needs of individuals.[118]

TRUST AS COMPLIANCE MOTIVATION

One of the most discussed concepts within the area of regulatory governance relates to trust. Trust is usually seen as a replacement for coercion, with the focus being on encouraging people to want to comply rather than forcing them to do so. On the

115 Jackson et al. "Why do people comply with the law?"

116 Tyler, Tom R., and Jeffrey Fagan. "Legitimacy and cooperation: Why do people help the police fight crime in their communities?" *Ohio State Journal of Criminal Law* 6 (2008): 231–276.

117 Jackson et al., "Why do people comply with the law?"

118 Losoncz, Ibolya. "Responses to institutional disrespect." In *Institutional disrespect: South Sudanese experiences of the structural marginalisation of refugee migrants in Australia*, Palgrave Pivot, 2019: 115–133.

other hand, it is also possible to argue that trust in institutions is not related to the behavior itself, but to the ability of citizens to believe that requests from those institutions are legitimate. Obeying a legal ordinance because one believes that the institution is functioning well and is professional, and therefore deserves trust, could be seen as noncoerced behavior. However, it does not necessarily mean that the person wants to behave in that way. The behavior itself may not be what the person wants, but rather they are acting in this way because the institution has asked them to.

A demonstration of that complexity can be seen in classical studies by K. Murphy, who has shown how trust can be considered an alternative to coercion. Murphy argues that using threats and coercion are ineffective in inducing compliance.[119] Using survey data collected from 2,292 taxpayers accused of tax avoidance, she demonstrated that variables such as trust need to be considered when managing noncompliance. If regulators are seen to be acting fairly, people will trust the motives of that authority and defer to their decisions voluntarily. Pautz and Wamsley have also studied the interaction between regulators and those they regulate, and have emphasized the importance of trust being developed between the two groups to ensure effective regulation.[120]

When we focus on the effect of trust as an alternative to control and deterrence, we must consider the ability of trust and deterrence to operate together. This issue is critical because it is difficult for states to base their policy on trust, given the fact that so many people are less likely to be affected by it. The attempt to simultaneously use both trust and deterrence is problematic because of the crowding-out argument. However, Andreas Glöckner and colleagues conducted studies that showed that both trust and deterrence had independent contributions to both legitimacy and deterrence, in addition to other factors.[121] Overall, their findings support the predictive power of all relevant factors, including legitimacy, self-control, and deterrence. Thus, trust is related to both legitimacy and to the functioning of deterrence.

The relationship between trust and motivation in the context of cooperation with a system is complex. Trust can be seen as an intrinsic motivator for cooperation because it originates from within the individual rather than from external rewards or punishments (see Figure 0.3). When people trust a system, their motivation to cooperate stems from this internal sense of trust rather than from external factors. This intrinsic nature of trust-based motivation distinguishes it from extrinsic motivations,

119 Murphy, Kristina. "The role of trust in nurturing compliance: A study of accused tax avoiders." *Law and Human Behavior* 28 (2004): 187–209.

120 Pautz, Michelle C., and Carolyn Slott Wamsley. "Pursuing trust in environmental regulatory interactions: The significance of inspectors' interactions with the regulated community." *Administration & Society* 44.7 (2012): 853–884.

121 de Puiseau, Berenike Waubert, Andreas Glöckner, and Emanuel V. Towfigh. "Integrating theories of law obedience: How utility-theoretic factors, legitimacy, and lack of self-control influence decisions to commit low-level crimes." *Judgment and Decision Making* 14.3 (2019): 318–334.

which are driven by external rewards or penalties. However, if the discussion is related to legal compliance, then trust in the system could be seen as an extrinsic reason to comply with the law, since trust is not related to the content of the law but rather to the system. This is different from trust in science, which is intrinsic: I take the vaccine because I believe it is good for my health.

A valuable conclusion can be drawn from research on trust by comparing it with the literature on intrinsic motivation and morality. The state faces many challenges in getting people to internalize that compliance is the moral thing to do, as not all acts of the state can be seen as such. However, trust, which is a much broader concept than just procedural justice and legitimacy, can be seen as a standard that states should aspire to maintain.

Essentially, it is easier to devise a legal theory that requires the state to earn the trust of the public. It is less likely that we can ask the state to ensure that everyone is convinced that they want to do what the state requires them to do. According to our typology, citizenship is the motivation behind why people comply – because they feel it is their duty. This is highly dependent on issues such as trust and legitimacy, and less so on morality and the content of the particular laws.

In this regard, approaches by regulators that provide reasons might be seen as more relevant for content than for procedure, although the two are clearly connected. If people cannot understand the rationale behind a certain legal requirement, they might come to question whether the state is trustworthy. Thus, it could be that it is more important for the state to explain things than to give people rationales.

MOTIVATIONAL POSTURES PARADIGM

Building on theories of procedural justice and legitimacy, the concept of motivational postures offers a broader understanding of what drives compliance. In their famous research on motivational postures, Valerie. Braithwaite, Kristina Murphy, and Monika Reinhart argue that the most effective regulatory outcome is achieved when the regulatory process can dampen the "taking control" and "feeling oppressed" sensibilities and strengthen the "thinking morally" sensibility.[122]

It is interesting to note that the motivational posture paradigm theory is very much related to the argument we made regarding procedural justice and legitimacy as being external to the law. This paradigm also focuses on the relationship with the system, rather than the law, making it extrinsic to the law itself. However, as suggested, some postures – as presented by Valerie Braithwaite – are consistent with motivation not being driven through processes of coercion. Braithwaite introduced the concept of motivational postures, which are signals that people send

[122] Braithwaite, Valerie, Kristina Murphy, and Monika Reinhart. "Taxation threat, motivational postures, and responsive regulation." *Law & Policy* 29.1 (2007): 137–158.

to authorities to indicate their willingness to comply with the authority's rules. Braithwaite identified five different motivational postures – commitment, capitulation, resistance, disengagement, and game playing.[123]

Some scholars have tried to use Braithwaite's motivational posturing framework to explain individuals' reactions to authorities.[124] This framework was also applied in the context of Australian agriculture and environmental regulation.[125] Postures were predictive of beyond-compliance behavior. While some were more likely to undertake beyond-compliance behaviors, the "gamers" were the least likely to do so.[126] Another study examined the perceptions of regulators and the regulated toward regulatory encounters in order to predict subsequent compliance with nursing home quality-of-care standards.[127] The argument was made in another study that self-determination theory may improve how the relation between trust and control is conceptualized in the dominant responsive regulation theory.[128]

The main problem with this approach, from the perspective of this book, is that it is not clear what the likelihood is that such a posture will stay stable over time, or how much of it is dependent upon the specifics of a legal ordinance. Moreover, in order to explore the theme of this book, it is important to examine the antecedents of posture, what sustains it, and the extent to which intrinsic motivation is connected to it. Can one's state of mind really affect one's posture?

This line of research suggests that gaining voluntary compliance is complicated because regulators must tailor their interventions to the level of intrinsic motivation of the people they are trying to regulate. The ability to tailor regulatory approaches to people's level of intrinsic motivation requires some indication of their level of motivation, as well as knowledge of how they behave.

123 Braithwaite, Murphy, and Reinhart. "Taxation threat, motivational postures, and responsive regulation."

124 Murphy, Kristina. "Turning defiance into compliance with procedural justice: Understanding reactions to regulatory encounters through motivational posturing." *Regulation & Governance* 10.1 (2016): 93–109.

125 A mail survey of 5,235 farmers across Australia was conducted to examine motivational postures and attitudes to government, environmental problems, environmental laws and regulations, and farm management behaviors. Four postures were empirically derived: one associated with compliance, here labeled "Aligned," and three associated with non- or creative compliance: one Disengaged, one Game playing, and one Resistant. Motivational postures were related to place, jurisdiction, and degree of regulatory alignment: the degree of agreement between regulatees and regulators on the latter's role and on the content, process, and aims of regulatory interventions.

126 Bartel, Robyn, and Elaine Barclay. "Motivational postures and compliance with environmental law in Australian agriculture." *Journal of Rural Studies* 27.2 (2011): 153–170.

127 Braithwaite, John, and Toni Makkai. "Trust and compliance." *Policing and Society: An International Journal* 4.1 (1994): 1–12.

128 See Weibel, Antoinette, and Frédérique Six. "Trust and control: The role of intrinsic motivation." In *Handbook of advances in trust research*, edited by Reinhard Bachmann and Akbar Zaheer, Edward Elgar Publishing, 2013: 57–81; see also Barak-Corren, Netta, and Yael Kariv-Teitelbaum. "Behavioral responsive regulation: Bringing together responsive regulation and behavioral public policy." *Regulation & Governance* 15 (2021): S163–S182.

Habit Formation and Voluntary Compliance

When discussing the different motivations for behavioral compliance, it is important to account for the role of habits in voluntary compliance. That is because many scholars have suggested that it is one of the best ways to lead to sustainable behavioral change. Although not the focus of the book, which attempts to take a motivational approach, it is important to consider the role of habits. Katy Milkman is a highly influential scholar in the field of habit formation. She contends that the best way to achieve behavioral change is to create habits that reduce the need to interact with the person every time cooperation is needed.[129]

This concept aligns closely with Benjamin van Rooij and Adam Fine's argument in their book *The Behavioral Code: The Hidden Ways the Law Makes Us Better or Worse*.[130] They describe how wearing seat belts became a habitual behavior through an intensive process involving various regulatory tools. This process was so effective that it reached a point where people's motivations for wearing seat belts were no longer consciously examined or analyzed.[131]

Thus, most of the focus in the habit formation literature seems to be on getting people to engage in the behavior, with little emphasis on the motivational approach needed to get them there. After the repetition of the action, people will engage in the behavior that is desirable for the state or the organization in a mindless way, whether it involves going to the gym, as Katherine Milkman writes about,[132] or wearing a seat belt as in van Rooije and Fine's mentioned book.[133] It is clear that going to the gym is not enforced like wearing a seat belt, but starting from a certain point, it is supposed to have a similar effect. A similar effort was made during the COVID pandemic when many people began wearing masks. This simple behavior became a habit for many people, as it was easy to do it automatically without thinking about it. Research has shown that the initial motivation for wearing masks originally was less important than the habit of doing it repeatedly.[134] A similar process can be observed, for example, in environmental contexts, such as when recycling becomes a habit.[135]

[129] Milkman, Katherine L., Julia A. Minson, and Kevin G. M. Volpp. "Holding the hunger games hostage at the gym: An evaluation of temptation bundling." *Management Science* 60.2 (2014): 283–299; Staats, Bradley R., et al. "Motivating process compliance through individual electronic monitoring: An empirical examination of hand hygiene in healthcare." *Management Science* 63.5 (2017): 1563–1585.

[130] Van Rooij, Benjamin, and Adam Fine. *The behavioral code: The hidden ways the law makes us better or worse*. Beacon Press, 2021.

[131] This model also targets the socially oriented individual discussed in Chapter 3.

[132] Milkman, Katherine L., et al. "Mega studies improve the impact of applied behavioral science." *Nature* 600.7889 (2021): 478–483.

[133] Van Rooij and Fine. *The behavioral code*.

[134] Li, Tianwen, et al. "Habitual mask wearing as part of COVID-19 control in Japan: An assessment using the self-report habit index." *Behavioral Sciences* 13.11 (2023): 951–963.

[135] Lally, Phillippa, and Benjamin Gardner. "Promoting habit formation." *Health Psychology Review* 7.supp. 1 (2013): S137–S158.

Despite the advantages of habit formation, the reliance on this process is not free of problems. When it comes to more complex behaviors, habit formation may be too problematic. This is especially true for very abstract types of behaviors, such as being honest.

The challenge of habit formation in regulatory policy raises several complex questions. First, how can we predict which behaviors will become habits and is it possible to break down complex behaviors into simpler, more manageable actions? Second, there are significant normative concerns: Is it appropriate for states to deliberately cultivate habits in their citizens? While encouraging habits like seat belt use has clear public benefits with minimal impact on autonomy, other behavioral interventions may pose greater challenges to individual freedom. Even from a democratic perspective that prioritizes personal autonomy there's a spectrum to consider – while creating habits around health and safety (like gym attendance or seat belt use) might seem acceptable, extending habit-forming interventions to broader areas of life raises serious concerns about governmental overreach and the normalization of behavioral control.

CONCLUSION

This chapter examines the multifaceted nature of compliance motivations, challenging reductionist approaches to understanding rule-following behavior. By exploring the interplay between intrinsic and extrinsic factors, as well as the nuanced roles of morality, social norms, and procedural justice, the discussion illuminates the complexity of human responses to legal and regulatory frameworks.

The analysis critically evaluates simplistic compliance models, demonstrating how factors such as institutional trust and perceptions of fairness can supersede traditional deterrence mechanisms. Through a rigorous examination of concepts like the obligation to obey and content-dependent motivations, the chapter offers a nuanced exploration of compliance decision-making processes.

This enriches our understanding of voluntary compliance. While existing literature acknowledges the role of intrinsic motivation in fostering voluntary compliance, the analysis reveals significant practical challenges in leveraging this potential. The findings suggest that cultivating trust and ensuring procedural fairness may offer more viable pathways to compliance than attempts to directly influence individual moral paradigms. However, the ongoing scholarly debate regarding the contextual efficacy of various motivational approaches underscores the need for further research in this domain.

This complexity sets the stage for Chapter 3's investigation of the crowding-out phenomenon and its relationship to trust. The forthcoming discussion will examine how well-intentioned regulatory efforts can inadvertently undermine intrinsic motivations. While a simplistic approach might suggest that regulators could combine multiple regulatory strategies to target different compliance motivations, the crowding-out paradigm reveals the potential impossibility of such an approach. One regulatory mechanism may actively diminish or negate the effectiveness of another, creating a complex paradox that further complicates the design of effective regulatory strategies. This understanding emphasizes the need for sophisticated approaches that account for the intricate dynamics of human motivation and behavior across diverse regulatory contexts.

3

Internalization versus Crowding Out

INTRODUCTION

In Chapter 2, we discussed the behavioral mechanisms underlying voluntary compliance and began to examine the interaction between intrinsic motivation and the likelihood of voluntary compliance. We also explored the advantages of intrinsic motivation for compliance in terms of its quality, durability, and ability to lead to a more meaningful internalization process that can also be relevant to other domains.[1]

Most studies on the interaction between internalization and compliance suggest that the state can achieve better results by focusing on intrinsic motivation.[2] Nonetheless, as we have suggested, some intrinsic motivations are better than others. For example, some of the research mentioned in the previous chapter, such as that of Margaret Levi and Tom Tyler,[3] highlights the benefits of compliance driven by institutional factors, such as legitimacy and fairness, rather than relying on morality, which can be more subjective and prone to variation.

Furthermore, it is arguable that the relationship between intrinsic motivation and actual compliance behavior doesn't exist or at least is very low in several settings. For example, as will be discussed in this chapter regarding environmental attitudes, many studies show that the relationship between environmental attitudes and actual environmental behavior is significant but not as strong as might have been expected, given the complexity of the factors moderating this relationship.[4]

1 See Feldman, Yuval. "The complexity of disentangling intrinsic and extrinsic compliance motivations: Theoretical and empirical insights from the behavioral analysis of law." *Washington University Journal of Law and Policy* 35 (2011): 11.

2 Cooter, Robert. "Do good laws make good citizens? An economic analysis of internalized norms." *Virginia Law Review* 86 (2000): 1577–1601.

3 Levi, Margaret, Tom R. Tyler, and Audrey Sacks. "The reasons for compliance with law." In *Understanding social action, promoting human rights*, edited by Ryan Goodman, Derek Jinks and Andrew K. Woods, Oxford University Press, 2012: 70–99.

4 Kollmuss, Anja, and Julian Agyeman. "Mind the gap: Why do people act environmentally and what are the barriers to pro-environmental behavior?" *Environmental Education Research* 8.3 (2002): 239–260.

However, other studies focusing on self-determination theory have found a positive relationship between environmental motivation and more frequent engagement in pro-environmental behaviors, such as recycling and energy conservation.[5] Similarly, in the context of tax morality, positive relationships have been found in countries with high tax morale and their levels of tax evasion.[6]

Overall, a variety of factors need to be considered when encouraging compliance, including intrinsic motivation, procedural justice, legitimacy, and the specific details of the behavior in question. A nuanced approach that takes these different factors into account is likely to be more effective than a one-size-fits-all approach based solely on intrinsic motivation, which clearly cannot lead to the needed compliance on its own. Rather, many factors, such as legitimacy and trust, contribute indirectly to compliance by moderating how a law affects intrinsic motivation. Thus, for example, highly trusted governments could more easily enhance intrinsic motivation through regulation.

With many seeing intrinsic motivation as leading to higher quality compliance,[7] the big question is how can both intrinsic motivation and extrinsic motivation be used at the same time when targeting those who lack intrinsic motivation. While, in the previous chapters, we have demonstrated that there are many types of intrinsic motivations, in this chapter we will focus on the effect of recognizing different intrinsic motivations. The mere recognition may have a significant impact on what happens when the law intervenes. In theory, intrinsic compliance motivation appears to positively affect actual compliance behavior. The question we will focus on in this chapter then, is why can't regulations combine the good value of intrinsic motivation with monitoring and extrinsic measures to achieve the best of all worlds?

We begin this analysis by examining a dichotomous and somewhat unsound way of internalization. We explore how the law can affect intrinsic motivation in the desired direction, as well as how it can lead to crowding out where the existence of the law undermines people's intrinsic motivations. We will demonstrate that when accounting for the variation between different compliance motivations and behaviors, many of the existing findings are expected to be limited or at least have limited predictability. We will also explain how two effects can coexist. The purpose is not intended to compare the two effects or to determine which is stronger, but rather to identify what in the law and in what context is more likely to increase or decrease internalized compliance.

5 Pelletier, Luc G., et al. "Why are you doing things for the environment? The motivation toward the environment scale (MTES) 1." *Journal of Applied Social Psychology* 28.5 (1998): 437–468.

6 Frey, Bruno S., and Benno Torgler. "Tax morale and conditional cooperation." *Journal of Comparative Economics* 35.1 (2007): 136–159.

7 Tyler, Tom R., and Jonathan Jackson. "Popular legitimacy and the exercise of legal authority: Motivating compliance, cooperation, and engagement." *Psychology, Public Policy, and Law* 20.1 (2014): 78–95.

SIMULTANEOUS CROWDING OUT AND PREFERENCE CHANGE?

To what extent is the law able to lead to preference change? What is unique in cases such as not smoking in public places, not picking wildflowers, buckling children into car seats, or even sexual harassment, where the law led to situations where people behaved better, even in contexts where they were less likely to be detected? Could this positive effect be related to visibility of behavior and hence social norms were more likely to function? Or could their success be related to a situation whereby no party benefits from any violation? Why does this positive effect not operate in cases relating to voluntary compliance with building code requirements? What is unique in those cases where a norm of voluntary compliance has emerged?

This chapter will also review some of the caveats regarding internalization. For example, opinions about compliance reasons were widely discussed regarding situations such as the COVID-19 pandemic context.[8] How is this debate on crowding out related to factors such as trust in science in cases where the science is contested? Will the introduction of sanctions will also crowd out the belief in science as it is expected to crowd out the belief in state authorities? We will also examine in what contexts coercive measures can create the greatest damage to intrinsic motivation and what type of intrinsic motivation is most likely to be inhibited by coercive measures.

Further discussion is needed not just to identify which approach can perform both functions simultaneously, but which approach is superior. In other words, if laws are crowding out intrinsic motivation, can they still lead to a change in preferences? In theory, both processes can coexist through many possible parallel pathways. For example, people might change their preferences due to their behavior or habit formation and not necessarily because of intrinsic motivation.[9]

WHY CAN'T WE HAVE IT ALL?

As suggested in the introduction to this chapter, the most important question we need to address when trying to find the right balance between different approaches toward intrinsic compliance motivation is why we need to choose between the different motivations to begin with. Why can't states focus on both coerced and internalized compliance at the same time?[10] When the state employs multiple regulatory

8 Bargain, Olivier, and Ulugbek Aminjonov. "Trust and compliance to public health policies in times of COVID-19." *Journal of Public Economics* 192 (2020): 104316.

9 Dynan, Karen E. "Habit formation in consumer preferences: Evidence from panel data." *American Economic Review* 90.3 (2000): 391–406.

10 Later on, approaches such as that of responsive regulation will be discussed, which basically suggest taking a consecutive approach to the different regulatory styles (compare with Feldman, Yuval. *The law of good people: Challenging states' ability to regulate human behavior*. Cambridge University Press, 2018).

approaches simultaneously – such as command and control, self-regulation, nudges, and sanctions – the question arises: Can these diverse strategies work in concert effectively? Our research aims to identify optimal combinations of regulatory approaches, considering what we know about the crowding-out effect.[11]

Rather than simply determining the best individual regulatory approach, we seek to understand which strategies aimed at fostering intrinsic motivation can most effectively coexist with external sanctions. For instance, instead of debating whether belief in science or moral conviction is superior in isolation, we must ask which of these intrinsic motivators is better suited to operate alongside monitoring and enforcement mechanisms.

This perspective shifts the focus from a unidimensional evaluation of regulatory tools to a more nuanced understanding of their interplay. It acknowledges that real-world policy implementation often involves multiple, concurrent strategies and that the effectiveness of such strategies may depend on how well they complement each other.[12]

By exploring these synergies and potential conflicts between different regulatory approaches, we can develop more sophisticated and effective policy designs. This approach recognizes the complex reality of governance, where multiple tools are often deployed simultaneously, and seeks to optimize their collective impact.[13]

Indeed, there are situations where a regulator can have all regulatory approaches working together, with no or relatively marginal destructive effects. For example, when the regulator can affirm both legitimacy and sanctions at the same time there might even be a mutual benefit rather than mutual destruction. We will further develop these differences in this chapter as well as in Chapter 4, which focuses on regulatory approaches to change behavior.

WHAT EXACTLY DOES CROWD OUT MEAN?

As suggested in the introduction to this chapter, most research on crowding-out motivation focuses on how incentives and compensation undermine people's intrinsic motivation to comply and to cooperate (such as in cases of civic duties).[14] That is, the introduction of extrinsic motivation on people who were originally motivated to cooperate influences how the intrinsic motivation operates, even completely

11 Frey, Bruno S., and Reto Jegen. "Motivation crowding theory." *Journal of Economic Surveys* 15.5 (2001): 589–611.

12 Baldwin, Robert, and Julia Black. "Really responsive regulation." *Modern Law Review* 71.1 (2008): 59–94.

13 Gunningham, Neil, and Darren Sinclair. "Regulatory pluralism: Designing policy mixes for environmental protection." In *Environmental law*, edited by Peter S. Menell, Routledge, 2019: 463–490.

14 Frey, Bruno S., and Felix Oberholzer-Gee. "The cost of price incentives: An empirical analysis of motivation crowding-out." *American Economic Review* 87.4 (1997): 746–755; Lafitte, François. "Richard M. Titmuss, *The gift relationship: From human blood to social policy*, Allen and Unwin, London, 1970." *Journal of Social Policy* 1.1 (1972): 81–84.

replacing it in extreme cases. The crowding-out effect is often considered one of the main reasons why legislation that focuses solely on extrinsic motivation without attempting to influence people's intrinsic motivation does not achieve the desired outcome.

Traditionally the safest regulatory approach is to focus on the common denominator. This means that a fear of punishment is the way to avoid the need to take a specific motivation into account. A legal approach that ignores the variation in intrinsic motivation is doomed to fail as it does not address the complexity and uncertainty associated with targeting individuals' presumed motivations.[15]

THE PROBLEM WITH THE CROWDING-OUT ARGUMENT

One of the omissions in the literature on crowding out relates to the question of what type of intrinsic motivation is being crowded out. Are all types of intrinsic motivation likely to be crowded out in the same way? Are there extrinsic motivations that are more likely to crowd out different types of intrinsic motivation?

Answering these questions is crucial to our ability to predict what we gain or lose from voluntary compliance in cases where the individual who is deciding whether to comply does not have a full view of the extrinsic motivation. People's compliance varies depending on whether and how social norms, citizenship, morality, or knowledge are being crowded out.

According to common findings in crowding-out research, a law that focuses on extrinsic motivation, such as incentives, is likely to undermine internalized compliance.[16] However, when the law focuses on intrinsic motivation, such as relying on science, it is likely to enhance internalized compliance.[17] However, it is important to note that many other scholars have suggested that examining processes such as habit formation or cognitive dissonance lead to a better understanding of the effect of law on people's preferences.[18] These processes are not related to any change in the individuals themselves.

This view is simplistic for a few reasons. First, in theory, law is a broad and multifaceted concept and it could target both types of motivation at the same time. A particular law could potentially cause a crowding out. However, this may not occur in every case. In addition, it's not certain that intrinsic motivation will be crowded out if legislation is present.

[15] Holmes, O. W. "The path of the law." *Harvard Law Review* 10.8 (1897): 457–478.

[16] Atiq, Emad H. "Why motives matter: Reframing the crowding out effect of legal incentives." *Yale Law Journal* 123 (2013): 1070–1116.

[17] Underhill, Kristen. "When extrinsic incentives displace intrinsic motivation: Designing legal carrots and sticks to confront the challenge of motivational crowding-out." *Yale Journal on Regulation* 33 (2016): 213–280.

[18] Compare with Lewinsohn-Zamir, Daphna. "The importance of being earnest: Two notions of internalization." *University of Toronto Law Journal* 65.2 (2015): 37–84.

Second, even models that focus on crowding out assume that people are intrinsically motivated to comply. However, this is not always the case and different people may respond differently to different situations.

Third, it is important to differentiate between what is being reduced: the intrinsic motivation, even in contexts where it already exists, or the desirable behavior. The reduction in intrinsic motivation may not be as relevant to policy if the crowding-out effect does not reduce desirable behavior. Of course, there are exceptions where intrinsic motivation plays a central role in the likelihood of compliance. This will be further developed in future chapters.

Fourth, morality or social norms might be crowded out by processes of signaling. Doing something moral solely because it is legal might undermine the social and the self-value of behaving morally.

In contrast to moral motivation to comply, scientific truth is less likely to be crowded out by the law. On the other hand, sanctions have been shown to influence morality but have no impact when scientific truth is an issue. Moreover, it is important to understand that the law may not always be extrinsically or intrinsically oriented. In many of the aspects, it can be both giving rationales to comply and signaling to people that lack of compliance will not be tolerated.

NOT ALL INTRINSIC MOTIVATIONS ARE CROWDED OUT EQUALLY

How exactly are intrinsic motivations crowded out and for how long? Is crowding out, with its many competing mechanisms, a social process or an individual one? Various accounts attempt to explain what types of intrinsic motivations are more likely to be crowded out. For example, one can speculate that intrinsic motivations, such as prosocial motivation, are more likely to be adversely affected by external interventions. Will an individual who believes that a certain institution is legitimate and is likely to comply with the laws it issues, cease to believe in that institution's legitimacy if there is legal reliance on external measures? Therefore, it is important to focus on understanding which intrinsic motivations we are discussing before we can make any predictions about the likelihood of crowding out.

THE MULTIPLE MOTIVES PROBLEM

Another issue with the crowding-out argument is that it assumes the law is one-dimensional and that people's motivation to comply is uniform. This assumption can be easily refuted. For example, while some studies show that there is some impact of enforcement on tax compliance,[19] very few people believe that deterrence

[19] Slemrod, Joel. "Tax compliance and enforcement." *Journal of Economic Literature* 57.4 (2019): 904–954.

is actually the only factor that explains tax compliance,[20] as many people are complying for cooperative reasons.[21] Specifically, as will be discussed in Chapter 9, the more updated view on tax compliance perceives some need for a balance between power and authorities and trust of authorities when attempting to understand the likelihood of tax compliance over time.[22] Even if a dominant motivation, such as cost-benefit, can be identified, it does not undermine the existence of parallel motivations to obey the law. States rarely rely on only one motivation when attempting to change people's behavior. The fine-is-a-price paradigm, first introduced in Gneezy and Rustichini's famous child-care study,[23] also exhibits these problems. While there are some concerns about generalization, this concept aligns with much of the discussion about crowding out in the behavioral economics literature.[24] For example, if an individual recycles because they believe it is important to protect the environment and to signal their virtue to their neighbors, adding sanctions for those who do not recycle will harm only the social-signaling motivation, but not the scientific motivation behind the importance of recycling to the future of the Earth. This analysis suggests that much of the crowding-out research has limitations.

VARIATION IN THE CROWDING-OUT EFFECT

The preceding discussion suggests that we must consider several moderating factors when trying to examine the likelihood of legal intervention changing people's intrinsic motivation. For example, when examining intrinsic motivation in the context of COVID, as will be developed in Chapter 8, one can discuss factors such as solidarity and morality on one hand,[25] and trust in science and scientists on the other.[26] While both could be defined as intrinsic compliance motivations, the crowding-out effect of each is likely to be different. One example of how extrinsic motivators can affect intrinsic motivation is in the application of sanctions. When sanctions are applied, some of the concern for solidarity (an intrinsic motivator) might diminish. This illustrates a potential crowding-out effect. However, it's important to note that

20 Scholz, John T., and Neil Pinney. "Duty, fear, and tax compliance: The heuristic basis of citizenship behavior." *American Journal of Political Science* (1995): 490–512.

21 Kirchler, Erich, Christoph Kogler, and Stephan Muehlbacher. "Cooperative tax compliance: From deterrence to deference." *Current Directions in Psychological Science* 23.2 (2014): 87–92.

22 Kirchler, Erich, Erik Hoelzl, and Ingrid Wahl. "Enforced versus voluntary tax compliance: The 'slippery slope' framework." *Journal of Economic Psychology* 29.2 (2008): 210–225.

23 Gneezy, Uri, and Aldo Rustichini. "A fine is a price." *Journal of Legal Studies* 29.1 (2000): 1–17. https://doi.org/10.1086/468061.

24 Frey, Bruno S. "Institutions and morale: The crowding-out effect." *Frontier Issues in Economic Thought* 3 (1997): 223–226.

25 Liekefett, Luisa, and Julia Becker. "Compliance with governmental restrictions during the coronavirus pandemic: A matter of personal self-protection or solidarity with people in risk groups?" *British Journal of Social Psychology* 60.3 (2021): 924–946.

26 Algan, Yann, et al. "Trust in scientists in times of pandemic: Panel evidence from 12 countries." *Proceedings of the National Academy of Sciences* 118.40 (2021): e2108576118.

different types of intrinsic motivation may be affected differently by extrinsic motivators. For instance, the crowding-out effects on solidarity-based motivation may differ from those on other types of intrinsic motivation, such as personal ethical standards. To better predict how extrinsic motivation affects intrinsic compliance motivation, several critical questions require examination. We must understand whether different types of intrinsic motivations, such as moral reasoning or scientific belief, vary in their susceptibility to being crowded out, and explore the underlying mechanisms of this crowding-out process, including over-justification and reactance. Essential considerations include whether crowding out leads to complete behavioral disappearance or merely reduced quality of compliance and how these effects manifest across different personality types and demographic groups. The evaluation framework must account for both quantitative and qualitative measures of compliance, comparing average quality against the number of individuals who become less cooperative. Temporal dimensions are crucial, as short-term and long-term effects may differ significantly, particularly in how behavioral changes relate to shifts in underlying attitudes and beliefs, including the internalization of norms. Understanding which specific aspects of legal implementation trigger crowding out is vital, as is examining the distinct processes that unfold when behaviors are legalized versus when sanctions are introduced. This comprehensive analysis would provide a more nuanced understanding of how regulatory interventions affect voluntary compliance motivation.

Self vs. Social Crowding-Out Processes

Many key questions about crowding-out effects have been overlooked in much of the research on motivation crowding. For example, researchers often haven't explored how different types of intrinsic motivation respond to extrinsic incentives, or how the mechanisms of crowding out might vary across contexts. Furthermore, most of this research has primarily focused on monetary interventions,[27] neglecting the more complex effects of using regulation and enforcement as motivational tools. While laws and incentives both represent extrinsic interventions, laws are far more complex in their ability to crowd out intrinsic motivation. The law itself communicates with intrinsic motivations,[28] and its effect cannot be reduced to simply increasing the price of behaviors that are against the law. Given the further complexity we see in the crowding-out effect created by laws, we will outline the different processes that could be triggered by law and that could be crowding-out motivations (see Table 3.1).

27 E.g., Frey, Bruno S. "Crowding out and crowding in of intrinsic preferences." *Reflexive Governance for Global Public Goods* 75 (2012): 75–83.

28 See, for example, Feldman, Yuval. "The expressive function of trade secret law: Legality, cost, intrinsic motivation, and consensus." *Journal of Empirical Legal Studies* 6.1 (2009): 177–212.

We believe that part of the confusion stems from a lack of theoretical clarity regarding the different mechanisms and processes that fall under the category of crowding out. To advance our understanding, these processes can be divided into two categories:

TABLE 3.1 *A taxonomy of crowding-out processes*

Over-justification:	The idea behind this process which, in a sense, is the original crowding-out paradigm,[29] is related to Edward Deci's original 1971 self-determination model.[30] In this model, people attribute their own behavior to extrinsic rather than intrinsic reasons. The existence of laws, especially when there is an enforcement mechanism, can have an effect like that of incentives. In the case of law, in contrast to that of incentives, it is less likely that the law will be removed. Therefore, the classical fear of the crowding-out effect when introducing incentives is weaker.
Attention:	Attention is somewhat related to the over-justification effect, where people focus their attention on the extrinsic incentives and fail to account for the effect of intrinsic motivation on their behavior.[31] The difference between the expected effects of incentives and laws seems to depend on their relative saliency. This difference may be affected by factors unrelated to the nature of either law or incentives, but rather to how they are being communicated. A related work on reminder nudges demonstrates that, in more complex decision-making settings, the removal of reminder nudges can create a negative spillover on people's behavior.[32]
Control and trustworthiness:	These are two important factors to consider when examining the effect of laws versus incentives.[33] Incentives can be viewed as giving people more autonomy on one hand, as individuals can choose whether to take the incentive. However, in terms of trustworthiness, law is more reliable. Because the law is general and not directed at the individual, there may be less of a problem of around the individual feeling untrustworthy. The law can be perceived as a form of guidance, rather than simply a lack of trust in an individual's ability to behave properly.

(*continued*)

29 Lepper, Mark R., and David Greene. "Over justification research and beyond: Toward a means–ends analysis of intrinsic and extrinsic motivation." In *The hidden costs of reward*, edited by Mark R. Lepper and David Greene, Psychology Press, 2015: 109–148.

30 Deci, Edward L., and Richard M. Ryan. *Intrinsic motivation and self-determination in human behavior*. Springer Science & Business Media, 2013.

31 Chao, Matthew. "Demotivating incentives and motivation crowding out in charitable giving." *Proceedings of the National Academy of Sciences* 114.28 (2017): 7301–7306.

32 Koch, Alexander K., Dan Mønster, and Julia Nafziger. "Spillover effects of reminder nudges in complex environments." *Proceedings of the National Academy of Sciences* 121.17 (2024): e2322549121.

33 Falk, Armin, and Michael Kosfeld. "The hidden costs of control." *American Economic Review* 96.5 (2006): 1611–1630.

TABLE 3.1 *(continued)*

Less spontaneous (such as in the context of prosocial behavior):	Another lesser-known mechanism, which has been called crowding out in the literature, involves people becoming more calculating and less spontaneous when extrinsic measures are present.[34] Rather than thinking about the behavior itself, they are thinking about what they might gain from it. Continuing the hypothetical discussion, this result is more likely to occur with incentives that are more strongly related to measurement than with those related to the legality effect, which might differ.
Cognitive dissonance:	Another important mechanism that is often overlooked is cognitive dissonance, which focuses on the discrepancy between free choice and attitudes.[35] Arguably, when people are either coerced or incentivized to behave in a certain way, they are less likely to feel that they have chosen the behavior. As a result, the likelihoods of cognitive dissonance being created and attitude change happening are reduced.
Decline in virtue signaling:	Virtue signaling involves the more social aspect of crowding out.[36] The decline in virtue signaling, such as the harm caused by monetary incentives to the social virtue of whistleblowing,[37] is mostly related to the fact that people engage in prosocial behavior to gain the approval of others. This approval is greater when the behavior is seen as voluntary. However, this is not the case when others perceive that the behavior is enacted for money or due to fear of the law. Even when the legal compliance required by enforcement is limited, people may still engage in some virtue signaling by complying with a legal requirement, even if they don't have to do so. This is less likely to happen with incentives, unless they are very small, as was the case in the original cognitive dissonance studies.[38]
Bureaucratization of behavior:	This important mechanism is related mostly to legal rather than incentive effects. It refers to the process that occurs when a social practice becomes legalized and its entire structure must become transparent, documented, equal, and so on. These values associated with legality are important. However, their presence is likely to change how people feel about engaging in these social practices. As my joint work with Rinat Markovitch and Eyal Pe'er has shown,[39] affidavits, which are more complex to use, were shown to create greater aversion to pledges, partly because of the greater administrative burden associated with them.[40]

34 Gråd, Erik, Arvid Erlandsson, and Gustav Tinghög. "Do nudges crowd out prosocial behavior?" *Behavioural Public Policy* 8.1 (2024): 107–120.

35 Elliot, Andrew J., and Patricia G. Devine. "On the motivational nature of cognitive dissonance: Dissonance as psychological discomfort." *Journal of Personality and Social Psychology* 67.3 (1994): 382–394.

36 Frey. "Institutions and morale."

37 Feldman, Yuval, and Orly Lobel. "The incentives matrix: The comparative effectiveness of rewards, liabilities, duties, and protections for reporting illegality." *Texas Law Review* 88 (2009): 1151–1212.

38 Metin, Irem, and Selin Metin Camgoz. "The advances in the history of cognitive dissonance theory." *International Journal of Humanities and Social Science* 1.6 (2011): 131–136.

39 Hilo-Merkovich, Rinat, Eyal Pe'er, and Yuval Feldman. "Affidavit aversion: Public preferences for trust-based policy instruments." *Regulation & Governance* 18.3 (2024): 970–986.

40 Herd, Pamela, and Donald P. Moynihan. *Administrative burden: Policymaking by other means*. Russell Sage Foundation, 2019.

Reactance:	The mechanism of reactance[41] (e.g., the provocative effect of law)[42] could be considered partly social and partly individualistic. According to the psychological reactance theory,[43] people react negatively to any attempt to limit their freedom of choice. Naturally, this is more likely to happen when certain laws threaten the values of a certain social groups, as seen in Israel in 2018 with the enactment of the Basic Law: Israel as the Nation-State of the Jewish People,[44] which drew negative reactions from non-Jewish Israeli citizens. According to reaction theory, such a negative reaction could be provoked on the individual level as well. However, such reactive extrinsic effects are less likely to occur when incentives are used.
Relational (e.g., fine is a price):	Another mechanism that could be seen as related to the idea of the difference between social and market relations is the use of incentives,[45] which could make change more likely to happen.[46] However, even if legal measures are not included in classical relational theory, they can certainly change the dynamic between friends who do each other favors as well as duty holders who demand that their requests be respected by the other party.

Self-Related Crowding Out and Social-Related Crowding Out

Is the effect of over-justification self-related or social-related? Over-justification affects the self-perception of an individual, making them question why they are behaving in a certain way. Alternatively, it can be social-related, undermining the virtue signaling that was present.

The foregoing general analysis discusses the differences between the more commonly discussed lines of research regarding crowding out in incentive and in legality contexts. One conclusion that can be drawn from this analysis is how difficult it is to predict whether a certain extrinsic intervention will lead to crowding out.

CAN COMPLIANCE BEHAVIOR BE CROWDED OUT?

The crowding-out paradigm for internalized compliance, which is based on research on motivation, has a problem. The original studies were related to various

41 Brehm, Sharon S., and Jack W. Brehm. *Psychological reactance: A theory of freedom and control*. Academic Press, 2013.

42 Barak-Corren, Netta, Yuval Feldman, and Noam Gidron. "The provocative effect of law: Majority nationalism and minority discrimination." *Journal of Empirical Legal Studies* 15.4 (2018): 951–986.

43 Brehm, Jack W. "Psychological reactance: Theory and applications." *Advances in Consumer Research* 16.1 (1989): 72–75.

44 See https://main.knesset.gov.il/EN/activity/documents/BasicLawsPDF/BasicLawNationState.pdf.

45 Gneezy and Rustichini. "A fine is a price."

46 Compare, for example, with Fiske, Alan P. "The four elementary forms of sociality: Framework for a unified theory of social relations." *Psychological Review* 99.4 (1992): 689–723.

tasks people had to do in a lab and then extrinsic measures were introduced.[47] This approach is different from the paradigm's application. The dynamics of crowding out in legal compliance contexts differ from those in other areas. In compliance situations, the state often defines the expected behavior and provides instructions for it. This contrasts with contexts where intrinsic motivations preexist state intervention.

Many compliance behaviors are very different than behaviors such as going to the gym or playing the piano and are very complex to execute. As a result, people's willingness to engage in them might not guarantee full compliance. As discussed in Chapter 2, there is great variation between the different types of motivation, whether they are related to morality, personal preferences, or belief in science. Similarly, procedural justice and legitimacy have often been strongly associated with intrinsic motivation in many studies.[48] This may be because people do not need external forces such as incentives or monitoring to behave in a certain way. As also discussed in the previous chapter about trust, many factors related to legitimacy and procedural justice fall into the same category, where many of the reasons for complying may not be considered to be intrinsic motivations to begin with. When we think about Deci's original meaning of intrinsic motivation, we focus on behaviors that are rewarding in and of themselves. As we will examine in this chapter, certain government actions might be perceived as crowding out alternative compliance motivations, even if these motivations are not strictly defined as intrinsic motivation. In other words, not all noninstrumental motivation can be seen as intrinsic motivation and not all crowding-out processes are similar to the one discussed in the original crowding-out approach. The following will further explore the difference between internalized and noncoerced compliance. This will help build the theoretical framework needed to understand when government interventions become dangerous.

INTERNALIZED VERSUS NONCOERCED COMPLIANCE

As discussed in Chapters 1 and 2, there is a big difference between internalized compliance, where the main motivation for compliance is intrinsic, and voluntary compliance, which, at a minimum, includes every situation where the individual doesn't feel coerced. When discussing crowding out in this chapter we are referring to the effect on *internalized compliance* rather than the broader definition of *noncoerced compliance* which is discussed in the first chapter. However, due to the importance of internalization in ensuring voluntary compliance, it is important to

47 Eckel, Catherine C., Philip J. Grossman, and Rachel M. Johnston. "An experimental test of the crowding out hypothesis." *Journal of Public Economics* 89.8 (2005): 1543–1560.

48 Zapata-Phelan, Cindy P., et al. "Procedural justice, interactional justice, and task performance: The mediating role of intrinsic motivation." *Organizational Behavior and Human Decision Processes* 108.1 (2009): 93–105.

understand what kind of regulatory interventions are likely to enhance or undermine such compliance.[49] At the same time, because of the gap between voluntary and internalized compliance, a certain regulatory intervention may be likely to adversely affect the process of internalization, while still contributing to the likelihood of voluntary compliance.

This might be related to the fact that the effect on the likelihood of internalization is more long term and depends on other factors, while the perception of voluntariness is shorter term. Moreover, as we discussed in Chapter 1, although intrinsic motivation is seen as an integral component of voluntary compliance, changing people's intrinsic motivations is not the purpose of the law. Additionally, the meaning of what is voluntary is open to interpretation. There is a narrow definition that focuses only on noncoercive compliance and, in that regard, even compliance through nudges and incentives might fall under the category of voluntary.

Indeed, the next chapter, focusing on broader accounts of regulation, will tackle the relationship between regulation and voluntary compliance, rather than internalized compliance, as understood in noncoerced compliance. However, the current chapter takes as its starting position the broader definition of voluntary compliance that includes people who intrinsically want to cooperate. Relying on this intrinsic motivation seems to be the way to achieve "effective voluntary compliance" that doesn't require continuous external intervention by the state.[50] This definition applies to every situation in which people are not subject to sanctions if they don't comply. The reason for our focus is the fear of the "crowding-out" effect of the law on intrinsic motivation, which can only be discussed in the context of internalized compliance.

CROWDING IN VS. CROWDING OUT

Most of the discussion here will focus on the two main processes we are interested in comparing, crowding in (internalization or preference change) versus crowding out.

In abstract terms, one could envision a situation where the law should be able to target only those whose current intrinsic motivation is in opposition to the values of the state. The law could then seek to change their attitudes without the risk of crowding out, as there is no intrinsic motivation that could be harmed. However, this abstract view is problematic on a few levels. First, people's level of intrinsic motivation is not truly binary: they don't either have it or not have it. Second, it is unclear how the state can identify in advance only people with intrinsic motivation. Third, even people with intrinsic motivation might need additional clarification

[49] Lewinsohn-Zamir. "The importance of being earnest."

[50] Which is part of what we referred to in Chapter 1 as *effective* voluntary compliance.

from the state and it cannot be assumed that they can sustain intrinsic motivation without state encouragement.

An alternative approach that will be developed in Chapters 8–10 is related to the acknowledgment that the level of popularity a given law enjoys is limited; therefore, the likelihood that people will enjoy a high level of intrinsic motivation is also limited. At the same time, since we have argued that even the concept of intrinsic motivation could mean more than one thing, it is not clear whether the effect of law on that intrinsic motivation is identical. For example, it is less likely that intrinsic motivation related to fairness and legitimacy might be affected or crowded out by external intervention by the law. The reason is that fairness and legitimacy are more related to the institution than to the law. Therefore, even the crowding out regarding a specific law is less likely to be substantial.

The Crowding-Out Effect of Intrinsic Motivation: Heterogeneity between People

Another important aspect of crowding out is related not to the heterogeneity of intrinsic motivations but rather to the difference between people. This refers to the interaction between a person's initial motivation and the likelihood that their compliance is driven by intrinsic motivations. For example, Lewis Kornhauser and colleagues conducted a lab study that manipulated the fine paid for breaching a contract in order to help clarify the mechanisms behind the crowding-out effect.[51] They identified a strong interaction between prosocial people and pro-self people. It has been demonstrated that people who are intrinsically committed to caring for others (high social value orientation) are more likely to be negatively affected by external incentives, such as paying a fine. This suggests that there is a challenge around incentivizing some people while ignoring others; this is a major issue that we seek to address in this book. Specifically, we are exploring what parts of the public can be trusted and what types of compliance can be expected from them.

FRAMING OF INCENTIVES AND CROWDING-OUT MOTIVATIONS

Another important question to answer is related to how extrinsic motivation is perceived by the public whose behavior we are trying to change.[52] It is possible to illustrate this by taking two classical examples of incentivizing people, which might lead to opposite effects. Consider a student who enjoys exploring new ideas and genuinely finds learning exciting. They dive into their studies because they're curious and want to understand more about the world, not just to get good grades.

[51] Kornhauser, Lewis, Yijia Lu, and Stephan Tontrup. "Testing a fine is a price in the lab." *International Review of Law and Economics* 63 (2020): 105931.

[52] Gneezy, Uri, Stephan Meier, and Pedro Rey-Biel. "When and why incentives (don't) work to modify behavior." *Journal of Economic Perspectives* 25.4 (2011): 191–210.

However, when a teacher offers an extrinsic reward (such as extra credit) for completing a task that the student would have undertaken in any event, a subtle shift occurs. The focus moves from the learning process to the outcome (the reward), potentially undermining the student's intrinsic motivation. Their love for learning may feel diminished. This scenario highlights the delicate balance between external incentives and the inherent joy of learning. In contrast, consider a musician deeply passionate about playing their instrument and creating music. Their intrinsic motivation fuels their artistic endeavors. Now, imagine that they receive a financial grant that enables them to continue pursuing their craft. Surprisingly, this external reward doesn't dampen their intrinsic drive; instead, it serves as validation of their dedication and talent. The grant becomes a catalyst, reinforcing their love for music. While our examples focus on monetary rewards, a similar shift in the impact of extrinsic interventions occurs in legal contexts. If individuals perceive their behavior as intrinsically driven, they are less likely to cease prosocial actions when there is a financial incentive. For example, a person volunteering at a homeless shelter out of genuine concern for others may continue to do so even if offered a small stipend. However, if the stipend becomes the primary reason for their involvement, its removal could diminish their motivation to continue volunteering.

It is challenging to understand the likelihood of a certain extrinsic motivation succeeding in changing behavior positively without undermining people's intrinsic motivation. This is especially true when accounting for the fact that people do not just have intrinsic motivation or not. Their level of intrinsic motivation will also affect their interpretation of extrinsic motivation. We can expect a difference when the intervention is targeting the individual rather than the public in general. When the policy is more general, it can be seen as not respecting the specific motivation of the individual to cooperate.

Because there are so many parallel processes of crowding out, it is also very difficult to know in advance when intrinsically motivated individuals will feel that extrinsic motivation enhances their willingness to voluntarily cooperate with legal requirements. Thus, for example, in the context of mask wearing, if a person upholds the law due to their belief in science, then the fact that there are laws or even sanctions that require the same things is unlikely to have an inadvertent effect. In fact, such laws could conversely enhance such people's belief that their scientific understanding is accurate and valid.

However, if they object to laws demanding cooperation, they might engage in some psychological reactance to it.[53] It seems plausible to predict that when people cooperate because they want to feel that they are moral people who choose to help others, clearly, when such cooperative behavior becomes a legal requirement, their ability to feel that they are helping others is reduced, as they are now forced to do

[53] Brehm, Sharon S., and Jack W. Brehm. Psychological reactance: A theory of freedom and control. Academic Press, 2013.

so by law. Another example can be found in Eugene Volokh's study,[54] which challenges the potential negative effect of Good Samaritan laws, showing that another interesting result regarding crowding out is related to how people perceive it.[55]

HOW DIFFERENT REGULATORY INTERVENTIONS CROWD OUT INTRINSIC MOTIVATION

Some recent research has begun examining how different nudges that either focus on social morals or simply a change in people's default response have changed people's intrinsic motivation. For instance, Erik Grad and his team discovered that in certain situations presenting nudges did not lead to a decrease in prosocial motivation.[56] If someone is being convinced to obey in a certain way, are they more likely to abandon their understanding because of some external intervention, such as a requirement or incentive?

Is it possible to see a reduction in societal feeling of morality because of intervention through nudges, which are mostly without awareness? Essentially, if people are motivated to do the right thing only because of external rewards or penalties, their internal sense of what is right and wrong may weaken over time. This can be problematic if the external incentives are removed or if individuals start to believe that they can engage in unethical behavior without suffering any consequences.

Also, the personal satisfaction of being a responsible citizen is reduced by extrinsic interventions, such as incentives or penalties. This can then affect people's intrinsic motivation to comply with laws and regulations, as people come to perceive the extrinsic intervention as the main reason for their compliance, rather than their sense of duty and responsibility as citizen.[57]

On the other hand, if science informs us about the benefits of getting vaccinated, it is important to consider the impact external factors might have on vaccination efforts. In fact, when a law is based on scientific evidence, it can increase public confidence in a particular policy.

CROWDING OUT VIRTUE SIGNALING

Payment for specific behavior can be seen as a signal to others and this can have a different type of crowding-out effect on the behavior of other individuals. The payment

[54] Volokh, Eugene. "Duties to rescue and the anti-cooperative effects of law." *Georgetown Law Journal* 88 (1999): 105–114.

[55] Lin, Stephanie C., Julian J. Zlatev, and Dale T. Miller. "Moral traps: When self-serving attributions backfire in prosocial behavior." *Journal of Experimental Social Psychology* 70 (2017): 198–203.

[56] Gråd, Erlandsson, and Tinghög. "Do nudges crowd out prosocial behavior?"

[57] Frey, Bruno S. "How intrinsic motivation is crowded out and in." *Rationality and Society* 6.3 (1994): 334–352.

may signal that the behavior needs to be incentivized, that is, it is not something that people would do voluntarily, which could undermine the social norm on which the behavior is based.[58] This is related to the concept of social norms and signaling analyzed by Eric Posner.[59] Social norms are often based on the idea of doing something because it is the right thing to do or because it is expected by others in the community. According to Posner, when extrinsic incentives are introduced, they can send a signal that the behavior is not actually a social norm, but something that is done only for the reward. This can lead to a reduction in the intrinsic motivation to engage in the behavior, as well as a reduction in the effectiveness of the social norm itself.

In a study of how incentives affect the intrinsic motivation of a whistleblower, Orly Lobel and I examined how getting paid for whistleblowing undermines the social status and image of a hero who cares only about fighting corruption.[60] Another famous field experiment by Tobias Cagala, testing the very different mechanism of pledges,[61] showed that when students were asked to make honesty pledges before exams, they were more likely to cheat. Presumably, the requirement to sign a pledge not to cheat led them to believe that others are probably cheating, thus making them more willing to do so as well.

WHAT DO WE KNOW ABOUT INCENTIVES AND CROWDING OUT?

In addition to the expected higher quality of performance, which is driven by voluntary compliance, there is a wealth of relatively consistence research that shows the negative impact of both punishment and incentives.[62] According to the "crowding-out" theory, exposing people to external motivation (either positive or negative) undermines their internal motivation.[63] For example, Bruno Frey found that residents were more likely to oppose a nuclear plant in their neighborhood if they were offered compensation.[64] In addition, Ernst Fehr and Armin Falk showed that in some contexts using incentives could harm the performance of agents as well as their compliance with various rules.[65] Moreover, in a meta-analysis of 128 studies examining the effects of extrinsic

58 Cagala, Tobias, Ulrich Glogowsky, and Johannes Rincke. "Does commitment to a no-cheating rule affect academic cheating?" Available at SSRN 3111855 (2019). https://papers.ssrn.com/sol3/papers.cfm?abstract_id=3111855.

59 Posner, Eric. *Law and social norms*. Harvard University Press, 2002.

60 Feldman and Lobel. "The incentives matrix," 1151.

61 Cagala, Tobias, Ulrich Glogowsky, and Johannes Rincke. "Detecting and preventing cheating in exams: Evidence from a field experiment." *Journal of Human Resources* 59.1 (2024): 210–241.

62 Gneezy, Uri, and Aldo Rustichini. "Incentives, punishment and behavior." In *Advances in behavioral economics*, edited by Colin F. Camerer, George Loewenstein and Matthew Rabin, Princeton University Press, 2004: 572–589.

63 Deci, Edward L. "Effects of externally mediated rewards on intrinsic motivation." *Journal of Personality and Social Psychology* 18.1 (1971): 105–115; Frey and Jegen. "Motivation crowding theory."

64 Frey. "Institutions and morale."

65 Fehr, Ernst, and Armin Falk. "Psychological foundations of incentives." *European Economic Review* 46.4–5 (2002): 687–724.

rewards on intrinsic motivation, Deci and colleagues found the robust negative effect of rewards on what they define as free choice intrinsic motivation, with some moderation effect related to the type of incentive and age of participants.[66] In contrast, Shu-Hua Tang and Vernon Hall took a different approach in their meta-analysis focusing on the concept of over-justification, as the main mechanism for crowding-out effect.[67] Additionally, Frey has conducted few reviews of the literature focusing on the problems associated with incentives in agency relationship.[68] Günther Schulze and Björn Frank demonstrated the crowding effect of deterrence and its destructive effect on the intrinsic motivation to behave honestly.[69] Another important review article applying a more economic than psychological approach is that of Samuel Bowles and Sandra Polanía-Reyes in the context of prosocial behavior, showing the contexts in which economic incentives might be counterproductive and have adverse effects.[70] They also suggest alternative explanations for why such effects might occur, which are unrelated to the classical crowding-out effect, such as framing and lack of internalization. It is also notable that other studies have sought to understand the mechanism through which people are intrinsically motivated to cooperate in social rather than individual behavior. These studies have found no variation within groups associated with individual's characteristics.[71]

RELATIONAL ACCOUNT OF CROWDING OUT (FINE IS A PRICE)

Another way that crowding out can happen is when people's relationships change from personal to financial. In the literature of behavioral economics, the famous and

[66] Deci, Edward L., Richard Koestner, and Richard M. Ryan. "A meta-analytic review of experiments examining the effects of extrinsic rewards on intrinsic motivation." *Psychological Bulletin* 125.6 (1999): 627–668. For a focus on joint effects of extrinsic and intrinsic motivation, see: Cerasoli, Christopher P., Jessica M. Nicklin, and Michael T. Ford. "Intrinsic motivation and extrinsic incentives jointly predict performance: A 40-year meta-analysis." *Psychological Bulletin* 140.4 (2014): 980–1008. For a discussion of the crowding-out effect in the context of environmental policy: Rode, Julian, Erik Gómez-Baggethun, and Torsten Krause. "Motivation crowding by economic incentives in conservation policy: A review of the empirical evidence." *Ecological Economics* 117 (2015): 270–282. For a discussion of the crowding effect, albeit with some reservation on the consistency of their effect, see: Promberger, Marianne, and Theresa M. Marteau. "When do financial incentives reduce intrinsic motivation? Comparing behaviors studied in psychological and economic literatures." *Health Psychology* 32.9 (2013): 950–957.

[67] Tang, Shu-Hua, and Vernon C. Hall. "The overjustification effect: A meta-analysis." *Applied Cognitive Psychology* 9.5 (1995): 365–404.

[68] Frey, Bruno S. "On the relationship between intrinsic and extrinsic work motivation." *International Journal of Industrial Organization* 15.4 (1997): 427–439.

[69] Schulze, Günther G., and Björn Frank. "Deterrence versus intrinsic motivation: Experimental evidence on the determinants of corruptibility." *Economics of Governance* 4 (2003): 143–160.

[70] Bowles, Samuel, and Sandra Polania-Reyes. "Economic incentives and social preferences: Substitutes or complements?" *Journal of Economic Literature* 50.2 (2012): 368–425.

[71] Henrich, Joseph, et al. "Cooperation, reciprocity and punishment in fifteen small-scale societies." *American Economic Review* 91.2 (2001): 73–78.

highly cited mechanism the "fine is a price," became a parallel for psychological research on the crowding-out effect. This well-known, albeit not too robust effect was documented in the context of daycare centers that imposed fines on parents who were late in picking up their children at the end of the day.[72] Imposing a fine on late parents was found to be counterproductive, resulting in an increased number of late pickups. Apparently, the fine caused parents to feel licensed to arrive late. In another study, the potentially disruptive effect of laws was examined. A related theory in the context of prosocial behaviors suggests that both rewards and punishments were shown to trigger an over-justification effect. This effect occurs when external rewards are present, causing people to question whether they actually have "true motivation."[73] In addition, this effect is more likely to occur when the behavior is done in private rather than in public.[74]

EXPRESSIVE LAW VERSUS CROWDING OUT

An important conceptual and somewhat contradictory approach that is crucial for this project on voluntary compliance involves comparing the crowding-out effect of incentives.[75] These are in many ways more coercive but in many others might seem less likely to shift the focus from thinking about the individual and why they should engage in a particular behavior.

As developed in more detail in Chapter 11, Tom Tyler and I have explored the contradiction between the law's ability to enhance social practices through expression and its potential to crowd out motivation by mandating voluntary acts, thereby reducing the signaling value of voluntary social practices.[76] We examined the association between employees' perceived fairness of pay and benefits procedures and their adherence to workplace rules. Specifically, we investigated whether this association differs when these procedures are enacted voluntarily by companies versus when they are mandated by law. Our results suggest that evaluations of procedural justice in performance appraisal hearings have a stronger influence on overall workplace fairness judgments, perceptions of management legitimacy, and employee rule-adherence behavior when employees believe fairer workplace procedures are mandatory and required by law.

72 Gneezy, Uri, and Aldo Rustichini. "Pay enough or don't pay at all." *Quarterly Journal of Economics* 115.3 (2000): 791–810.

73 Bénabou, Roland, and Jean Tirole. "Incentives and prosocial behavior." *American Economic Review* 96.5 (2006): 1652–1678.

74 Ariely, Dan, Anat Bracha, and Stephan Meier. "Doing good or doing well? Image motivation and monetary incentives in behaving prosocially." *American Economic Review* 99.1 (2009): 544–555.

75 Frey and Oberholzer-Gee. "The cost of price incentives."

76 Feldman, Yuval, and Tom R. Tyler. "Mandated justice: The potential promise and possible pitfalls of mandating procedural justice in the workplace." *Regulation & Governance* 6.1 (2012): 46–65.

DUTY TO ENLIST: THE CASE STUDY OF THE ULTRA-ORTHODOX

Jointly with Netta Barak-Corren and Shelli Robson, we examined how intrinsic motivation might affect the likelihood that making military service mandatory could change the nature of ultra-Orthodox motivation to serve in the Israel Defense Forces (IDF).[77]

The issue of military conscription for ultra-Orthodox (Haredi) youth in the IDF presents a classic example of the crowding-out dilemma. When examining this complex issue, we faced a fundamental question: Would efforts to persuade the Haredi community to embrace military service voluntarily prove more effective than mandatory conscription, particularly given that forced service could trigger serious social and political backlash?

Understanding how different interventions might affect intrinsic motivation in this context is particularly challenging. The complexity stems from dealing with a large community that has traditionally resisted military service, making it crucial to carefully consider strategies for encouraging participation. Our research framework explored several critical aspects in developing a new conscription policy, including how military service affects Haredi soldiers' social standing, marriage prospects, and religious identity within their community. We specifically examined how Haredi youth perceive IDF service and what factors influence their decisions regarding enlistment.

Our analysis examined the various intrinsic motivations shaping Haredi youth's attitudes toward military service, including personal, ideological, and normative factors, as well as the prevailing social norms within their community. The findings revealed an interesting gap: While approximately one in four Haredi youth expressed interest in serving in the IDF, only 10 percent demonstrated actual readiness to enlist. Most Haredi youth showed mixed motivations regarding military service, with their attitudes influenced by personal convictions, ideological beliefs, and community norms. This complex interplay of multiple motivations alongside a general resistance to mandatory conscription makes policy decisions about using coercion particularly challenging.

CONFLICTING STUDIES ON CROWDING-OUT EFFECTS

In previous studies, I have compared two possible conflicting effects of law on behavior. On one hand, we have argued that *when* legal requirements "crowd out" the influence of social norms, their overall effect is not sufficient to ensure compliance with the law. For example, when legal requirements are the only influence on employee behavior, the important role of voluntary adherence to social norms

[77] "Conscription to the IDF through an Ultra-Orthodox Lens: Attitudes, Opinions, and Social Perspectives Shelley Robinson | Netta Barak-Corren | Yuval Feldman," idi.org.il/media/25015/conscription-to-the-idf-through-an-ultra-orthodox-lens-attitudes-opinions-and-social-perspectives.pdf.

in shaping compliance is undermined.[78] Following a similar line of reasoning, Meir Dan-Cohen argues that the positive reputation associated with being a Good Samaritan will disappear if assisting others in need becomes a legal requirement.[79] This argument implies that if employers are compelled by law to treat their employees in a certain way, the social reputation that employers gain from treating their employees fairly is lost. Knowing that their efforts will go unappreciated, employers will have no reason to act on behalf of employees beyond legal requirements, as they will receive no credit for such behavior.[80]

On the other hand, the law can also have an expressive effect on behavior by shaping people's attitudes and beliefs about what is right and wrong.[81] This can lead to voluntary compliance with legal requirements even when they are not strictly enforced. However, this effect is not guaranteed. Therefore, to minimize any negative effects on voluntary adherence to social norms, it is important to consider how legal requirements might be perceived by individuals and organizations. Ultimately, the goal should be to strike a balance between using the law to promote ethical behavior and avoiding unintended consequences that could undermine the effectiveness of legal regulation.

CROWDING OUT, FAIRNESS, AND LACK OF TRUST

In the studies examined in this chapter, we have also focused on the crowding-out mechanism of the signaling of mistrust that is associated with imposing law. For example, Falk and Kosfeld have demonstrated that when a principal signals distrust to an agent, the agent's performance is reduced.[82] Frey and Feld have made a similar argument in the context of tax compliance from a reverse direction.[83] Their research has demonstrated the importance of giving people fair treatment and a voice to increase the likelihood that they will engage in voluntary compliance. Along those lines, Margaret Blair and Lynn Stout have demonstrated that regulation and monitoring can have an inadvertent effect on executive behavior, a finding relevant to current corporate law.[84] They suggest that the mistrust signaled through

78 Frey. "On the relationship between intrinsic and extrinsic work motivation."

79 Dan-Cohen, Meir. "Responsibility and the boundaries of the self." *Harvard Law Review* 105 (1991): 959–1003.

80 Blair, Margaret M., and Lynn A. Stout. "Director accountability and the mediating role of the corporate board." *Washington University Law Quarterly* 79 (2001): 403–448.

81 Sunstein, Cass R. "On the expressive function of law." *University of Pennsylvania Law Review* 144.5 (1996): 2021–2053.

82 Falk and Kosfeld. "The hidden costs of control."

83 Feld, Lars P., and Bruno S. Frey. "Trust breeds trust: How taxpayers are treated." *Economics of Governance* 3 (2002): 87–99.

84 Blair, Margaret M., and Lynn A. Stout. "Trust, trustworthiness, and the behavioral foundations of corporate law." *University of Pennsylvania Law Review* 149 (2000): 1735–1810. Blair and Stout. "Director accountability and the mediating role of the corporate board," 403.

harsh regulation serves as a self-fulfilling prophecy. A policy that threatens people overlooks the possibility that a threatened punishment is perceived as a signal that noncompliance is widespread.[85]

REACTANCE THEORY AS AN ALTERNATIVE TO CROWDING OUT

The reactance theory provides an alternative approach to the potential effects of regulation, especially restrictive ones, on people's behavior. According to reactance theory, people resist restrictions. This suggests a negative effect of the law on behavior. Interestingly, when the concept of perceived legitimacy is considered, it is shown that both legitimate and nonlegitimate restrictions create reactance. However, the difference is in the type of mechanism employed against it: according to one study the reactance to the illegitimate intervention was immediate, while longer cognitive deliberation was needed regarding the legitimate one.[86]

A more legally relevant example of this can be found in a joint work with Netta Barak-Corren and Noam Gidron,[87] where we developed the concept of inexpressive law. This is expressed in situations where the national law causes left-wing individuals to experience a feeling of reaction, which leans to greater support for anti-discrimination law. It is important to note that in that context, the focus was reversed to reflect the classical crowding out. The law was in a direction consistent with the intrinsic beliefs of the right in Israel, but in a direction contrary to the intrinsic beliefs of the left in Israel. The polarizing effect itself demonstrates that there is complexity when it comes to predicting behavior.

We conducted a study to investigate the impact of majority nationalism laws on the patterns of minority discrimination.[88] We used the Israeli draft Nation Law as a case study. This law was introduced in response to the ethnic and religious diversification experienced by Western societies, specifically in Israel, in recent decades. The law aims to protect the cultural heritage of the majority by defending the local dominant culture. Based on two experimental surveys conducted with a representative sample of Israel's majority population, our findings provide limited support for the hypothesis that laws promoting majority nationalism heighten bias against minorities. We also found modest support for the hypothesis that such laws generate unintended spillover effects across different minority groups and from the public to the private sphere. A key finding of our research was how majority nationalism laws triggered strong negative reactions among their opponents. We termed this the

85 Depoorter, Ben, and Sven Vanneste. "Norms and enforcement: The case against copyright litigation." *Oregon Law Review* 84 (2005): 1127–1180.

86 Sittenthaler, Sandra, Christina Steindl, and Eva Jonas. "Legitimate vs. illegitimate restrictions: A motivational and physiological approach investigating reactance processes." *Frontiers in Psychology* 6 (2015): 1–11.

87 Barak-Corren, Feldman, and Gidron. "The provocative effect of law."

88 Barak-Corren, Feldman, and Gidron. "The provocative effect of law."

"provocative effect of law" and examined its significance for expressive law theory. Our analysis revealed that these laws affect different ideological groups in distinct ways, leading to varying patterns of discriminatory behavior across different social spheres. When legal intervention is used to change people's intrinsic motivation, it can sometimes lead to a backlash if the law does not align with the target group's intrinsic motivation. This provides another theoretical route to understanding the complexity of predicting whether the law will enhance or destroy intrinsic motivation. This is why it is so important to consider the diverse reactions to legal interventions and their potential unintended consequences when we are trying to address these issues.

CROWDING OUT BY GIVING ALTERNATIVE REASONS?

Daphna Lewinsohn-Zamir and colleagues explored the effectiveness of reason giving in promoting compliance with legal norms.[89] While sanctions alone often fall short in ensuring adherence, recent attention has shifted toward nudges – a subtle measure that leverages people's automatic System 1 thinking to influence behavior without resorting to punitive measures. However, nudges have proven both ineffective and contentious. Their article examines how providing information about the underlying reasons behind legal norms can enhance compliance, primarily through deliberative System 2 thinking. They argue that giving reasons can significantly increase compliance while reducing the need for costly enforcement mechanisms. After exploring the theory, their empirical investigation employed vignette studies to demonstrate the feasibility and effectiveness of the reason-giving technique. Their findings reveal that people are more likely to follow legal norms when sound reasons to comply are given, compared to situations where reasons are not provided. It is important to note that persuasive reasons can encourage compliance, but questionable reasons may have the opposite effect.

RELIGION AND REASON GIVING

Religious traditions have long recognized the potential problems with providing reasons for divine laws.[90] The concern was that if the given reasons proved unconvincing, people might question not only those specific reasons but also the divine authority of the religious code itself. This insight raises an important consideration for modern regulation: When people are already intrinsically motivated to follow a

[89] Lewinsohn-Zamir, Daphna, Eyal Zamir, and Ori Katz. "Giving reasons as a means to enhance compliance with legal norms." *University of Toronto Law Journal* 72.3 (2022): 316–355.

[90] Adams, Robert Merrihew. "Divine command metaethics modified again." *Journal of Religious Ethics* (1979): 66–79.

law for one reason, introducing a different justification might actually weaken their original motivation. While further research is needed to fully understand this effect, existing crowding-out literature suggests that introducing new rationales that differ from a person's original motivations could indeed diminish their compliance.

Sanctions That Enhance Morality

To render the picture even more complex, some research suggests that not only do sanctions not crowd out morality, but they could potentially increase our perception of the immorality of the act.[91] In a series of three experiments, Laetitia Mulder and colleagues examined the influence of sanction severity. They found that severe sanctions lead to stronger moral judgments regarding rule-breaking behavior and stronger social disapproval of rule-breakers than mild sanctions. Interestingly, there was some moderation in the level of trust in institutions.

While fascinating, these findings are limited in a few ways. First, when relying on trust in authorities, the strong sanction may be perceived as a credible signal. Second, as we discussed earlier, there is an open question as to the extent to which we can view morality as an intrinsic motivation to obey a particular rule, as it might be more part of the intrinsic motivation to obey legitimate authority. Thus, it might be the case that if people believed in the actual law, they would have assessed their behavior differently.

FAIRNESS OF THE LAW AS AFFECTING THE LIKELIHOOD OF CROWDING OUT

In their famous study, Valerie Braithwaite and colleagues concluded that nursing home managers were more likely to comply with requests when they felt that they were treated fairly.[92] On the surface, this seminal study appears to answer the main questions of this book: How can voluntary compliance be achieved and what is the best way to maintain it? The main problem with the study is that the managers who felt they were trustworthy may have only been trustworthy to the regulators and not to the rest of the organization. This doesn't solve the regulators' dilemma when they need to decide the best approach in cases where there is a lack of information about the integrity and trustworthiness of the particular entity they are interested in regulating.

In a study from 2009, Neil Gunningham and Darren Sinclair examined what happens when inspectors, focused on the more intrinsically oriented "advise-and-persuade" approach, switch to the more extrinsically oriented deterrence-based

91 Mulder, Laetitia B., Peter Verboon, and David De Cremer. "Sanctions and moral judgments: The moderating effect of sanction severity and trust in authorities." *European Journal of Social Psychology* 39.2 (2009): 255–269.

92 Braithwaite, Valerie, et al. "Regulatory styles, motivational postures and nursing home compliance." *Law & Policy* 16.4 (1994): 363–394.

approach because of some disaster that happens and public demand for a tougher approach.[93] They found that this change in approach has led to problematic consequences and the decline of trust has led to a decline in the regulatory effectiveness. Carol Heimer and J. Lynn Gazley have emphasized the importance of meaningful interaction between inspectors and regulators.[94] This interaction can enhance information gathering and improve compliance.

PARETO SELF-IMPROVEMENT AND THE EFFICACY OF CHANGING INTRINSIC MOTIVATION

Robert Cooter has been working on the notion of "Pareto self-improvement";[95] that is, people must be authentic in their ethical preference change to be able to behave in authentically and systematically ways.[96] Cooter proposes that the law can shape ethical behavior through an instrumental mechanism involving preference change. His theory suggests that people have both low-order preferences (immediate desires) and high-order preferences (longer term aspirations, including the desire for social status). When laws create social conditions where virtue is recognized and valued, people seeking to improve their social standing will work to be perceived as virtuous. This desire for social recognition can lead individuals to modify their low-order ethical preferences to align with their high-order preference for elevated social status. This process, which Cooter terms the "Pareto self-improvement mechanism," exemplifies a rational choice approach to understanding how laws can influence moral behavior.[97] This perspective suggests that people logically change their preferences in response to new information or new social opportunities.[98]

The effectiveness of this mechanism in improving intrinsic ethicality depends critically on whether people cannot falsely present themselves as virtuous when they are not genuinely so.[99] Therefore, Cooter argues that if the best way to appear moral is to actually be moral, then people will want to become moral and change their ethical preferences.[100] Therefore, close social groups are important for observing people's true morality and improving ethical preferences.[101] The state can improve compliance with the law by enacting laws that have moral implications. This is

93 Gunningham, Neil, and Darren Sinclair. "Organizational trust and the limits of management-based regulation." *Law & Society Review* 43.4 (2009): 865–900.
94 Heimer, Carol A., and J. Lynn Gazley. "Performing regulation: Transcending regulatory ritualism in HIV clinics." *Law & Society Review* 46.4 (2012): 853–887.
95 This text is based on an analysis done in Feldman. "The expressive function of trade secret law."
96 Cooter, Robert. "Expressive law and economics." *Journal of Legal Studies* 27.S2 (1998): 585–607.
97 Cooter, Robert. *Expressive law and economics*. University of California Press, 1998.
98 Cooter. *Expressive law and economics*.
99 Scott, Robert E. "The limits of behavioral theories of law and social norms." *Virginia Law Review* 86 (2000): 1603–1648.
100 Cooter. "Do good laws make good citizens?," 1577.
101 Cooter. "Do good laws make good citizens?," 1577.

done by piggybacking on social mechanisms. If people want to appear moral to others, they will change their preferences to align with the law, which is often equated (at least somewhat) with morality.[102]

We must ask ourselves whether sanctions threaten this process. Are sanctions making it less likely for cognitive dissonance to occur, causing people to avoid thinking about why they want to obey the law? How do we explain the fact that we have probably internalized the need to put on a seat belt simply through habit formation? What about repetition? Is internalizing through repetition different? The law that prevented sexual harassment used sanctions from the beginning, which led to a change in how sexual harassment is viewed. This is all related to the previous discussion on the contradiction between the expressive function of the law and the crowding-out effect.

IS A CHANGE IN INTRINSIC MOTIVATION NEEDED FOR SUSTAINABLE BEHAVIORAL CHANGE?

When discussing the impact of incentives or regulations on intrinsic motivation, it is important to consider whether intrinsic motivation needs to be altered for behavior to change over time. As already discussed in more detail, Cooter argues that for behavioral change to be sustainable, intrinsic motivation must be altered.

However, this argument overlooks certain facts. For example, the literature on habit formation does not include the classical approach to intrinsic motivation. According to Cooter, people need to believe that their behavior is consistent with their values. However, when looking for studies on behavioral change, this does not seem to be the case. Instead, habit formation is viewed as a more sustainable approach.[103]

ALTERNATIVE MECHANISMS OF ATTITUDE CHANGE

For example, scholars like Kathy Milkman have researched behavioral change through habit formation.[104] This approach is seen as the best way to create stable behavioral change that can withstand various external counter effects. Daphna Lewinsohn-Zamir's work on internalization, which was discussed earlier in this

[102] Cooter. "Do good laws make good citizens?," 1598. Similar arguments are advanced by Paul Robinson and John Darley, who argue that legal rules are more effective when they converge with conventional morality: Robinson, Paul H., and John M. Darley. "The utility of desert." In *Criminal law*, edited by Thomas Morawetz, Routledge, 2019: 381–428. See also Tom R. Tyler, *Why people obey the law*. Princeton University Press, 1990: 65; Lessig, Lawrence. "The new Chicago School." *Journal of Legal Studies* 27.S2 (1998): 661–691; Lessig, Lawrence. "The regulation of social meaning." *University of Chicago Law Review* 62.3 (1995): 943–1045; Lessig, Lawrence. "Social meaning and social norms." *University of Pennsylvania Law Review* 144 (1995): 2181–2190.

[103] Gardner, Benjamin, and Amanda L. Rebar. "Habit formation and behavior change." In *Oxford research encyclopedia of psychology*. Oxford University Press, 2019.

[104] Milkman, Katy. *How to change: The science of getting from where you are to where you want to be*. Penguin, 2021.

chapter, refers to another approach that is similar to the classical effect of cognitive dissonance.[105] According to this approach, behavioral change must precede internal change and internal change is more likely to occur without strong external pressure. This effect has led Lewinsohn-Zamir to argue that a command-and-control sanctions-based approach is less likely to lead to internal change, making it less intrusive and problematic. Interestingly, the assumption is that an internal change is problematic from a rule of law perspective. This issue will be discussed in Chapter 11, which focuses on normative implications.

In addition to the literature on habit formation, models of attitude change also suggest a mixed picture.[106] According to many studies, it is difficult to identify one process through which such change happens.[107] This undermines some of the original models of persuasion and attitude change that sought to differentiate different attributes of messages (such as quality of argument versus source of message).[108]

WHAT REGULATORY INTERVENTIONS ARE MORE LIKELY TO CHANGE PREFERENCES?

Thus, if sanctions are not necessarily the only means to crowd out motivation, as the law might have a similar crowding-out effect, we need to understand what other factors might explain this potential effect. In the following section, which begins by identifying the regulatory toolbox choices, we will examine which regulatory aspects will have a stronger effect on behavior. A related question is what regulatory instrument will have a positive effect on people's intrinsic motivation (which is sometimes referred to as preference change in economic terminology), and what regulatory instrument will have a negative effect on people's intrinsic motivation (which is usually referred to in law and behavioral economics as crowding-out motivation).[109]

IS THERE A REGULATORY INSTRUMENT BEST SUITED TO CHANGE PREFERENCES?

As we showed in Chapter 2, each regulatory instrument has more than one dimension. Therefore, it is difficult to argue that one legal tool is preferable to another

[105] Lewinsohn-Zamir. "The importance of being earnest."

[106] Petty, Richard E., and Pablo Briñol. "Attitude change." In *Advanced social psychology: The state of the science*, edited by R. F. Baumeister and E. J. Finkel, Oxford University Press, 2010: 217–259.

[107] Kruglanski, Arie W., and Erik P. Thompson. "Persuasion by a single route: A view from the unimodel." *Psychological Inquiry* 10.2 (1999): 83–109; Petty, Richard E., S. Christian Wheeler, and George Y. Bizer. "Is there one persuasion process or more? Lumping versus splitting in attitude change theories." *Psychological Inquiry* 10.2 (1999): 156–163.

[108] Briñol, Pablo, and Richard E. Petty. "A history of attitudes and persuasion research." In *Handbook of the history of social psychology*, edited by Arie W. Kruglanski and Wolfgang Stroebe, Psychology Press, 2012: 283–320.

[109] Zamir, Eyal, and Doron Teichman. *Behavioral law and economics*. Oxford University Press, 2018.

when it comes to preference change. Traditionally, it has been assumed that providing an explanation to people regarding compliance is the best way to change preferences. However, recent research has challenged the connection between what people believe and what they actually do.[110] This raises questions about whether the extra effort needed for preference change is the most effective way to achieve the desired policy outcome.

In a sense, our approach advocates for preference change as a desired goal. This is not necessarily because it will lead to greater cooperation, but because it will improve people's sense of belonging and identification with the state.

As policymakers seek tools to promote thoughtful preference change, the "nudge-plus" approach offers a framework that combines behavioral interventions with reflective thinking.[111] While this approach adds deliberation, it is not suggesting doing so because of empirical evidence. Rather, it suggests that adding deliberation is likely to lead to an increase in an important behavioral component of democracy – the feeling that you understand what is expected of you. It is not necessarily because this might lead to a better or higher quality of compliance.

For instance, a government might initiate a campaign to encourage citizens to consume more fruits and vegetables by disseminating information about the health benefits of such a diet. Additionally, they could make it easier to choose healthier options by placing fruits and vegetables at eye level in grocery stores and adding labels that highlight their nutritional value. The nudge-plus approach combines nudges with education and information to encourage positive changes in behavior.

BEHAVIORAL ETHICS AND THE LIMITS OF USING LAW TO SHAPE PREFERENCES

In joint work with Yotam Kaplan, we have criticized the axiom common to all studies on internalization that people will behave more ethically if their preferences become more ethical.[112] This axiom underlies much of the attempt to change people's preferences. It is impossible to argue against the greater good that comes to the world with more people who have ethical preferences. We have argued that ethical preferences do not necessarily guarantee ethical behavior. Instead, we believe that the design of the situation in which people operate is of greater importance. In short, the argument is that even people who have a strong preference for ethical behavior can end up behaving unethically.

[110] Conner, Mark, and Paul Norman. "Understanding the intention–behavior gap: The role of intention strength." *Frontiers in Psychology* 13 (2022): 923464.

[111] Banerjee, Sanchayan, and Peter John. "Nudge plus: Incorporating reflection into behavioral public policy." *Behavioral Public Policy* 8.1 (2024): 69–84.

[112] Feldman, Yuval, and Yotam Kaplan. "Preferences change and behavioral ethics: Can states create ethical people?" *Theoretical Inquiries in Law* 22.1 (2020): 21–14.

Research across cognitive and social psychology, behavioral ethics, and behavioral economics challenges the assumption of internal consistency in human decision-making. This is particularly evident in how people make ethical choices, where behavior often proves more complex and less predictable than traditional models suggest.[113] This point is closely related to the growing literature on deliberative, semi-deliberative, and nondeliberative choice.[114] It is possible for a person to have an explicit preference for one state of affairs yet systematically make choices that seem to contradict this preference. In the context of ethical decision-making, it is possible (and even common) for a person to hold an explicit preference for ethical behavior, but at the same time to have an implicit habit, or a nondeliberative tendency, to lie and cheat.[115] Similarly, people can have a preference for helping others, yet behave selfishly due to various semi-deliberative cognitive processes.[116] This could also happen due to self-deception mechanisms, where individuals might misinterpret their own actions, viewing them as helpful when they are in fact egoistic.[117] Preferences are not monolithic, but fragmented. People behave in ways that indicate the existence of fractions or inconsistencies in their preferences, even within a single time. This insight is also related to the literature on situational wrongdoing, which highlights the effects of minor situational changes on people's levels of moral commitment.[118]

In other words, we argued that the current approach of attempting to change people's preferences to improve ethical behavior is oversimplified and not always effective. People's preferences can be fragmented and inconsistent and holding a conscious preference for ethical behavior does not necessarily lead to behaving ethically. Efforts to improve ethical behavior should focus on maintaining moral awareness and changing social norms, institutions, and organizations. The law can play a role in improving ethical awareness indirectly by changing social norms and

113 Funder, David C., and C. Randall Colvin. "Explorations in behavioral consistency: Properties of persons, situations, and behaviors." *Journal of Personality and Social Psychology* 60.5 (1991): 773–794; Byrka, Katarzyna. *Attitude–behavior consistency: Campbell's paradigm in environmental and health domains*. Technische Universiteit Eindhoven, 2009.

114 Haidt, Jonathan. "The emotional dog and its rational tail: A social intuitionist approach to moral judgment." *Psychological Review* 108.4 (2001): 814–834 (arguing that moral reasoning is typically the result of quick, automatic evaluation and that rational justifications are only made after the fact); Kahneman, Daniel. *Thinking, fast and slow*. Macmillan, 2011.

115 Feldman. The law of good people: 1 ("various psychological and social mechanisms … prevent people from recognizing their wrongdoing and encourage them to feel as if they are far more moral, unbiased, and law abiding than they actually are").

116 Merritt, Anna C., Daniel A. Effron, and Benoît Monin. "Moral self-licensing: When being good frees us to be bad." *Social and Personality Psychology Compass* 4.5 (2010): 344–357 (showing that individuals can use past good deeds to justify future violations of moral norms).

117 Tenbrunsel, Ann E., and David M. Messick. "Ethical fading: The role of self-deception in unethical behavior." *Social Justice Research* 17 (2004): 223–236.

118 Bazerman, Max H., and Ann E. Tenbrunsel. *Blind spots: Why we fail to do what's right and what to do about it*. Princeton University Press, 2011.

institutions.[119] Therefore, improving a person's expressed beliefs or preferences, or encouraging a "taste for fairness,"[120] will not necessarily result in a positive behavior change. This means that the effort to improve ethical behavior should become more nuanced. Improving behavior can require constant maintenance of moral awareness, rather than a discrete intervention designed to alter expressed attitudes.

Our conclusion, which is very relevant to the conclusion of this chapter, is that the law may be ill-equipped to produce an overall improvement in people's internal drive to behave ethically and legally. Instead, we suggest an alternative approach to the role of law. Rather than directly improving ethical awareness, the law should indirectly change conventional social norms, institutions, and organizations.

CONCLUSION

This chapter explores the complex relationship between intrinsic motivation and external regulatory interventions, challenging the traditional view that crowding-out effects are uniform and predictable. Through detailed analysis, we discover that the interaction between internal drives and external pressures varies significantly across contexts and individuals. Most notably, different forms of intrinsic motivation exhibit varying levels of resilience to external intervention – scientific beliefs, for instance, often prove more resistant to crowding out than moral motivations, while legitimacy-based compliance responds differently than purely voluntary cooperation.

The crowding-out process itself operates through multiple interconnected mechanisms at both individual and social levels. At the individual level, we observe self-related processes such as over-justification, attention shifts, and changes in perceived autonomy. These personal responses are complemented by broader social processes, including the diminishment of virtue-signaling opportunities and the bureaucratization of behavior. Understanding these mechanisms reveals why the effectiveness of regulatory interventions depends heavily on perception and framing – the same intervention might enhance compliance in one context while undermining it in another, based largely on whether the target population perceives it as supportive or controlling. This variability is further complicated by individual differences, as people with strong prosocial orientations often react quite differently to external incentives than those with more individualistic tendencies.

119 Traditional preference-change literature recognizes external constraints on people's preferences. That is, it might be that a person holds a preference for helping others, but they are not able to act on that preference since they do not possess the necessary financial means. Our argument in this chapter adds another layer, that of internal constraints, to the factors limiting people's ability to realize their preferences. That is, we argue that even if a person has a preference for helping others, and that person is able to realize this preference without being externally constrained, it might still be the case that cognitive biases will interrupt and limit that person's ability to realize their explicit preference.

120 Cooter. "Do good laws make good citizens?," 1577.

These findings point to the need for a more sophisticated approach to regulation. Rather than viewing crowding out as a universal phenomenon, policymakers must carefully consider how specific interventions might affect different groups and various types of motivation. This understanding opens the possibility of combining regulatory approaches in ways that reinforce rather than undermine voluntary compliance.

Looking ahead to Chapter 4, we will examine how specific regulatory tools affect intrinsic motivation and voluntary compliance. By deepening our understanding of the interplay between rules, incentives, and natural motivations, we can design regulatory systems that enhance rather than suppress human nature's positive inclinations. Ultimately, our goal extends beyond achieving mere compliance to building regulatory frameworks that strengthen the social fabric that makes willing cooperation possible.

The chapter concludes by arguing that successful regulation requires a more sophisticated understanding of how different regulatory tools interact with various types of intrinsic motivation. Rather than viewing crowding out as a universal phenomenon, policymakers need to consider how specific interventions might affect different groups and different types of motivation, potentially combining approaches in ways that reinforce rather than undermine voluntary compliance.

In Chapter 4, we'll examine specific regulatory tools' effects on intrinsic motivation and voluntary compliance. By understanding how rules and incentives interact with people's natural motivations, we can design approaches that bring out the best in human nature rather than suppress it. The goal is to develop systems that not only achieve compliance but also strengthen the social fabric that makes willing cooperation possible in the first place.

4

Regulatory Design, Trust, and Voluntary Compliance

INTRODUCTION

Chapter 3 explored how different regulatory approaches affect compliance motivation, particularly examining the potential for regulations to crowd out intrinsic motivation. This chapter shifts focus to examine how regulatory changes can build trust between the public and government, with particular attention to citizens' subjective experiences and perceptions of government trustworthiness.

While considerable research exists on the interaction between trust and regulation, a significant gap remains in our understanding of their causal relationship. Most existing research examines how trust influences regulatory development and implementation, or how regulations can be designed to build upon existing trust. However, there is notably less examination of the reverse relationship – how regulatory implementation affects societal trust levels. Key questions remain unexplored: Do stricter regulations increase or decrease public trust in institutions? How do different regulatory approaches distinctly impact trust? What are the long-term effects of regulatory policies on societal trust?

This research gap is particularly challenging given the lack of theoretical and empirical frameworks for predicting which regulatory interventions will effectively build trust. The challenge is further complicated by the difficulty of identifying and measuring the broader, lasting effects of regulatory choices on public response. These limitations underscore the need for more targeted research into how regulations shape trust, rather than solely examining how trust shapes regulation.

THE EFFECTIVE VOLUNTARY COMPLIANCE PARADIGM: A REGULATORY DILEMMA

1. The effective *voluntary* compliance paradigm presents a complex regulatory challenge with multiple interrelated considerations:
2. **Population Effectiveness**: Policymakers must evaluate which regulatory tools best achieve "effective voluntary compliance" both immediately and across

different domains. This evaluation should examine not only average effects but also how regulatory interventions reshape the distribution of compliance behavior across the population. This distributional analysis is particularly crucial in voluntary compliance frameworks, where we expect to see significant gaps between intrinsically motivated "true believers" and instrumentally motivated compliers.

3. **Sustainability**: The long-term impact of these tools on voluntary compliance requires careful evaluation and is currently missing from most types of studies. This includes considering whether the chosen approach will foster or hinder a culture of self-regulation over time. Additionally, potential spillover effects into other regulatory domains should be examined to understand the broader implications of these strategies.
4. **Broader Societal Carry-Over Implications**: It's crucial to examine how the selected regulatory strategy might affect public behavior and trust in institutions beyond the immediate target area. This holistic view helps anticipate unintended consequences and ensures that efforts to improve compliance in one area don't inadvertently undermine other societal goals.
5. **Adaptability**: Regulatory approaches should be flexible enough to maintain effectiveness as societal attitudes and behaviors evolve. This involves considering how different strategies – from trust-based regulation to more traditional command-and-control methods involving monitoring and coercion – can be adjusted or combined. The goal is to create a regulatory framework that can respond to changing circumstances while consistently promoting voluntary compliance.

By addressing these interconnected aspects, policymakers can develop a more comprehensive and nuanced approach to promoting effective voluntary compliance. This multifaceted strategy recognizes that successful regulation isn't just about short-term results, but also about fostering a sustainable culture of compliance that adapts to societal changes and maintains public trust.

This chapter is an important part of the book's broader agenda. It emphasizes the importance of understanding the theory behind regulatory dilemmas, rather than relying solely on extensive data collection. While undoubtedly important, such empirical evidence only indicates regulation's immediate impact on behavior, while neglecting the long-term response. This gap highlights the critical need for a robust theoretical framework in regulatory interventions. While empirical studies yield valuable data, they often lack the predictive power that a well-developed theory could provide. Enhancing our understanding of when voluntary compliance is most effective could contribute significantly to the development of a theoretical framework, thereby improving our ability to predict the outcomes of various interventions. While empirical studies often focus on short-term behavioral changes, theoretical approaches can better account for long-term adaptations and complex interactions within regulatory systems. Theory allows us to model and predict outcomes beyond the immediate observable effects, providing a more comprehensive understanding of regulatory dynamics.

Building on this understanding of the limitations of purely empirical approaches, it's important to consider the multifaceted nature of regulatory dilemmas. Although there are many dimensions to the dilemma of regulatory dichotomy, current research usually treats it as one-dimensional. For example, the important work of Erich Kirchler on the legitimate versus coercive dimension largely assumes that regulatory styles are dichotomous and that voluntary compliance is more likely when approaches are balanced along this single dimension.[1] There are many dimensions to consider when designing regulatory tools and it is not entirely clear how each of them contributes to the level of trust they might generate.

The interaction of trust-based regulatory approaches with these domains of voluntary compliance is not cohesive. Traditionally, coercion and sanction-based regulation can be considered antidotes to voluntary compliance. However, there are many open questions with regard to these relationships; for example, it is not entirely clear whether noninstrumental motivations, such as guilt, could be considered voluntary?

One aim of this book is to create a better connection between research on regulation and research on compliance. This more comprehensive approach can enhance our understanding of the different regulatory tools and how they affect the *likelihood of voluntary compliance* (see Table 4.1).

Table 4.1 provides a comparative analysis across five policy domains to guide the decision between trust-based and coercion-based regulatory approaches. The domains examined include environmental compliance, tax compliance, commercial ethics, COVID-19 mask wearing, and COVID-19 vaccination. For each domain, various factors are evaluated, such as quality and proportion of compliance, cost of mistakes, time frame, population heterogeneity, need for social support, possibility for nudges, feasibility of sequential approaches, alignment with intrinsic motivation, and feasibility of monitoring. This comprehensive assessment aims to determine the suitability of trust-based regulation in each context. For instance, in areas like commercial ethics and COVID-19 mask wearing, where intrinsic motivation alignment is highly important and the quality of compliance is high, trust-based approaches might be more effective. Conversely, in domains like tax compliance, where monitoring feasibility is very high and alignment with intrinsic motivation is least important, coercion-based methods might be more appropriate. This nuanced approach recognizes that the effectiveness of trust-based regulation varies significantly across different policy areas and depends on a complex interplay of factors.

[1] Kirchler, Erich, Erik Hoelzl, and Ingrid Wahl. "Enforced versus voluntary tax compliance: The 'slippery slope' framework." *Journal of Economic Psychology* 29.2 (2008): 210–225.

TABLE 4.1 *How to decide between trust and coercion in five policy domains*

Legal doctrine	Environmental compliance	Tax compliance	Commercial ethics	COVID (mask)	COVID (vaccine)
Quality of compliance	High	Moderate	High	High	Low relevance
Proportion of compliance	The more the merrier	The more the merrier	High	Very high	High
Cost of mistakes	Moderate	Low	Moderate	High	Moderate
Long/short term	Long	Moderate	Long	Long	Short
Heterogeneity of regulated population	Very high	Very high	Very high	High	High
Need for social support	Very high	Moderate	High	High	Moderate
Possibility for nudges	High	Moderate	Moderate	High	High
Feasibly of sequential approach	Moderate	High	Moderate	Moderate	High
Alignment with intrinsic motivation	Moderately important	Least important	Highly important	Highly important	High
Feasibility of monitoring	Usually high	Very high	Moderate	Low	High

CAN WE PREDICT WHICH REGULATORY APPROACH WILL ENHANCE VOLUNTARY COMPLIANCE?

Predicting the effect of each regulatory approach on broader aspects of society, such as the creation of trust between the state and the public, remains a daunting task. In the next few paragraphs, we examine an even more fundamental problem arising from the limitations of predicting the results of regulatory choices. One of the best, albeit most frustrating, examples of the need for a trial-and-error approach is the work of Katherine Milkman, who compares the impact of dozens of interventions on various behaviors. Behavioral science studies, such as the one examining flu vaccination reminders, reveal valuable insights into effective intervention strategies. Her recent mega study involving 689,693 Walmart Pharmacy customers found that text-based reminders can encourage pharmacy flu vaccinations.[2] In this case, sending two reminder texts, spaced three days apart and emphasizing that a vaccine was "waiting for you," proved most effective in increasing vaccination rates. However,

[2] Milkman, Katherine L., et al. "A 680,000-person mega study of nudges to encourage vaccination in pharmacies." *Proceedings of the National Academy of Sciences* 119.6 (2022): e2115126119.

the fact that experts failed to predict this outcome highlights a significant gap in our understanding of behavioral interventions.

We argue that the best way to understand what makes regulation work is to look at how much pressure is needed to get people to follow the rules. Different situations call for different approaches – sometimes people willingly comply, while other times strict enforcement is necessary. The key is finding the right balance for each specific situation, considering how resistant people are to changing their behavior. By analyzing the relationship between the level of coercion and behavioral outcomes across different regulatory contexts, we can begin to construct a more nuanced and predictive theoretical model. This model would not only help in selecting the most appropriate regulatory tools for given situations but also in anticipating potential challenges and resistances to various interventions.

The need for such a theoretical framework becomes even more apparent when considering the complexities of human behavior in response to regulations. Understanding voluntary compliance, for instance, requires a nuanced approach that goes beyond simple cause-and-effect relationships. A comprehensive theory would need to account for various factors, including psychological, social, and contextual elements that influence decision-making and behavior.

In conclusion, while empirical studies like the flu vaccination reminder experiment provide valuable insights, they also highlight the limitations of a purely data-driven approach. To truly advance our understanding of regulatory interventions and their impact on behavior, we need to develop a theoretical paradigm that can explain the mechanisms behind successful interventions, predict the effectiveness of new strategies, guide the design of more targeted and efficient regulatory approaches, and facilitate the transfer of knowledge across different regulatory domains.

By investing in the development of such a theoretical framework, we can move beyond trial-and-error approaches and toward a more systematic and effective method of designing and implementing regulatory interventions. This would not only improve the success rate of these interventions but also enhance our overall understanding of human behavior in response to regulatory efforts.

COERCIVE POWER VS. LEGITIMATE POWER

The most crucial dimension in distinguishing between various regulatory interventions appears to be the focus of the approach: whether it emphasizes the ability to impose costs on noncooperators or aims to induce positive willingness to cooperate through factors such as fairness, trust, and legitimacy.

Studies suggest that trust and legitimacy can positively affect not only voluntary compliance, but also the effectiveness of enforced regulation. For example, Eva Hoffman and others found that legitimate power increases science and reason-based trust, voluntary cooperation, and success in enforcing compliance.[3] These results challenge the assumption of other researchers that trust and coercion are competing and are mutually exclusive.[4]

The primary paradigm we are examining is the approach that best achieves compliance, in line with the research of Kirchler and colleagues.[5] The distinction between coercive and legitimate powers does not suffice to fully explain the relationship between regulatory approaches and people's motivation to comply. Parallel to this examination is one regarding *voluntary vs. nonvoluntary* compliance that seeks to determine through which of these powers – coercive or legitimate – regulators can increase public compliance.

It should be noted that there is a gap between extrinsic–intrinsic and coercive vs. legitimate compliance methods. While the coercive method is clearly an extrinsic force, legitimate power is not necessarily exercised to create intrinsic motivation. This distinction highlights the complexity of motivational factors in compliance scenarios. Some of the knowledge gap in this topic is due to conceptual confusion in the literature differentiating between extrinsic and instrumental motivations and intrinsic and non-instrumental motivations (e.g., moral motivation could be seen as intrinsic or extrinsic motivation). The thinking is that people might comply with a legitimate power because they believe others might comply and not because they have intrinsic motivations within the action. This perspective underscores the nuanced nature of human motivation and compliance behaviors. It shows that the relationships between these concepts are not always straightforward, creating areas where our understanding is incomplete.

VOLUNTARY COMPLIANCE AND "ORDER WITHOUT LAW" LITERATURE

Another important paradigm to consider when examining regulatory approaches that allow for voluntary compliance is the approach taken by scholars such as Lisa Bernstein in her study of the diamond industry.[6] Bernstein found that social norms can serve as a substitute for formal laws in achieving compliance. The diamond industry is unique in that it can use reputation and social bonds at a low cost, creating a system that enables most transactions to be completed entirely outside the legal system. It has been suggested that, historically, Jewish merchants controlled

3 Hofmann, Eva, et al. "Enhancing tax compliance through coercive and legitimate power of tax authorities by concurrently diminishing or facilitating trust in tax authorities." *Law & Policy* 36.3 (2014): 290–313.

4 Rousseau, Denise M., et al. "Not so different after all: A cross-discipline view of trust." *Academy of Management Review* 23.3 (1998): 393–404; discussing, among other things, the concept of deterrence-based trust.

5 Muehlbacher, Stephan, Erich Kirchler, and Herbert Schwarzenberger. "Voluntary versus enforced tax compliance: Empirical evidence for the 'slippery slope' framework." *European Journal of Law and Economics* 32 (2011): 89–97.

6 Bernstein, Lisa. "Opting out of the legal system: Extralegal contractual relations in the diamond industry." *Journal of Legal Studies* 21.1 (1992): 115–157.

this industry due to their ability to form an effective external reputation mechanism. This means that within the Jewish merchant community there was a strong system of trust and accountability based on shared cultural and religious values, as well as close-knit family and community ties. Thus, contracts were thought to be enforced primarily through trust-based relationships and the fear of reputational damage within the community, rather than by legally based coercive measures. This reputation mechanism was supported by a distinctive set of industry, family, and community institutions that facilitated information sharing and collective enforcement of norms.[7] An alternative explanation can be found in a study on the diamond exchange economy, where there is an ethnically homogeneous middleman group that provides alternatives to contract law. Perceived as a club-like structure, this unique arrangement is based on mutual trust and reputation.[8] In a subsequent study on the cotton industry, Bernstein argued that the industry's reliance on an alternative legal system, rather than a market-driven trust system, was the primary reason for minimal use of formal courts.[9] Very similar findings on extralegal functioning, came from Robert Ellickson has shown how considerations of efficiency caused neighbors in Shasta County in northern California to cooperate beyond what was required by law.[10] In Shasta County, research reveals that, in accordance with the Coase theorem,[11] law plays a lesser role than expected in neighborly relationships. People largely govern themselves using informal rules and social norms that develop without the aid of a state or other central coordinators.[12]

Another study has demonstrated that individuals' concern for their reputation can facilitate the formation of contracts between trading partners, even when one or both parties are committed to or dependent on the trading relationship.[13] In a similar vein, Mark Suchman's sociological study of lawyers in Silicon Valley presents an alternative view of the legal profession, describing it as engaging in the venture capital financing of "new technology-based corporations." In this context, lawyers are viewed favorably by their clients and are perceived as adding value to a transaction rather than arguing over how to divide the transactional pie.[14]

7 Richman, Barak D. "How community institutions create economic advantage: Jewish diamond merchants in New York." *Law & Social Inquiry* 31.2 (2006): 383–420.

8 Landa, Janet T. "A theory of the ethnically homogeneous middleman group: An institutional alternative to contract law." *Journal of Legal Studies* 10.2 (1981): 349–362.

9 Bernstein, Lisa. "Private commercial law in the cotton industry: Creating cooperation through rules, norms, and institutions." *Michigan Law Review* 99.7 (2001): 1724–1790.

10 Ellickson, Robert C. *Order without law: How neighbors settle disputes*. Harvard University Press, 1991.

11 Cooter, Robert D. "Coase theorem." In *The world of economics*, edited by John Eatwell, Murray Milgate and Peter Newman, Palgrave Macmillan, 1991: 51–57.

12 Ellickson. *Order without law*.

13 McMillan, John, and Christopher Woodruff. "Private order under dysfunctional public order." *Michigan Law Review* 98.8 (2000): 2421–2458.

14 Suchman, Mark C., and Mia L. Cahill. "The hired gun as facilitator: Lawyers and the suppression of business disputes in Silicon Valley." *Law & Social Inquiry* 21.3 (1996): 679–712. See also Bernstein, Lisa. "The Silicon Valley lawyer as transaction cost engineer." *Oregon Law Review* 74 (1995): 239–256.

While many consider this order without law paradigm not easily translated to other spheres where reputation systems are not as effective, it does suggest the importance of accounting for community governance as a potential alternative to state command and control. As we will demonstrate in Chapters 8 and 10 on COVID-19 and environmental behavior, community governance can be used as an important alternative tool to state regulation. It could help achieve voluntary compliance more effectively.

DO SANCTIONS KILL VOLUNTARY COMPLIANCE?

One of the most important regulatory dilemmas is related to sanctions and their possible effect on people's ability to develop an autonomous feeling of choosing to comply voluntarily with regulations. What characterizes the type of regulatory instruments that are likely to lead to voluntary compliance both in the short term and in the long term? What can we learn from current research about which types of regulatory instruments, such as reminders, pledges, technological interventions, and others are likely to harm voluntary compliance in both the short and long term? Does compliance become nonvoluntary every time sanctions are used? In the next few paragraphs, we will explore some aspects of these dilemmas.

CAN WE CREATE COERCION-FREE REGULATION?

The short answer to the question on sanctions is no. Although alternative regulatory strategies exist, they are not as effective as responsive law approaches in influencing behavior.[15] The larger question, which existing empirical research has not yet answered, is what is the optimal way to locate deterrence in a place where it can be effective?

When discussing whether governments can trust the public, it is important to consider whether coercion is effective. While some may argue that coercion is the safest and best choice for regulators, there is ample research on the negative effects of deterrence on people's intrinsic motivation and moral commitment.[16] However, another perspective demanding discussion is whether deterrence is effective. In their recent book, *The Behavioral Code*, Adam Fine and Benjamin van Rooij dedicate two chapters to discussing recent statistical studies of the deterrent effect of policies such as "three strikes and you are out" and capital punishment. Their findings reveal mixed results, with the majority of studies failing to establish a significant deterrence impact of severe punishment.[17] The book focuses on the argument that

[15] Braithwaite, John. "The essence of responsive regulation." *UBC Law Review* 44 (2011): 475–520.

[16] Atiq, Emad H. "Why motives matter: Reframing the crowding out effect of legal incentives." *Yale Law Journal* 123 (2013): 1070–1116.

[17] Van Rooij, Benjamin, and Adam Fine. *The behavioral code: The hidden ways the law makes us better or worse*. Beacon Press, 2021.

deterrence-based approaches have negative effects and that their long-term drawbacks outweigh any short-term benefits of immediate compliance.

When the need for punishment arises, we should focus on various factors such as the harm caused and the immediacy of the response needed. For example, when the regulated activity carries significant potential for immediate harm to others, sanctioning might be the safest approach and focusing on deterrence might be more justifiable. On the other hand, if the desired behavior requires the goodwill of the people and their behavior beyond compliance, relying on deterrence is not desirable. Instead, greater focus should be placed on reaching people through regulatory measures that support their dominant motivation. Additionally, we should consider whether the targeted behavior is enforceable. When compliance is relatively easy to measure and assess in terms of quality, and the cost of enforcement is low, there is less needed to focus on voluntary compliance. In such cases, enforcement costs are naturally reduced.

Furthermore, some behaviors are less likely to be crowded out by any type of regulation because they depend on knowledge and motivation that comes from wanting to behave according to the knowledge communicated through the regulation and knowledge is less likely to be crowded out. In other words, when the regulation does not provide an additional motivation to comply, it is simply offering instruction as to what behavior would be viewed as the right thing to do. For example, imagine that someone is interested in driving safely. Without enforcement, both that individual and other drivers will likely drive faster. The first step is to determine the safest driving speed for each context. The second step is to acknowledge that speeding may result in a penalty, which motivates the driver to ensure compliance with the speed limit. People are less likely to be intrinsically motivated to drive at a certain arbitrary speed.

Finally, given the differences between individuals suggested, a preliminary analysis of the attitudes of the target populations could shed light on the likely effect of each model on the aggregated compliance behavior.[18]

ENFORCEMENT EFFORTS AND VOLUNTARY COMPLIANCE

A potential obstacle to achieving voluntary compliance could come not from regulation, but from the way enforcement bodies work. In collaboration with Yotam Kaplan, we have identified ethical blind spots and regulatory traps, highlighting the potential disparity between enforced and intrinsic motivation.[19] This observation

[18] Feldman, Yuval. "Five models of regulatory compliance motivation: Empirical findings and normative implications." In *Handbook on the politics of regulation*, Vol. 1, edited by David Levi-Faur, Elgar, 2011: 335–346; Feldman, Yuval. "The complexity of disentangling intrinsic and extrinsic compliance motivations: Theoretical and empirical insights from the behavioral analysis of law." *Washington University Journal of Law and Policy* 35 (2011): 11–52.

[19] Feldman, Yuval, and Yotam Kaplan. "Ethical blind spots and regulatory traps: On distorted regulatory incentives, behavioral ethics and legal design." In *Law and economics of regulation*, edited by Klaus Mathis Avishalom Tor, Springer International Publishing, 2021: 37–54.

presents a nuanced perspective on regulatory enforcement. While there's often an emphasis on strictly enforcing legal standards across the board, this approach may not always be the most effective. In some cases, it may be more beneficial to focus enforcement efforts on those who are already intrinsically motivated to comply with regulations. Revisiting the example of speeding, people who are focused only on extrinsic measures may be less likely to get caught. Regulators will find it easier to enforce regulations and catch those who want to drive safely but might misunderstand the speed limit because of a gap between reality and the law.

To reduce such wrongdoings, regulators should aim to eliminate ethical blind spots in their work; ethical blind spots are scenarios and situations in which ordinary law-abiding people find it difficult to identify the harmfulness of their actions. This can be done by removing ambiguity and changing the conditions that contribute to unethical behavior.

However, policymakers may be incentivized to conserve these ethical blind spots and build regulatory traps around them in order to increase the perception of their effectiveness by demonstrating intense and rapid enforcement activity.[20] By ignoring the underlying cognitive causes of unethical behavior, we are allowing wrongdoing to continue. We should not simply sanction those who repeatedly fall into this trap. Instead, we should be identifying the root causes of these ethical blind spots and addressing them.

For example, consider speeding tickets. Speed limits are usually intuitive and easy to follow if people care to comply with the law. However, in some situations, such as when the speed limit drops for a small section of a highway, speed limits can be confusing or unintuitive. This is an ethical blind spot in the sense that, in such a location, many law-abiding people will find the law difficult to understand because the ethical mechanism behind it will be less clear. These ethical blind spots will likely lead to an increase in wrongdoing, as more people will struggle to recognize the intrinsic problems with disobeying the law. In such cases, regulators should ideally act to reduce ambiguity and address these ethical blind spots. For instance, one way to improve safety in these areas is to ensure that road signs are highly visible and easy to understand. However, in many cases, police officers may exploit drivers' ethical blind spots by creating traps for wrongdoers and issuing multiple tickets. This approach can transform what was initially an ethical blind spot into a regulatory trap.

Kaplan and I argue in our paper that technological advancements in law enforcement can exacerbate these distortions between intrinsic motivation to comply and likelihood of enforcement. Automated law enforcement technologies, such as speed cameras or automated auditing tools, are particularly effective at easily identifying and sanctioning recurring violations. The use of these mechanisms makes it easier

[20] Feldman and Kaplan. "Ethical blind spots and regulatory traps."

for law enforcement to create situations where people unknowingly break the law and then are punished for it, especially when those violations are reoccurring and follow known patterns. In other words, speed cameras are most effective when installed at locations where people frequently violate the speed limit. These locations are often overlooked and difficult to monitor, making them ethical blind spots. Violations in these areas are common and, with the availability of speed cameras, sanctions are inexpensive. These can make regulatory traps an even more dominant and profitable strategy for police and other law enforcers. Therefore, when speed cameras are available, regulators are often reluctant to diffuse ethical blind spots on the road because they are too profitable. Similarly, tax authorities might use technological resources to focus on the most ambiguous clauses, where more people are likely to underreport, rather than on the places where intentional and malicious tax evasion is likely to happen.

In our paper, Kaplan and I showed that similar issues are relevant in many areas of law, from financial regulation to tax compliance, consumer protection, and regulation. To combat these disturbing trends regarding regulatory traps, we must be more aware of regulatory incentive structures and the way regulators and enforcement agencies are affected by the introduction of new law enforcement technologies.

Auditing-Based Corporate Voluntary Compliance Program

Another important regulatory approach is auditing-based voluntary compliance, where corporations opt into programs offering enhanced guidance in exchange for a more cooperative compliance approach. Several examples of such programs exist among US administrative agencies. For instance, the Environmental Protection Agency's Audit Policy Program, which allows companies to voluntarily disclose violations in exchange for reduced penalties, has led to the discovery and correction of violations at thousands of facilities since its inception.[21] Another example is the Inland Revenue Service's Compliance Assurance Process, where corporate taxpayers pledge to maintain transparency in exchange for real-time tax guidance, the process has shown a decrease in tax uncertainty (measured through the money reserves they've put for challenges by tax authority).[22] Similarly, the Food and Drug Administration's Voluntary Qualified Importer Program uses trust-based certification to expedite food imports to the US for international companies with strong safety records.[23] Similarly, the Securities and Exchange Commission's 2010

[21] Short, Jodi L., and Michael W. Toffel. "Coerced confessions: Self-policing in the shadow of the regulator." *Journal of Law, Economics, & Organization* 24.1 (2008): 45–71.

[22] Beck, Paul J., and Petro Lisowsky. "Tax uncertainty and voluntary real-time tax audits." *The Accounting Review* 89.3 (2014): 867–901.

[23] Fortin, Neal. "The US Food Safety Modernization Act: Implications in transnational governance of food safety, food system sustainability, and the tension with free trade." *Duke Environmental Law & Policy Forum* 25 (2014): 313–338.

Cooperation Program, offering leniency for self-reporting securities violations, has improved the effectiveness of securities enforcement.[24] This evidence suggests that when properly structured, corporate-based trust-based regulatory tools can achieve both instrumental goals (reducing enforcement costs) and normative ones (fostering cooperation and compliance culture).[25] While this book primarily examines individual compliance, trust-based regulatory programs show greater promise when applied to corporations. This increased potential stems from two key factors: corporations are repeat players who are more sensitive to reputational consequences, and they generally cannot claim violations of personal autonomy or dignity when their compliance history influences regulatory treatment (for a detailed discussion of technology-based differentiated enforcement using past behavior, see Chapter 7).

PREVENTIVE APPROACH TO VOLUNTARY COMPLIANCE

Preventative regulatory approaches have been used to make noncompliance a remote possibility. This practice may undermine voluntary compliance, either in the short or long term. In the short run, if one cannot comply because noncompliance is not possible, then no voluntary act is present. This raises the question: Does long-term exclusion of choice have a negative effect on people's choice about whether to comply? For example, many people whose main income comes from wages cannot avoid paying taxes. Is such a practice good or bad for their future tax morale?

Indeed, a possible solution is to take a preventative approach that focuses on intrinsic motivation rather than extrinsic motivation.[26] This approach aligns with the instrumental perspective on compliance motivation while being less prone to disrupting other factors that drive compliance. In a preventive approach, regulators use technological tools and structural design to eliminate opportunities for lawbreaking before they occur. Edward Cheng's structural law approach illustrates this strategy by making socially undesirable behavior more difficult through design rather than relying on after-the-fact enforcement.[27] For example, rather than imposing fines for mail theft, this approach focuses on designing mailboxes that prevent unauthorized access. Similar preventive strategies include tax withholding to prevent tax evasion and technological barriers to prevent illegal file sharing.

This approach, while still treating individuals as rational actors who might violate laws when costs are low, differs from traditional enforcement models. By removing the possibility of noncompliance through design, it may be less likely to trigger the

[24] Leone, Andrew J., Edward Xuejun Li, and Michelle Liu. "On the SEC's 2010 enforcement cooperation program." *Journal of Accounting and Economics* 71.1 (2021): 1–22.
[25] Short, Jodi L. "The paranoid style in regulatory reform." *Hastings Law Journal* 63 (2011): 633–694.
[26] Katyal, Neal Kumar. "Digital architecture as crime control." *Yale Law Journal* 112 (2002): 2261–2290.
[27] Cheng, Edward K. "Structural laws and the puzzle of regulating behavior." *Northwestern University Law Review* 100 (2006): 655–718.

negative psychological effects associated with explicit enforcement, such as crowding out intrinsic motivation. When compliance becomes the only viable option, individuals quickly adapt their behavior accordingly.

Importantly, despite its highly restrictive nature, this preventive approach often feels less coercive than traditional enforcement methods. This is because when alternative actions are structurally impossible, individuals don't experience the psychological burden of being forced to make a choice. The effectiveness of this approach lies in its ability to prevent both opportunistic noncompliance by ordinary citizens and deliberate violations by those more inclined to break rules.

Incentives and Voluntary Compliance

While Chapter 3 examined the relationship between incentives and crowding out, this chapter will explore whether incentives that give people choice in cooperation can help maintain voluntary compliance long term, even in areas where incentives aren't available. When considering behaviors like vaccination or recycling, we need to examine several critical issues: how offering rewards affects participation, whether these rewards might discourage unpaid cooperation in the future, and whether using market-like incentives could be seen as weakening government authority. We'll explore how this market-based approach to compliance might affect public perception of state legitimacy and regulatory effectiveness. Research by scholars such as Michael Sandel and Dagan and Fisher could lead us to believe that incentives can have a negative effect both on the specific behavior and, more importantly, on how participants treat the system that offers them rewards for their participation.[28]

Although many people have argued that deterrence is not effective, moving away from using it as the sole regulatory approach doesn't necessarily mean that policymakers and researchers have abandoned the idea that individuals make decisions based on cost-benefit calculations. Even when other regulatory tools are introduced, there's still an underlying assumption that people weigh pros and cons in their decision-making process. For example, assuming that human motivation is the same, various modern methods of governance have been created, including environmental taxation and different forms of self-governance programs that do not always carry direct sanctions.[29] Other scholars have suggested revisiting the concept of deterrence from a broader perspective and taking into account various social

[28] Sandel, M. *What money can't buy: The moral limits of markets*. Farrar, Straus and Giroux (2012): 1–36; Dagan, Tsilly, and Talia Fisher. "Rights for sale." *Minnesota Law Review* 96 (2011): 90–140.

[29] Revesz, Richard L., and Robert N. Stavins. "Environmental law and public policy." In *Handbook of law and economics*, rev. ed., edited by A. Mitchell Polinsky and Steven Shavell, Elsevier Science, 2004: 499–589; King, Andrew A., and Michael J. Lenox. "Industry self-regulation without sanctions: The chemical industry's responsible care program." *Academy of Management Journal* 43.4 (2000): 698–716.

factors and sanctions that might make deterrence more effective.[30] In this context, the environmental field has been especially interesting, as deterrence has been used in particularly sophisticated ways through various regulations that force organizations to publicize their emission levels and face sanctions from the public.[31]

In this book, incentives are viewed as interesting tools that allow people to choose and cooperate, even when coercion is involved. However, if our goal is to foster internalized voluntary compliance rather than coerced behavior, we need to carefully consider the role of incentives. Traditional incentives may not always lead to internalized compliance. External rewards can shift motivation from intrinsic to extrinsic, potentially undermining long-term commitment to the behavior. People might view incentivized actions as transactional rather than moral or civic duties. Moreover, once incentives are removed, the motivation to continue the behavior may decrease. As discussed in Chapter 3, there are instances where incentives can crowd out cooperative behavior. This phenomenon occurs when external motivations replace or diminish intrinsic ones.

However, we will demonstrate that there are ways to design and implement incentives that can increase the likelihood of internalized voluntary compliance. These methods involve aligning incentives with existing values and norms, using nonmonetary rewards that reinforce social recognition and gradually phasing out incentives as behaviors become habitual.[32] By addressing these factors, it's possible to use incentives as a tool to foster genuine, internalized voluntary compliance rather than mere temporary behavioral change.[33]

THE POTENTIAL RISK TO COMPLIANCE OF MORALITY AND FAIRNESS

This book reviews several models and it is important to focus on those that are less likely to interfere with other models that have unintended effects. For example, the concept of procedural justice, which has been widely studied by scholars such as Tom Tyler and Margaret Levi, is likely to increase legitimacy and compliance, with

30 Kahan, Dan M. "Social influence, social meaning, and deterrence." In *Criminal law,* edited by Thomas Morawetz, Routledge, 2019: 429–476; McAdams, Richard H. "An attitudinal theory of expressive law." *Oregon Law Review* 79 (2000): 339–390.

31 Peterson, Sonja. "Monitoring, accounting and enforcement in emissions trading regimes." In *Greenhouse gas emissions trading and project-based mechanisms.* OECD, 2003: 189–205; Feldman, Yuval, and Oren Perez. "How law changes the environmental mind: An experimental study of the effect of legal norms on moral perceptions and civic enforcement." *Journal of Law and Society* 36.4 (2009): 501–535.

32 See, for example, Carrera, Mariana, et al. "The structure of health incentives: Evidence from a field experiment." *Management Science* 66.5 (2020): 1890–1908. See also John, Leslie K., et al. *The role of incentive salience in habit formation.* Harvard Business School, 2016.

33 Frey, Bruno S., and Felix Oberholzer-Gee. "The cost of price incentives: An empirical analysis of motivation crowding-out." *American Economic Review* 87.4 (1997): 746–755.

less likelihood of interfering with the effective functioning of deterrence.[34] Similarly, informing people of the harm associated with their behavior may be effective for some, without inducing resentment toward the law. Despite these approaches, some scholars suggest that emphasizing morality could give people the impression that the state is unable to enforce the law, which could have potentially unintended consequences.[35] Therefore, regulators should aim to identify policies that target as many motivations as possible while recognizing the challenge of achieving complete success in this mission.

TRUST-BASED REGULATION

It is acknowledged that there is no one regulatory solution that fits all situations and that there is a need for initial data collection. When collecting data, we must consider the quality of cooperation, the cost of enforcement, and the contribution to the regulator's legitimacy. How well does the tool interact with population heterogeneity? Is trust necessary for trust-based regulation to work? To what extent is trust-based regulation likely to work better in the long run? Do we know if it is indeed stable enough over time? To what extent we can rely on the "trust but verify" approach and still call it trust? In what situations we can say that can use multiple methods at the same time?

NUDGES AND VOLUNTARY COMPLIANCE

In Chapter 2, we differentiated between two types of voluntary compliance: noncoerced and internalized. Nudges are an excellent example of a regulatory approach that doesn't involve coercion, but also doesn't require intrinsic motivation to comply.[36] However, is there a difference between the various types of nudges regarding both the meaning of coercion and the meaning of intrinsic motivation? For example, people may end up choosing a certain option without much thought, simply because it's presented as the default. This choice isn't necessarily forced upon them; theoretically, they could have selected a different option. However, the key question is how much effort would be required to deviate from this default option.

Think of the mechanism on Netflix that automatically offers the next episode. According to their results, this mindlessness dramatically increases the number of people who watch the next episode. Many people could easily stop their Netflix from running, but they choose not to. Is this behavior voluntary or not? In other

[34] Grimes, Marcia. "Organizing consent: The role of procedural fairness in political trust and compliance." *European Journal of Political Research* 45.2 (2006): 285–315.

[35] Bardach, Eugene. "Moral suasion and taxpayer compliance." *Law & Policy* 11.1 (1989): 49–69.

[36] The interaction between nudges and deliberation is more complex; see, for example, Jung, Janice Y., and Barbara A. Mellers. "American attitudes toward nudges." *Judgment and Decision Making* 11.1 (2016): 62–74.

words, are nudges that encourage people to do the right thing using a mindless approach (in the context of Netflix, watching more is the right thing) perceived as reducing the voluntariness of people's compliance?

Another way to look at nudges is through the lens of Milkman's research on habit formation and examining whether nudges can mindlessly cause people to behave in a certain way.[37] Over time, repeated behavior may cause individuals to internalize their actions. Through processes such as cognitive dissonance, they may change their attitudes toward the act. Thus, nudges can indirectly cause this internalization process.

Researchers have long been debating whether nudges are indeed cost-effective. For the most part, the main questions have involved how to measure and compare the cost-effectiveness of nudges in relation to traditional interventions.[38] What is missing from the current discussion is an exploration of the long-term effects of nudges on people's attitudes toward the state and on their behaviors in contexts where nudges are less likely to be effective.

What is the cost of blindly complying with a law that relies mostly on nudges? For example, when we use auditory signals to remind and alert people to wear seat belts, what effect does this have on road behaviors that do not and cannot use signals to influence conduct? This may be concerning, as people will learn to expect nudges that help them understand what they are expected to do. However, this argument does not suggest that intrinsic motivation is the only way to create sustainable compliance. Rather, it challenges the idea that other types of regulatory interventions might undermine it.

When trying to understand the relationship between nudges and voluntary compliance, it is impossible to ignore a more fundamental question about the effect of nudges on behavior. As discussed, one way that nudges could enhance the likelihood of voluntary compliance is by changing behavior. This can later lead to an internal change in attitudes. For such a change to occur, nudges must have a significant impact on the desired change in behavior. However, it seems that the fact itself is questionable. In the following paragraphs, we will examine this aspect.

Shlomo Benartzi and colleagues argued for a "save more tomorrow" nudge, which has often been presented as one of the most effective and simple ways to understand nudges that increase the amount of long-term savings by people.[39] According

[37] Duckworth, Angela L., Katherine L. Milkman, and David Laibson. "Beyond willpower: Strategies for reducing failures of self-control." *Psychological Science in the Public Interest* 19.3 (2018): 102–129. Wood, Wendy, and David T. Neal. "Healthy through habit: Interventions for initiating and maintaining health behavior change." *Behavioral Science & Policy* 2.1 (2016): 71–83.

[38] Benartzi, Shlomo, et al. "Should governments invest more in nudging?" *Psychological Science* 28.8 (2017): 1041–1055. Also see Tor, Avishalom, and Jonathan Klick. "When should governments invest more in nudging? Revisiting Benartzi et al. (2017)." *Review of Law & Economics* 18.3 (2022): 347–376.

[39] Thaler, Richard H., and Shlomo Benartzi. "Save more tomorrow™: Using behavioral economics to increase employee saving." *Journal of Political Economy* 112.S1 (2004): S164–S187.

to them, nudging is a cost-effective approach that should be used more often in conjunction with traditional policies. However, further calculations are required to determine the relative effectiveness of nudging.

It should be noted that not only is this claim being challenged by Tor and Klick, but they argue that the problems in the methods being used to measure cost-effectiveness are misguided from a theoretical economic approach.[40]

SYSTEM 1 VERSUS SYSTEM 2 NUDGES

It is possible to distinguish between nudges that change your attitudes and nudges that attempt to change your behavior. Some nudges seek to change your behavior without awareness, while others attempt to do so by influencing people's awareness.[41] The literature on nudges and behavioral public policy reveals a distinction between two main approaches. The first focuses on changing behaviors through small adaptations to the environment, often referred to as "choice architecture." The second approach, in contrast, aims to enhance individuals' reasoning skills and self-awareness. This latter strategy, sometimes called "boosting," seeks to empower people to make better decisions by improving their cognitive abilities and understanding of their own thought processes. In Chapter 1, we focused on different approaches to the definition of voluntary compliance. Now, we need to understand to what extent the different approaches to voluntary compliance could help us understand the different types of nudges.

NUDGE PLUS AND SELF-REFLECTION

Due to the ethical problems associated with lack of awareness to nudges, Sanchayan Banerjee and Peter John have outlined a modified version of behavior change called nudge plus,[42] which incorporates an element of reflection as part of the delivery of a nudge. Nudge plus builds on recent work advocating for educative nudges and boosts.[43] The argument is based on Evans' seminal work on dual systems.[44] That presents a more nuanced relationship between fast and slow thinking than what is commonly portrayed in the classic literature on behavioral public policy. Banerjee and John's argument advocates for a combination of System 1 nudges and techniques that promote deliberation and reasoning.

[40] See Tor and Klick "When should governments invest more in nudging?"

[41] Hausman, Daniel M., and Brynn Welch. "Debate: To nudge or not to nudge." *Journal of Political Philosophy* 18.1 (2010): 123–136.

[42] Banerjee, Sanchayan, and Peter John. "Nudge plus: Incorporating reflection into behavioral public policy." *Behavioural Public Policy* 8.1 (2021): 69–84.

[43] Grüne-Yanoff, Till, and Ralph Hertwig. "Nudge versus boost: How coherent are policy and theory?" *Minds and Machines* 26.1 (2016): 149–183.

[44] Evans, Jonathan St B. T. "Dual-processing accounts of reasoning, judgment, and social cognition." *Annual Review of Psychology* 59.1 (2008): 255–278.

Pledges and Trust-Enhancing Nudges

In a series of collaborative papers with Eyal Pe'er and colleagues,[45] we researched the effectiveness of honesty nudges, particularly in contexts where the temptation to cheat is high. The challenge is to determine the appropriate level of trust to place in people's self-reports. When faced with this challenge, regulators are often risk-averse and impose stringent requirements when granting permits and licenses. While ex ante commitments to ethical behavior have been suggested to combat dishonesty and noncompliance, some have raised concerns that these commitments might undermine trust.[46]

Our research aims to investigate the effectiveness of ethical pledges. We examined the impact of these ex ante commitments on ethical behavior. One of our studies consists of two separate experiments we conducted to comprehensively analyze the relationship between pledges and ethical behavior over time.[47] The first study involved two phases of data collection. The second study introduced a time delay between making a pledge and the opportunity to cheat.

The results were promising. Pledges not only reduced dishonesty in one-time decisions but also in sequential ones. Their effectiveness was notable even over long periods of time and when individuals were exposed to multiple pledges. Moreover, introducing a time delay after pledging did not diminish its impact. This suggests that pledges primarily discourage dishonesty by reducing ambiguity, rather than merely serving as moral reminders.

It is important to ensure that pledges and sanctions are used together in a coordinated way. Their role is vital in ensuring regulatory practices complement pledges effectively. Since sanctions might not work well with pledges, it will be very hard to use them in real-life settings. In our studies, the effect of nudges was not diminished by fines.[48] Pledges were also effective for people who are less inclined to follow rules and norms. Therefore, pledges can be a valuable tool for regulating dishonesty and reducing regulatory burdens. They can also foster trust between the government and the public, even in situations with high incentives and opportunities for cheating.

In a more recent paper on pledges, conducted with Eyal Pe'er, Nina Mazar, and Dan Ariely, we present findings from four preregistered experiments with a collective sample size exceeding 5,000 participants.[49] Our research systematically

45 Pe'er, Eyal, et al. "How pledges reduce dishonesty: The role of involvement and identification," *Journal of Experimental Social Psychology* 113 (2024): 104614.

46 For the most recent and extensive review of contexts where this might happen, see Zickfeld, Janis H., et al. "Effectiveness of ex ante honesty oaths in reducing dishonesty depends on content." *Nature Human Behaviour* 9.1 (2025): 169–187.

47 Pe'er, Eyal, and Yuval Feldman. "Honesty pledges for the behaviorally based regulation of dishonesty." *Journal of European Public Policy* 28.5 (2021): 761–781.

48 Pe'er and Feldman. "Honesty pledges for the behaviorally based regulation of dishonesty."

49 Pe'er et al. "How pledges reduce dishonesty," 104614.

examines the impact of pledges with varying levels of identification and involvement on participants' self-reports about a cheating task. Our results demonstrate that pledges that require a transcribed pledge text and personal identification are more effective than those that only require individuals to acknowledge the text's content. Notably, the effects of high-involvement pledges endured over time, even after a short delay between taking the pledge and the initiation of the cheating task. The study's results provide valuable guidance to managers and policymakers on how to effectively mitigate dishonesty in self-reports.

Our research investigates the effectiveness and durability of ex ante pledges in preventing dishonest behavior. We specifically address a critical yet understudied aspect of ethical nudges: the longevity of their impact. The potential for ethical nudges to serve as a viable alternative to traditional command-and-control regulations depends fundamentally on their ability to produce lasting effects, which is the central focus of our study.

While existing research on pledges has largely focused on one-time decisions, there has been limited exploration of their long-term consequences, particularly regarding potential "ethical decay."[50] To address this research gap, we conducted two experiments using a matrices task where participants either had to provide exact solutions for rewards or simply report finding solutions, with a 10 percent chance of being audited.

Our findings revealed that participants in the self-report condition claimed to solve approximately twice as many problems compared to the control group. However, implementing a pre-task honesty pledge reduced this cheating gap by half. Notably, the pledge's effectiveness remained stable across all ten problems, demonstrating no decay in its impact over time.

BEHAVIORAL CHANGE VS. PREFERENCE CHANGE

The previous discussion explored the idea that nudges should allow for some reflection on one's behavior to change one's intrinsic motivation. This perspective suggests that nudges can ultimately influence individuals' attitudes and preferences by altering their behavior through defaults or other mechanisms.[51]

An alternative perspective suggests that changes in behavior may precede shifts in intrinsic motivation. This idea aligns with cognitive dissonance theory, which posits that when our actions don't match our beliefs, we often adjust our beliefs to match our actions.[52] In this context, behavior can change first and preferences may follow suit. Daphna Lewinsohn-Zamir, in her paper on law and preference change,

50 E.g., Zickfeld, et al. "Effectiveness of ex ante honesty oaths in reducing dishonesty depends on content."

51 Lewinsohn-Zamir, Daphna. "The importance of being earnest: Two notions of internalization." *University of Toronto Law Journal* 65.2 (2015): 37–84.

52 Aronson, Elliot. "The theory of cognitive dissonance: A current perspective." In *Advances in experimental social psychology*, Vol. 4, edited by Leonard Berkowitz, Academic Press, 1969. 1–34.

suggests that people change their behavior when they feel they have a choice to do so.[53] In such cases, cognitive dissonance often comes into play, potentially leading to behavioral change.

In our collaborative work with Yotam Kaplan, we presented a different perspective.[54] We questioned the value of trying to alter people's preferences when they can reinterpret their actions in a way that benefits themselves. In that paper, we relied on research in behavioral ethics, which showed that wrongdoing often originates from semi-deliberative or nondeliberative cognitive processes.[55] These findings suggest that the process of changing preferences through the law is more complex and nuanced than previously thought. For example, even if an employer's explicit discriminatory stance was changed, discriminatory behavior might still occur if it originated from semiconscious, habitual, or nondeliberative decision-making mechanisms.[56] Therefore, changing behavior may require close engagement with people's level of moral awareness. We also explored how these insights impact institutions and norms and assessed their relevance to using various legal mechanisms to shape preferences.

REGULATION AND TRUST

This section explores the complex relationship between trust and regulation. We'll examine two key questions: Does a lack of trust in society or institutions drive a greater demand for regulatory measures? Conversely, does the implementation of regulations tend to erode trust? By investigating these interconnected issues, we aim to shed light on how trust and regulation influence each other.

Many studies have examined the relationship between regulation and trust, but most rely on correlations, which limits the ability to understand causality. However, much of the most recent research does provide some insight.[57] Not only is the state's ability to create trust uncertain, but many studies have argued that trust has eroded for several reasons beyond the state's limitations.[58] As a result, regulation has been introduced to compensate for this lack of trust and to, in effect, create a demand for trust. Essentially, it can be argued that there is an inverse relationship between the amount of trust in a society and the amount of regulation that is needed: the less trust that is present, the

53 Lewinsohn-Zamir. "The importance of being earnest."

54 Feldman, Yuval, and Yotam Kaplan. "Preference change and behavioral ethics: Can states create ethical people?" *Theoretical Inquiries in Law* 22.2 (2021): 85–110.

55 Sezer, Ovul, Francesca Gino, and Max H. Bazerman. "Ethical blind spots: Explaining unintentional unethical behavior." *Current Opinion in Psychology* 6 (2015): 77–81.

56 E.g., Jackson, Sarah M., Amy L. Hillard, and Tamera R. Schneider. "Using implicit bias training to improve attitudes toward women in STEM." *Social Psychology of Education* 17 (2014): 419–438.

57 Six, Frédérique. "Trust in regulatory relations: How new insights from trust research improve regulation theory." *Public Management Review* 15.2 (2013): 163–185.

58 Twenge, Jean M., W. Keith Campbell, and Nathan T. Carter. "Declines in trust in others and confidence in institutions among American adults and late adolescents, 1972–2012." *Psychological Science* 25.10 (2014): 1914–1923.

more regulation is called for.[59] We also see that interpersonal trust is highly related to regulation and punishment.[60] This observation is consistent with a theme that is developed throughout this book – that social norms and what we think others will do constitute the main driving forces behind the public's willingness to cooperate.

REGULATORS' PUNITIVENESS AND INSTITUTIONAL TRUST

As will be discussed also in Chapter 6 in the context of culture, the research of Daniel Balliet and Paul Van Lange is important for understanding the relationship between regulation and trust.[61] It also important for understanding the "no one policy fits all" approach to regulation is more likely to enhance voluntary compliance. After examining the efficacy of punishment across high- and low-trust societies, they concluded that high trust in government is needed for punishment to be effective. After analyzing eighty-three studies on public good experiments across eighteen societies, researchers found that, contrary to expectations, punishment is more effective in promoting cooperation in societies with high trust than in societies with low trust. The explanation is probably that if there is high trust, individuals also trust that they will be punished because they have faith in the efficacy of the government, while if there is low trust, the public may think that they have a higher chance with getting away with illegal behavior.

Taking a slightly different approach, we collaborated with Libby Maman and David Levi-Faur to find that people are more inclined to trust market actors when self-regulation is in place and they trust the regulators.[62] However, under a regulatory regime with sanctions, the level of trust in the regulator is irrelevant. Although our study did not focus on the regulators, it was centered on the people who are supposed to be protected by market regulations. The study demonstrates the interdependency between regulatory style and the level of trust. Both lines of research emphasize the critical role of trust in shaping the effects of regulatory factors, such as sanctions. This is even more the case with softer approaches, such as self-regulation.

TYPES OF TRUST AND RELATIONSHIPS WITH VOLUNTARY COMPLIANCE

In this book, we focus on research examining governments' ability to trust the public. However, it's crucial to understand the interrelationship between various types

[59] Six, Frédérique, and Koen Verhoest. *Trust in regulatory regimes: Scoping the field.* Edward Elgar Publishing, 2017.

[60] Spadaro, Giuliana, et al. "Enhancing feelings of security: How institutional trust promotes interpersonal trust." *PLOS One* 15.9 (2020): e0237934.

[61] Balliet, Daniel, and Paul A. M. Van Lange. "Trust, punishment, and cooperation across 18 societies: A meta-analysis." *Perspectives on Psychological Science* 8.4 (2013): 363–379.

[62] Maman, Libby, Yuval Feldman, and David Levi-Faur. "Varieties of regulatory regimes and their effect on citizens' trust in firms." *Journal of European Public Policy* 30.12 (2023): 2807–2831.

of trust and explore how a country's trust levels influence the government's choice of regulatory tools. Research has shown that trust in state institutions has a causal effect on social trust.[63] Specifically, when the public trusts their government and its institutions, this fosters greater trust among people within the same society. While there is limited evidence supporting a reverse relationship (i.e., lower trust in government leading to less trust among people in society), the primary direction of influence appears to be from institutional trust to social trust. In this study conducted in Denmark, it was found that an increase in trust in the country was one of the factors that caused an increase in the public's trust in institutions. It also found that institutions, rather than culture, matter more for social trust.[64] According to the study, trust can serve as a key mechanism in ensuring the accountability of the state to the citizen and, as a result, improve the latter's cooperation.[65]

In another study, six leading theories regarding the determinants of social trust were tested against survey data from seven societies in 1999–2001.[66] Among the six theories of trust examined in this research, three demonstrated stronger explanatory power while three showed weaker performance. The findings indicate that social trust is predominantly high among individuals who perceive less severe societal divisions and experience greater personal security. Moreover, participation in informal social networks correlates positively with trust levels, and individuals who have achieved success in life typically display higher trust levels, presumably due to their positive life experiences.

A notable finding from the study is that the explanatory power of different trust theories varies according to the society's overall trust levels. In high-trust societies, theories focusing on individual factors tend to be more effective, while, in low-trust environments, theories emphasizing societal factors demonstrate greater explanatory power. This pattern may be understood through the lens of recent historical developments. These broad societal changes appear to have more significantly influenced individual circumstances and trust perceptions in these countries compared to more stable, high-trust societies.

THE MALLEABILITY OF SOCIAL AND INSTITUTIONAL TRUST

The development of trust, as discussed in more detail in Chapter 6, is inextricably linked to research on culture and its malleability – a core focus of that chapter. For our current discussion on the relationship between trust and regulation, we must

63 Sønderskov, Kim Mannemar, and Peter Thisted Dinesen. "Trusting the state, trusting each other? The effect of institutional trust on social trust." *Political Behavior* 38 (2016): 179–202.

64 Nannestad, Peter, et al. "Do institutions or culture determine the level of social trust? The natural experiment of migration from non-Western to Western countries." *Journal of Ethnic and Migration Studies* 40.4 (2014): 544–565.

65 See also Brown, Rob. "The citizen and trust in the (trustworthy) state." *Public Policy and Administration* 35.4 (2020): 384–402.

66 Delhey, Jan, and Kenneth Newton. "Who trusts? The origins of social trust in seven societies." *European Societies* 5.2 (2003): 93–137.

also consider the dynamic interaction between these two elements.[67] Sønderskov and Dinesen have examined the relationship between social and interpersonal trust and the level of trust in institutions. Their research contributes to the broader study of trust mechanism typology. Using a panel data approach spanning eighteen years, they investigated the relationship between social trust and institutional trust.

Their findings indicate that trust in people does not necessarily predict trust in the state. However, trust in state institutions tends to predict an individual's ability to trust other people. This suggests that government policymakers could play a significant role in increasing interpersonal trust by improving institutional design.

In contrast, scholars like Geert Hofstede have argued that the culture of trust in certain countries can be traced back to ancient history, potentially limiting the impact of institutional design.[68] This presents an important regulatory dilemma: States must not only adapt their regulatory interventions to their existing culture but also shape these interventions to influence societal trust levels.

Regarding the high levels of trust in Nordic countries, long-term data analysis at both individual and collective levels reveals several contributing factors.[69] These include high levels of education, better state institutions, increased trust in these institutions, and generational replacement. For example, these factors have played a crucial role in the increased trust observed in Denmark over the past century.

Other research has suggested that trust eroded and was replaced by regulation in the second half of the twentieth century, indicating that lack of trust invites regulation rather than preventing it.[70] Another argument is that governments shift away from cooperative regulatory styles because of the lack of trust between the relevant stakeholders.[71] This view is reflected in a twenty-year case study of the mines inspectorate conducted by Neil Gunningham and Darren Sinclair. Addressing the issue of whether the lack of trust between regulators and the regulated can lead to changes in regulatory styles, they demonstrated the centrality of trust in regulatory effectiveness, how it can be lost, and how it can best be regained.[72] A study conducted by Niklas Harring across multiple countries suggests that a reward-based regulatory approach is more popular when citizens have greater trust in their government's

[67] Sønderskov, Kim Mannemar, and Peter Thisted Dinesen. "Trusting the state, trusting each other? The effect of institutional trust on social trust." Political Behavior 38 (2016): 179–202.

[68] Hofstede, Geert. *Culture's consequences: Comparing values, behaviors, institutions, and organizations across nations*. SAGE Publications, 2001.

[69] Martela, Frank, et al. "The Nordic exceptionalism: What explains why the Nordic countries are constantly among the happiest in the world." *World Happiness Report* 2020 (2020): 129–146.

[70] Capie, Forrest. "Trust, financial regulation, and growth." *Australian Economic History Review* 56.1 (2016): 100–112.

[71] Gouldson, Andy. "Cooperation and the capacity for control: Regulatory styles and the evolving influence of environmental regulations in the UK." *Environment and Planning C: Government and Policy* 22.4 (2004): 583–603.

[72] Gunningham, Neil, and Darren Sinclair. "Regulation and the role of trust: Reflections from the mining industry." *Journal of Law and Society* 36.2 (2009): 167–194.

ability to execute it.[73] Moreover, Marc Hetherington demonstrated that low trust levels can create significant barriers to government action in certain policy areas. This creates a political environment in which it is more difficult for leaders to succeed.[74] Peter Huang has argued that imposing duties on security professionals can cause them to behave in accordance with regulatory goals without the need to use penalties.[75] He argues that it is vital to analyze the emotional, moral, and psychological consequences of broker-dealers' fiduciary duties. Along these lines, Bettina Lange and Andy Gouldson have argued that trust-based regulation is important not only because it fosters trust between regulators and the regulated but also because it encourages the regulated to engage in various collective efforts to achieve the goals, particularly in the context of environmental protection.[76] Several other studies have also demonstrated the benefits of trust in the interaction between inspectors and regulates.[77]

In another study using data from the World Values Survey/European Values Study for approximately 130,000 individuals in 40 OECD (Organisation for Economic Co-operation and Development) and EU countries to determine the causal relationship between social and institutional trust,[78] evidence was found that social trust depends upon institutional trust. Moreover, this study's experimental evidence, presented using a sophisticated behavioral game theory involving a buyer and seller who must trust each other in a setting with and without regulation, demonstrates that regulation is not just negatively correlated with trust. This supports the argument of many other studies that have claimed the existence of causal effects on the level of trust.[79]

TRUST IN INSTITUTIONS AND LEGITIMACY

Among other studies, that of John Braithwaite and Toni Makkai focusing on nursing homes is notable for having argued that being treated as trustworthy will increase

73 Harring, Niklas. "Reward or punish? Understanding preferences toward economic or regulatory instruments in a cross-national perspective." *Political Studies* 64.3 (2016): 573–592.

74 Hetherington, Marc J. "The political relevance of political trust." *American Political Science Review* 92.4 (1998): 791–808.

75 Huang, Peter H. "Trust, guilt, and securities regulation." *University of Pennsylvania Law Review* 151.3 (2003): 1059–1095.

76 Lange, Bettina, and Andy Gouldson. "Trust-based environmental regulation." *Science of the Total Environment* 408.22 (2010): 5235–5243.

77 Pautz, Michelle C., and Carolyn Slott Wamsley. "Pursuing trust in environmental regulatory interactions: The significance of inspectors' interactions with the regulated community." *Administration & Society* 44.7 (2012): 853–884; De Boer, Noortje. "How do citizens assess street-level bureaucrats' warmth and competence? A typology and test." *Public Administration Review* 80.4 (2020): 532–542.

78 Pitlik, Hans, and Ludek Kouba. "Does social distrust always lead to a stronger support for government intervention?" *Public Choice* 163 (2015): 355–377.

79 Six and Verhoest. *Trust in regulatory regimes*: 1–36; Van Swol, Lyn M. "The effects of regulation on trust." *Basic and Applied Social Psychology* 25.3 (2003): 221–233.

the likelihood of voluntary compliance among individuals.[80] Margaret Levi and colleagues have argued that two interrelated factors influence the likelihood of voluntary compliance.[81] The first factor is the individual's perception of the government's legitimacy. The second factor is the individual's conception of the government's trustworthiness, which significantly affects their view of the legitimacy of the regulation.

Similarly, Frédérique Six demonstrates how trust in the regulator and control may complement each other in their effect on regulating compliance.[82] Along those lines, in collaboration with David Levi-Faur and Libby Maman,[83] we examined various regulatory regimes that could be used to enhance trust. It is important to note that, in our studies, the public expressed a preference for the government to engage in some form of active oversight, rather than relying solely on firms to cooperate voluntarily. In that study, we began by distinguishing between regulatory designs, which are usually conceptualized as a dichotomous choice between state and self-regulation. The theory of regulatory capitalism proposes regulatory controls, which often conflate state regulation with private forms of regulation.[84] Various mechanisms can be employed to enhance self-regulation. This enhanced approach to self-regulation involves organizations leveraging intermediaries and stakeholders. These external parties help monitor and sanction the behavior of regulated entities, improve policy implementation and compliance, and reduce agency drift.[85]

SELF-REGULATION: TRUST IN INSTITUTIONS VS. TRUST IN MARKETS

While the role of regulatory design in shaping behavior has been extensively studied, its impact on public trust remains largely unexplored. This gap in scholarship is significant because trust plays a crucial role in facilitating market relationships and transactions.[86] Thus, the Maman, Feldman, and Levi-Faur study, mentioned before, sought to analyze the extent to which public trust is affected by various forms of regulation, examining an advanced framework of enhanced self-regulation. In

80 Braithwaite, John, and Toni Makkai. "Trust and compliance." *Policing and Society: An International Journal* 4.1 (1994): 1–12.

81 Levi, Margaret, Tom R. Tyler, and Audrey Sacks. "The reasons for compliance with law." In *Understanding social action, promoting human rights*, edited by Ryan Goodman, Derek Jinks, and Andrew K. Woods, Oxford University Press, 2012: 70–99.

82 Six. "Trust in regulatory relations."

83 Maman, Feldman, and Levi-Faur. "Varieties of regulatory regimes and their effect on citizens' trust in firms."

84 Levi-Faur, David. "The global diffusion of regulatory capitalism." *Annals of the American Academy of Political and Social Science* 598.1 (2005): 12–32; Braithwaite, John. *Regulatory capitalism: How it works, ideas for making it work better*. Edward Elgar Publishing, 2008.

85 Levi-Faur, David, Yael Kariv-Teitelbaum, and Rotem Medzini. "Regulatory governance: History, theories, strategies, and challenges." In *Oxford research encyclopedia of politics*. Oxford University Press, 2021: 1–58.

86 Warren, Mark E. *Democracy and trust*. Cambridge University Press, 1999.

that study, we used two web-based experimental surveys on a representative sample of Israeli society (approximately 1,200 subjects in two studies) to investigate public trust in a fictitious fintech company operating under different regulatory designs.

The findings of the first study revealed several key insights into the relationship between market trust and different types of regulation. First, we observed that knowledge about any form of regulation positively impacts trust in the market. Second, our examination of state regulations with varying levels of monitoring revealed that higher levels of monitoring are associated with increased trust in the market. Low levels of monitoring in state regulation rely on the regulatees' commitments and do not foster the same level of trust. Finally, we observed a significant interaction effect between trust in the regulator and the level of monitoring state regulation. This was particularly true for situations with low monitoring. This suggests that state regulators can effectively maintain public trust in regulated firms by utilizing self-regulatory tools when the public has a high level of trust in the regulator. The study highlights the importance of considering the interaction between different regulatory approaches and their impact on market trust.

In the second study, we sought to further test the possibility that enhanced self-regulation can provide a similar level of trust in state regulation. We examined six different potential enhancements of self-regulation and tested the effect on trust using a combination of between and within subject analysis, with state regulation used as a control group. Our results show that all forms of self-regulation are less trusted by the public than a state regulatory regime. However, within self-regulatory designs, we find that a self-regulatory constellation includes the possibility of sanctioning that increases trust.

The results of the second study reinforced those of the first, showing that public trust in regulated firms increases when state regulation exists, while self-regulation (even if enhanced) leads to lower levels of public trust. The interaction effects we found suggest that governments play an important role in ensuring public trust in the market. This is true not only with governments as regulators, but also when combining self-regulatory instruments such as pledges. Our paper demonstrated that more government regulation leads to more trust. Additionally, trust in self-regulation and perhaps deregulation depends on the public's trust in the government.

The rise of self-regulation suggests that there is potential for voluntary compliance for those who are willing to adopt greater transparency and accountability.

Adapting the type of regulatory supervision is one of the most complex challenges. The regulator needs to protect the public while also helping businesses thrive. The concept of responsive regulation allows for a more customized and targeted approach. A pyramid approach is based on the idea that you should start with softer means. Ideally, most people will cooperate with these approaches. We argue that when attempting to find the best regulatory tool, we usually focus on three aspects: the extent to which the regulated knows and understands the actions expected of them; the extent to which they are capable of cooperating with the rules; and the extent of their willingness to do so. Christine Parker's study found that spontaneous compliance can occur without enforcement and can be broken down into three main dimensions: two control dimensions focusing on how enforcement might affect compliance and a third punitive approach dimension in which the effect of sanctions on compliance is expected to work.[87] In another study, Ian Bartle and Peter Vass propose a "new regulatory paradigm" based on the concept of regulatory "subsidiarity." This approach advocates for delegating regulatory outcomes to regulated organizations and self-regulatory bodies, while simultaneously strengthening public regulatory oversight through enhanced accountability and transparency measures.[88]

Many scholars have argued that states play a central role in enhancing trust toward market actors in cases when regulators are perceived as third-party providers.[89] Bart Nooteboom has argued that regulatory intervention is needed to help boost the ability of the public to trust market actors.[90] Other scholars have demonstrated that the public's trust in regulators is important in increasing trust.[91] According to Piotr Sztompka,[92] trust in regulators depends upon factors such as transparency, accountability, protection of private autonomy, and regulatees' rights. Other scholars have argued that it is important for regulators to be seen as not being too close to the industry in order to maintain public trust.[93]

Overall, when endeavoring to understand the factors that predict public trust in institutions, some have argued that such trust is dependent on the personal experience with the institutions and on the public's perception of the institutions as being objective and representative.[94] Other scholars have focused on demographic and family-related factors as being the main predictors of institutional trust.[95]

87 Parker, Christine. *The open corporation: Effective self-regulation and democracy*. Cambridge University Press, 2002.

88 Bartle, Ian, and Peter Vass. "Self-regulation within the regulatory state: Towards a new regulatory paradigm?" *Public Administration* 85.4 (2007): 885–905.

89 Six and Verhoest. *Trust in regulatory regimes*.

90 Nooteboom, Bart. "The dynamics of trust: Communication, action and third parties." In *Trust: Comparative Perspectives*, edited by Masamichi Sasaki & Robert M. Marsch, Brill, 2012: 9–30.

91 Braithwaite and Makkai. "Trust and compliance."

92 Sztompka, Piotr. *Trust: A sociological theory*. Cambridge University Press, 1999.

93 Van der Meer, T. W. G. "Economic performance and political trust." In *The Oxford handbook of social and political trust*, edited by E. M. Uslaner, Oxford University Press, 2018: 599–615; Six and Verhoest. *Trust in regulatory regimes*.

94 Bradford, Ben, Jonathan Jackson, and Mike Hough. "Trust in justice." *The Oxford Handbook of Social and Political Trust, Oxford Legal Studies Research Paper* 43, edited by Eric M. Uslaner, Oxford University Press, 2016: 633–654.

95 Dinesen, Peter Thisted, and Kim Mannemar Sønderskov. "Ethnic diversity and social trust: A critical review of the literature and suggestions for a research agenda." In *The Oxford handbook of social and political trust*, edited by E. M. Uslaner, Oxford University Press, 2018: 175–204; Ermisch, John, and Diego Gambetta. "Do strong family ties inhibit trust?" *Journal of Economic Behavior & Organization* 75.3 (2010): 365–376.

RULES, STANDARDS, AND VOLUNTARY COMPLIANCE

Another angle of the trust between regulators and regulates is related to optimal level of discretion. Is it good to give people discretion? Is it likely to increase voluntary compliance? When giving people regulatory instruction, should vague terminology be used to give people greater flexibility?

In a joint paper with Henry Smith and Constantine Boussalis, we experimentally examined the effect of vagueness and good faith on how participants react to instructions.[96] To test these hypotheses, we used a factorial experimental design. Participants were instructed to edit a document with either general or detailed instructions. The instructions either included a reference to good faith or did not have such a reference. Participants could engage in different levels and types of editing, enabling us to measure compliance and performance separately. When participants needed information and guidance, such as when editing, we found that being specific improved performance compared to the vague standard condition. In our work, we discussed the characteristics of the regulatory frameworks, such as good faith in contract performance, to which our findings are especially relevant.

In a similar vein, Laetitia Mulder, Jennifer Jordan, and Floor Rink have argued that specific rules have a stronger effect on ethical decisions than general rules.[97] Their conclusion is based on a series of five studies that demonstrated that specifically framed rules elicited more ethical decisions compared to generally framed rules. This research contributes to a broader understanding of how rule framing impacts ethical behavior in organizations. In a related line of inquiry, Ann Tenbrunsel and David Messick examined the effects of surveillance and sanctioning systems on cooperative behavior in dilemma situations. Their work, while focusing on different aspects of organizational control, complements the findings on rule specificity by exploring how external monitoring mechanisms influence ethical decision-making. Their studies demonstrated that a weak sanctioning system results in less cooperation than a no-sanctioning system.[98] Results from the second study suggest that sanctions affect the type of decision people perceive they are making. Sanctions can lead them to perceive their decision as being driven by financial rather than ethical considerations.

CONCLUSION

This chapter has explored a wide range of topics related to regulatory approaches and their impact on voluntary compliance. We began by examining the interplay

[96] Boussalis, Constantine, Yuval Feldman, and Henry E. Smith. "Experimental analysis of the effect of standards on compliance and performance." *Regulation & Governance* 12.2 (2018): 277–298.

[97] Mulder, Laetitia B., Jennifer Jordan, and Floor Rink. "The effect of specific and general rules on ethical decisions." *Organizational Behavior and Human Decision Processes* 126 (2015): 115–129.

[98] Tenbrunsel, Ann E., and David M. Messick. "Sanctioning systems, decision frames, and cooperation." *Administrative Science Quarterly* 44.4 (1999): 684–707.

between trust and coercion in regulatory strategies, discussing the effectiveness of various approaches such as deterrence, incentives, and trust-based regulation. The chapter delved into the concept of "order without law" and its implications for voluntary compliance, as well as the potential risks and benefits of sanction-free regulation. We explored the role of nudges in shaping behavior, distinguishing between different types of nudges and their effects on intrinsic motivation. The chapter also examined the complex relationship between trust and regulation, considering how different forms of trust – interpersonal, social, and institutional – interact with regulatory approaches. Finally, we discussed the impact of rules versus standards on compliance behavior and the potential for ethical blind spots in regulatory enforcement.

Looking forward, this exploration reveals several key areas for future research and policy development. There is a clear need for more robust theoretical frameworks that can predict the outcomes of different regulatory approaches across various contexts and cultures. Longitudinal studies are crucial to assess the long-term impacts of regulatory strategies on trust and consequently on voluntary compliance. Future research should also focus on developing more sophisticated methods for balancing coercive and trust-based approaches in regulatory design.

By addressing these research gaps and continuously refining our understanding of the complex dynamics between regulation, trust, and compliance, we can work toward more effective, efficient, and trust-enhancing regulatory systems that serve the public interest while respecting individual autonomy. Along these lines, as technology continues to evolve, in Chapter 7 we will investigate the role of digital tools in fostering voluntary compliance while maintaining privacy and autonomy will be essential. Policymakers and researchers alike should work toward creating technologically based adaptive regulatory systems that can respond to changing societal norms and behaviors while promoting sustainable voluntary compliance.

5

What Are the Perils of Voluntary Compliance?

INTRODUCTION

This chapter will discuss some of the potential disadvantages of utilizing voluntary compliance. For example, when relying on voluntary compliance, which is based on limited monitoring and enforcement by the state, an increase in inequality between "good" and "bad" people may rise, as many people will continue to obey while others might not. This could lead to a situation where there is a growing gap between the formal law and social norms. In addition, while in previous chapters the notions of voluntary compliance and trust-enhancing regulatory approaches were associated with substantial changes in trust in society, this chapter focuses on their potential harmful effects to society and the rule of law. For example, if governments need to persuade people that laws should be obeyed, then this practice may be counterproductive as it expects states to be more intrusive. Of course, in many studies on factors such as legitimacy and fairness, where states behave in a trustworthy way, changing people's attitudes toward the law by explaining its importance is not always necessary.[1]

In addition, this chapter will examine to what extent the reduction in the usage of sanctions by states will be replaced by nonformal sanctions which could, in some contexts, be more problematic than formal sanctions (e.g., reliance on reputation might be more harmful to some people than to others).[2] While most of the discussion on crowding out assumes some interplay between extrinsic sanctions and intrinsic motivation, we will argue that in many contexts this could be the opposite, where formal sanctions will be replaced by informal ones.[3] Those sanctions, while

1 Tyler, Tom R. *Why people obey the law*. Princeton University Press, 2006. See also Tyler, Tom R. "Evaluating consensual models of governance." *Nomos* 61 (2019): 257–292.

2 Charny, David. "Nonlegal sanctions in commercial relationships." *Harvard Law Review* 104.2 (1990): 373–467. On the variation problem see Cooter, Robert, and Ariel Porat. "Should courts deduct nonlegal sanctions from damages?" *Journal of Legal Studies* 30.2 (2001): 401–422.

3 Iacobucci, Edward M. "On the interaction between legal and reputational sanctions." *Journal of Legal Studies* 43.1 (2014): 189–207.

being somewhat more effective and less costly to enforce, could have far more problematic results in terms of procedure, evidentiary rules, and proportionality.[4] Many of the discussions about the power of communities and social norms are such that there is a very limited opportunity to understand the control mechanisms at play. For example, there is a great variation in the strictness of the community in which one lives. Community-based governance can lead to significant variations in how closely people's behavior is monitored.[5]

HETEROGENEITY: THE CHALLENGE TO VOLUNTARY COMPLIANCE

Given the expected heterogeneity in population response, the main challenge for policymakers will be how this gap affects the level of trust both among cooperators and among noncooperators as well as regarding the interaction between them. Furthermore, as discussed in the next paragraph, research on cooperation shows that many of the cooperators are, in fact, conditional cooperators,[6] and hence at a certain point, many may shift their behavioral patterns based on the cooperation of others. To that end, estimating what proportion of the population are conditional cooperators is difficult. In one of the most influential papers on this topic, Fischbacher and colleagues demonstrate that 50 percent of participants in public good experiments are conditional cooperators – individuals who increase their contributions when they observe higher average contributions from other group members.[7] While many studies in this field identify a substantial proportion of conditional cooperators in their populations, they often refrain from specifying exact percentages. This approach is understandable, as the precise proportion of conditional cooperators can vary significantly based on multiple factors, including experimental design, cultural context, and participant demographics.[8]

Conditional cooperators make up a significant portion of participants in public goods experiments, with estimates ranging from 25 percent to 62 percent. These individuals exhibit sophisticated behavior, adjusting their contributions based on others' actions to maximize group earnings while avoiding inefficient outcomes.[9]

4 Frye, Harrison. "The problem of public shaming." *Journal of Political Philosophy* 30.2 (2022): 188–208.

5 Bliss, John, et al. "Community-based ecosystem monitoring." *Journal of Sustainable Forestry* 12.3–4 (2001): 143–167.

6 Fischbacher, Urs, Simon Gächter, and Ernst Fehr. "Are people conditionally cooperative? Evidence from a public goods experiment." *Economics Letter* 71.3 (2001): 397–404. In that paper, focusing on one-shot public goods, the authors argue that half of the subjects could be seen as conditional cooperators and about third of the subjects as free riders.

7 Fischbacher, Urs, Simeon Schudy, and Sabrina Teyssier. "Heterogeneous reactions to heterogeneity in returns from public goods." *Social Choice and Welfare* 43 (2014): 195–217.

8 See also Zhang, Huanren, and Matjaž Perc. "Evolution of conditional cooperation under multilevel selection." *Scientific Reports* 6.1 (2016): 1–13.

9 Fallucchi, Francesco, R. Andrew Luccasen III, and Theodore L. Turocy. "The sophistication of conditional cooperators: Evidence from public goods games." *Games and Economic Behavior* 136 (2022): 31–62.

Their decisions are influenced by both financial incentives and social norms, demonstrating a nuanced understanding of social dilemmas. Conditional cooperators demonstrate increased contributions when informed about the presence of other cooperative individuals in their group. This behavioral pattern indicates that transparency regarding group composition could effectively promote cooperation. However, the strategic interactions between conditional cooperators can produce complex outcomes – potentially enabling free-riding behavior or transforming collective action situations into coordination problems. The research also highlights the importance of distinguishing genuine conditional cooperation from confusion-driven behavior or a general tendency to follow others.[10] These findings underscore the need for careful consideration of the heterogeneity in cooperative behaviors when designing policies or interventions aimed at promoting collective action in public goods scenarios.

To deal with the negative consequences of an approach focusing on intrinsic motivation or even just coercion-free voluntary compliance, states will, in certain contexts, still need to employ monitoring mechanisms to determine if they can continue with the "hands-off" approach. As such, states must maintain oversight to prevent exploitation of trust-based regulation – essentially adopting a "trust but verify" approach. However, this oversight may diminish some of the efficiency benefits that pure trust-based systems aim to achieve. Furthermore, voluntary compliance could lead to situations where there could be what has been termed a "chilling effect," where some people might be unsure of what is expected of them and, ultimately, comply to a greater extent than is required.[11] For example, people might cover their faces with masks even in contexts where the risk is minimal. Alternatively, others may enjoy the more lenient approach and would comply less, leading to a situation where "good" law-abiding people will suffer more, while "bad" people will suffer less.

Such a shift may suggest that the gap between good doers and bad doers will only arise when regulatory approaches, primarily relevant to the bad doers, are reduced. Within a simple schematic perspective of "good" and "bad" doers, the undermining of extrinsic measures and the increase of intrinsic measures, as part of the voluntary compliance approach, creates an unbalanced approach toward the population. Part of the regulatory dilemma is that current research on the proportion of good and bad doers is quite limited. Even in well-studied, easy-to-quantify contexts such as tax evasion, where states could reasonably be expected to know how many people evade taxes, it is very hard for policymakers to come up with concrete numbers as to how many tax evaders there are.[12] The net benefit of transitioning to trust-based regulation

[10] For a different view see Chaudhuri, Ananish, and Tirnud Paichayontvijit. "Conditional cooperation and voluntary contributions to a public good." *Economics Bulletin* 3.8 (2006): 1–14.

[11] Youn, Monica. "The chilling effect and the problem of private action." *Vanderbilt Law Review* 66 (2013): 1473–1540.

[12] Slemrod, Joel. "Cheating ourselves: The economics of tax evasion." *Journal of Economic Perspectives* 21.1 (2007): 25–48.

depends on two key factors: the proportion of compliant versus noncompliant actors in society for the regulated activity and the relative social and behavioral benefits of voluntary compliance compared to the costs of reduced enforcement efforts associated with voluntary compliance. A responsible regulation with a sequential approach that uses increasingly severe enforcement actions is clearly not a perfect solution, as the information on who will cooperate in each situation is missing and can even be misleading.

An additional point of concern regarding voluntary compliance relates to the definition of compliance as based on intrinsic motivation. If the state needs to cause people to intrinsically believe in the law, this may require the state to engage in a far more intrusive process of educating people and leading them to see the value in obeying. Thus, the state will need to not only cause people to change their behavior but also their belief system, a far more problematic process from many points of view.

There is, of course, a difference between the state providing information on how tax revenue is used versus attempting to explain the reasoning behind a certain law. The latter could raise concerns about a slippery slope, where states feel compelled to shape public beliefs to align with government policies. However, if the state focuses solely on regulating behavior rather than attempting to influence attitudes, the fear of brainwashing is diminished. By not viewing itself as responsible for aligning public attitudes with state values, the government can avoid overreach.

Indeed, if the state aligned its laws to fit with the values of society, rather than the other way around,[13] this is clearly something that doesn't raise the criticism suggested. However, the focus of the argument regarding the fear of intrusive intervention is the reverse, where states would have chosen to change public preferences. For example, during the COVID pandemic, many individuals' preferences were to move openly, engage in social interactions, and fly abroad. States needed to demonstrate to their citizens how noncompliance would undermine public health efforts to contain the pandemic. While often overlooked in behavioral public policy literature, this process of building public understanding is central to enhanced approaches to nudge theory such as the "nudge plus."[14] The need to focus on deliberation and reflection, rather than merely changing behavior, becomes evident when we consider the implications of people internalizing values differently.

When governments attempt to project trustworthiness, particularly when unwarranted, it raises significant ethical concerns. Such behavior may mask ulterior motives behind a facade of public trust. When a regime relies solely on public goodwill for cooperation, it might resort to manipulation – alternating between propaganda and appeasement to secure public support.

[13] This is related, of course, to the discussion about literature on whether laws are created by societal norms or whether the state creates societal norms (e.g., Hart's theory discussion in Chapter 11).

[14] Banerjee, Sanchayan, and Peter John. "Nudge plus: Incorporating reflection into behavioral public policy." *Behavioral Public Policy* 8.1 (2024): 69–84.

VOLUNTARILY COOPERATING: VARIANCE IN PEOPLE'S RESPONSES

As stated in the introduction, this chapter focuses on how people react differently to law in the absence of sanctioning systems.

Even with current enforcement approaches, there is significant variation in how people respond to legal requirements. Some individuals are more adept at evading enforcement and more likely to do so based on factors like their attitudes toward risk and their respect for the rule of law.[15] Therefore, concerns about distributive justice are not unique to voluntary compliance or reduced coercive measures.

Various theories of social preference compare people's preference to cooperate, free ride, and respond to cooperation (conditional cooperators).[16] Given the prevalence of conditional cooperators discussed, governments that wish to treat the public using trust-based approaches face a significant challenge. However, the argument put forward here is that without extrinsic motivation such as sanctions, there is more room for intrinsic motivation to influence cooperation. As suggested with regard to the existence of different types of cooperators – conditional ones, those who tend to free ride, and those who always comply – intrinsic motivation is expected to have far greater variation between people based on their personalities, culture, and contextual factors.[17] In contrast, price as affecting compliance, being external to the person, is more likely to create equalization between people,[18] even if their economic status obviously differs.

This heterogeneity could create a few problems:

First, the proportion of wrongdoers may be too high to be tolerated by the state, leading to increased costs to the majority of the public.

Second, many cooperators are what's called conditional cooperators,[19] where their cooperation depends on that of others.[20] With an increase in the number

15 Bogaert, Sandy, Christophe Boone, and Carolyn Declerck. "Social value orientation and cooperation in social dilemmas: A review and conceptual model." *British Journal of Social Psychology* 47.3 (2008): 453–480; Heilman, Renata M., and Petko Kusev. "Personal values associated with prosocial decisions." *Behavioral Sciences* 10.4 (2020): 77–86.

16 Fischbacher, U., and Gächter, S. "Social preferences, beliefs, and the dynamics of free riding in public good experiments." *American Economic Review* 100 (2010): 541–556.

17 Fine, Adam D., and Benjamin van Rooij. "Legal socialization: Understanding the obligation to obey the law." *Journal of Social Issues* 77.2 (2021): 367–391; Tyler, Tom R. "Multiculturalism and the willingness of citizens to defer to law and to legal authorities." *Law & Social Inquiry* 25.4 (2000): 983–1019; Jiang, Shanhe, Yuning Wu, and Jin Wang. "Citizens' obligation to obey the law: An empirical study of Guangzhou, China." *International Journal of Offender Therapy and Comparative Criminology* 57.4 (2013): 495–518.

18 Price effect is, of course, also dependent on factors which are different for different people, such as income.

19 Fischbacher, Schudy, and Teyssier. "Heterogeneous reactions to heterogeneity in returns from public goods."

20 Chaudhuri and Paichayontvijit. "Conditional cooperation and voluntary contributions to a public good."

of wrongdoers who might exploit the trust given to them by the state, conditional cooperators might follow and stop cooperating as well.[21]

Third, we might encounter a situation where people misinterpret the true content of social norms, either due to false signals or overestimation of wrongdoing. As a result, they might stop cooperating, not because others are actually uncooperative, but because they believe others would likely not cooperate under less scrutiny from authorities.[22]

HETEROGENEITY IN HONESTY

Beyond differences in cooperation levels, there's also significant variation in honesty among people. This heterogeneity likely affects how much governments can trust the public without more specific data on the distribution of cooperative and honest individuals in each population.

In my previous book,[23] I examine differing accounts in the literature. Some studies suggest a substantial level of dishonesty albeit with variation across the different experimental paradigms,[24] while Abeler and colleagues seem to believe that honesty is less prevalent.[25] The relationship between honesty and cooperation is an important consideration, as discussed in Chapters 1 and 2.[26]

In that context of individual difference, Jacquemet and colleagues found that individuals who engage in occasional or moderate dishonesty – rather than systematic lying – are influenced by a truth-telling oath as a nonprice commitment device.[27] Through experiments examining income reporting and tax declarations, researchers used response time analysis and sequential decision patterns to demonstrate that moderate dishonesty reflects a weak preference for profitable honesty. The oath effectively transforms these occasional deceivers into committed truth-tellers. However, in my work with Eyal Pe'er (discussed further in Chapter 4), we discovered a broader effect: pledges reduced dishonesty more effectively than fines, impacting even habitual liars. This effect proved consistent across multiple time periods, varying degrees of dishonesty, and different individual characteristics.[28]

21 Chaudhuri and Paichayontvijit. "Conditional cooperation and voluntary contributions to a public good."

22 Fallucchi, Luccasen III, and Turocy. "The sophistication of conditional cooperators."

23 Feldman, Yuval. *The law of good people: Challenging states' ability to regulate human behavior*. Cambridge University Press, 2018.

24 Gerlach, Philipp, Kinneret Teodorescu, and Ralph Hertwig. "The truth about lies: A meta-analysis on dishonest behavior." *Psychological Bulletin* 145.1 (2019): 1–44.

25 Abeler, Johannes, Daniele Nosenzo, and Collin Raymond. "Preferences for truth-telling." *Econometrica* 87.4 (2019): 1115–1153.

26 Köbis, Nils C., et al. "Intuitive honesty versus dishonesty: Meta-analytic evidence." *Perspectives on Psychological Science* 14.5 (2019): 778–796.

27 Jacquemet, Nicolas, et al. "Who'll stop lying under oath? Empirical evidence from tax evasion games." *European Economic Review* 124 (2020): 1–14.

28 Pe'er, Eyal, and Yuval Feldman. "Honesty pledges for the behaviorally based regulation of dishonesty." *Journal of European Public Policy* 28.5 (2021): 761–781.

WHAT IS THE PREVALENCE OF DISHONESTY IN SOCIETY?

Regarding the prevalence of dishonesty in society, research has examined statistics on unethical behavior in the US.[29] For example, in a 2004 poll done by the popular magazine *Readers' Digest*,[30] 93 percent reported engaging in one or more kinds of dishonesty at work or school, such as calling in sick when not feeling ill (63 percent), taking office supplies from work (63 percent), and lying on their résumés (18 percent).

In contrast to the perspective which views unethicality as prevalent and contagious among normative people, Abeler and colleagues combined data from ninety experimental studies in economics, psychology, and sociology, and showed that, in fact, people lie surprisingly little.[31] The study's empirical evidence suggests that a preference for being seen as honest is the main motivation for truth-telling.

Similarly, Ostrom presents a comprehensive overview of research, and some of the key insights include the fact that not all individuals are purely rational egoists and that social norms can evolve to support cooperation.[32] For example, in a prisoner's dilemma experiment, 40 percent of the subjects ranked the cooperative outcome higher than the outcome of defecting while the other cooperates, and 27 percent were indifferent between these outcomes, even though their individual payoff was substantially higher in the latter. According to Ostrom, this finding confirms that not all players enter a collective action situation as pure forward-looking rational egoists who make decisions based solely on individual outcomes. Some bring with them a set of norms and values that can support cooperation. In addition, Ostrom shows that conditional cooperators are apparently also a substantial proportion of the population, with rates ranging from 40 to 60 percent.

In another important question regarding honesty from a more economist perspective, Gibson and colleagues sought to solve the question of whether the world is populated by exactly two fixed types: economic types and ethical types, and whether there is heterogeneity in the preferences of the people to lie or to tell the truth, depending on consequences.[33] The type-based model and the model with heterogeneous preferences for truthfulness lead to very different implications.[34] Therefore, it is important to determine which of these two models offers a more accurate description of reality.

[29] Serota, Kim B., Timothy R. Levine, and Franklin J. Boster. "The prevalence of lying in America: Three studies of self-reported lies." *Human Communication Research* 36.1 (2010): 2–25. https://static1.squarespace.com/static/53143e7de4b0d2c24316913f/t/531eca51e4b069e27c30717c/1394526801975/Serota_etal_2010_Few-Prolific_liars.pdf.

[30] Kalish, Nancy. "How honest are you?" *Reader's Digest* 164.981 (2004): 114–119.

[31] Abeler, Nosenzo, and Raymond. "Preferences for truth-telling."

[32] Ostrom, Elinor. "Collective action and the evolution of social norms." *Journal of Economic Perspectives* 14.3 (2000): 137–158.

[33] Gibson, Rajna, Carmen Tanner, and Alexander F. Wagner. "Preferences for truthfulness: Heterogeneity among and within individuals." *American Economic Review* 103.1 (2013): 532–548.

[34] Gneezy, Uri. "Deception: The role of consequences." *American Economic Review* 95.1 (2005): 384–394.

To address this question, they conducted a decision-theoretic laboratory experiment in which each participant was placed in the situation of a CEO who had to announce their firm's earnings to a passive market. The participants were informed of the true level of earnings. Participants were informed that misreporting higher earnings was illegal but would result in larger payouts compared to truthfully reporting their lower earnings. It was expected that economic types would always lie in our experiment because truthfulness was designed to be economically costly; also, it was expected that ethical types would always tell the truth.

They observed that, in a situation where the standard economic model predicts that everybody will lie, 32 percent of the participants chose not to do so, thus forgoing a larger variable compensation. Importantly, the aggregate percentage of truth-tellers decreased as the costs of truthfulness increased. That implies that the marginal effect of a cost increase on the probability of an individual telling the truth is significantly negative, even after controlling for various demographic and psychological factors. These results are at odds with the type-based model but are consistent with a model that posits heterogeneous preferences for truthfulness. The models' primary contribution, therefore, is to provide evidence for the notion that people occupy a spectrum of preferences for truthfulness rather than only two opposite positions.

WHY DO SO MANY PEOPLE CHEAT?

Competing literature varies between different meta-analysis studies, as well as in more field-oriented studies that show that in certain contexts a large proportion of the population lies.[35] Jacobsen and colleagues present six main theories explaining why people cheat:[36]

1. **The Economic Theory**: This represents a rational approach to cheating, where individuals weigh the costs and benefits of dishonest behavior.
2. **The Moral Balance Theory**: This introduces a psychological perspective, suggesting that people engage in a form of ethical accounting, allowing themselves to cheat if they feel they have accumulated moral credit.
3. **The Self-Maintenance Theory**: This focuses on preserving one's self-image, indicating that individuals will cheat only to the extent that it doesn't force them to revise their self-perception as honest.
4. **The Self-Justification Theory**: This extends the idea of self-maintenance, proposing that people can rationalize their cheating behavior, even after the fact, to maintain cognitive consistency.

[35] Gerlach, Teodorescu, and Hertwig. "The truth about lies," 1.

[36] Jacobsen, Catrine, Toke Reinholt Fosgaard, and David Pascual-Ezama. "Why do we lie? A practical guide to the dishonesty literature." *Journal of Economic Surveys* 32.2 (2018): 357–387.

5. **The Moral Disconnection Theory**: This highlights the human capacity for moral disengagement, where individuals exempt themselves from the ethical standards they expect others to follow.
6. **The Limited Morality and Moral Blindness Theory**: This addresses the role of awareness and self-reflection in ethical behavior, suggesting that some individuals may cheat due to a lack of moral awareness or failure to critically examine their own actions.

Together, these theories illustrate that cheating is not simply a matter of economic calculation, but a complex interplay of psychological, moral, and cognitive factors that can vary significantly across individuals and situations.

Jacobson and colleagues concluded that people regularly engage in dishonest behavior, but that this behavior is highly malleable because it is sensitive to elements such as decision contexts, behavior of others, state of mind, and ego depletion.[37] In other words, changes in regulatory culture or industry norms can significantly impact behavior. For instance, an industry where cutting corners becomes the norm might see a rapid increase in such practices.

While the concept of conditional cooperators has been extensively studied, the idea of conditional cheaters has received comparatively less attention.[38] Despite this imbalance in research focus, there are notable similarities between these two bodies of literature. These similarities allow us to speculate that environmental factors likely influence the prevalence of dishonesty in ways similar to how they affect cooperation.

The key contrast lies in the depth of research: conditional cooperation is well documented, while conditional cheating, though studied,[39] lacks the same level of comprehensive investigation. However, the parallels between these phenomena suggest that social and environmental cues probably shape dishonest behavior just as they do cooperative behavior.

To sum up, research on heterogeneity of honesty and cooperation is diverse and many models of human cooperation have accounted for the fact that different people come with different motivations. However, individual differences are not the only concern; equally important is the potential distributive effect when trust is extended to those who shouldn't be trusted. As we discuss in Chapter 7, this creates a paradox: If privacy and autonomy considerations force us to trust everyone uniformly, we might ultimately end up trusting no one.

[37] Cantarero, Katarzyna, and Wijnand A. P. Van Tilburg. "Too tired to taint the truth: Ego-depletion reduces other-benefiting dishonesty." *European Journal of Social Psychology* 44.7 (2014): 743–747.

[38] Earley, Ryan L. "Social eavesdropping and the evolution of conditional cooperation and cheating strategies." *Philosophical Transactions of the Royal Society B: Biological Sciences* 365.1553 (2010): 2675–2686.

[39] Innes, Robert, and Mitra Arnab. "Is dishonesty contagious?" *Economic Inquiry* 51.1 (2013): 722–734; Gino, Francesca, Shahar Ayal, and Dan Ariely. "Contagion and differentiation in unethical behavior: The effect of one bad apple on the barrel." *Psychological Science* 20.3 (2009): 393–398.

In line with the perception against dichotomy and for a spectrum, an important study claims that there are more diverse profiles of liars than has been accepted so far in the literature.[40]

In an experimental study examining dishonest behavior, participants were instructed to roll a die, with financial rewards proportional to the reported outcome. The findings revealed distinct patterns of honest and dishonest behavior. While one group maintained complete honesty, others exhibited various forms of dishonest behavior: Some participants rolled multiple times without misreporting (reporting the first, less profitable result); others misreported their single roll; and a third group both rolled multiple times and misreported their results.

The researchers identified a behavioral spectrum across these categories and explored participants' motivations. Of particular interest was the distinction between those who repeatedly rolled until achieving their desired outcome versus those who directly misreported results without rolling. This behavior suggests different psychological mechanisms regarding self-image maintenance when dealing with actual versus hypothetical dishonesty.

The study demonstrated consistency in dishonest behavior profiles across different populations while highlighting that honesty is not a unidimensional trait. Individuals often simultaneously violate rules while maintaining a self-perception of honesty. This heterogeneity in honest behavior, previously considered problematic for voluntary compliance, may inform the development of optimal policy solutions, particularly in the context of Chapter 11's compliance mechanisms.

HETEROGENEITY IN COMPLIANCE

The previous sections have discussed heterogeneity in prosocial behavior and dishonesty. Now, we'll examine these factors in the context of compliance. Compliance is not merely a combination of prosocial behavior and honesty; it also involves people's perceptions of their relationship with authority and their duty to obey the law. In Chapter 2 we discussed the work of van Rooij and colleagues in the context of compliance motivation, which is also important for the heterogeneity.[41] In that context, we have examined variations in people's sense of obligation to obey the law (OOL). The OOL plays a vital role in people's responses to the legal system and their compliance decision-making. So far, most studies have linked the OOL to people's experiences and views of the legal system.[42] This chapter seeks to expand our understanding of

[40] Pascual-Ezama, David, et al. "Cheaters, liars, or both? A new classification of dishonesty profiles." *Psychological Science* 31.9 (2020): 1097–1106.

[41] Fine, Adam, et al. "Rule orientation and behavior: Development and validation of a scale measuring individual acceptance of rule violation." *Psychology, Public Policy, and Law* 22.3 (2016): 314–329.

[42] Suddaby, Roy, Alex Bitektine, and Patrick Haack. "Legitimacy." *Academy of Management Annals* 11.1 (2017): 451–478.

the OOL by analyzing how such variation relates to personal and moral differences, differences in socialization in higher education, and differences in political preferences. Throughout a series of 4 studies with a total of 5,085 participants, Fine and colleagues found that the OOL is not solely dictated by experiences with and perceptions of the legal system but is comparatively more related to personal and political differences.[43] Indeed, as discussed in more detail in this paper, an important source of variation between people in the US is related to political orientation, where conservative moral values, such as loyalty, authority, and purity,[44] may lead to a preference for obedience,[45] stricter punishment, and more trust in law enforcement.[46] Research consistently links political affiliation with perceptions of the law and law enforcement,[47] with Republicans being more "tough on crime" compared to Democrats. One could only predict that such variation will have a huge impact on heterogeneity in compliance which might end up increasing the gap between the different political groups. Such an increase in the gap might be exacerbated when accounting for the rise of polarization in many countries around the world.[48]

Heterogeneity in Compliance Based on Age and Gender

Another area with lots of research on heterogeneity in compliance is driving violations, where both age and gender were shown to be significant. Research on driver behavior has also indicated that there are some cross-cultural factors that affect compliance.[49] A study exploring methods to reduce parking violations examined the effectiveness of various strategies, including signage, warnings, volunteer patrols, fines, and increased enforcement by police. The findings suggest that vertical signs, particularly those warnings of severe financial consequences for illegal parking, can lower the violation rate. However, low enforcement rates continue to be an issue.[50]

43 Fine, et al. "Rule orientation and behavior," 314.

44 Frimer, Jeremy A., Danielle Gaucher, and Nicola K. Schaefer. "Political conservatives' affinity for obedience to authority is loyal, not blind." *Personality and Social Psychology Bulletin* 40.9 (2014): 1205–1214.

45 Gerber, Monica M., and Jonathan Jackson. "Authority and punishment: On the ideological basis of punitive attitudes towards criminals." *Psychiatry, Psychology and Law* 23.1 (2016): 113–134.

46 Pickett, Justin T. "Public opinion and criminal justice policy: Theory and research." *Annual Review of Criminology* 2.1 (2019): 405–428.

47 Unnever, James D., and Francis T. Cullen. "Executing the innocent and support for capital punishment: Implications for public policy." *Criminology & Public Policy* 4.1 (2005): 3–38; Moule Jr., Richard K., Bryanna Hahn Fox, and Megan M. Parry. "The long shadow of Ferguson: Legitimacy, legal cynicism, and public perceptions of police militarization." *Crime & Delinquency* 65.2 (2019): 151–182.

48 Compare with Maman, Libby, Yuval Feldman, and Tom Tyler. "Polarization and voluntary compliance: The impact of ideological extremity on the effectiveness of self-regulation." *Regulation & Governance* (in press) on trust-based regulation in polarized counties.

49 Sagberg, Fridulv, et al. "A review of research on driving styles and road safety." *Human Factors* 57.7 (2015): 1248–1275. For more discussion on the interaction between culture and compliance see Chapter 6.

50 Fletcher, Donna. "Illegal parking in spaces reserved for people with disabilities: A review of the research." *Journal of Developmental and Physical Disabilities* 8 (1996): 151–165.

Furthermore, a survey of 3,360 drivers' parking habits revealed that the frequency of illegal parking decreased after fines were introduced. Notably, males and young drivers have consistently demonstrated a higher likelihood of illegally parking in spaces reserved for people with disabilities.[51] While insurance companies are known to use both age and gender in their car insurance practices, it is less clear that regulators can use age and gender as factors in their approaches.[52]

HETEROGENEITY IN MORAL REASONING

The propensity to morally disengage refers to an individual's tendency to use cognitive mechanisms that allow them to distance themselves from their own unethical actions. It involves a set of cognitive processes that enable individuals to justify or rationalize their unethical behavior, thereby reducing feelings of guilt or responsibility.[53]

Moral disengagement is a common phenomenon that can be found in all segments of society. Drawing on Bandura's moral disengagement theory,[54] research has examined this phenomenon across schools, businesses, and prisons. For example, a study found that 85 percent of college students used moral disengagement strategies to justify cheating on exams.[55]

In the seminal work by Moore and colleagues,[56] they examined the influence of individuals' propensity to morally disengage on a broad range of unethical organizational behaviors. They concluded that considering an individual's propensity for moral disengagement can help in understanding and predicting a wide range of undesirable behaviors. This variation in moral disengagement acts as another predictor of behavior. Consequently, without enforcement, we are likely to see a much greater gap between people's actions.

HETEROGENEITY IN SOCIAL VALUE ORIENTATION

As discussed in Chapter 3, social value orientation plays a crucial role in predicting cooperative behavior and compliance. Within the Big Five personality model, social

51 Fletcher, Donna. "A five-year study of effects of fines, gender, race, and age on illegal parking in spaces reserved for people with disabilities." *Rehabilitation Psychology* 40.3 (1995): 203–210.

52 However, see Ben-Shachar, Omri, and Ariel Porat, *Personalized law: Different rules for different people*. Oxford University Press, 2021, as well as Chapter 7, for discussions about the use of technology in improving personalized compliance.

53 Moore, Celia, et al. "Why employees do bad things: Moral disengagement and unethical organizational behavior." *Personnel Psychology* 65.1 (2012): 1–48.

54 Bandura, Albert. "Moral disengagement in the perpetration of inhumanities." *Personality and Social Psychology Review* 3.3 (1999): 193–209.

55 McCreary, Gentry Russell. *The impact of moral judgment and moral disengagement on hazing attitudes and bystander behavior in college males*. The University of Alabama Press, 2012.

56 Moore, et al. "Why employees do bad things."

value orientation represents the most recent addition that is particularly relevant to understanding voluntary compliance behaviors.[57]

Another important personality dimension related to cooperation is honesty-humility, which appears as the first dimension in the HEXACO (honesty-humility [H], emotionality [E], extraversion [X], agreeableness [A], conscientiousness [C], and openness to experience [O]) personality model.[58] This trait is defined as the tendency to be fair, genuine, and sincere in dealing with others.

For example, Hilbig and Zettler investigated the predictive ability of the honesty-humility personality trait in relation to economic and cooperative behavior.[59] They hypothesized that this trait would explain how individuals allocate valuable resources between themselves and others in two different scenarios: the dictator game and the ultimatum game.[60] Furthermore, they predicted that honesty-humility would account for the differences in behavior between these two games, where the recipient's power to retaliate varies.

Their study involved 134 participants and yielded results that supported both hypotheses. Participants who scored low in honesty-humility made more self-centered decisions and only shifted toward a more equitable distribution when the other party had the power to punish uncooperative behavior. In contrast, those who scored high in honesty-humility consistently chose a fairer allocation, even when they could have acted selfishly without fear of repercussions.

Lastly, the study found that social value orientations partially mediated the observed effects, suggesting that an individual's preference for certain social outcomes played a role in the relationship between honesty-humility and economic decision-making.

An additional study, by Lainidi and colleagues, found that people who were high in honesty-humility were more likely to cooperate with others in a prisoner's dilemma game, even though they knew that they could potentially earn a larger reward by defecting. This suggests that people who are high in honesty-humility are more likely to cooperate with others, even when it is not in their best interests to do so.[61]

In a meta-analysis of studies on the relationship between honesty-humility and prosocial behavior, Fang and colleagues found that honesty-humility is positively correlated with prosocial behavior such as helping others in need, cooperating with others, and donating to charity.[62]

57 Hilbig, Benjamin E., and Ingo Zettler. "Pillars of cooperation: Honesty–humility, social value orientations, and economic behavior." *Journal of Research in Personality* 43.3 (2009): 516–519.

58 Ashton, Michael C., and Kibeom Lee. "The HEXACO model of personality structure and the importance of the H factor." *Social and Personality Psychology Compass* 2.5 (2008): 1952–1962.

59 Hilbig and Zettler. "Pillars of cooperation."

60 Larney, Andrea, Amanda Rotella, and Pat Barclay. "Stake size effects in ultimatum game and dictator game offers: A meta-analysis." *Organizational Behavior and Human Decision Processes* 151 (2019): 61–72.

61 Lainidi, Olga, Eirini Karakasidou, and Anthony Montgomery. "Dark triad, impulsiveness and honesty-humility in the prisoner's dilemma game: The moderating role of gender." *Merits* 2.4 (2022): 387–399.

62 Fang, Yuan, Yan Dong, and Lanran Fang. "Honesty-humility and prosocial behavior: The mediating roles of perspective taking and guilt-proneness." *Scandinavian Journal of Psychology* 60.4 (2019): 386–393.

HETEROGENEITY OF SOCIAL NORMS

In other studies, conducted for example with Barak-Corren and Gidron,[63] we show how pluralistic and nonhomogeneous are the effect of norms on different parts of society. From the perspective of voluntary compliance, this suggests an important caveat to consider, that is, how much we can rely on social norms to replace formal laws.

Additionally, many argue that religious mandates have contributed to a decline in public support for religion and have triggered public resistance to perceived attempts at top-down control.[64]

This argument suggests that for practices like circumcision, Leil HaSeder observance, and refraining from driving on Yom Kippur, there is no need for legal enforcement. The social norms surrounding these practices are strong enough to guide behavior without legal intervention. However, in areas where there is likely to be a prohibition, such as the law against eating bread during Passover, noncompliance is prevalent.

The Yom Kippur example in Israel illustrates the complexities of relying solely on social norms for regulation. While there's a strong norm among secular Jews not to drive on Yom Kippur, transforming roads into spaces for cycling,[65] this practice has led to unforeseen consequences. With 20 percent of Israel's population being Arab and not observing this norm, there have been tragic accidents in recent years.

This situation highlights a key challenge: societies often comprise diverse groups with different beliefs and practices. The effectiveness of norms in changing behavior is limited when society isn't homogeneous. In the Yom Kippur case, the absence of cars led children to cycle on roads without considering potential dangers from the minority still driving.[66]

This example relates to the taxonomy discussed in chapter 11 of *The Law of Good People*, where we compared legal contexts requiring cooperation from everyone (like trade secrets), a few (whistleblowing), or the more the better (e.g., tax compliance). The Yom Kippur scenario falls into the category needing universal cooperation, making it difficult to rely solely on intrinsic motivation without formal compliance measures.

Furthermore, when there's no consensus in the population and a law is passed to enforce a behavior that only some are motivated by social values to follow, much of its effectiveness may be lost due to social reactance theory.[67]

63 Barak-Corren, Netta, Noam Gidron, and Yuval Feldman. "Majority nationalism laws and the equal citizenship of minorities: Experimental, panel, and cross-sectional evidence from Israel." *Journal of Legal Studies* 51.2 (2022): 371–401.

64 Cohn, Haim H. "Religious freedom and religious coercion in the state of Israel." In *Judaism and human rights*, edited by Miton R. Konvitz, Routledge, 2018: 291–334.

65 www.theguardian.com/world/2023/sep/25/yom-kippur-israel-cyclists.

66 www.jpost.com/israel-news/article-824278.

67 Barak-Corren, Netta, Yuval Feldman, and Noam Gidron. "The provocative effect of law: Majority nationalism and minority discrimination." *Journal of Empirical Legal Studies* 15.4 (2018): 951–986.

REGULATING HETEROGENEOUS POPULATIONS EFFECTIVELY: INSIGHTS FROM RESEARCH ON HONESTY PLEDGES

Along with research on the factors that predict the likelihood of cooperation among different individuals, there is hope in the work I have done with Eyal Pe'er on the effect of pledges on brazen liars, whom one might predict would be less affected by trust-based regulation such as pledges. We have analyzed whether pledges work primarily for honest people or also for brazen liars. We hypothesized that pledges, which raise awareness of honesty's morality, might only be effective for those with a strong commitment to ethics. Previous findings also suggested that pledges might only affect minor cheaters.[68] However, we found that pledges significantly influenced behavior across individual differences in rule-following tendencies and cheating extents. This implies that trust-based regulation could be equally effective for people with low commitments to the law. The overall reduction in brazen liars was similar, with no interaction found between individual differences in commitment to obey the law. The percentage of "high-extent cheaters" (defined as 75 percent or higher) was largest in the self-report group, considerably smaller with a pledge or fine, and smallest with both. These differences remained significant when the "high-extent cheater" threshold was defined between 60 percent and 90 percent, suggesting that pledges and fines affect even those who exhibit high degrees of cheating. This contradicts the perspective that trust-based regulation might increase the gap between ethical and nonethical people.

SOCIAL PUNISHMENT AS A REPLACEMENT FOR STATE PUNISHMENT

A possible solution to the problem we have raised about voluntary compliance without punishment and monitoring by the state in a heterogeneous society, where not all members are equally committed to the cooperate with the requests of the state, is social punishment, which could be substituted for state enforcement.

Social punishment is widely discussed in the field of behavioral game theory where the idea of altruistic punishment is being developed and it was argued that it could lead to stable cooperation.[69] Some other studies have focused on the usage of shaming as an alternative to state enforcement in various domains.[70] However, the question is whether such altruistic punishment can really be used to ensure voluntary compliance given the complexity of many forms of compliance, especially with regards to

[68] Jacquemet, et al. "Who'll stop lying under oath?," 103369.

[69] Fehr, Ernst, and Simon Gächter. "Altruistic punishment in humans." *Nature* 415.6868 (2002): 137–140; Bowles, Samuel, and Herbert Gintis. "The evolution of strong reciprocity: Cooperation in heterogeneous populations." *Theoretical Population Biology* 65.1 (2004): 17–28.

[70] Yadin, Sharon. "Regulatory shaming." *Environmental Law* 49.2 (2019): 407–451.

corporations,[71] as will be developed in more detail in Chapter 7. This approach was subject to lots of criticism for not always being accurate and proportional.[72]

UNDESIRABLE OUTCOMES OF HETEROGENEITY IN VOLUNTARY COMPLIANCE

In voluntary compliance regimes, nonintrinsically motivated actors may increase their noncompliant behavior. This can trigger a cascade effect where conditional cooperators, observing free-riding or misconduct, reduce their own compliance. Such dynamics can escalate perceived distributive injustice as compliance gaps between different groups widen.

The impact of others' behavior on compliance varies significantly across regulatory domains. Tax compliance demonstrates a particularly strong "sucker effect," where individuals are highly sensitive to others' free-riding behavior and may withdraw their own compliance in response. Environmental regulations, however, often elicit more independent compliance decisions, less influenced by others' behavior.

In domains requiring collective cooperation, such as protecting trade secrets within professional communities, uneven compliance can undermine the entire system's effectiveness. For instance, when some business association members breach confidentiality while others maintain it, the value of information protection diminishes for all participants.

Governments face a fundamental dilemma in addressing these varying cooperation levels. While effective policy implementation requires detailed information about individual backgrounds and behavioral patterns (as Chapter 8 will explore), collecting such comprehensive personal data raises significant privacy concerns.

THE FEAR OF BRAINWASHING

In the research about nudges there is always the fear that there will be harm to autonomy, but in voluntary compliance the fear might be greater for various reasons related to overreliance on intrinsic motivation. When many people need to be intrinsically committed so are more likely to engage in social enforcement, cooperation, and compliance, the government might need to resort to various techniques to cause as many people as possible to be committed to the purposes of the state. When the government focuses on sanctioning and monitoring such a shift might be less needed.

[71] Corlett, J. Angelo, and J. Angelo Corlett. *Corporate responsibility and punishment*. Springer Netherlands, 2001.

[72] Skeel, David A. "Shaming in corporate law." *University of Pennsylvania Law Review* 149.6 (2001): 1811–1868.

The Double-Edged Sword of Moral Conviction

Research on moral conviction provides important insights into the challenges faced by regulatory regimes that depend on public support.[73] While intrinsic motivation for compliance can enhance regulatory effectiveness, it presents a potential risk: Excessive moral certainty among citizens might lead them to prioritize their personal moral imperatives over established legal frameworks.

At first glance, the idea of moral conviction, where people become overzealous about paying taxes, might seem far-fetched. However, we can envision more plausible scenarios where intrinsic motivation leads to problematic outcomes. For instance, individuals deeply motivated to protect the environment might sanction firms that comply with the letter of the law but fall short of their personal environmental standards. Similarly, employees overly committed to their organizations might violate corporate governance rules, or citizens excessively loyal to their country might disregard international law or tax treaties.

These examples illustrate the delicate balance required in fostering compliance. We aim for a level of commitment that encourages adherence to rules without tipping into overcompliance or conflict with other important values. This balance is crucial for maintaining a functional and fair regulatory system that respects both the letter and spirit of the law, while also fostering public cooperation.[74]

OVERRELYING ON MORAL COMPLIANCE

Focus should be given to some of the models reviewed in this chapter which are less likely to interfere with other models and carry unintended effects, as was demonstrated regarding sanctions or incentives. For instance, the concept of procedural justice, widely studied by scholars such as Tyler and others,[75] is likely to increase legitimacy and compliance with less likelihood of interfering with effective functioning of deterrence. Similarly, informing people of the harm associated with their behavior may be relevant for some people without inducing resentment toward the law. Nevertheless, even with these approaches, some scholars propose the possibility

[73] Skitka, Linda J. "The psychology of moral conviction." *Social and Personality Psychology Compass* 4.4 (2010): 267–281.

[74] Armour, John, Jeffrey Gordon, and Geeyoung Min. "Taking compliance seriously." *Yale Journal on Regulation* 37 (2020): 1.

[75] Murphy, Kristina, and Tom Tyler. "Procedural justice and compliance behaviour: The mediating role of emotions." *European Journal of Social Psychology* 38.4 (2008): 652–668; Walters, Glenn D., and P. Colin Bolger. "Procedural justice perceptions, legitimacy beliefs, and compliance with the law: A meta-analysis." *Journal of Experimental Criminology* 15 (2019): 341–372.

that emphasizing morality might give people the impression that the state is unable to enforce the law; that is, these approaches may potentially backfire.[76] Thus, regulators should strive to identify the policy which will target as many motivations as possible while acknowledging the challenge of achieving complete success in this mission.

THE PROBLEM OF BIASED MORALITY

An additional challenge with intrinsic motivation and moral conviction arises from allowing individuals to use moral reasoning to guide their behavior. This approach assumes a universal agreement on moral standards, which is problematic. While there may be clear consensus on straightforward issues like the obligation to pay taxes, many situations present more complex dilemmas. In these cases, we must consider how people will ultimately apply their moral judgments and whether they will do so appropriately.

As already suggested in my previous book, *The Law of Good People*, since people's interest is to not view themselves in a negative light, they are likely to engage in various biased cognitive process related to reasoning, memory, and vision. In that book, I outline various biases which could explain the distortion of people's evaluation of what is moral.[77] Thompson and Loewenstein have shown that people were more likely to remember information that was related to their own position, with the result that their opinion of what was fair aligned with their interest in the outcome of a settlement.[78] The fact that these biases operate without awareness makes it difficult for people to notice the process. Moore and Loewenstein were among the first to show that self-interest and concern for others affect behavior through different cognitive systems and that self-interest, unlike concern for others, is automatic, viscerally compelling, and often unconscious.[79] By comparing people's private beliefs and public behavior, Moore demonstrated that people truly believed their own biased judgments, and did not recognize any problems in their responses.[80]

[76] Bardach, Eugene. "Moral suasion and taxpayer compliance." *Law & Policy* 11.1 (1989): 49–69.

[77] For example, Batson, C. Daniel, et al. "Moral hypocrisy: Appearing moral to oneself without being so." *Journal of Personality and Social Psychology* 77.3 (1999): 525–537; Tenbrunsel, Ann E., and David M. Messick. "Ethical fading: The role of self-deception in unethical behavior." *Social Justice Research* 17 (2004): 223–236.

[78] Thompson, Leigh, and George Loewenstein. "Egocentric interpretations of fairness and interpersonal conflict." *Organizational Behavior and Human Decision Processes* 51.2 (1992): 176–197.

[79] Moore, Don A., and George Loewenstein. "Self-interest, automaticity, and the psychology of conflict of interest." *Social Justice Research* 17 (2004): 189–202.

[80] Moore, Don A., Lloyd Tanlu, and Max H. Bazerman. "Conflict of interest and the intrusion of bias." *Judgment and Decision Making* 5.1 (2010): 37–53; Epley, Nicholas, and Eugene M. Caruso. "Egocentric ethics." *Social Justice Research* 17 (2004): 171–187.

As this review reveals, there is a growing recognition that many ethical decisions are the result of implicit, not explicit, choices.[81] Given that people's unethical behavior is frequently accompanied by a limited and distorted view of their own conduct, it is particularly important to focus on legal violations by otherwise good employers in the context of employment law. Indeed, this study will show that many of those mechanisms, which are particularly likely to increase the likelihood of good people behaving with limited awareness of the full legal and ethical meaning of their actions, are especially problematic in the context of employment. In the employer–employee relationship, issues such as ambiguity, repeated smaller violations, and the strong effect of workplace norms, which may not necessarily conform to those of the employees', are likely to have significant impacts on employees' conduct.[82]

REGULATORY MISTAKES AND PUBLIC SAFETY

An essential aspect to consider when discussing voluntary compliance, as explored in Chapter 4, is the complex interaction between regulation, trust, and public safety. A significant concern in regulatory research is the potential harm to the public when regulators place excessive trust in businesses. This issue arises from the possibility that regulated entities might exploit the increased flexibility granted by regulators to act against public interests.[83]

81 This argument was the foundation of *The Law of Good People*. Some of the additional literature on this topic is, for example, Mazar, Nina, On Amir, and Dan Ariely, "The dishonesty of honest people: A theory of self-concept maintenance." *Journal of Marketing Research* 45.6 (2008): 633–644; Bersoff, David M. "Why good people sometimes do bad things: Motivated reasoning and unethical behavior." *Personality and Social Psychology Bulletin* 25.1 (1999): 28–39; Kidder, Rushworth M. *How good people make tough choices: Resolving the dilemmas of ethical living* (2009); Pillutla, Madan M. "When good people do wrong: Morality, social identity, and ethical behavior." In *Social psychology and organizations*, edited by David De Cremer, Rolf van Dick and J. Keith Murnighan, Routledge, 2011: 385–402; James Hollis, *Why good people do bad things: Understanding our darker selves*. Gotham Books, 2008; Banaji, Mahzarin R., and Anthony G. Greenwald, *Blindspot: Hidden biases of good people*. Delacorte Press, 2013. Many others do not use the term "good people" in their titles but make the same argument in the text (see, e.g., Pillutla, "When good people do wrong"). This is also the view held by Bazerman, Max H., George Loewenstein, and Don A. Moore. "Why good accountants do bad audits." *Harvard Business Review* 80.11 (2002): 96–103. Note that the "good people" scholarship is usually different from the type of research conducted by Zimbardo on the Lucifer effect: see Philip Zimbardo, *The Lucifer effect: How good people turn evil*. Random Books, 2007. Their work generally tries to explain how ordinary people end up doing evil or at least engage in gross criminal behaviors.

82 For example, Dana, Weber, and Kuang have shown in a series of experiments one dominant strategy people use to maintain their self-concept while engaging in self-driven behavior – moral wiggle room. See Dana, Jason, Roberto A. Weber, and Jason Xi Kuang. "Exploiting moral wiggle room: Experiments demonstrating an illusory preference for fairness." *Economic Theory* 33 (2007): 67–80.

83 Sharma, Lisa L., Stephen P. Teret, and Kelly D. Brownell. "The food industry and self-regulation: Standards to promote success and to avoid public health failures." *American Journal of Public Health* 100.2 (2010): 240–246.

This concern aligns with our earlier discussion on heterogeneity in compliance motivations. When the government extends trust to regulated entities that don't genuinely merit public confidence, the consequences can be severe:

1. It may jeopardize public safety, which regulators are primarily tasked with protecting.
2. It could erode public trust in both the regulatory system and the regulated industries.
3. It might discourage public engagement in economic activities due to perceived risks.

The cost of regulatory mistakes in such scenarios extends beyond immediate safety concerns. It can lead to long-term damage to the relationship between the public, businesses, and regulatory bodies, potentially undermining the entire regulatory framework's effectiveness.

THE LIMITS OF FAIRNESS AND ALTRUISM

Another possible criticism on the reliance on voluntary compliance is related to studies which show that it is unreliable to focus on fairness in costly decisions.[84] How likely are people to base their behavior on intrinsic motivation when what's being requested from them is very costly and requires a sacrifice? Is it true that most regulators currently believe voluntary compliance motivations are not truly reliable? Indeed, research on honesty usually shows that the amount of money is not crucial, but is it clear enough to show that costs don't matter?[85] Other lines of research, for example those developed in economics and behavioral economics on fairness as a constraint on profit seeking, do tend to understand the tension between profit and fairness.[86] Furthermore, there is an obvious problem with the fact that experimental lab studies are limited in measuring high prices.[87] Another important debate about fairness concerns the self-interested interpretation of what constitutes "fair," as explored in *The Law of Good People*. According to this view, fairness is inherently limited because it is subjective and therefore may not effectively constrain opportunistic behavior.[88] However, Tyler's research on procedural

[84] Jimenez, Peggy, and Govind S. Iyer. "Tax compliance in a social setting: The influence of social norms, trust in government, and perceived fairness on taxpayer compliance." *Advances in Accounting* 34 (2016): 17–26.

[85] Wright Whelan, Clea, Graham F. Wagstaff, and Jacqueline M. Wheatcroft. "Subjective cues to deception/honesty in a high stakes situation: An exploratory approach." *Journal of Psychology* 149.5 (2015): 517–534.

[86] Kahneman, Daniel, Jack L. Knetsch, and Richard Thaler. "Fairness as a constraint on profit seeking: Entitlements in the market." *American Economic Review* 76.4 (1986): 728–741.

[87] Lusk, Jayson L., and Ted C. Schroeder. "Are choice experiments incentive compatible? A test with quality differentiated beef steaks." *American Journal of Agricultural Economics* 86.2 (2004): 467–482.

[88] Wade-Benzoni, Kimberly A., Ann E. Tenbrunsel, and Max H. Bazerman. "Egocentric interpretations of fairness in asymmetric, environmental social dilemmas: Explaining harvesting behavior and the role of communication." *Organizational Behavior and Human Decision Processes* 67.2 (1996): 111–126.

justice suggests that perceptions of fairness can transcend self-interest – both those who benefit from a decision and those who do not (e.g., winners and losers in court) tend to view procedurally fair decisions as more legitimate.[89]

MANAGING HETEROGENEITY RISKS

Finally, it is important, as will be developed in more detail in Chapter 11, that there are various mitigations to many of the concerns discussed thus far. Without the focus on people's background, it will be very hard for governments to know whom they can trust. In work with Orly Lobel and Ori Aronson,[90] discussed in more detail in Chapter 7, we found one approach which could help governments deal with this issue. We identified personality traits of people we can trust more. In that work we explore various ways to examine what kind of people are more likely to be cooperative and receptive to voluntary compliance initiatives. However, it is not clear whether, given privacy concerns, it is realistic for governments to treat people based on personality traits.

An alternative approach to determining trustworthiness was developed in collaboration with Yotam Kaplan.[91] We argued that it is more effective to adopt a differentiated approach that compares situations rather than one that evaluates people based on their past behavior. In Chapter 7, we explore technological approaches to voluntary compliance and discuss the potential for creating a more nuanced approach to voluntary cooperation. This approach recognizes that different situations pose varying levels of risk for voluntary compliance, potentially offering a mitigation strategy for the risks discussed earlier.

In higher risk situations, where the disparity between voluntary and nonvoluntary compliance might be more significant, we might reduce our emphasis on voluntary compliance and allocate more resources to alternative enforcement strategies. Thus, understanding the contexts in which people are less likely to voluntarily cooperate with the government could provide at least a partial solution to addressing the gaps discussed at the beginning of this chapter.

CONCLUSION

The heterogeneity in people's responses to voluntary compliance presents significant challenges to regulatory approaches that rely on intrinsic motivation and trust. This chapter has highlighted various dimensions of this heterogeneity, including

89 Lind, E. Allan, and Tom R. Tyler. *The social psychology of procedural justice*. Springer Science & Business Media, 1988.

90 Aronson, Ori, Yuval Feldman, and Orly Lobel. "The behavioral challenges of trust-based regulation: Navigating the complexities of past behavior as a predictor." Working paper, 2025 (on file with author).

91 Feldman, Yuval, and Yotam Kaplan. "Big data and bounded ethicality." *Cornell Journal of Law and Public Policy* 29 (2019): 39–94.

differences in honesty, moral reasoning, social value orientation, and compliance attitudes. These variations among individuals can lead to undesirable outcomes, such as increased inequality between "good" and "bad" actors, erosion of trust among conditional cooperators, and potential exploitation of trust-based systems by those less inclined to comply voluntarily.

While voluntary compliance approaches offer many benefits, including reduced enforcement costs and increased social capital, they also carry risks. These include the potential for brainwashing, overreliance on moral conviction, and the limits of fairness and altruism in costly decisions. The chapter has also explored how social punishment might replace state punishment in some contexts, but this too comes with its own set of challenges. Despite these concerns, the potential benefits of voluntary compliance suggest that rather than abandoning such approaches, regulators should seek ways to mitigate risks and tailor strategies to account for population heterogeneity.

To address the challenges posed by heterogeneity in voluntary compliance, future research should focus on several key areas. First, more comprehensive studies are needed to accurately measure the distribution of different types of cooperators (e.g., conditional cooperators, free riders, and altruists) across various regulatory contexts. Second, research should explore how to effectively combine voluntary compliance approaches with targeted enforcement strategies, perhaps using AI and big data to identify high-risk individuals or situations while respecting privacy concerns. Third, investigations into the long-term effects of voluntary compliance strategies on social norms and individual behavior are crucial to understanding their sustainability. Finally, cross-cultural studies examining how heterogeneity in compliance attitudes varies across different societies could provide valuable insights for designing more universally effective regulatory approaches. This research agenda would help policymakers develop more nuanced, adaptive regulatory strategies that can harness the benefits of voluntary compliance while mitigating its risks in heterogeneous populations.

6

Cross-Cultural Level

INTRODUCTION

This chapter examines the profound influence of culture on key factors underlying voluntary compliance, with a particular emphasis on prosocial behavior, rule of law, values, and culture.[1] This examination is important because it will help us understand, both descriptively and normatively, what lessons can be learned from cross-country comparison when examining the level of success of various trust-based regulatory tools, which are built on the need to trust the public's willingness to engage in voluntary compliance.

Machiavelli introduced the model of the lion, representing force, and the fox, representing cunning, to illustrate how the discourse on power can be tailored, considering the variations in power's significance within a given culture.[2] Indeed, the role of culture is an important component to examine when determining whether states can allow themselves to relinquish any of their coercive power. Intuitively, many scholars recognize the close association between the topics raised in previous chapters and culture. While, in some countries, a positive relationship between the state's expectations and the public's voluntary compliance is the norm, in other

1 OECD. "Society at a glance 2019." *OECD Social Indicators.* www.oecd.org/social/society-at-a-glance-19991290.htm (2019); Weingast, Barry R. "Why developing countries prove so resistant to the rule-of-law." In *Global perspectives on the rule of law,* edited by James J. Heckman, Robert L. Nelson and Lee Cabatingan, Routledge-Cavendish, 2013: 44–68; Moors, Guy, and Charlotte Wennekers. "Comparing moral values in Western European countries between 1981 and 1999. A multiple group latent-class factor approach." *International Journal of Comparative Sociology* 44.2 (2003): 155–172; De Groot, Judith I. M., and Linda Steg. "Value orientations and environmental beliefs in five countries: Validity of an instrument to measure egoistic, altruistic and biospheric value orientations." *Journal of Cross-cultural Psychology* 38.3 (2007): 318–332; Vauclair, Christin-Melanie, and Ronald Fischer. "Do cultural values predict individuals' moral attitudes? A cross-cultural multilevel approach." *European Journal of Social Psychology* 41.5 (2011): 645–657; Álvarez, Gloria, Yasuhiro Kotera, and Juan Pina. *World index of moral freedom, WIMF 2022.* Fundación para el Avance de la Libertad, 2020; Harrington, Jesse R., and Michele J. Gelfand. "Tightness–looseness across the 50 United States." *Proceedings of the National Academy of Sciences* 111.22 (2014): 7990–7995.

2 Lukes, Timothy J. "Lionizing Machiavelli." *American Political Science Review* 95.3 (2001): 561–575.

countries, trust between the government and the public is low and it would be futile to expect any major cooperation. This chapter aims to examine which factors may predict those cultures in which voluntary compliance is likely to be successful.

The variations between states in terms of how culture relates to predictors of effective voluntary compliance are dramatic.[3] This chapter will explore and compare the impact of culture in countries with varying levels of voluntary compliance, whether high, moderate, or low. It will analyze how this cultural impact is related to other predictors of voluntary compliance and various measures of trust,[4] as well as how it affects the perception of the rule of law in these countries.[5] Finally, we will compile and compare possible predictors across some prominent cultures. This should enable us to determine the true impact of culture on voluntary compliance.

Research supports the view that an individual's response to voluntary compliance is a function of their cultural background. According to Coleman and Freeman,[6] understanding and integrating cultural nuances and values, such as attitudes toward taxes, perceptions of fairness, and peer influences, can enhance voluntary compliance programs. Additionally, taking into account cultural factors, such as holding the system accountable and increasing transparency about spending, can improve the outcomes of compliance efforts.[7] Studies suggest that interpersonal trust, while reflecting an individual's positive expectation of others for overall well-being, plays a pivotal role in shaping behavioral tendencies.[8] Interpersonal trust fosters cooperation by reducing the individual's fear of being exploited by others.[9] Evidence suggests that the individual's cultural context can moderate the relationship between interpersonal trust and willingness to comply voluntarily, as in

3 For an elaboration, see OECD. "Society at a glance, 2011." *OECD Social Indicators*. www.oecd.org/social/societyataglance2011.html (2011); Gallup World Poll: www.gallup.com; OECD, "Growing unequal? Income distribution and poverty in OECD countries." www.oecd.org/els/social/inequality (2008).

4 Marien, Sofie, and Marc Hooghe. "Does political trust matter? An empirical investigation into the relation between political trust and support for law compliance." *European Journal of Political Research* 50.2 (2011): 267–291; Bjørnskov, Christian. "Determinants of generalized trust: A cross-country comparison." *Public Choice* 130 (2007): 1–21; Delhey, Jan, and Kenneth Newton. "Predicting cross-national levels of social trust: Global pattern or Nordic exceptionalism?" *European Sociological Review* 21.4 (2005): 311–327.

5 Dinesen, Peter Thisted, and Kim Mannemar Sønderskov. "Ethnic diversity and social trust." In *The Oxford handbook of social and political trust*, edited by Eric M. Uslaner, Oxford University Press, 2018: 175–204.

6 Coleman, Cynthia, and Lynne Freeman. "Cultural foundations of taxpayer attitudes to voluntary compliance." *Australian Tax Forum* 13 (1997): 311–336.

7 There are many studies in this tradition, for example: Coleman and Freeman. "Cultural foundations of taxpayer attitudes to voluntary compliance," 311–336.

8 Dineson, P., and Rene Bekkers. "The foundations of individuals' generalized social trust: A review." In *Trust in social dilemmas*, edited by Paul A. M. van Lange, Bettina Rockenbach, and Toshio Yamagishi, Oxford University Press, 2017: 77–100.

9 Yamagishi, Toshio, and Kaori Sato. "Motivational bases of the public goods problem." *Journal of Personality and Social Psychology* 50.1 (1986): 67–73.

the case of COVID-19 regulations, for example.[10] It was found that interpersonal trust served as a mediator between risk perception and self-restraint during the pandemic.[11] Tight cultures, characterized by strong norms, adherence to regulations, and a low tolerance for deviant behavior, have been associated with lower mortality rates during the pandemic.[12] However, it remains less clear whether a tight culture inherently fosters a sense of voluntary compliance. Recent research has investigated how cultural factors influenced people's willingness to voluntarily comply with COVID-19 regulations, exploring when and under what cultural conditions certain voluntary components are accepted and implemented.[13]

In the context of taxation, studies have suggested that a taxpayer's willingness to comply with regulations is linked to their trust in the government and their belief that the authorities have the right to monitor them. When there is a high level of trust in the authorities, taxpayers are more likely to have the intention to voluntarily pay taxes. Voluntary compliance arises from the taxpayer's willingness to cooperate effectively and fulfill both their moral and their civil obligations to contribute to the "public good."[14]

CULTURE AND PROSOCIAL BEHAVIOR

Contrary to what might be intuitively expected, it has been found that individualistic societies tend to trigger higher levels of prosocial behaviors rather than collectivist societies.[15] The longevity of cultural norms significantly influences their resistance to change, potentially affecting patterns of voluntary compliance. Importantly, these norms, which vary across countries, play a vital role in shaping prosocial behavior beyond mere legal obligations. Cross-cultural psychology research emphasizes that community norms, developed uniquely in different societies, can foster a culture that encourages voluntary actions that extend beyond legal requirements. This study shows that cultural dimensions are interrelated and together affect the likelihood of prosocial actions within a society.[16]

10 Yuan, Hang, et al. "Different roles of interpersonal trust and institutional trust in COVID-19 pandemic control." *Social Science & Medicine* 293 (2022): 1–10.

11 Diotaiuti, Pierluigi, et al. "Perception of risk, self-efficacy and social trust during the diffusion of COVID-19 in Italy." *International Journal of Environmental Research and Public Health* 18.7 (2021): 1–17.

12 Gelfand, Michele J., et al. "The relationship between cultural tightness–looseness and COVID-19 cases and deaths: A global analysis." *The Lancet Planetary Health* 5.3 (2021): e135–e144.

13 Besley, Timothy, and Chris Dann. "Why political trust and voluntary compliance have been key to government pandemic responsiveness in Europe." LSE European Politics and Policy (EUROPP) blog (2023).

14 Kirchler, Erich, and Ingrid Wahl. "Tax compliance inventory TAX-I: Designing an inventory for surveys of tax compliance." *Journal of Economic Psychology* 31.3 (2010): 331–346.

15 Luria, Gil, Ram A. Cnaan, and Amnon Boehm. "National culture and prosocial behaviors: Results from 66 countries." *Nonprofit and Voluntary Sector Quarterly* 44.5 (2015): 1041–1065.

16 Luria, Cnaan, and Boehm. "National culture and prosocial behaviors."

Norms that have developed in different countries can play a crucial role in cultivating a culture that promotes voluntary actions beyond legal obligations. This observation aligns with cross-cultural psychology research, which demonstrates that human behavior is significantly influenced not only by legal frameworks but also by community norms of prosocial behavior.[17]

COMPARING DIFFERENT COUNTRIES' PROSOCIAL BEHAVIOR

As discussed, it is widely acknowledged that culture exerts an influence on individuals' behavior.[18] Some studies show that the impact of national culture on behavior is greater than any organizational or environmental factor.[19] Researchers often use five measuring tools to conduct a societal culture study: Individualism; Power Distance; Uncertainty Avoidance; Masculinity versus Femininity; and Future Orientation.[20]

In addition, the cultural aspect of voluntary compliance shares similarities with a broader and well-known argument regarding the role of civic society in US democracy. Studies have shown that citizens' active involvement in family, school, work, voluntary associations, and religion has a notable impact on their participation as voters and protesters.[21] Generally, studies show that there has been a systematic decline in civic engagement among America's younger generations compared to previous ones. This decrease in social and political involvement is attributed to a combination of technological, social, and economic changes, such as increased media consumption, changing family structures, and greater economic pressures.[22] It has also been observed that since the mid 1960s (post-Vietnam War), Americans' distrust in their government has steadily increased. One study has suggested that the decline of trust in government and lack of confidence in leaders and institutions among the American people reflect a growing skepticism toward many forms of power.[23]

An Organisation for Economic Co-operation and Development (OECD) questionnaire that collected data from 140 countries on prosocial and antisocial behavior around the world found the highest levels of prosocial behavior in five Anglophone

[17] Bowles, Samuel, and Herbert Gintis. "The moral economy of communities: Structured populations and the evolution of pro-social norms." *Evolution and Human Behavior* 19.1 (1998): 3–25.

[18] House, Robert J. "Culture, leadership, and organizations: The GLOBE study of 62 societies." (2004); Ashkanasy, Neal M., Celeste P. M. Wilderom, and Mark F. Peterson, eds. *Handbook of organizational culture and climate*. SAGE, 2000.

[19] Gelfand, Michele J., Miriam Erez, and Zeynep Aycan. "Cross-cultural organizational behavior." *Annual Review of Psychology* 58.1 (2007): 479–514.

[20] Hofstede, G., and Hofstede, G. J. *Cultures and organizations: Software of the mind, revised and expanded* (2nd ed.). McGraw-Hill, 2005.

[21] Verba, Sidney. *Voice and equality: Civic voluntarism in American politics*. Harvard University Press, 1995.

[22] Putnam, Robert D. *Bowling alone: The collapse and revival of American community*. Simon & Schuster, 2000.

[23] Cook, Timothy E., and Paul Gronke. "The skeptical American: Revisiting the meanings of trust in government and confidence in institutions." *Journal of Politics* 67.3 (2005): 784–803.

countries (the United States, Ireland, Australia, New Zealand, and the United Kingdom).[24] In contrast, Chile and Mexico stood out as having high levels of antisocial behavior. Surprisingly, the Nordic countries, often considered leaders in various social indicators, showed comparatively average performance in this area. On the other hand, Mediterranean and Eastern European countries, including Israel, typically had lower levels of prosocial behavior.

However, it appears that there is no correlation between countries with high levels of prosocial behavior and low levels of antisocial behavior, or vice versa. It was also found that countries with higher income levels exhibited more prosocial behavior. However, it was found that the positive correlation between income inequality and antisocial behavior is weak.[25]

Social norms were found to have an impact on prosocial behavior. To comprehend the workings of law "outside of sanction or direct coercion," one must recognize that the law typically does not affect individual conduct in isolation from the social environment. For example, one study has shown that promoting seat belt use is more effective when addressing all relevant beliefs that shape people's attitudes and social norms about seat belts, rather than simply raising awareness about driving risks.[26] A study conducted in Turkey explored the reasons why a significant number of car passengers do not use seat belts despite their proven effectiveness in reducing injury severity during road traffic accidents. The study confirmed that attitudes and subjective norms have a positive correlation with the intention of using seat belts.[27]

Along those lines, Janice Nadler's research on the expressive function of the law suggests that, unlike the instrumental view of law, which sees legal systems as directly influencing autonomous individuals through incentives, the social groups perspective argues that legal compliance is primarily shaped by group dynamics.[28] This view contends that an individual's response to legal demands stems from the interplay of law, social influence, and motivational goals tied to in-group commitments. Law, in this context, operates expressively by shaping group norms and values, which in turn affect individual attitudes and behaviors. Thus, the relationship

[24] OECD. "Pro- and anti-social behaviour." In "Society at a Glance 2011." *OECD Social Indicators* (2011): 94–39. https://doi.org/10.1787/soc_glance-2011-en.

[25] Krueger, Robert F., Brian M. Hicks, and Matt McGue. "Altruism and antisocial behavior: Independent tendencies, unique personality correlates, distinct etiologies." *Psychological Science* 12.5 (2001): 397–402.

[26] Stasson, Mark, and Martin Fishbein. "The relation between perceived risk and preventive action: A within-subject analysis of perceived driving risk and intentions to wear seatbelts." *Journal of Applied Social Psychology* 20.19 (1990): 1541–1557.

[27] Şimşekoğlu, Özlem, and Timo Lajunen. "Social psychology of seat belt use: A comparison of theory of planned behavior and health belief model." *Transportation Research Part F: Traffic Psychology and Behaviour* 11.3 (2008): 181–191.

[28] Nadler, Janice. "Expressive law, social norms, and social groups." *Law & Social Inquiry* 42.1 (2017): 60–75.

between people and the law is mediated by the complexities of group life rather than through direct individual interaction.

CULTURE AND CIVIC ENGAGEMENT

Robert D. Putnam's study on the decline of social capital in the United States since the 1950s provides valuable insights into the changing nature of civic engagement and its impact on democracy. In *Bowling Alone: America's Declining Social Capital*, Putnam explores the concept of social capital, which encompasses networks, trust, and norms that facilitate effective collaboration among individuals. Putnam's comprehensive analysis reveals a significant decrease in face-to-face social interactions, which have been essential for constructing and sustaining the social fabric of American society. He contends that this decline has had a profound impact on active participation in civic life, a vital component of a thriving democracy and citizen engagement. The consequences of this decline are evident in various aspects of civic life, such as reduced voter turnout, lower attendance at public meetings, decreased participation in committees, and diminished political cooperation. Furthermore, Putnam highlights a growing public distrust toward the government, suggesting that while some of this may be attributed to political changes since the 1960s, there are more profound, systemic issues at play. Putnam's work underscores the critical role of social capital in maintaining a robust democratic society and highlights the need for renewed efforts to foster civic engagement. This research not only provides a framework for understanding the erosion of social ties but also serves as a call to action for policymakers and citizens alike to reinvigorate community connections.

THE IMPORTANCE OF CULTURE IN EXPLAINING VOLUNTARY COMPLIANCE

Our analysis examines how countries differ in their levels of trust, legitimacy, and compliance with specific policies, particularly in areas like taxation and environmental protection. For instance, a well-known cross-cultural study on punishment and cooperation found that during public goods games, countries with stronger rule of law traditions showed higher levels of cooperation among their citizens. The rule of law influenced two types of punishment: antisocial punishment (penalizing those who cooperate or contribute to the public good) and social punishment (penalizing those who don't cooperate or contribute). The effect of the rule of law on antisocial punishment was more prominent, which overshadowed its impact on social punishment.[29] In addition to the role of culture, we must also address whether policymakers can foster a shift in culture toward greater cooperation through softer regulatory approaches (this question will be discussed in the next chapter).

[29] Herrmann, Benedikt, Christian Thoni, and Simon Gächter. "Antisocial punishment across societies." *Science* 319.5868 (2008): 1362–1367.

Can We Change Culture?

In countries where cultural norms don't support trusting citizens, policymakers implementing trust-based regulations must consider whether their policies can catalyze cultural change. A key question emerges: Can adopting more trusting regulatory approaches gradually shift societal attitudes? If evolutionary and environmental factors shape these cultural mechanisms, we need to understand both the likelihood and conditions under which such changes might occur?[30]

The implications for regulators and policymakers extend far beyond merely matching regulatory approaches to existing cultural contexts, if indeed, there is a chance that their choices may actively reshape how society relates to state institutions. This transformative potential means policymakers must consider not only which regulatory approaches suit current cultural norms, but also how the widespread adoption of specific regulatory strategies might fundamentally alter the culture of compliance and institutional trust.

The scholarship on this issue presents a mixed perspective, with some studies supporting the ability to change culture and others concluding the opposite. Notably, in our discussions later in this chapter on the "Nordic model," we will explore research that highlights the potential for cultural change.[31] In contrast, we will also delve into studies supporting the idea that cultural norms may be traced back hundreds and even thousands of years in history. As a result, the ability to change them is far more limited.

Can Trust Mechanisms Change Culture?

The work of the famous Dutch social psychologist Geert Hofstede stands at the forefront of research on how cultural values persist over time. His influential studies on how culture shapes workplace behavior show that culture acts as a collective mindset, distinguishing members of one group from another.[32] His perspective on culture leans toward determinism, asserting that cultural influences are inescapable.

Hofstede, in collaboration with Michael Minkov and their research teams,[33] developed one of the earliest and most popular frameworks for measuring cultural differences between countries. This framework encompasses six dimensions: Power Distance,

30 Varnum, Michael E. W., and Igor Grossmann. "Cultural change: The how and the why." *Perspectives on Psychological Science* 12.6 (2017): 956–972.

31 Mjøset, Lars. "Nordic economic policies in the 1970s and 1980s." *International Organization* 41.3 (1987): 403–456, at 403.

32 Minkov, Michael, and Geert Hofstede. "Is national culture a meaningful concept? Cultural values delineate homogeneous national clusters of in-country regions." *Cross-Cultural Research* 46.2 (2012): 133–159.

33 Minkov, Michael, and Geert Hofstede. "The evolution of Hofstede's doctrine." *Cross Cultural Management: An International Journal* 18.1 (2011): 10–20.

Individualism, Uncertainty Avoidance, Masculinity, Long-Term Orientation, and Indulgence vs. Restraint.

Hofstede's framework, utilized in both academic and professional management settings throughout the world, represents what he terms "the software of the mind."[34] Through it, he seeks to explain how culture affects behavior. For example, according to Hofstede,[35] countries in which Romance languages (Italian, Spanish, and French) were spoken had scored significantly higher on Uncertainty Avoidance (preference for structure, clear rules, and predictability) than did countries in which Germanic languages (German, Dutch, and English) were spoken. It could be argued that the enduring influence of the Roman Empire's strict legal system led to a greater tendency among citizens many centuries later to avoid uncertainty. In addition, Romance-language-speaking countries scored higher on Power Distance compared to Germanic-language-speaking ones, suggesting greater acceptance of hierarchy and centralized authority among citizens of these countries. Both sets of results suggest a greater preference for command-and-control compliance than for intrinsically motivated voluntary compliance in countries speaking Romance languages. The World Values Survey measures additional sets of dimensions related to the work of Hofstede, Ronald Inglehart, and Wayne Baker. According to this survey, Romance-language-speaking countries tend to favor Traditional and Survival values while Germanic-language-speaking countries lean more toward Secular-Rational and Self-Expression values.[36] For example, Romance-language-speaking France, Italy, and Spain are located in the Catholic Europe cluster, which emphasizes traditional values, while Germanic-language-speaking Germany, the Netherlands, and Sweden are in the Protestant Europe cluster, characterized by secular-rational and self-expression-oriented values. This distinction seems relevant to understanding voluntary compliance, though further research is needed to confirm its impact. Importantly, the longevity of cultural norms plays a crucial role in determining how susceptible a culture is to change. Older, more established norms may be more resistant to modification, potentially affecting the dynamics of voluntary compliance. When examining some strands of the research on culture, one of the most significant findings is that many of the characteristics that differ between countries are nearly impossible to change. Indeed, as mentioned earlier in this chapter, some of Hofstede's research implies the continuing influence of some of Europe's Roman Empire ancestry.[37] If this is the case, what is the point of even

34 Hofstede, Geert. *Cultures and organizations* (rev. ed.). McGraw-Hill, 1997.

35 Hofstede, Geert. "Dimensionalizing cultures: The Hofstede model in context." *Online Readings in Psychology and Culture* 2.1 (2011): 1–26.

36 Inglehart, Ronald, and Wayne E. Baker. "Modernization, cultural change, and the persistence of traditional values." *American Sociological Review* 65.1 (2000): 19–51.

37 Hofstede. "Dimensionalizing cultures"; Minkov, Michael, and Geert Hofstede. "Nations versus religions: Which has a stronger effect on societal values?" *Management International Review* 54 (2014): 801–824.

arguing that adopting a trust-based regulatory approach might lead to a sustainable change in a country's culture?

Nonetheless, other scholars provide a different point of view,[38] suggesting that the idea of trust can be influenced both positively and negatively by more flexible elements, such as effective governance, population homogeneity, and equal income distribution. The presence of these factors helps explain the high trust levels in Nordic countries.[39] This perspective is consistent with research suggesting that the high levels of interpersonal trust observed in Scandinavian countries is a relatively recent phenomenon, emerging since around the mid 1980s, as these characteristics have become more prominent in these countries.[40]

CREATION OF A TRUST CULTURE IN THE NORDIC COUNTRIES

As research and surveys indicate, the Nordic countries serve as a dynamic model for building trust, offering an optimistic message regarding the efficacy of trust-enhancing approaches.[41] Nordic countries are characterized by a "virtue" cycle in which various key institutional and cultural indicators of a good society mutually reinforce each other. These include a well-functioning democracy, generosity, effective social welfare benefits, low levels of crime and corruption, and satisfied citizens who feel free and who trust each other and their governmental institutions. It has been suggested that the historical fact that the Nordic countries did not have an underclass of slaves or cheap labor imported from colonies may have played a role in shaping the development of their welfare societies.

In addition, Nicholas Charron and Bo Rothstein's research suggests that the impact of ethnic diversity on social trust diminishes significantly when factors related to the quality of government are considered. This indicates that in countries with high-quality institutions, like the Nordic countries, ethnic diversity may not affect social trust.[42] Trust in state institutions has been found to have a positive impact on social trust, although evidence for the reverse relationship is limited. A study from Denmark found that increased citizen trust in institutions was one of the factors contributing to higher social trust in the country.[43]

38 Norris, Pippa. *Democratic deficit: Critical citizens revisited*. Cambridge University Press, 2011.

39 Delhey and Newton. "Predicting cross-national levels of social trust."

40 Inglehart, Ronald, and Karlheinz Reif, eds. *Eurobarometer: The dynamics of European public opinion essays in honour of Jacques-René Rabier*. Springer, 2016.

41 Martela, Frank, et al. "The Nordic exceptionalism: What explains why the Nordic countries are constantly among the happiest in the world." *World Happiness Report* 2020 (2020): 129–146.

42 Charron, Nicholas, and Bo Rothstein. "Regions of trust and distrust: How good institutions can foster social cohesion" In *Bridging the prosperity gap in the EU*, edited by Ulf Bernitz, Moa Mårtensson, Lars Oxelheim and Thomas Persson, Edward Elgar Publishing, 2018: 220–242.

43 Sønderskov, Kim Mannemar, and Peter Thisted Dinesen. "Trusting the state, trusting each other? The effect of institutional trust on social trust." *Political Behavior* 38 (2016): 179–202.

Other studies show that cultural traditions evolve in response to new laws and policies, suggesting that by trusting their citizens more in their regulatory and compliance approaches, governments might spearhead cultural change. For example, a recent influential work concluded that the terms of pension plans may alter certain saving customs.[44] Another important study summarizing over half a century of cross-cultural research has shown specific changes at a group level in psychological and behavioral phenomena such as values, attention, and neural responses.[45]

POWER DISTANCE AND VOLUNTARY COMPLIANCE

A very relevant factor influencing the likelihood of voluntary compliance within a culture is the level of "Power Distance" in each country. High Power Distance countries are often associated with authoritarian values. In contrast, low Power Distance countries are less likely to emphasize obedience, thereby creating opportunities for other factors to play a role in compliance.[46] Although obedience is typically associated with positive attributes, such as honesty and civility, the relationship between obedience and these qualities is not always straightforward. Power Distance significantly influences societal expectations and behaviors. In high Power Distance societies, individuals readily accept a hierarchical order without questioning its justification and each person is expected to occupy a specific place within this hierarchy. Conversely, low Power Distance societies strive for equal power distribution, with members often challenging perceived inequalities.

This cultural dimension affects how people respond to authority and engage in collective behaviors. In low Power Distance contexts, individuals are more likely to express concerns about power dynamics, seeking consensus before conforming to group behaviors. Consequently, the willingness to comply voluntarily is closely tied to perceptions of equal treatment and respect. The impact of Power Distance on voluntary compliance is thus twofold: First, it shapes expectations about power distribution and the acceptability of hierarchies. Second, it influences individuals' demands for equal treatment, which in turn affects their likelihood of engaging in voluntary compliance.[47]

Power Distance is a crucial dimension of cultural variation that reflects how societies manage inequality. It measures the extent to which less powerful members of a society accept and expect unequal power distribution. This dimension significantly influences the likelihood of voluntary compliance within different cultural contexts.

[44] Bau, Natalie. "Can policy change culture? Government pension plans and traditional kinship practices." *American Economic Review* 111.6 (2021): 1880–1917.

[45] Varnum and Grossmann. "Cultural change."

[46] Brockner, Joel, et al. "Culture and procedural justice: The influence of power distance on reactions to voice." *Journal of Experimental Social Psychology* 37.4 (2001): 300–315.

[47] Fiala, Andrew. "The fragility of civility: Virtue, civil society, and tragic breakdowns of civility." *Dialogue and Universalism* 3 (2013): 109–122.

In the context of voluntary compliance, cultural attitudes toward hierarchical relationships play a crucial role, particularly through the lens of Power Distance. Research by De Meulenaer and colleagues (2018)[48] reveals that societies with high Power Distance, where hierarchical relationships are more readily accepted and justified, may facilitate easier persuasion for compliance with authority. This dynamic stands in marked contrast to low Power Distance societies, where individuals typically require substantial justification from authorities before accepting hierarchical structures. The degree of Power Distance in a given cultural context fundamentally shapes how hierarchical relationships are perceived and justified, as well as the level of justification expected from governmental authorities. These cultural variations in Power Distance have profound implications for governance strategies and policy implementation, as approaches that prove effective in high Power Distance societies may falter in low Power Distance contexts. This understanding suggests the critical importance of developing culturally tailored strategies for promoting voluntary compliance that accounts for these fundamental differences in how authority is perceived and accepted.

Cultural Orientation and Voluntary Compliance

Power Distance and the Collectivism–Individualism spectrum are two interrelated cultural factors that can significantly influence collective decision-making, such as the adoption of COVID-19 preventive measures.[49]

Furthermore, research suggests that in cultures with an individualistic orientation, people may prioritize personal convenience or preference over collective welfare, potentially leading to a reduced willingness to comply for the public good, such as wearing face masks during the pandemic.[50] However, individuals can still exhibit prosocial behavior through their commitment to personal values and fulfilling individual responsibilities.[51] Additionally, studies suggest that there is a correlation between individualism and both charitable donations and volunteer activity.[52]

48 De Meulenaer, Sarah, Patrick De Pelsmacker, and Nathalie Dens. "Power distance, uncertainty avoidance, and the effects of source credibility on health risk message compliance." *Health Communication* 33.3 (2018): 291–298.

49 Zhu, Nan, Skyler T. Hawk, and Judith G. Smetana. "The influence of power on US and Chinese individuals' judgments and reasoning about intersocietal conflicts." *Journal of Cross-Cultural Psychology* 51.1 (2020): 77–105.

50 Lu, Jackson G., Peter Jin, and Alexander S. English. "Collectivism predicts mask use during COVID-19." *Proceedings of the National Academy of Sciences* 118.23 (2021): 1–8.

51 Waterman, Alan S. "Individualism and interdependence." *American Psychologist* 36.7 (1981): 762–773; Adams, Gerald. "Alan S. Waterman: The psychology of individualism. New York: Praeger: 1984." *Journal of Adolescence* 9.1 (1986): 107—107.

52 Kemmelmeier, Markus, Edina E. Jambor, and Joyce Letner. "Individualism and good works: Cultural variation and volunteering across the United States." *Journal of Cross-Cultural Psychology* 37.3 (2006): 327–344.

Similarly, it has been found that people with an independent self-concept displayed a higher willingness to wear face masks.[53]

In the context of voluntary compliance with COVID-19 measures,[54] many required behaviors, such as social distancing and hygiene practices, are inherently collective. They depend on individuals' willingness to adopt strict practices while considering their broader community impact. The cultural dimension of collectivism versus individualism plays a significant role in shaping these behaviors.

Individuals in collectivist societies are generally better equipped to undertake collective action, as these societies place high value on unity and strong interpersonal connections within the wider community.[55] Collectivists are often more receptive to actions involving greater personal sacrifice if it improves the well-being of the greater society.

Conversely, in more individualistic societies, people may prioritize personal freedoms and individual needs over collective well-being. This cultural orientation can potentially impact the adoption of and compliance with community-focused health measures.[56]

It's important to note that while these cultural tendencies exist, individual behaviors can vary within both collectivist and individualistic societies. The degree of collectivism or individualism in society can influence, but does not entirely determine, individual responses to public health measures.

Masculine vs. Feminine Cultures and Voluntary Compliance

Gender identity appears to be an additional cultural dimension strongly associated with the likelihood of voluntary compliance in a country.

Research suggests that men and women often perceive their environment differently. Women frequently view themselves as part of a wider network of social relationships and feel a moral obligation to contribute to the network's well-being. In contrast, men tend to prioritize individual rights over group needs and view their environment as a system of hierarchical relationships.[57] Generally, it is commonly

53 Kemmelmeier, Markus, and Waleed A. Jami. "Mask wearing as cultural behavior: An investigation across 45 US states during the COVID-19 pandemic." *Frontiers in Psychology* 12 (2021): 1–24.

54 As discussed in Chapter 8.

55 Castle, Cassandra, Corrado Di Guilmi, and Olena Stavrunova. "Individualism and collectivism as predictors of compliance with COVID-19 public health safety expectations." *Ultimo, Australia: University of Technology Sydney* 2021/03 (2021).

56 Dheer, Ratan, Carolyn Egri, and Len J. Treviño. "A cross-cultural exploratory analysis of pandemic growth: The case of COVID-19." *Journal of International Business Studies* 52.9 (2021): 1871–1892.

57 Gilligan, Carol. *In a different voice: Psychological theory and women's development*. Harvard University Press, 1993; Rosener, J. B. "Ways women lead." *Harvard Business Review* 68.1 (1990): 119–125. See also the ensuing debate in the Epstein, Cynthia Fuchs. "Ways men and women lead." *Harvard Business Review* 69.1 (January–February 1991): 150–160.

believed that women show a greater interest in cooperation and working with others, particularly in countries with a high likelihood of voluntary cooperation.[58]

Broadening this perspective, Hofstede's cultural dimensions theory offers insights into how gender-related cultural traits might influence voluntary compliance. Hofstede distinguishes between national cultures based on Masculinity versus Femininity. This dimension reflects the overall "toughness" and competitiveness of society, with "masculine cultures" tending to be more aggressive and ambitious, while "feminine cultures" are typically more modest and nurturing.[59]

In masculine cultures, competition is viewed from a distributive perspective where the world is seen as consisting of winners and losers. Moreover, in these cultures, cooperative alliances are typically formed under the guise of a win-win situation.[60] This perspective on cooperation and competition could potentially impact attitudes toward voluntary compliance, especially in situations requiring collective action for the common good.

Interestingly, research indicates that entrepreneurs from more masculine and individualistic societies exhibit a lower appreciation for cooperative strategies compared to entrepreneurs from feminine and collectivist societies.[61] This finding suggests that the Masculinity–Femininity dimension of culture could play a role in shaping attitudes toward voluntary compliance and cooperative behaviors at a societal level.

GALLUP DATA ON CULTURAL DIFFERENCES

As could be seen from data from the Gallup World Poll as reported in the OECD publication,[62] it is possible to see the different dimensions of the relationship between culture and compliance. This data offers insights into the cultural and regulatory landscapes of these nations, highlighting differences in social behavior, trust levels, and environmental policies.

Prosocial behavior is represented as a percentage, indicating the proportion of the population engaging in altruistic or helpful actions. The United States leads with 60 percent, followed closely by the United Kingdom at 57 percent, while Greece shows the lowest rate at 13 percent.

[58] However, it should be noted that a careful meta-analysis on this very question in the context of social dilemmas didn't find an overall significant main effect. Balliet, Daniel, et al. "Sex differences in cooperation: A meta-analytic review of social dilemmas." *Psychological Bulletin* 137.6 (2011): 881.

[59] Doney, Patricia M., Joseph P. Cannon, and Michael R. Mullen. "Understanding the influence of national culture on the development of trust." *Academy of Management Review* 23.3 (1998): 601–620.

[60] Hamel, Gary, Yves L. Doz, and Coimbatore K. Prahalad. "Collaborate with your competitors and win." *Harvard Business Review* 67.1 (1989): 133–139.

[61] Steensma, H. Kevin, Louis Marino, and K. Mark Weaver. "Attitudes toward cooperative strategies: A cross-cultural analysis of entrepreneurs." *Journal of International Business Studies* 31 (2000): 591–609.

[62] OECD. "Pro- and anti-social behaviour."

The perception of voluntary environmental "codes of conduct" by citizens is also expressed as a percentage. Greece surprisingly tops this category at 59 percent, with Denmark following at 57 percent, suggesting strong environmental awareness among their populations.

Trust is measured on a scale where positive numbers indicate higher trust levels. The Netherlands shows the highest trust at 0.30, while Italy has the lowest at –0.7, indicating significant variations in social trust across these countries.

Social cohesion is measured on a scale up to 10, with higher numbers indicating stronger cohesion. The Netherlands leads with 7.15, while Israel has the lowest score at 4.29. International tax evasion is measured in billions of euros, with Italy showing the highest amount at 3.1 billion, while Denmark has the lowest at 0.2 billion.

The environmental regulatory regime is represented by an index, with the Netherlands having the strongest regime at 1.747 and Greece the weakest at –0.619.

PROSOCIAL BEHAVIOR ≠ ENVIRONMENTAL COMPLIANCE

As mentioned, opinions on a voluntary environmental "code of conduct" vary significantly among countries, as reflected in the rates of positive opinions ranging from high to low. Greece emerges as the leading nation, with 59 percent of its population holding a positive opinion. Following closely is Denmark, where 57 percent of the population expresses a positive opinion, followed by Austria with a 53 percent approval rate. The Netherlands also demonstrates significant support, as 50 percent of the respondents endorse this code of conduct. Italy, while still supportive, ranks lower, with 44 percent of its population expressing positive opinions toward voluntary environmental standards.

Examining both sources of information, it is apparent that there are diverse attitudes toward prosocial behavior and environmental awareness and no correlation seems to emerge between them. For example, the Netherlands has a high prosocial behavior rate (55 percent) but is not ranked high in environmental awareness relative to other countries. Denmark and Austria both demonstrate strong prosocial behavior (46 percent and 43 percent) and support for environmental codes (57 percent and 53 percent). In contrast, Greece has the lowest prosocial rate (13 percent) but the highest approval for environmental codes (59 percent), indicating that prosocial behavior does not necessarily predict environmental attitudes.[63]

CROSS-CULTURAL TRUST

The inconsistency among various measures available in cross-country datasets is not limited to tax morale; it is also evident in the context of trust. Countries that

[63] Based on OECD. "Pro- and anti-social behaviour." Data sourced from Gallup World Poll 2010.

score highly on certain social measures do not necessarily maintain this ranking across all metrics.

For instance, in our VCOMP (Voluntary Compliance Lab)[64] research group, high rates of trust are observed in countries such as Denmark and the Netherlands (0.30), and slightly lower ones in countries such as Austria (0.15), while countries such as Israel (-0.5), Italy (-0.7), and Greece (-0.35) demonstrate even lower levels of trust. At the upper end of the spectrum, in nations like Norway and Sweden, over 60 percent of respondents in the World Values Survey agree that most people can be trusted.

Data from European nations reveal a nuanced and somewhat inconsistent picture of institutional trust. Generally, people exhibit higher levels of trust in law enforcement compared to political and legal systems. Except for Switzerland, trust in the political system is notably low across all countries, significantly below the level of interpersonal trust. Conversely, there is a remarkably high level of confidence in the police, with the majority of European countries demonstrating greater trust in law enforcement than in fellow citizens.[65] On the opposite end, in countries such as Colombia, Brazil, Ecuador, and Peru, fewer than 10 percent of respondents share this belief in law enforcement.[66] Data from the United States suggests that people have less trust in each other now than they did in the 1980s.[67] This decline in interpersonal trust in the United States has been accompanied by a long-term reduction in public trust in government.[68]

High rates of social cohesion were shown in several countries, with Canada achieving the highest score (9.42), followed by the United States (8.34), the Netherlands (7.15), Denmark (7.08), Germany (7.0), Italy (6.55), and Austria (6.35). However, low rates of social cohesion were shown in Israel (4.29) and China (5.52), and the lowest score was given to Greece (5.39).[69]

CULTURE DYNAMICS

As mentioned previously, Hofstede's theory suggests that a culture may have deep historical roots, which can limit its capacity for change. However, some economists and political scientists believe that institutional design can influence the level of trust in a country. As mentioned, the transformation of Scandinavian countries in the twentieth century offers the most well-known example of such institutional

[64] Funded by the ERC: Advanced Grant VCOMP 101054656: www.voluntary-compliance-lab.org/.

[65] Haerpfer, Christian, et al. "World values survey wave 7 (2017–2020) cross-national data-set." (2020). www.worldvaluessurvey.org/WVSDocumentationWV7.jsp.

[66] Ortiz-Ospina, Esteban, and Max Roser. "Trust." (2016). https://ourworldindata.org/trust.

[67] The General Social Survey has been gathering information about trust attitudes since 1972.

[68] According to estimates compiled by the Pew Research Center since 1958.

[69] Foa, Roberto Stefan. "The economic rationale for social cohesion: The cross-country evidence" (2011) doi:10.17863/CAM.90182, roughly corresponds with their prosocial rates. See also www.oecd.org/development/pgd/46908575.pdf.

influence on cultural trust.[70] This change accompanied the enactment of their famous welfare systems and the ensuing reduction in inequality. Following these institutional changes, these countries soon vaulted to the top levels in many of the values related to solidarity and trust.

DEMOGRAPHICS OF HONESTY AND COOPERATION

In addition to culture, various other factors that have been described in the literature influence behaviors associated with voluntary compliance.[71] For example, Joshua Bourdage and colleagues (2018) suggested that age might affect honesty in job interviews.[72] According to their findings, older individuals may be less inclined to lie in job interviews because they possess more job knowledge and are perceived as more competent in their jobs. Allen Huffcutt and colleagues (2011) have argued that education is also relevant regarding honesty.[73] Similarly studying job applicants, they found that well-educated applicants are more likely to prioritize honesty in the context of demonstrating that they meet the job requirements. Additionally, factors like income, education, and age can predict how likely people are to believe they should deceive during interviews, as well as their confidence in their ability to do so successfully to improve their evaluation outcomes. In general, studies indicate that trust and cooperation vary with sex, schooling, age, household size, quality of living, and placement on a psychological cooperation scale.[74] Additionally, we have observed a correlation between prosocial behavior and several factors, such as home ownership, community homogeneity, past participation in community projects, the relationship between individuals and their neighbors, and community leadership.[75]

70 Gärtner, Svenja, and Svante Prado. "Unlocking the social trap: Inequality, trust and the Scandinavian welfare state." *Social Science History* 40.1 (2016): 33–62.

71 For a very recent contribution to the predictor of honesty and the relationship with compliance see Shalvi, S. et al. "The science of honesty-setting the agenda." *Advances in Experimental Social Psychology* (in press).

72 Bourdage, Joshua S., Nicolas Roulin, and Rima Tarraf. "'I (might be) just that good': Honest and deceptive impression management in employment interviews." *Personnel Psychology* 71.4 (2018): 597–632.

73 Huffcutt, Allen I., Chad H. Van Iddekinge, and Philip L. Roth. "Understanding applicant behavior in employment interviews: A theoretical model of interviewee performance." *Human Resource Management Review* 21.4 (2011): 353–367.

74 Sutter, Matthias, and Martin G. Kocher. "Trust and trustworthiness across different age groups." *Games and Economic Behavior* 59.2 (2007): 364–382; Ho, Jordan L., and Deborah Powell. "A test of expectancy theory and demographic characteristics as predictors of faking and honesty in employment interviews." *Personnel Assessment and Decisions* 7.2 (2021): 1–10; Croson, Rachel, and Uri Gneezy. "Gender differences in preferences." *Journal of Economic Literature* 47.2 (2009): 448–474.

75 Carpenter, Jeffrey P., Amrita G. Daniere, and Lois M. Takahashi. "Cooperation, trust, and social capital in Southeast Asian urban slums." *Journal of Economic Behavior & Organization* 55.4 (2004): 533–551.

Cultural variations within a nation can result from different communal identities or geographic factors. Studies have shown that foreign shoppers are more likely to engage in fraudulent behavior in grocery stores in urban centers compared to other neighborhoods. This pattern may reflect the reduced likelihood of repeated encounters in urban areas, demonstrating how environmental context can shape ethical decision-making.[76]

From various data sources which were accumulated during COVID,[77] analysis reveals an inverse relationship between interpersonal trust and excess mortality across countries. Poland shows the highest excess mortality (around 15) combined with low trust (about 1.3), while Spain and Portugal follow a similar pattern of high mortality and low trust.

In contrast, countries with higher interpersonal trust show lower excess mortality. Nordic nations, particularly Denmark and Norway, demonstrate the highest trust levels (around 1.8) alongside the lowest excess mortality scores (near 0 or slightly negative).

Some exceptions exist: The United States shows higher excess mortality than its trust level would suggest, while New Zealand achieved negative excess mortality despite moderate trust levels.

The Netherlands, Sweden, and Switzerland form a cluster characterized by high trust and low excess mortality, while Germany, Ireland, and Austria occupy middle positions on both scales. This pattern suggests that societies with higher interpersonal trust may be more resilient in managing mortality risks.

The data indicates that cultural background and interpersonal trust influence voluntary compliance, highlighting the importance of understanding cultural attitudes toward governance when developing compliance strategies.

CULTURE AND PUNISHMENT LIKELIHOOD

Important work carried out by Daniel Balliet and Paul Van Lange examines the relationship between society's cultural trust and punishment.[78] They show that punishment encourages people to contribute to public goods, but its effectiveness varies across different societies. The variation has been thought to depend on the levels of trust within these societies and how punishment, as a means of enforcing social norms, encourages cooperative behavior. Some theories suggest that punishment is more likely to encourage cooperation in low-trust societies, where people might contribute to public goods only if they face significant incentives or consequences.

[76] Vranka, Marek, et al. "Cheating customers in grocery stores: A field study on dishonesty." *Journal of Behavioral and Experimental Economics* 83 (2019): 1–7.

[77] See generally, Casey, Bernard H. "COVID-19: Did higher trust societies fare better?" *Discover Social Science and Health* 3.1 (2023): 1–17.

[78] Balliet, Daniel, and Paul A. M. Van Lange. "Trust, punishment, and cooperation across 18 societies: A meta-analysis." *Perspectives on Psychological Science* 8.4 (2013): 363–379.

Conversely, others have argued that punishment is more effective in high-trust societies, where people tend to cooperate and support public interests while being willing to punish those who do not. This raises an important question: Is punishment more effective in fostering cooperation in societies with high trust or low trust? To tackle this issue, in their comprehensive meta-analysis they reviewed 83 studies, including 7,361 participants from 18 different societies, examining the impact of punishment on public goods dilemmas.[79]

Their study concluded that punishment generally has a positive effect on cooperation, with its effectiveness varying based on factors such as group size, punishment severity, and communication opportunities. Although it may seem more logical to assume that punishment is more successful in countries with low trust levels, some meta-analyses indicate the opposite: In societies where trust is high, punishment is more common. This is likely because high-trust societies tend to view norm enforcement actions positively. In these societies, people often see punishment as a necessary step toward the common good, rather than a personal attack.

This openness to punishment can increase its effectiveness in promoting adherence to social norms and promoting collective well-being, which can encourage further cooperative behavior. In contrast, in low-trust societies, punitive measures might be viewed with skepticism or hostility, reducing their ability to encourage cooperation. The importance of societal trust is emphasized in the Balliet and colleagues' studies, as it acts as a foundational element that affects the effectiveness of norm enforcement mechanisms, such as punishment.

The findings clearly show that punishment significantly enhances cooperation in high-trust societies more than in low-trust ones.[80] Furthermore, beyond formal punishment drawing on the work of scholars like Simon Gächter and others,[81] who have explored social punishment, we can anticipate that when regulators allow for flexibility, individuals are less likely to shirk their responsibilities due to the high probability of social enforcement.

VOLUNTARISM VS. VOLUNTARY COMPLIANCE

It is possible to expect that there would be a correlation between people who voluntarily comply with laws and their willingness to do things for others that are not required. Generally, there are different varieties of prosocial behaviors and it's usually measured by three aspects: volunteering for organizations, donating to charities, and helping strangers.[82] It appears that people with higher social and economic

79 Balliet and Van Lange. "Trust, punishment, and cooperation across 18 societies."

80 Balliet and Van Lange. "Trust, punishment, and cooperation across 18 societies."

81 Herrmann, Thoni, and Gächter. "Antisocial punishment across societies."

82 Jones, Keely S. "Giving and volunteering as distinct forms of civic engagement: The role of community integration and personal resources in formal helping." *Nonprofit and Voluntary Sector Quarterly* 35.2 (2006): 249–266; Putnam. *Bowling alone*; Verba. *Voice and equality*.

status tend to volunteer more.[83] Religious participation is also assumed to enhance prosocial behaviors.[84] Other explanations that have been advanced for prosocial behavior include trust, altruism, age, family structure, norms, solicitation, response to disaster or crisis, and more.[85]

CROSS-CULTURAL HETEROGENEITY IN COMPLIANCE

A study conducted in Sweden examined how reduced enforcement affects the extent to which regulated actors comply with government regulations. It unexpectedly found that removing an unenforced law had a negative impact on employers' vacancy-posting behavior. This finding contradicts the emphasis placed on the role of effective punishment in standard deterrence models of regulatory compliance, highlighting instead the significance of organizational factors such as culture and norms.[86]

Studies of organizational culture show how it influences compliance behavior. For example, research comparing different government sectors found that local government employees, who typically work in environments with stronger law-abiding cultures, were more likely to follow regulations even without enforcement than their counterparts in central government. This is particularly noticeable in the context of advertising job vacancies.[87] Further analyses has shown that local governments characterized by a more law-abiding organizational culture and stronger commitment to social responsibility are more likely to comply with regulations that are not enforced.[88]

DOES POLARIZATION THREATEN VOLUNTARY COMPLIANCE?

In a work in progress with Tom Tyler and Libby Maman,[89] we investigated how polarization and extreme ideology affect trust, cooperation, and the effectiveness

83 Wilson, John. "Volunteering." *Annual Review of Sociology* 26.1 (2000): 215–240.

84 Bekkers, René, and Pamala Wiepking. "Who gives? A literature review of predictors of charitable giving part one: Religion, education, age and socialization." *Voluntary Sector Review* 2.3 (2011): 337–365; Musick, Marc A., John Wilson, and William B. Bynum Jr. "Race and formal volunteering: The differential effects of class and religion." *Social Forces* 78.4 (2000): 1539–1570; Putnam, Robert D., and David E. Campbell. *American grace: How religion divides and unites us*. Simon & Schuster, 2012.

85 Bekkers, René, and Pamala Wiepking. "A literature review of empirical studies of philanthropy: Eight mechanisms that drive charitable giving." *Nonprofit and Voluntary Sector Quarterly* 40.5 (2011): 924–973; Smith, Joanne R., and Andreè McSweeney. "Charitable giving: The effectiveness of a revised theory of planned behaviour model in predicting donating intentions and behaviour." *Journal of Community & Applied Social Psychology* 17.5 (2007): 363–386.

86 Cronert, Axel. "When the paper tiger bites: Evidence of compliance with unenforced regulation among employers in Sweden." *Regulation & Governance* 16.4 (2022): 1141–1159.

87 Cronert. "When the paper tiger bites."

88 See Cronert. "When the paper tiger bites."

89 Maman, Libby, Yuval Feldman, and Tom Tyler. "Polarization and voluntary compliance: The impact of ideological extremity on the effectiveness of self-regulation." Available at SSRN 4822965 (2024). https://onlinelibrary.wiley.com/doi/10.1111/rego.70020.

of self-regulatory tools in governance. We have used data from the World Value Survey and the European Social Survey.[90]

Contrary to initial expectations, holding extreme ideological views did not necessarily reduce trust. Right-wing views were associated with increased trust in institutions while left-wing views appeared to have no significant impact on trust.

The study shows that ideological extremism can significantly affect how authority is perceived. Specifically, the study found that left-wing extremism increased the significance of trust in legal authorities when deciding to comply. On the other hand, right-wing extremism has resulted in a reduction in the significance of trust in legal authorities. At the aggregate level, countries with higher levels of left-wing extremism showed a stronger correlation between trust in legal authorities and cooperation; on the other hand, countries with a higher degree of right-wing extremism showed a weaker correlation. Regarding cooperative behavior, an association was found between left-wing extremity and increased cooperation, while right-wing extremity showed a similar trend.

Finally, we examined whether the political party in power had an impact on this relationship and discovered that individuals with extreme views placed a greater emphasis on this factor when making decisions regarding trust and compliance. Consistent with our expectations, extremity reduced the willingness to trust and show deference to "others."

According to these findings, polarization and extremism may not directly erode trust, but they can make self-regulation and voluntary compliance more vulnerable to changes in trust levels. Our study found that extremism does not adversely affect trust, but it does alter the dynamics of authority, where the relationship between individual trust and cooperation intensifies, making cooperation more dependent on the perceptions of the government.

This heightened sensitivity could potentially jeopardize the effectiveness of self-regulatory measures in highly polarized societies, especially if trust in the government were to decline. Our analysis also reveals significant overall differences between left- and right-wing ideologies. In extreme left-wing societies, trust plays a crucial role, whereas extreme right-wing societies tend to place less emphasis on trust. Thus, our study suggests that policymakers in polarized societies who are considering self-regulatory tools should be aware of the varying effects of left- and right-wing extremism on the importance of trust in decisions related to compliance and cooperation.

When we look at Niklas Luhmann's work and what we've discussed about trust and social capital,[91] we see a striking difference in how trust works in small communities versus big cities. In small villages, trust tends to develop naturally – people know their neighbors, understand who's reliable, and share common values. This

90 www.worldvaluessurvey.org/wvs.jsp; www.europeansocialsurvey.org/.

91 Luhmann, Niklas. "Familiarity, confidence, trust: Problems and alternatives." *Trust: Making and Breaking Cooperative Relations* 6.1 (2000): 94–107.

fits with what we've seen about how tight-knit communities build trust through day-to-day interactions and shared expectations.

The story is quite different in urban areas, where we often don't know the people around us personally. Here, the power of reputation isn't as strong and building trust becomes more complicated. As we explored earlier when discussing modern society's challenges, we need to create systems that help us figure out who we can rely on in specific situations, even when we don't know them personally.

This difference between urban and rural settings really brings home one of the main challenges in encouraging voluntary compliance in today's diverse and complex societies. It shows just how important it is to build institutions and norms that can help strangers trust and work together – essentially trying to create the same kind of trust that naturally exists in smaller communities.

SUMMARY AND CONCLUSION

This chapter has explored the complex relationship between culture and voluntary compliance across different societies. Several key themes and findings emerged in this chapter. First, cultural dimensions: Hofstede's cultural dimensions, particularly Power Distance, Individualism–Collectivism, and Masculinity–Femininity, appear to significantly influence propensities for voluntary compliance. Low Power Distance, individualistic, and feminine cultures tend to exhibit higher levels of voluntary compliance and prosocial behavior.[92]

Second, the relationship between trust and social capital: Societies with higher levels of interpersonal and institutional trust generally demonstrate greater voluntary compliance. The "Nordic model" exemplifies how trust can be cultivated through effective governance and social policies, leading to increased cooperation.[93]

Third, the ability to change culture – cultural malleability: While some cultural traits appear deeply rooted, evidence suggests that cultural change is possible, as demonstrated by the relatively recent increases in trust and social cohesion in Nordic countries. This offers hope for the potential of policy interventions to shape cultural norms over time.[94]

Fourth, when focusing on cross-cultural variation it is important to account also for heterogeneity within cultures. Significant variation exists within cultures regarding compliance behaviors. Factors such as education, age, and socioeconomic status interact with cultural norms to influence individual propensities for voluntary compliance.[95]

92 Hofstede. "Dimensionalizing cultures," 8.

93 Sønderskov, Kim Mannemar, and Peter Thisted Dinesen. "Danish exceptionalism: Explaining the unique increase in social trust over the past 30 years." *European Sociological Review* 30.6 (2014): 782–795.

94 Varnum and Grossmann. "Cultural change."

95 Carpenter, Daniere, and Takahashi. "Cooperation, trust, and social capital in Southeast Asian urban slums"; Luria, Cnaan, and Boehm. "National culture and prosocial behaviors."

Fifth, the interplay of formal and informal institutions: The effectiveness of formal rules and enforcement mechanisms is heavily moderated by cultural norms and informal institutions. Understanding this interplay is crucial for designing effective compliance strategies.[96]

Sixth, a crucial observation is that while trust is generally considered more important for voluntary compliance than for command-and-control approaches, the effectiveness of punitive measures in promoting cooperation varies across cultures. Interestingly, we have reviewed research that high-trust societies tend to respond more positively to punishment than low-trust ones, challenging the intuitive assumption about the relationship between trust and enforcement strategies.[97]

In conclusion, while culture plays a significant role in shaping voluntary compliance, it is neither deterministic nor immutable. Policymakers seeking to enhance voluntary compliance must consider the cultural context in which they operate, recognizing both the constraints and opportunities it presents. The success of the Nordic model suggests that trust-building measures and inclusive governance can, over time, foster a culture more conducive to voluntary compliance.

However, there is no one-size-fits-all approach. Strategies that work in high-trust, individualistic societies may be less effective or even counterproductive in low-trust, collectivist contexts. Thus, a nuanced, culturally informed approach is necessary, combining elements of trust-building, appropriate enforcement mechanisms, and targeted interventions that align with local cultural values and norms.

Future research on culture and compliance should focus on identifying specific policy levers that can effectively shape cultural norms toward greater voluntary compliance while respecting the diversity of cultural contexts. Additionally, more cross-cultural comparative studies are needed to better understand how different aspects of culture interact with various regulatory approaches.

[96] Helmke, Gretchen, and Steven Levitsky. *Informal institutions and comparative politics: A research agenda*. Edward Elgar Publishing, 2012.

[97] Balliet and Van Lange. "Trust, punishment, and cooperation across 18 societies."

7

Technology, Nudges, Reputation, and Voluntary Compliance

INTRODUCTION

This chapter explores whether technology can be used to enhance noncoercive compliance by creating more effective reputational mechanisms and technological nudges. The discussion focuses on two main questions about technology usage. We first ask whether it is possible to monitor and enforce regulations while minimizing the impact of crowding out, at least as being subjectively perceived by the individual. The second question is whether technology can help identify which parts of the population can be trusted to comply voluntarily; a concept related to differentiated trust, as we have explored earlier in this book. It is important to note that, on the surface, the second goal may appear to resemble the Chinese social credit system (SCS) that seeks to exploit technology in order to enable the state to monitor and control people's social behavior (see the section "China's Social Credit System: Trustworthiness"). However, our focus on technology aims for quite a different situation, as we are looking for ways in which the state can become less coercive and more trusting toward more people.

Generally speaking, using technology to enhance compliance could lead to two developments. On the one hand, improved technological monitoring could reduce the need to rely on people's voluntary compliance. By providing clear instructions and analyzing behavioral patterns, this technology could complement research on personalization and technology-based enforcement.[1] This could potentially facilitate various types of cooperation among people, which could reduce or eliminate the need for state monitoring or the use of sanctions as part of a command-and-control approach.

[1] Porat, Ariel, and Lior Jacob Strahilevitz. "Personalizing default rules and disclosure with big data." *Michigan Law Review* 112 (2013): 1417–1478. Some workplaces use wearable wireless sensors that relay data to algorithms in order to emotionally monitor their employees. By tracking employees' emotional states, managers can analyze the effectiveness of company policies and procedures. In China, brain surveillance is conducted without consent. See Nelson, J. S. "Management culture and surveillance." *Seattle University Law Review* 43 (2019): 631–682.

On the other hand, technology can help foster a more trusting relationship between citizens and the state, allowing officials to grant people greater discretion while avoiding direct monitoring of their activities. By using personalized data on past behavior, as discussed in the work with Aronson and Lobel on trust-based regulation, the state can achieve a balance between allowing greater freedom for more people without harming those who are less deserving of this trust.[2]

Research conducted in the field of algorithmic management has produced mixed results regarding the potential crowding-out effect of rating and monitoring procedures.[3] This poses a challenge to the idea that technology can enhance intrinsically motivated compliance, as these procedures may only minimally reduce the need for state-imposed sanctions. While it is true that technology can replace certain forms of enforcement, much of the current research suggests that it may also lead to alienation among people.[4] Therefore, in this chapter, we will examine the potential pitfalls of using technology as a substitute for state enforcement.

THE OVER-MONITORING DILEMMA

As noted, the primary challenge in using technology is determining whether we can achieve a high level of monitoring that renders the need to trust people unnecessary by enabling us to monitor nearly all actions individuals take. As we have argued, this new ability of the state could have divergent implications. It could either lead toward perfect monitoring, which would eliminate the need for trust, or it could allow the state to have faith in individuals whose past actions have been proven trustworthy. At the same time, in our normative analysis, we need to acknowledge that there is no such thing as perfect technological monitoring, at least not yet. This due to several aspects: First, people are not being monitored all the time; and second, there are instances where strict compliance is essential, but monitoring compliance can prove to be challenging for the state without violating privacy rights. For example, in the context of COVID, even the states that allowed themselves to use rather intrusive technology, such as contact tracing, could not monitor how people behaved in their own homes, where much of the virus's spread occurred.[5] Therefore, the state found it easier to monitor areas where voluntary compliance posed less of a problem, as it was epidemiologically less risky (e.g., open-air public

[2] Feldman, Yuval, Orly Lobel, and Ori Aronson. "The behavioral challenges of trust-based regulation: Navigating the complexities of past behavior as a predictor." Available at SSRN 5117987 (2025). https://papers.ssrn.com/sol3/papers.cfm?abstract_id=5117987.

[3] Dickinson, David, and Marie-Claire Villeval. "Does monitoring decrease work effort? The complementarity between agency and crowding-out theories." *Games and Economic Behavior* 63.1 (2008): 56–76.

[4] Rowe, Frantz, Ojelanki Ngwenyama, and Jean-Loup Richet. "Contact-tracing apps and alienation in the age of COVID-19." *European Journal of Information Systems* 29.5 (2020): 545–562.

[5] See, for example, www.ox.ac.uk/news/2020-09-03-new-research-shows-tracing-apps-can-save-lives-all-levels-uptake; www.bundesregierung.de/breg-de/themen/corona-warn-app/corona-warn-app-englisch.

spaces). It was much more difficult for the state to enforce COVID regulations in closed spaces where more of the virus transfer could happen.[6] The need for voluntary compliance is especially important in areas where enforcement, especially technological enforcement, is most difficult.

One of the concerns we have about voluntary compliance is related to the need to convince people who are not initially supportive of the government's policy to act in a trustworthy manner. This process may undermine people's autonomy and it should be compared to the negative impact that algorithmic regulation can have on autonomy. Therefore, the comparison between the two approaches should focus on which approach is more detrimental to people's freedom of choice in deciding whether to comply with state laws and regulations. The comparison becomes even more complex when considering the role of technology, including big data approaches, in identifying people who may not need convincing, as their behavior should influence the decision between a technology-based approach and a trust-based approach. For those individuals, regulations based on trust – a concept that was explained in more detail in Chapter 4 – do not require any internalization process. Therefore, such people may find the use of technology far less desirable.

In this chapter, we will explore several critical aspects of the interaction between technology and voluntary compliance. Technology fundamentally shapes the relationship between citizens and government, sometimes constraining human decision-making flexibility. In traditional human-mediated interactions, inconsistent treatment based on personal characteristics may be more prevalent and harder to trace compared to technological solutions.

The advancement of technological enforcement capabilities has paradoxically increased the importance of voluntary compliance, while simultaneously enabling governments to differentiate their approach based on individuals' compliance histories. This development aligns with a broader trend toward personalized regulation, where technological solutions facilitate more individualized regulatory approaches that better align with personal preferences and circumstances.

Furthermore, technological progress has enhanced the ability to design and implement sophisticated incentive systems, creating new pathways for encouraging voluntary compliance. These technological innovations in incentive design may foster the long-term internalization of compliant behavior, potentially transforming temporary compliance into sustained voluntary cooperation. The combination of improved enforcement capabilities, personalization, and sophisticated incentive systems creates new opportunities for promoting and sustaining voluntary compliance while addressing traditional challenges in regulatory implementation.

[6] For the general problem of enforcement focusing on the wrong place, see Feldman, Yuval, and Yotam Kaplan. "Ethical blind spots and regulatory traps: On distorted regulatory incentives, behavioral ethics & legal design." In *Law and economics of regulation*, edited by Klaus Mathis and Avishalom Tor, Springer International Publishing, 2021: 37–54.

TECH-ENABLED CIVIC ENGAGEMENT

Extensive research in the intersection of technology and governance has focused on e-government, a relatively new mode of citizen-to-government contact that takes advantage of information and communications technologies. Similarly, Im and colleagues (2014)[7] investigated the impact of internet use on government trust and citizen compliance in South Korea. They found that increased internet use led to decreased trust and compliance, but e-government programs could effectively counter these problems.

The success of e-government is based on governments' trust in their citizens and on how citizens view the government in terms of their technological experience when working with the government.[8] Findings suggest that although e-government may help improve citizens' confidence in an agency's future performance, it does not necessarily result in greater satisfaction with interaction with an agency, nor does it correlate with greater overall trust in the federal government.[9] To the best of our knowledge, most current research in these areas focuses on ethical issues related to the technological monitoring of citizens as well as the extent to which citizens are satisfied with the more efficient technological services being offered by governments.[10]

TECHNOLOGY: MORE MONITORING, LESS TRUST?

In many ways, the combined role of law and technology revolves around questions of differentiated trust and people's ability to trust technology. On one hand, as mentioned in the introduction to this chapter, technology is likely to reduce the incentive for people to cheat, ultimately resulting in reduced reliance on the government to trust in people's compliance.[11] A classic example of how technology improves monitoring is using cash. From a tax evasion standpoint, the cash economy is the most difficult to monitor. Several methods are being utilized to replace cash with more traceable alternatives, although this does not consider

7 Im, Tobin, et al. "Internet, trust in government, and citizen compliance." *Journal of Public Administration Research and Theory* 24.3 (2014): 741–763.

8 Welch, Eric W., Charles C. Hinnant, and M. Jae Moon. "Linking citizen satisfaction with e-government and trust in government." *Journal of Public Administration Research and Theory* 15.3 (2005): 371–391.

9 Morgeson III, Forrest V., David VanAmburg, and Sunil Mithas. "Misplaced trust? Exploring the structure of the e-government–citizen trust relationship." *Journal of Public Administration Research and Theory* 21.2 (2011): 257–283.

10 Asgarkhani, Mehdi. "The effectiveness of e-service in local government: A case study." *Electronic Journal of e-Government* 3.4 (2005): 157–166.

11 Bamberger, Kenneth A. "Technologies of compliance: Risk and regulation in a digital age." *Texas Law Review* 88 (2010): 669–739.

newer advancements such as Bitcoin, which are even more challenging to monitor by authorities.

As another example, compared to traditional taxi drivers those who work for Uber or other ridesharing apps are less likely to commit tax fraud when their earnings are received through the app.[12] Similarly, renting through booking websites like Airbnb is less likely to be vulnerable to tax evasion.[13] Furthermore, services like Airbnb, Uber, and Lyft not only help to reduce tax evasion but also offer ways for the public to determine whom they can trust based on social reputation and social-reporting systems.[14] For one, Alm's study examines the effects of technological progress on tax avoidance and evasion.[15] This work looks at these effects on individual taxpayers and the state, and it finds that technology has two effects: the first is that it increases the amount of information taken in by the government which makes tax evasion more difficult as the state can better combat tax evasion. While this means that most taxpayers will evade taxes less, this paper argues that technology also allows for a small group of taxpayers to more easily avoid taxes. This paper correlates wealth with the ability to do this, which means that in a more unequal society the wealthy can more easily avoid taxation.

SMART MONITORING REDUCES ENFORCEMENT

The goal of technology is to simplify the process by which states can have confidence in people, not necessarily because they inherently trust them, but because an algorithm suggests that less strict enforcement may be appropriate due to the fact that everything is being recorded. With the various privacy concerns, can we reduce the negative effects of technological surveillance? Can we raise the threshold for minor offenses so that they can be more easily overlooked? For example, the noncash shift may change the need for trust in taxation, as people might have harder time evading taxation, not to mention the even more dramatic blockchain revolution.[16] Similarly, we must ask ourselves if we are better off with contact-tracing apps than with epidemiological interviews with people who got infected?[17]

[12] https://morganjones.co.uk/2022/09/22/tax-dodging-taxi-drivers/.

[13] Alm, James. "Tax evasion, technology, and inequality." *Economics of Governance* 22.4 (2021): 321–343.

[14] Hawlitschek, Florian, Benedikt Notheisen, and Timm Teubner. "The limits of trust-free systems: A literature review on blockchain technology and trust in the sharing economy." *Electronic Commerce Research and Applications* 29 (2018): 50–63.

[15] Alm. "Tax evasion, technology, and inequality."

[16] Mohanta, Bhabendu Kumar, Soumyashree S. Panda, and Debasish Jena. "An overview of smart contract and use cases in blockchain technology." In *2018 9th International Conference on Computing, Communication and Networking Technologies (ICCCNT)*, IEEE, 2018: 1–4.

[17] Daisuke, Takagi, Amemiya Mamoru, and Shimada Takahito. "What do security cameras provide for society? The influence of cameras in public spaces in Japan on perceived neighborhood cohesion and trust." *Journal of Experimental Criminology* 18.1 (2022): 129–147.

REGULATING SITUATIONS VS. REGULATING PEOPLE

The recent s-frame paper by Nick Chapter and George Lowenstein supports the view that technological advancements may reduce the need to change intrinsic motivation.[18] When discussing corporate climate change responsibility, the authors advocate prioritizing technologies that reduce the burden on individuals to address environmental challenges. Digital technologies could potentially replace traditional trust-based compliance mechanisms. With enhanced technological enforcement capabilities, governments may be able to move beyond questions of trustworthiness and focus instead on improving the quality of compliance outcomes, as explored in Chapter 1.

PROPORTIONALITY AND BEHAVIORAL BIG DATA

In a work in progress with Ori Aronson and Orly Lobel,[19] we study the concept of differentiated trust – a concept related to using people's past behavior – to decide whether trust-based regulatory attempts will be successful. In that paper, we analyze whether it's constitutional to treat people differently based on how their group has behaved in the past, rather than looking at their individual track record. This raises important questions about using group-level data to make trust-based decisions about individuals. We also examined how AI-powered data analytics can transform regulatory approaches to assessing individual and group trustworthiness. While traditional regulatory systems often rely on information concealment to protect privacy and equality, we propose that advanced algorithmic capabilities offer a new paradigm.

This new approach, sometimes called "fairness through awareness," leverages AI's sophisticated pattern recognition to process multiple data points while still protecting individual privacy. However, this capability raises important ethical questions: How do we ensure these systems promote genuine fairness rather than amplifying existing biases? How do we manage the risks of privacy breaches and discriminatory outcomes?

A key example is the use of machine learning to create individual "compliance scores" by aggregating various behavioral indicators. These scores typically evaluate factors such as accuracy of reporting, legal compliance, and ethical conduct. While such comprehensive profiling could enhance regulatory effectiveness, it also raises significant social and ethical concerns. For instance, how might minor norm violations affect an individual's overall trustworthiness assessment? And how do we ensure these scoring systems remain transparent and accountable?

18 Chater, Nick, and George Loewenstein. "The i-frame and the s-frame: How focusing on individual-level solutions has led behavioral public policy astray." *Behavioral and Brain Sciences* 46 (2023): 1–26.

19 Feldman, Lobel, and Aronson. "The behavioral challenges of trust-based regulation."

Group-level trust assessments analyze patterns between regulatory compliance and group characteristics. While this data-driven approach aims for objectivity, it presents serious ethical challenges. Historical biases in data collection and interpretation could lead to discriminatory outcomes. For example, if past enforcement disproportionately targeted certain communities, these patterns might be incorrectly interpreted as reflecting inherent compliance differences. Moreover, automated systems might amplify existing socioeconomic disparities by applying stricter scrutiny to already disadvantaged groups, creating a self-reinforcing cycle of distrust. In my work with Kaplan,[20] we addressed an important gap in big data research – its potential role in regulatory decision-making. We examined how big data analytics could help identify trustworthy individuals in trust-based regulatory systems, using the COVID-19 pandemic as a key example. During the pandemic's early stages, governments needed to assess whether the public would voluntarily follow safety protocols rather than requiring strict enforcement.

Big data analysis offers unprecedented capabilities to differentiate between individual and group behaviors, enhancing our ability to predict voluntary compliance in trust-based regulatory systems. This predictive power becomes especially valuable in regulatory approaches that rely less on coercion and more on cooperation. Trust relationships are inherently reciprocal – when regulators demonstrate trust in the public, individuals often respond with increased trustworthy behavior. While this reciprocal dynamic is widely recognized, the empirical evidence examining how suspicion affects individual behavior remains limited.

This section examines the ethical dimensions of using data-driven approaches to regulate trust. Our analysis focuses on how differentiated regulatory strategies, based on data analytics, raise fundamental ethical questions.

Several key considerations emerge: First, how should we interpret and act upon statistical measures of trust? Second, what threshold of statistical significance justifies policy interventions? Third, what level of correlation between data points should be required before implementing differential treatment?

The justification for using predictive analytics varies by policy context. For instance, stronger privacy intrusions might be warranted for national security purposes than for improving tax collection efficiency. This aligns with the constitutional proportionality doctrine, which permits greater infringement on individual rights when pursuing objectives of higher public importance.[21]

Overall, the differentiated trust work in progress with Aronson and Lobel highlights the key ethical concerns related to differentiated lawmaking and regulation, particularly concerning trust regulation based on data. In our data-driven world, policymakers

[20] Feldman, Yuval, and Yotam Kaplan. "Big data and bounded ethicality." *Cornell Journal of Law and Public Policy* 29 (2019): 39–94.

[21] Jackson, Vicki C. "Constitutional law in an age of proportionality." *Yale Law Journal* 124 (2014): 3094–3197.

and regulators must be able to navigate these complexities to promote fairness, transparency, and equity. We explore real-world examples, such as predictive systems that identify potential harassers and cases like COMPASS (Cooperation on Migration and Partnerships to Achieve Sustainable Solutions) to gain insight into the ethical and regulatory challenges of trust mechanisms driven by algorithmic data.[22] This discussion provides an apt approach to exploring the country that is most commonly associated with data-driven regulations, particularly in ethical contexts – China.

CHINA'S SOCIAL CREDIT SYSTEM: TRUSTWORTHINESS

The SCS in China provides an important example of how technology can be integrated into regulatory governance. The system combines elements of both automated monitoring and behavioral incentives to promote compliance with legal and social norms.

Initial implementations of the SCS in selected cities integrated traditional financial credit scoring with broader behavioral metrics. The system uses both positive and negative incentives to encourage certain behaviors, offering insights into how technological tools can influence social conduct within specific cultural contexts.[23] This approach reflects a unique cultural context where trust in central government institutions remains relatively high, as evidenced by Kostka's survey findings.[24]

Sheng Zou's study on algorithmic ratings in China argues that the SCS exemplifies the reduction of social issues to numerical metrics, potentially undermining fundamental moral values like trust and trustworthiness.[25] This aligns with our broader discussion on the challenges of fostering genuine voluntary compliance in technologically mediated environments.

What seems to be coming from the studies focusing on SCS is that the widespread adoption of it in China, with four out of five respondents using commercial versions, suggests a cultural predisposition toward accepting technologically driven governance solutions.[26] This acceptance may be rooted in China's collectivist culture and high Power Distance, as discussed in our analysis of Hofstede's cultural dimensions in Chapter 6.

The Chinese case also presents a stark contrast to the Nordic model of trust building that was also discussed in Chapter 6. While both approaches aim to enhance

22 www.iom.int/compass.

23 Wong, Karen Li Xan, and Amy Shields Dobson. "We're just data: Exploring China's social credit system in relation to digital platform ratings cultures in Westernised democracies." *Global Media and China* 4.2 (2019): 220–232.

24 Kostka, Genia. "China's social credit systems and public opinion: Explaining high levels of approval." *New Media & Society* 21.7 (2019): 1565–1593.

25 Zou, Sheng. "Disenchanting trust: Instrumental reason, algorithmic governance, and China's emerging social credit system." *Media and Communication* 9.2 (2021): 140–149.

26 See discussion in Kostka. "China's social credit systems and public opinion."

societal cooperation, they employ fundamentally different mechanisms shaped by their respective cultural contexts. Analysis of regulatory approaches in different regions reveals distinct mechanisms for promoting compliance. China's SCS utilizes data-driven monitoring and structured incentive systems, implemented through digital infrastructure. The Nordic regulatory framework, by comparison, builds upon established institutional relationships and community-based compliance norms. These differing approaches reflect how regulatory systems often develop in response to existing social and institutional structures. This variation in regulatory design invites empirical examination of several key questions: What is the end goal, to improve behaviors or also to change intrinsic motivation, social capital, and trust? How do preexisting institutional trust levels affect regulatory outcomes? What role do historical governance patterns play in determining the effectiveness of automated compliance systems? Systematic comparative research across jurisdictions could help identify which elements of technological compliance systems are universally applicable and which require adaptation to local institutional contexts.

BIG DATA AND VOLUNTARY COMPLIANCE

Considering the previous discussion on China's SCS in the already mentioned work with Yotam Kaplan, we examined how big data can be used in ways that are less invasive to individuals' privacy and autonomy.[27] Our research explores the transition from personalization to a situational approach in the context of big data and ethical boundaries. Recent years have seen a remarkable rise in big data's use for predictive decision-making in diverse sectors such as finance, healthcare, and law enforcement.[28] As Julie Cohen notes,[29] big data involves both advanced technology and a process that rapidly analyzes massive data volumes, identifies patterns, and applies data-driven predictions. This results in a wealth of synthesized knowledge.

Big data analytics involves working with immense datasets, often reaching into petabytes, as well as integrating information from various sources.[30] Some of the current applications of big data analytics include spam and fraud detection, credit scoring, insurance pricing, and data-driven law enforcement, such as predicting gun violence and other serious crimes.[31] Using big data for predictive regulation enables regulators

[27] Feldman and Kaplan. "Big data and bounded ethicality," 39.

[28] Christin, Angèle. "From daguerreotypes to algorithms: Machines, expertise, and three forms of objectivity." *ACM Sigcas Computers and Society* 46.1 (2016): 27–32.

[29] Cohen, Julie E. "What privacy is for." *Harvard Law Review* 126.7 (2013): 1904–1933.

[30] For other definitions of big data, see Lazer, David, and Jason Radford. "Data ex machina: Introduction to big data." *Annual Review of Sociology* 43.1 (2017): 19–39 (emphasizing the context dependence of any definition of big data); Mayer-Schönberger, Viktor, and Kenneth Cukier. *Big data: A revolution that will transform how we live, work, and think*. Houghton Mifflin Harcourt, 2013.

[31] Papachristos, Andrew V., David M. Hureau, and Anthony A. Braga. "The corner and the crew: The influence of geography and social networks on gang violence." *American Sociological Review* 78.3

to preemptively engage with potential violators by issuing alerts before any wrongdoing takes place. We argue that this data-driven approach effectively tackles many of the ethical challenges suggested earlier in this chapter. Another important concept that Kaplan and I developed is targeted regulation, which allows regulators to focus on specific risks and behaviors through data-driven law enforcement, rather than random enforcement. This targeted approach is needed to prevent ethical desensitization and enhance ethical deliberation. Additionally, we explore the idea of *tailored regulation*, which involves using data-driven law enforcement to choose appropriate regulatory measures based on insights gained from specific instances of misconduct.

While the focus of my joint work with Kaplan, as discussed, was on the concept of bounded ethicality, the newfound ability to overcome ethical numbing is crucial.[32] To improve ethical deliberation, regulatory intervention must be targeted and specific, rather than broad and general. For example, organizational ethical alerts are effective only if they are targeted and infrequent, rather than routine and constant.[33] If everyone is randomly bombarded with ethical messages, those messages will quickly lose their meaning and impact.[34] Big data analysis can provide a significant advantage here by enabling a regulatory scheme that is activated only when analysis of the background information suggests its involvement is necessary.

TAILORED REGULATION

Using data to inform law enforcement can help overcome the challenge of selecting the most effective methods for promoting thoughtful consideration and addressing ethical limitations. This will be crucial for deciding on the most appropriate legal response, based on the ethical bias that prevents open and honest discussion.

Kaplan and I argue that big data analysis can provide regulators with a wealth of information regarding instances of misconduct, allowing them to develop the most suitable regulatory response. Situations where many of the likely transgressors are first-time offenders tend to involve ethical blind spots, compared to situations where the transgressor is a repeat offender. In these cases, it is less likely that one would be unfamiliar with the underlying ethical problem behind the behavior. In addition, by utilizing big data, we can gain insights into the past transgressions of frequent

(2013): 417–447 (offering a network model that predicts the identity of individuals most likely to participate in gang violence). See also Perry, Walt L. *Predictive policing: The role of crime forecasting in law enforcement operations*. Rand Corporation, 2013.

32 Ayal, Shahar, et al. "Three principles to REVISE people's unethical behavior." *Perspectives on Psychological Science* 10.6 (2015): 738–741.

33 See, for example, in environmental context, Ricart, Sandra, Jorge Olcina, and Antonio M. Rico. "Evaluating public attitudes and farmers' beliefs towards climate change adaptation: Awareness, perception, and populism at European level." *Land* 8.1 (2018): 1–24.

34 Banaji, Mahzarin R., and Anthony G. Greenwald. *Blindspot: Hidden biases of good people*. Bantam, 2016.

offenders and identify the most effective ethical nudges to encourage ethical behavior. Essentially, the history of the violations of the typical transgressor could be used to improve our ability to predict not only the situational characteristics that may lead to more unethical behavior, but also the specific interventions that are likely to be effective based on their past efficacy across different situations.[35]

Further, policymakers may be able to determine indirectly which mechanism is operative by using big data analysis together with an *experimental regulation* approach.[36] Randomized content can be created using experimental design protocols and analyzed for varying effects through big data analysis. By deploying randomized messages, statistical analysis can yield insights into the effectiveness of each message.

INTEGRATED DATASETS

Another aspect that Kaplan and I discuss is the integration of data from previously separate institutional sources.[37] Law enforcement has always been data-driven to an extent. That is, police have traditionally used limited datasets, documenting fingerprints, past convictions, or other relevant information.[38] The trend toward big data involves combining information from multiple sources and analyzing it in a systematic and integrated way.[39] An integrated system like this enables users to track disparate data points in relation to each other and study correlations among data points that originate from different datasets.

In our paper, Kaplan and I demonstrate that the recent trend of using big data for law enforcement purposes marks a departure from traditional approaches. Specifically, there is now a growing move to gather and analyze information about individuals with no prior contact with law enforcement authorities,[40] which is crucial given the recognition that bounded ethicality is far more prevalent, as discussed in the concept of good people in the law.[41]

In that paper, we show how the growing availability of data enables new ways to study patterns of unethical behavior. A great example is Cantalupo and Kidder's

35 Feldman and Kaplan. "Big data and bounded ethicality," 39.

36 The more common term is experimental legislation, see Ranchordás, Sofia. "The whys and woes of experimental legislation." *Theory and Practice of Legislation* 1.3 (2013): 415–440, but the term experimental *regulation* is also mentioned frequently and fits under the same analytical framework (415). In both cases, the term refers to the idea that policymakers should aspire to evaluate the effects of legislation or regulation either prior to or after their implementation (417).

37 Ferguson, Andrew Guthrie. "Big data and predictive reasonable suspicion." *University of Pennsylvania Law Review* 163 (2014): 327–410.

38 Berk, Richard. "Balancing the costs of forecasting errors in parole decisions." *Albany Law Review* 74 (2010): 1071–1086 (discussing the use of historical data to identify future offenders).

39 Brayne, Sarah. "Big data surveillance: The case of policing." *American Sociological Review* 82.5 (2017): 977–1008.

40 Brayne, "Big data surveillance," 992.

41 Feldman, Yuval. *The law of good people: Challenging states' ability to regulate human behavior*. Cambridge University Press, 2018.

2018 study of faculty sexual harassment in academia. They combined different types of data – news reports, federal investigations, and court cases – to reveal systematic patterns of misconduct. Their approach shows how legal research can now use any collection of documented wrongdoing or disputes as a valuable source for analysis. Contemporary law enforcement entities increasingly possess access to extensive databases – both internally generated and commercially sourced – comprising an exponential magnitude of discrete data points. Through rigorous empirical analysis, these comprehensive datasets enable the identification of contextual variables that correlate with or potentially precipitate unethical conduct. This methodological integration of diverse data repositories represents a significant epistemological advancement in comprehending and addressing multifaceted ethical infractions across varied institutional contexts, thereby offering more sophisticated and efficacious approaches to regulatory compliance and enforcement protocols.

The paper discusses also the work of James Jacobs and Tamara Crepet regarding the fact that private commercial actors may also maintain databases that could prove useful.[42] Financial institutions maintain detailed and extensive records, directly and indirectly documenting the actions, preferences, and behavior of both employees and consumers.[43] Similar datasets are maintained and used by retailers, pharmaceutical companies, and technology firms.[44] Some private companies, especially in the financial sector, have already begun implementing situational regulation of their employees. For example, JPMorgan Chase provides ethical reminders to employees, cautioning them when they are approaching the limits of legitimate business practices. Such warnings, which seek to prevent wrongdoing before it occurs, are based on "predictive-monitoring" algorithms.[45] Other financial institutions are beginning to adopt similar mechanisms based on big data analysis.[46]

THE PERSONALIZED LAW APPROACH

Omri Ben-Shahar and Ariel Porat's influential book on personalized law focuses on the use of technology, particularly big data, as a solution to the fact that people's

[42] Jacobs, James, and Tamara Crepet. "The expanding scope, use, and availability of criminal records." *NYU Journal of Legislation and Public Policy* 11.2 (2008): 177–214.

[43] Jacobs and Crepet. "The expanding scope, use, and availability of criminal records."

[44] Kline, Candice L. "Security theater and database-driven information markets: A case for an omnibus US data privacy statute." *University of Toledo Law Review* 39 (2007): 443–496; Kamin, Sam. "The private is public: The relevance of private actors in defining the Fourth Amendment." *Boston College Law Review* 46 (2004): 83–148 (discussing databases that retailers compile in order to store consumer information).

[45] See, generally, Bennett Moses, Lyria, and Janet Chan. "Algorithmic prediction in policing: Assumptions, evaluation, and accountability." *Policing and Society* 28.7 (2018): 806–822.

[46] Credit Suisse is developing a compliance program with Palantir Technologies, a Silicon Valley tech company focused on data analysis for police and intelligence services; Jeffrey Vogeli, "Credit Suisse, CIA-Funded Palantir to target rogue bankers." *Bloomberg* (March 22, 2016). www.bloomberg.com/news/articles/2016–03–22/credit-suisse-cia-funded-palantir-build-joint-compliance-firm.

preferences differ across many legal domains.[47] In their book, they demonstrate how big data analytics can help the law provide tailored solutions to various factors that predict people's preferences and align them with fairness constraints. Although the book doesn't address people's ethics and willingness to cooperate, it's worth considering how the authors' approach could justify a situation in which past cooperation determines the level of trust the government should have in the public's willingness to cooperate voluntarily.

The concept of personalization could also be incorporated into various technologies, such as modifying the type of a pledge and providing the option to opt-out or omit certain sections. Tax authorities could gain insights into effective practices for promoting ethical behavior among individuals who share similar characteristics. As people increasingly interact with the government through digital platforms, personalization should aim to enhance ethical standards rather than simply learning people's preferences and establishing a legal framework based on that.

EMPATHY IN THE DIGITAL ADMINISTRATIVE STATE

Another important factor in technology's ability to improve voluntary compliance is empathy, which is often absent when algorithms make policy decisions affecting people. In her influential paper, Sofia Ranchordás writes that making mistakes is a fundamental human trait, especially when dealing with complex government forms like tax returns and benefit applications.[48] Nevertheless, the ability to overlook these mistakes is diminishing as government services become more digitized and automated. The author asserts that empathy has been a contentious but vital factor in enabling public officials to strike a balance between administrative priorities and the needs of citizens, particularly underserved groups such as people with disabilities, the elderly, minorities, and those with a low socioeconomic status. In the digital administrative state, the erosion of empathy could potentially hinder vulnerable citizens from being able to access their rights through the digital bureaucracy.

Ranchordás argues that preserving empathy, defined as the capacity to comprehend legal scenarios from various angles and relate to others, is pivotal in the realm of administrative law, especially within the context of the digital administrative state. Empathy can significantly enhance procedural due process, equitable treatment, and the legitimacy of automated systems. Administrative empathy does not promote emotional-based exceptions or individualized justice. Instead, it suggests strategies

[47] Ben-Shahar, Omri, and Ariel Porat. *Personalized law: Different rules for different people*. Oxford University Press, 2021.

[48] Ranchordás, Sofia. "Empathy in the digital administrative state." *Duke Law Journal* 71 (2021): 1341–1390.

This analysis provides crucial insights into the growing complexity of technology-enabled compliance systems.

ALGORITHMIC POLICING

Furthermore, in examining algorithmic regulation, we must consider how automated enforcement affects compliance and trust. While technology offers the promise of more efficient and consistent enforcement, research indicates it may actually erode public trust and create new challenges for voluntary compliance – dynamics we'll examine in detail in the next section.

These concerns are particularly evident in law enforcement, where new technologies can amplify existing social inequities.[57] Consider predictive policing algorithms, which analyze crime data to anticipate likely crime locations and guide police deployment.[58] While seemingly objective, these systems learn from historical data that reflects long-standing racial biases in policing practices, thereby risking the perpetuation and automation of discriminatory patterns. The equity challenge extends to facial recognition technologies used by police departments – these systems have shown significantly lower accuracy rates when identifying people of color, increasing the risk of wrongful identification and prosecution.[59] Recognizing these systemic risks, researchers are now developing comprehensive frameworks to evaluate the equity impact of police technologies before deployment.[60]

In another survey, the participants expressed doubts about an algorithm's ability to identify good candidates, reasoning that it would lack human intuition and make judgments based on keywords or ignore qualities that are hard to quantify. These results indicate that people have a lower level of trust in algorithms performing such tasks.[61] Other studies have examined police responses to new technology, focusing on the benefits of data integration as well as on the number of risks associated with different pathways. These algorithmic biases can disproportionately harm vulnerable populations, magnifying existing social and economic disadvantages.[62]

57 Bennett Moses and Chan. "Algorithmic prediction in policing."

58 Benbouzid, Bilel. "To predict and to manage: Predictive policing in the United States." *Big Data & Society* 6.1 (2019): 1–13.

59 Kevorkian, Martin. *Color monitors: The black face of technology in America.* Cornell University Press, 2018.

60 Moy, Laura M. "A taxonomy of police technology's racial inequity problems." *University of Illinois Law Review* (2021): 139–192.

61 Lee, Min Kyung. "Understanding perception of algorithmic decisions: Fairness, trust, and emotion in response to algorithmic management." *Big Data & Society* 5.1 (2018):1–16.

62 Chan, Janet, and Lyria Bennett Moses. "Making sense of big data for security." *British Journal of Criminology* 57.2 (2017): 299–319.

TECHNOLOGICAL SURVEILLANCE AND TRUST

Governments use technological surveillance as a substitute for trusting people.[63] This shift is particularly evident in the evolution from traditional panoptic surveillance to newer forms of environmental monitoring, as exemplified by predictive policing. Predictive policing aims to forecast where and when future crimes will occur. However, finding the appropriate balance between predictive accuracy and protecting historically disadvantaged groups is a challenging and subjective task. Moreover, research has highlighted concerns about law enforcement officers' compliance with necessary safeguards.[64] Given the public's distrust of these systems, independent judicial oversight may be necessary. As a model for building public confidence, governments could apply the same rigorous controls to these new surveillance systems that they use for handling online tax returns.[65]

The New York City Police Department has transitioned from traditional policing methods to those based on predictive analytics in response to a growing demand for police services. This has resulted in regularly suspecting certain groups of people based on their perceived risks and threats.[66] In addition to the problematic nature of predicting analytics, there is also the problem of transparency in these algorithms, which is sometimes lacking in AI-driven policing.[67]

TRANSPARENCY AND TRUST

Research has shown that higher levels of citizen satisfaction with the level of interaction with government are associated with higher levels of trust in government. Similarly, the more citizens believe that government websites are reliable sources of information, the greater their level of trust in government.[68]

The increasing adoption of e-government strategies has significant implications for public administration and citizen engagement. Research suggests that the use of government websites may lead to positive attitudes toward e-government, which

63 Trüdinger, Eva-Maria, and Leonie C. Steckermeier. "Trusting and controlling? Political trust, information and acceptance of surveillance policies: The case of Germany." *Government Information Quarterly* 34.3 (2017): 421–433.

64 Ferguson, "Big data and predictive reasonable suspicion," 327.

65 Warkentin, Merrill, et al. "Encouraging citizen adoption of e-government by building trust." *Electronic Markets* 12.3 (2002): 157–162.

66 Sanders, Carrie B., and James Sheptycki. "Policing, crime and 'big data': Towards a critique of the moral economy of stochastic governance." *Crime, Law and Social Change* 68.1 (2017): 1–15.

67 E.g., Berk, Richard A. "Artificial intelligence, predictive policing, and risk assessment for law enforcement." *Annual Review of Criminology* 4 (2021): 209–237.

68 Welch, Eric W., and Charles C. Hinnant. "Internet use, transparency, and interactivity effects on trust in government." In *Proceedings of the 36th Annual Hawaii International Conference on System Sciences*, edited by Ralph H. Sprague Jr, IEEE, 2003: 144a.1–144a.7.

in turn can foster improved trust and confidence in governments generally.[69] This digital transformation has the potential to enhance the provision of many types of public services, making them more accessible and efficient.

A study by Tolbert and Mossberger (2006)[70] supports this view, arguing that the growing number of government websites at the federal level correlates with a rise in the perception of government transparency. This increased perception of transparency is crucial, as it can lead to greater citizen participation and a more informed electorate.

However, as governments increasingly rely on digital tools and data analytics to inform decision-making and service delivery, new challenges emerge. For instance, many analysis tools used in public administration tend to focus on specific locations rather than on individual citizens.[71] While this approach can be useful for urban planning and resource allocation, it may overlook the nuanced needs of diverse populations.

Furthermore, it is crucial to acknowledge that achieving complete neutrality in data-driven governance may be impossible, particularly when dealing with historical data. Such data often includes evidence of past discrimination, which can inadvertently perpetuate biases if not carefully addressed. This challenge highlights the need for critical examination of the data and algorithms used in e-government initiatives.[72]

The ability to predict the geographic distribution of future crimes, regardless of accuracy, alters the context in which police strategies are developed. Some predictive programs focus on mobilizing police patrols to specific blocks using predictive analytics instead of trying to comprehend the underlying causes of crime in a particular area.[73] While police resistance may hinder the implementation of predictive policing, empirical evidence demonstrates that hot spot policing effectively reduces crime levels.[74] Hot spots should be limited in size, so they can be patrolled effectively, and there should not be too many of them.

In the context of taxes, numerous research findings suggest that enforcing regulations too strictly, with high audit rates and heavy fines, may result in reactance and resistance-provoking compliance.[75] Research shows that the successful

[69] Tan, Chee Wee, Izak Benbasat, and Ronald T. Cenfetelli. "Building citizen trust towards e-government services: Do high quality websites matter?" In *Proceedings of the 41st Annual Hawaii International Conference on System Sciences (HICSS 2008)*, edited by Ralph H. Sprague Jr, IEEE, 2008: 217–217.

[70] Tolbert, Caroline J., and Karen Mossberger. "The effects of e-government on trust and confidence in government." *Public Administration Review* 66.3 (2006): 354–369.

[71] West, Darrell M. "E-government and the transformation of service delivery and citizen attitudes." *Public Administration Review* 64.1 (2004): 15–27.

[72] Bennett Moses and Chan. "Algorithmic prediction in policing."

[73] Brayne, Sarah. *Predict and surveil: Data, discretion, and the future of policing*. Oxford University Press, 2020.

[74] Brayne, Sarah. *Predict and surveil.*

[75] Murphy, Kristina. "Enforcing tax compliance: to punish or persuade?" *Economic Analysis and Policy* 38.1 (2008): 113–135.

implementation of e-audits depends on acceptance by both taxpayers and tax auditors.[76] Precise and accurate tax audits can significantly increase public trust in tax authorities without making the authorities appear more coercive. As discussed in previous chapters, trust promotes voluntary compliance, while enforcement capacity ensures compliance through deterrence. Nevertheless, tax authorities must maintain sufficient enforcement capabilities to ensure overall compliance.[77]

Taxpayers who already have a high level of trust in tax authorities are more likely to support e-audits and respond to them by increasing their trust even further.[78] There is a positive association between electronic participation and people's perceptions of government responsiveness and their trust in the local government providing the program.[79] E-participants who receive quality feedback and responses from government officials are more likely to perceive that they have obtained useful policy information that helps them better understand government agencies and community issues. The quality of government responses to citizen participants can help boost e-participants' self-esteem.[80]

By improving the frequency and quality of its communication with citizens, the government can strengthen its relationship with the people and demonstrate that its actions are in their best interest. This sense of connection with the government could also contribute to increased trust among citizens.

There is a significant gap in research on the factors that build trust and lead to the successful adoption of e-government services. While studies have shown that trust in e-government is influenced by various factors – including gender, education, perceived risk, and citizens' expectations and beliefs – very few have examined how trust affects satisfaction, continued usage, and successful e-government adoption.[81] The accuracy, completeness, reliability, and accessibility of information on government websites are crucial factors that influence citizens' trust. In addition, timely updates to the system can also influence the level of trust citizens have in the information provided.

Further research on the correlation between trust and technology indicates that citizens' trust in the government rises when they receive information about

76 De Santis, Federica, and Giuseppe D'Onza. "Big data and data analytics in auditing: In search of legitimacy." *Meditari Accountancy Research* 29.5 (2021): 1088–1112.

77 Brezina, Paul, Eva Eberhartinger, and Maximilian Zieser. *The future of tax audits? The acceptance of online-based, automated tax audits and their effects on trust and power.* WU Vienna University of Economics and Business, 2021.

78 Brezina, Eberhartinger, and Zieser. The future of tax audits?

79 Kim, Soonhee, and Jooho Lee. "E-participation, transparency, and trust in local government." *Public Administration Review* 72.6 (2012): 819–828.

80 Kim and Lee. "E-participation, transparency, and trust in local government."

81 Alzahrani, Latifa, Wafi Al-Karaghouli, and Vishanth Weerakkody. "Analysing the critical factors influencing trust in e-government adoption from citizens' perspective: A systematic review and a conceptual framework." *International Business Review* 26.1 (2017): 164–175.

government actions and processes. Having the users participate in the process, as well as consulting them for their views, is an imperative approach to creating trust.[82]

If government agencies expect citizens to provide sensitive information and carry out personal transactions online, they must recognize and enhance citizens' views concerning the reliability of e-government services.[83] Government agencies must acquire and advertise features that increase citizens' perceptions of the site's trustworthiness as well.[84]

SUMMARY

This chapter looks at how technology affects people's willingness to follow rules without being forced. We pay special attention to two main tools: systems that track reputation and subtle prompts that encourage certain behaviors. While technology can help promote compliance without heavy-handed enforcement, it creates an interesting dilemma. Better technological monitoring might mean we need to rely less on trust, but it could also weaken people's natural motivation to cooperate voluntarily.[85]

We examined the promise and perils of big data and algorithmic regulation in identifying trustworthy individuals and tailoring regulatory approaches. We then addressed the ethical concerns surrounding data-driven trust mechanisms, including privacy issues and potential reinforcement of biases.[86] The importance of transparency and empathy in digital governance to maintain public trust is emphasized, along with the challenges of balancing technological efficiency with human discretion and empathy in administrative processes.[87]

In this chapter, we explore how new technologies fit into our overall understanding of voluntary compliance. While technology gives us new ways to encourage rule following, we need to be thoughtful about how we use these tools. As we've seen throughout the book, getting people to willingly follow rules depends on their inner motivation and trust in the system. Technology could either help build these qualities or wear them down, depending on how it's used.

FUTURE RESEARCH DIRECTIONS

Future research should focus on empirical studies examining technological personalization and the long-term effects of technological nudges and reputation systems

[82] Alzahrani, Al-Karaghouli, and Weerakkody. "Analysing the critical factors influencing trust in e-government adoption from citizens' perspective."

[83] Bélanger, France, and Lemuria Carter. "Trust and risk in e-government adoption." *Journal of Strategic Information Systems* 17.2 (2008): 165–176.

[84] Bélanger and Carter. "Trust and risk in e-government adoption."

[85] Yeung. "Algorithmic regulation."

[86] Barocas and Selbst. "Big data's disparate impact," 671.

[87] Ranchordás. "Empathy in the digital administrative state," 1341.

on enhancing intrinsic motivation and voluntary compliance. Comparative analyses of different technological approaches to compliance across various cultural contexts would build on the insights from Chapter 6, providing a more comprehensive understanding of how cultural factors interact with technological interventions.[88]

Investigations into the optimal balance between algorithmic decision-making and human discretion in regulatory processes are crucial, as are explorations of how emerging technologies such as blockchain and AI might reshape voluntary compliance paradigms.[89] Studies on the psychological impact of continuous technological monitoring on individuals' sense of autonomy and trust in institutions would provide valuable insights into the potential unintended consequences of these approaches.

Research should also focus on designing technology-enhanced regulatory systems that preserve or enhance intrinsic motivation and on developing ethical frameworks for the use of big data in predictive compliance models, with a focus on fairness and privacy preservation. Examination of how different demographic groups across different regulatory contexts respond to technologically mediated compliance strategies would help ensure that these approaches are inclusive and effective across diverse populations.[90]

Future research should examine whether technology can help create regulatory approaches that match different people's values and preferences. We also need to better understand how people's comfort with technology affects their acceptance of digital compliance systems. These insights would help clarify the benefits and limitations of using technology to encourage voluntary compliance in today's increasingly digital environment.

[88] Luria, Gil, Ram A. Cnaan, and Amnon Boehm. "National culture and prosocial behaviors: Results from 66 countries." *Nonprofit and Voluntary Sector Quarterly* 44.5 (2015): 1041–1065.

[89] Hawlitschek, Notheisen, and Teubner. "The limits of trust-free systems."

[90] Ferguson, Andrew Guthrie. "Whom we police: person-based predictive targeting." In *The rise of big data policing: Surveillance, race, and the future of law enforcement*. New York University Press, 2017: 34–61.

8

Voluntary Compliance and the COVID-19 Pandemic

INTRODUCTION

The COVID-19 pandemic served as an unprecedented testing ground for regulatory approaches beyond traditional command-and-control mechanisms. Government efforts to promote radical behavioral changes, particularly social distancing, represented a unique regulatory challenge. Never had authorities needed to implement such sweeping modifications to fundamental human social behaviors on a global scale.

In responding to this unprecedented challenge, governments worldwide developed an array of innovative regulatory approaches to influence public behavior. As state intervention in daily life reached extraordinary levels, policymakers recognized that success hinged not on enforcement alone, but on fostering voluntary cooperation from citizens. This shift toward voluntary compliance proved especially critical in situations where traditional enforcement mechanisms were either impractical or counterproductive, particularly in private spaces like homes and indoor gatherings, where the risk of virus transmission was highest yet direct monitoring was virtually impossible. The limitations of conventional enforcement mechanisms became especially apparent in high-risk scenarios. How could authorities effectively monitor private indoor gatherings without creating additional health risks or violating basic privacy rights? These practical constraints forced policymakers to innovate, developing new approaches to promote voluntary compliance through public health messaging, social norms, and community engagement.

This chapter examines the various regulatory strategies governments employed to influence behavior during the COVID-19 pandemic, as well as in other public health contexts. By analyzing these approaches, we can better understand the effectiveness of different regulatory tools in situations where voluntary compliance is not just desired but essential for public health outcomes. The pandemic experience offers valuable insights into the potential and limitations of trust-based regulatory approaches in addressing complex social challenges.

COVID-19

The COVID-19 virus, officially declared a pandemic by the World Health Organization on March 11, 2020, after more than 118,000 cases of infection and 4,291 deaths across 114 countries, has had a profound impact on global health and public policy.[1] Nearly five years later, the death toll has reached over a staggering 7 million, solidifying its position as one of the deadliest pandemics in human history.[2] The pandemic has brought to the forefront a fundamental debate regarding the extent to which government intervention and overreach into individuals' decision-making can be considered proportionate to the threat. Policymakers have grappled with the question of whether alternative means of enforcing health provisions could prove effective in curbing the spread of the virus. As the discourse has evolved over the past few years, there has been a notable shift toward encouraging voluntary compliance, reflecting a growing recognition of the limitations of COVID-19 regulations and the government's ability to directly influence individual behavior.[3] This chapter aims to explore the complexities of public policies during the COVID-19 pandemic, focusing on the delicate balance between government intervention and individual autonomy. By examining the effectiveness of various health provisions and the factors that contribute to voluntary compliance, we seek to shed light on the lessons learned and the potential implications for future public health crises.

Public health focus on the compliance literature in general and public health research on adherence in particular, could greatly benefit from analyzing the extensive comparative data regarding adherence to COVID-19 regulations. Using such data gathered from countries around the world, we can enhance our understanding of the potential of voluntary compliance. Data detailing the varying levels of strictness across countries during the COVID-19 pandemic, including Google data on compliance with regulations, may help in ascertaining whether the restrictions imposed influenced people's avoidance of certain behaviors and places. It may also help clarify whether stricter COVID-19 restrictions ultimately led to a counterreaction. It has further been suggested that women leaders enjoyed greater "success" in fighting the coronavirus, a result which is at least stereotypically associated with solidarity and empathy.[4]

1 "CDC Museum COVID-19 timeline." Centers for Disease Control and Prevention (August 16, 2022). www.cdc.gov/museum/timeline/covid19.html.

2 See: "CDC Museum COVID-19 timeline."

3 Clark, Cory, et al. "Predictors of COVID-19 voluntary compliance behaviors: An international investigation." *Global Transitions* 2 (2020): 76–82.

4 Johnson, Carol, and Blair Williams. "Gender and political leadership in a time of COVID." *Politics & Gender* 16.4 (2020): 943–950; Sergent, Kayla, and Alexander D. Stajkovic. "Women's leadership is associated with fewer deaths during the COVID-19 crisis: Quantitative and qualitative analyses of United States governors." *Journal of Applied Psychology* 105.8 (2020): 771–783.

CROSS-NATIONAL COMPARISON

The relationship between the strictness of COVID-19 regulations with the level of adherence has been extensively studied across nations.[5] The first task is to identify common themes related to the success and failure of regulatory efforts to address COVID-19 based on the studies. For example, some studies have suggested that stricter government regulations can lead to increased compliance,[6] while others have claimed that imposing more restrictive guidelines can sometimes be less effective.[7] Various studies showed that some of the factors we focus on in the book are highly relevant for COVID compliance. For example, areas with high social capital tended to exhibit greater compliance with COVID-19 regulations.[8] High levels of cohesion in an area were found to be related to high compliance.[9]

FEAR APPEALS

Various meta-analyses have examined the usage and efficacy of fear appeals in health policy, particularly in vaccination campaigns, which use persuasive messages that emphasize the negative consequences of failing to follow recommended health behaviors. These appeals aim to motivate individuals to take protective actions by highlighting potential threats to their well-being.[10]

In the context of vaccination, fear appeals can be effective in increasing intention to vaccinate, especially when combined with high-efficacy messages that emphasize the vaccine's ability to prevent disease. These appeals often focus on the risks of not vaccinating (e.g., severe illness, hospitalization) rather than the benefits of vaccination.[11]

While fear appeals can be powerful motivators, they raise ethical concerns about potential manipulation and anxiety induction. Excessive fear-based messaging may

[5] Coccia, Mario. "Effects of strict containment policies on COVID-19 pandemic crisis: Lessons to cope with next pandemic impacts." *Environmental Science and Pollution Research* 30.1 (2023): 2020–2028.

[6] Pak, Anton, Emma McBryde, and Oyelola A. Adegboye. "Does high public trust amplify compliance with stringent COVID-19 government health guidelines? A multi-country analysis using data from 102,627 individuals." *Risk Management and Healthcare Policy* 14 (2021): 293–302.

[7] Haug, Nina, et al. "Ranking the effectiveness of worldwide COVID-19 government interventions." *Nature Human Behaviour* 4.12 (2020): 1303–1312.

[8] Makridis, Christos A., and Cary Wu. "How social capital helps communities weather the COVID-19 pandemic." *PLOS One* 16.1 (2021): 1–18. See also Pitas, Nicholas, and Colin Ehmer. "Social capital in the response to COVID-19." *American Journal of Health Promotion* 34.8 (2020): 942–944.

[9] Gelfand, Michele J., et al. "The relationship between cultural tightness–looseness and COVID-19 cases and deaths: A global analysis." *The Lancet Planetary Health* 5.3 (2021): e135–e144.

[10] Tannenbaum, Melanie B., et al. "Appealing to fear: A meta-analysis of fear appeal effectiveness and theories." *Psychological Bulletin* 141.6 (2015): 1178–1204.

[11] Yang, Chun. "Exploring communication strategies to encourage COVID-19 vaccination: Motivation-based message appeals, incidental emotions, and risk perception." *Health Communication* 38.9 (2023): 1731–1743.

lead to denial or avoidance behaviors in some individuals, potentially reducing vaccine uptake.[12] The effectiveness of fear appeals varies across demographics and cultures, necessitating tailored approaches. Fear appeals are often most effective when used in conjunction with other communication strategies, such as addressing vaccine hesitancy concerns and providing clear, factual information.[13] The approach to COVID-19 public health policy drew heavily on a long history of research into behavioral change strategies in health contexts. While fear appeals might seem at odds with trust-based or cooperative regulation, they share a common goal: influencing people's intrinsic motivation. As discussed earlier in this book, these strategies, including fear appeals, are not necessarily contradictory to trust-based approaches. Instead, they represent different tools in the policymaker's arsenal for encouraging beneficial health behaviors.

Governmental Rhetoric and Public Cooperation

When discussing ways to encourage voluntary compliance with regulations, it is crucial to examine the influence of government rhetoric. The central dilemma faced by those seeking to motivate voluntary compliance is reflected in the importance of relational concerns, such as legitimacy versus deterrence. Should the rhetoric emphasize instilling fear of sanctions or strive to generate social solidarity and a moral commitment?[14] Some research has shown that fear-based appeals can be effective in general,[15] particularly in the case of compliance with COVID-19 restrictions. Despite these findings, in other contexts there is strong empirical evidence to suggest that people are more likely to comply with health regulations not only due to fear of sanctions, but also if they perceive the requesting entity as one that represents their moral values and a group to which they feel they belong.[16] The concept of social solidarity is also closely tied to the power of social norms and has been shown to be highly influential in guiding individuals' behavior.[17] Additionally, during the pandemic, people demonstrated higher levels of

[12] Ruiter, Robert A. C., et al. "Sixty years of fear appeal research: Current state of the evidence." *International Journal of Psychology* 49.2 (2014): 63–70.

[13] Kok, Gerjo, et al. "Finding theory-and evidence-based alternatives to fear appeals: Intervention mapping." *International Journal of Psychology* 49.2 (2014): 98–107.

[14] Or Cohen-Sason, Rinat Markovitch, and I are working on a large language model approach to COVID rhetoric (on file with author).

[15] Harper, Craig A., et al. "Functional fear predicts public health compliance in the COVID-19 pandemic." *International Journal of Mental Health and Addiction* 19.5 (2021): 1875–1888.

[16] Sunshine, Jason, and Tom R. Tyler. "The role of procedural justice and legitimacy in shaping public support for policing." *Law & Society Review* 37.3 (2003): 513–547.

[17] Fehr, Ernst, and Urs Fischbacher. "Social norms and human cooperation." *Trends in Cognitive Sciences* 8.4 (2004): 185–190; Rand, David G., and Martin A. Nowak. "Human cooperation." *Trends in Cognitive Sciences* 17.8 (2013): 413–425; Reynolds, Katherine J. "Social norms and how they impact behaviour." *Nature Human Behaviour* 3.1 (2019): 14–15.

compliance with governmental measures aimed at mitigating the pandemic when they perceived the measures to be legitimate and felt they were being treated fairly and with respect.[18]

The Use of Incentives in the COVID-19 Context

To understand the importance of intrinsic voluntary motivation in COVID-19 contexts, we must first acknowledge the successful use of incentives before examining their limitations. Understanding the effectiveness of incentives requires analyzing evidence of how they encourage testing and vaccination, while considering key questions: What was the reach of the incentive? Did it lead to repeated behaviors? Were community-based programs implemented that required cooperation? For example, the widespread deployment of COVID-19 vaccination incentives offers valuable insights into program effectiveness. Recent research has analyzed how different compliance approaches affected vaccination rates and identified key factors that determined whether incentives succeeded. In a study on the Israeli Green Pass, which can be considered a type of incentive, as it saves time, avoids quarantine, and allows for easier access to malls and restaurants, researchers examined the response to the exemption announcement and found a correlation with an increase in vaccine uptake.[19] Research demonstrates that perceived policy effectiveness serves as a stronger predictor of public compliance than appeals to solidarity in public health contexts. Studies have shown that individuals are more inclined to adhere to health measures when they believe in their efficacy, rather than acting primarily from a sense of communal responsibility. Although social solidarity remains a valuable factor, evidence suggests that emphasizing and clearly communicating the effectiveness of health policies may be more instrumental in securing public support and compliance during health emergencies.[20]

Another study of 1,096 adult Americans examined how the interplay of the characteristics of the COVID-19 vaccine (including manufacture, reports of adverse effects, and so on), financial incentives, and misinformation on vaccination effectiveness and safety, affected individuals' vaccination preferences.[21] A higher efficacy rate

[18] McCarthy, Molly, et al. "Policing COVID-19 physical distancing measures: Managing defiance and fostering compliance among individuals least likely to comply." *Policing and Society* 31.5 (2021): 601–620.

[19] Saban, Mor, et al. "Issues surrounding incentives and penalties for COVID-19 vaccination: The Israeli experience." *Preventive Medicine* 153 (2021): 1–6.

[20] Mantzari, Eleni, et al. "Personal financial incentives for changing habitual health-related behaviors: A systematic review and meta-analysis." *Preventive Medicine* 75 (2015): 75–85. See also Vlaev, Ivo, et al. "Changing health behaviors using financial incentives: A review from behavioral economics." *BMC Public Health* 19 (2019): 1–9.

[21] See Kreps, Sarah, et al. "Public attitudes toward COVID-19 vaccination: The role of vaccine attributes, incentives, and misinformation." *npj Vaccines* 6.1 (2021): 1–7. https://doi.org/10.1038/s41541-021-00335-2.

of vaccine intake resulted in a 13 percent increase in the willingness to be vaccinated. Manufacturer identity had no impact, while reports of more minor side effects reduced vaccination willingness by 5 percent. In addition, introducing a $100 incentive did not have any noticeable effect on increasing vaccine uptake. On the other hand, imposing a mandatory $20 co-payment for the vaccine seemed to discourage people from getting vaccinated. This study provides evidence to support the idea that increasing the effectiveness of vaccines and raising public awareness about these improvements can be an effective strategy for increasing voluntary vaccine rates.

In addition, a survey of 2,000 North American residents was conducted to investigate the impact of COVID-19 vaccine pricing, financial incentives, and vaccine efficacy on demand. The survey measured willingness to pay and willingness to accept compensation.[22] Most of the individuals (60 percent) indicated they were willing to pay a positive amount for the vaccine; 13.7 percent said they would only accept the vaccine if it were free. The amount of $500 would motivate 48 percent of those in the latter group and $1,000 would motivate 74 percent. The acceptance of vaccines was significantly influenced by their efficacy. Based on the study, it is recommended to tailor incentives to some but not all of the population, as 70 percent of people are inclined to vaccinate without incentives, while offering $500 to $1,000 incentives is sufficient for the remaining percentage.

Another study in the United States involving 2,461 participants supported this approach and suggested that incentives of $1,000 could increase vaccination rates to 86 percent, an increase of 16 percent. Both studies found that offering monetary incentives would not persuade individuals who are categorically opposed to getting vaccinated.[23] The aforementioned research indicates that age plays an important role in the effectiveness of incentives in a public health context. Building on this insight, researchers have examined several methods to enhance global vaccine acceptance. These studies consider how age-related differences in response to incentives might improve vaccine uptake across different demographic groups.[24]

Is Intrinsic Motivation Important in Public Health Contexts?

In the context of practicing safe medical behavior, using multifaceted approaches that include education along with written material, reminders, and ongoing performance feedback can have a significant impact on handwashing compliance and

[22] Carpio, Carlos E., et al. "COVID-19 vaccine demand and financial incentives." *Applied Health Economics and Health Policy* 19 (2021): 871–883.

[23] Iyer, Ganesh, Vivek Nandur, and David Soberman. "Vaccine hesitancy and monetary incentives." *Humanities and Social Sciences Communications* 9.1 (2022): 1–10. https://doi.org/10.1057/s41599-022-01074-y.

[24] Larson, Heidi J., et al. "Understanding vaccine hesitancy around vaccines and vaccination from a global perspective: A systematic review of published literature, 2007–2012." *Vaccine* 32.19 (2014): 2150–2159.

rates of hospital-acquired infections.[25] A study in this area found that interventions based on arousing disgust were considerably more effective in promoting hygienic handwashing compared to educational posters.[26] Moreover, implementing "gentle reminders" can significantly enhance safety measures – in this study, team members agreed to gently remind their coworkers whenever they deviated from safety norms.[27]

A recent study found that more conscientious people were more likely to adhere to COVID-19 regulations, both directly and indirectly, through increased self-efficacy in following the rules.[28] Moreover, it appears that higher levels of perceived social approval of the guidelines, favorable attitudes toward the guidelines, and stronger intentions to adhere to them were associated with increased adherence.[29] When discussing the topic of compliance with less fear, several studies have demonstrated that self-efficacy is the most significant predictor in the relationship. Examining representative samples across many countries, this factor was the leading one for people who are not in a risk group themselves.[30]

THE INTERACTION BETWEEN INCENTIVES AND INTRINSIC MOTIVATION

Many countries implemented a system using some combination of incentives and restrictions. One example is referred to as the Green Pass system, which allows those who had been vaccinated to be subject to fewer restrictions than those who had not.[31] Studies have shown that while normative messages can come from various sources like experts, family, and friends, expert messaging tends to be most effective in influencing behavior.[32]

Research on COVID-19 compliance illustrates the power of intrinsic motivation. A large international study of over 8,000 participants found that belief in the effectiveness of preventive measures was the strongest predictor of compliance behavior. This

25 Naikoba, Sarah, and Andrew Hayward. "The effectiveness of interventions aimed at increasing handwashing in healthcare workers: A systematic review." *Journal of Hospital Infection* 47.3 (2001): 173–180.

26 Porzig-Drummond, Renata, et al. "Can the emotion of disgust be harnessed to promote hand hygiene? Experimental and field-based tests." *Social Science & Medicine* 68.6 (2009): 1006–1012.

27 Erev, Ido, et al. "The value of gentle enforcement on safe medical procedures." *Quality and Safety in Health Care* 19.5 (2010): 1–3.

28 Tedesco, Lisa A., Michele A. Keffer, and Cynthia Fleck-Kandath. "Self-efficacy, reasoned action, and oral health behavior reports: A social cognitive approach to compliance." *Journal of Behavioral Medicine* 14 (1991): 341–355.

29 Bogg, Tim, and Elizabeth Milad. "Demographic, personality, and social cognition correlates of coronavirus guideline adherence in a US sample." *Health Psychology* 39.12 (2020): 1026–1036. osf.io/preprints/psyarxiv/yc2gq.

30 Jørgensen, Frederik, Alexander Bor, and Michael Bang Petersen. "Compliance without fear: Individual-level protective behaviour during the first wave of the COVID-19 pandemic." *British Journal of Health Psychology* 26.2 (2021): 679–696. doi.org/10.1111/bjhp.12519.

31 Saban, et al. "Issues surrounding incentives and penalties for COVID-19 vaccination," 1–6.

32 Salali, Gul Deniz, and Mete Sefa Uysal. "Effective incentives for increasing COVID-19 vaccine uptake." *Psychological Medicine* 53.7 (2023): 3242–3244.

finding extends beyond the pandemic context, reinforcing broader research showing that internal motivation often drives compliance more effectively than external pressures. Based on a sample of 2,461 individuals across the United States aimed to evaluate the effectiveness of monetary incentives,[33] research found that a $1,000 incentive could increase vaccination rates to 86.9 percent. However, the study identified two distinct groups: vaccine-hesitant individuals who responded to monetary incentives and those firmly opposed who wouldn't vaccinate regardless of payment.[34] In a comprehensive review of the behavioral economics literature on health behavior, Ivo Vlaev and colleagues explored the role of incentives and identified the types of behaviors that are most likely to be positively influenced by incentives.[35] Financial incentives work better for one-time actions, like getting vaccinated, than for ongoing behaviors like maintaining a healthy diet. During the COVID-19 pandemic, some programs successfully combined individual and community incentives, rewarding municipalities that achieved high vaccination and testing rates.[36] Belief in the efficacy of vaccination has been found to be more important than incentives in influencing vaccination decisions among US participants.[37]

Research on public health incentives shows they can effectively change habitual behaviors, with effects lasting up to eighteen months during implementation. However, behavioral changes typically disappear three months after financial incentives end. The effectiveness of incentives also depends heavily on their size – incentives that are too small may backfire, requiring policymakers to ensure rewards are substantial enough to justify their cost.[38] Studies have also found that mandating vaccinations can trigger public resentment, leading policymakers to seek alternative approaches.[39]

MASKS VS. VACCINES: DIFFERENT COMPLIANCE

Masks and vaccines differ in that people must wear masks properly, over time, and in situations where enforcement may be limited. In contrast, vaccine compliance is a specific, one- or multi-time, albeit limited, behavior that is 100 percent monitored.

33 See: Iyer, Nandur, and Soberman. "Vaccine hesitancy and monetary incentives."

34 Khazanov, Gabriela K., et al. "The effectiveness of financial incentives for COVID-19 vaccination: A systematic review." *Preventive Medicine* 172 (2023): 1–16. See also Iyer, Nandur, and Soberman. "Vaccine hesitancy and monetary incentives."

35 Vlaev, et al. "Changing health behaviors using financial incentives."

36 See Saban, et al. "Issues surrounding incentives and penalties for COVID-19 vaccination," 106763. See also: Salali and Sefa Uysal. "Effective incentives for increasing COVID-19 vaccine uptake."

37 Kreps, et al. "Public attitudes toward COVID-19 vaccination," 73.

38 Mantzari, et al. "Personal financial incentives for changing habitual health-related behaviors."

39 Lytras, Theodore, et al. "Interventions to increase seasonal influenza vaccine coverage in healthcare workers: A systematic review and meta-regression analysis." *Human Vaccines & Immunotherapeutics* 12.3 (2016): 671–681. In the context of COVID see Klüver, Heike, et al. "Incentives can spur COVID-19 vaccination uptake." *Proceedings of the National Academy of Sciences* 118.36 (2021): 1–3.

The fact that mask mandates are problematic was acknowledged even in the popular press. The problems included the fact that people can always choose to use cheap masks, wear them improperly, or not wear them consistently.[40]

Public Discretion in Mask Wearing and Voluntary Compliance

Mask policies that target high-risk settings while allowing more flexibility in low-risk environments are likely to increase public adherence. This approach acknowledges the potential downsides of face masks while maximizing their protective benefits where most needed. Bakhit and colleagues conducted a systematic review and meta-analysis of face mask drawbacks and potential mitigation strategies, providing valuable insights for policy development.[41] Along those lines, Seale and colleagues examined factors influencing engagement with nonpharmaceutical interventions during COVID-19, offering guidance on improving the impact of such measures.[42] Finally, a comprehensive review by Escandón and colleagues further emphasizes the importance of nuanced, evidence-based policymaking in COVID-19 response plans, supporting the need for sensitive and targeted mask policies.[43]

The Mask Mandate Debate

As already mentioned regarding the discussion on the gap between vaccines and masks, a classic example of a COVID-19-related regulatory challenge involves mandates for wearing masks.[44] For masks to work, they need to be worn in close spaces, over time, and the masks need to be very high-quality ones that cover the whole face.[45]

Mask wearing is a very low-cost intervention.[46] However, in many countries, there were concerns regarding the ability of masks to actually stop transmission, given that people tended to remove their masks during several activities, such as eating and in

[40] Leonhardt, David. "Why masks work, but mandates haven't." *New York Times* (May, 2022). www.nytimes.com/2022/05/31/briefing/masks-mandates-us-covid.html.

[41] Bakhit, Mina, et al. "Downsides of face masks and possible mitigation strategies: A systematic review and meta-analysis." *BMJ Open* 11.2 (2021): 1–12.

[42] Seale, Holly, et al. "Improving the impact of non-pharmaceutical interventions during COVID-19: Examining the factors that influence engagement and the impact on individuals." *BMC Infectious Diseases* 20 (2020): 1–13.

[43] Escandón, Kevin, et al. "COVID-19 false dichotomies and a comprehensive review of the evidence regarding public health, COVID-19 symptomatology, SARS-CoV-2 transmission, mask wearing, and reinfection." *BMC Infectious Diseases* 21.1 (2021): 1–47.

[44] Teichman, Doron, and Kristen Underhill. "Infected by bias: Behavioral science and the legal response to COVID-19." *American Journal of Law & Medicine* 47.2–3 (2021): 205–248.

[45] Brooks, John T., and Jay C. Butler. "Effectiveness of mask wearing to control community spread of SARS-CoV-2." *JAMA* 325.10 (2021): 998–999.

[46] Aldila, Dipo, et al. "Analyzing the MERS disease control strategy through an optimal control problem." *International Journal of Applied Mathematics and Computer Science* 28.1 (2018): 169–184.

social gatherings, where most of the transmission occurs.[47] Furthermore, numerous studies have indicated that the vast majority of people did not wear masks properly.[48]

"Smart Masking" vs. "Universal Masking"

A dilemma that is highly related to intrinsic motivation, voluntary compliance, and COVID is related to whether to trust people to know when it is important to cover their faces (e.g., smart masking) or whether to reduce people's discretion and give them instructions to always wear masks (e.g., universal masking). It seems from current research that publications advocating universal masking for the public leave out important details about viral transmission dynamics, risk communication, and the sustainability of policies.[49] Mask policies that target high-risk settings rather than low-risk activities are more likely to encourage people. To increase acceptance and compliance with mask-wearing mandates, it's crucial to address the main areas of concern. These include discomfort barriers, external factors, and usability issues. By focusing on these aspects, policymakers can work to reduce mask-related discomfort and fatigue, potentially improving overall adherence to mask mandates.[50] Therefore, face mask mandates are accepted only as a temporary measure in liberal Western societies and should be enforced only when epidemiologically necessary.[51]

MIXED EVIDENCE ON THE INTRINSIC MOTIVATION PREDICTORS OF COVID-19 COMPLIANCE

Several strategies have been employed to encourage compliance with preventive measures like social distancing, better hand hygiene, and vaccination. Research has shown that rhetoric, including appeals to fear, unity, and solidarity, can influence public health compliance.[52] In addition, the more individuals perceive that social norms or authority figures support guidelines, the more positive their attitudes are toward the guidelines, and the more likely they are to intend to follow them.[53]

47 Zimmermann, Bettina Maria, et al. "Face mask uptake in the absence of mandates during the COVID-19 pandemic: A qualitative interview study with Swiss residents." *BMC Public Health* 21 (2021): 1–10.

48 Huynh, Toan Luu Duc. "'If you wear a mask, then you must know how to use it and dispose of it properly!': A survey study in Vietnam." *Review of Behavioral Economics* 7.2 (2020): 145–158.

49 Escandón, et al. "COVID-19 false dichotomies and a comprehensive review of the evidence regarding public health."

50 Esmaeilzadeh, Pouyan. "Public concerns and burdens associated with face mask-wearing: Lessons learned from the COVID-19 pandemic." *Progress in Disaster Science* 13 (2022): 1–11.

51 Zimmermann, et al. "Face mask uptake in the absence of mandates during the COVID-19 pandemic."

52 Harper, et al. "Functional fear predicts public health compliance in the COVID-19 pandemic."

53 Bogg, and Milad. "Demographic, personality, and social cognition correlates of coronavirus guideline adherence in a US sample," 1026; Salali and Sefa Uysal. "Effective incentives for increasing COVID-19 vaccine uptake."

Especially, in the context of health, people's belief in the efficacy of preventive measures, which is a classic example of an intrinsic motivation, has been identified as a strong predictor of compliance.[54] Research shows that increasing people's sense of self-efficacy – their belief in their ability to take protective actions – leads to better adoption of preventive measures, especially among groups resistant to health policies.[55]

REMINDERS FOR HEALTH WORKERS

Research on behavioral change in public health includes studies focused not only on the public but also on healthcare workers. Various approaches have been employed for interventions aimed at improving hygiene practices, such as handwashing and mask wearing. A combined approach utilizing written materials, reminders, and continued feedback on performance has been found effective.[56] As mentioned in the discussion on motivation in public health, disgust-based interventions have been shown to be significantly better at promoting hand hygiene compared to educational posters.[57] "Gentle reminders" have also been used to encourage safe medical procedures.[58]

TRUST AND VOLUNTARY COMPLIANCE IN THE COVID-19 CONTEXT

Our discussion of trust and voluntary compliance in the COVID-19 context begins with the study of Cory Clark and colleagues.[59] They surveyed an international sample to examine which of five belief predictors – effectiveness of health precautions, health importance, invulnerability, disruptiveness, and government trust – correlate with voluntary compliance. However, having faith in the effectiveness of precautions was strongly associated with compliance with government recommendations, taking health precautions (such as wearing masks and quarantining), and encouraging others to do the same. Therefore, their findings emphasize the crucial role

54 See: Iyer, Nandur, and Soberman. "Vaccine hesitancy and monetary incentives."

55 Fathian-Dastgerdi, Zohreh, Banafsheh Tavakoli, and Maryam Jaleh. "Factors associated with preventive behaviors of COVID-19 among adolescents: Applying the health belief model." *Research in Social and Administrative Pharmacy* 17.10 (2021): 1786–1790. Ozdemir, Semra, et al. "Adoption of preventive behaviour strategies and public perceptions about COVID-19 in Singapore." *International Journal of Health Policy and Management* 11.5 (2020): 579–591; Rabin, Carolyn, and Sunny Dutra. "Predicting engagement in behaviors to reduce the spread of COVID-19: The roles of the health belief model and political party affiliation." *Psychology, Health & Medicine* 27.2 (2022): 379–388.

56 Naikoba and Hayward. "The effectiveness of interventions aimed at increasing handwashing in healthcare workers."

57 Porzig-Drummond, et al. "Can the emotion of disgust be harnessed to promote hand hygiene?"

58 Erev, et al. "The value of gentle enforcement on safe medical procedures."

59 Clark, et al. "Predictors of COVID-19 voluntary compliance behaviors."

of the public's confidence in the effectiveness of health behaviors in encouraging compliance with COVID-19 mandates, especially in policies that rely on voluntary adherence.[60]

In their influential and extensive paper, Timothy Besley and Sacha Dray expanded on this idea, emphasizing the importance of both interpersonal and governmental trust, in addition to factors such as state capacity to offer responses and COVID-19 mortality rates.[61]

Besley's definition of state capacity is broad and encompasses various factors, such as the capacity to levy taxes. In the context of interpersonal trust, the authors posit that the stronger the mutual trust and cooperation ingrained within the civic culture, the better the state's performance during the pandemic. This study does not clarify whether there is any additional factor that influences both civic culture and pandemic performance; however, it highlights the importance of promoting a culture of trust.

How law shapes civic virtue is a fundamental question in legal and regulatory frameworks. This broader issue invites us to examine how legal systems can foster civic-mindedness among citizens. The relationship between state capacity and citizen support is particularly relevant here. As Besley argues, growing state capacity requires increasing cooperation from citizens, particularly through mutual obligations and reciprocity. The strength of these relationships depends heavily on levels of trust and social solidarity within the nation, which in turn shape citizens' preferences and willingness to cooperate with state institutions.

According to Besley's research, an expected pattern emerges:[62] Countries with strong accountability and open debate sometimes had higher COVID-19 mortality rates than those with fewer civil liberties and lower incomes. This highlights why voluntary compliance is crucial – not just because coercion often proves ineffective, but because governments cannot sometimes enforce measures. The challenge is particularly acute in nations that need high public cooperation but suffer from low mutual trust, as limited government trust restricts policy options while simultaneously increasing the need for public cooperation.

TRUSTING WHAT EXACTLY?

Understanding the relationship between trust and voluntary compliance helps identify which types of trust matter most when selecting policy tools. There are many different aspects to trust within the COVID context. First, it relates to

60 On trust and health-related behavior, see, more generally, Jarrett, Caitlin, et al. "Strategies for addressing vaccine hesitancy: A systematic review." *Vaccine* 33.34 (2015): 4180–4190.

61 Besley, Timothy, and Sacha Dray. "Institutions, trust and responsiveness: Patterns of government and private action during the COVID-19 pandemic." *LSE Public Policy Review* 1.4 (2021): 1–11.

62 Besley and Dray. "Institutions, trust and responsiveness," 10.

trusting the capacity of policymakers and the technical and organizational skills of the government,[63] as well as trusting information from government sources.[64] With distrust in government extending to vaccines,[65] there are studies showing an overall positive correlation between trust in government and vaccine uptake.[66] Other studies have shown that the perception of trust is often intertwined with an individual's political views and that partisanship can affect one's trust.[67] It is also noteworthy that other studies on trust have examined trust in science, in the scientists, and in the healthcare workers.[68] Generally, these studies anticipate that having trust in science is linked with compliance with COVID-19 guidelines.[69] There are also COVID-related studies on the crisis of trust in science, particularly about denialism and discrediting experts,[70] which also discuss how to restore trust in science.[71] The last form of trust in science in the context of COVID is trust in the product of science – the vaccine.[72] Finally, trust in others is an important aspect of trust in a pandemic situation.[73]

HETEROGENEITY IN INTRINSIC MOTIVATION DURING COVID-19

There is an intriguing correlation between how incentives affect people who hold different attitudes toward vaccinations. For example, Tali Goren and colleagues have shown that there are differences in the effects of negative and positive incentives on

63 Mesch, Gustavo S., and Kent P. Schwirian. "Confidence in government and vaccination willingness in the USA." *Health Promotion International* 30.2 (2015): 213–221.

64 Lazarus, Jeffrey V., et al. "COVID-SCORE: A global survey to assess public perceptions of government responses to COVID-19 (COVID-SCORE-10)." *PLOS One* 15.10 (2020): 1–18.

65 Freimuth, Vicki S., et al. "Determinants of trust in the flu vaccine for African Americans and whites." *Social Science & Medicine* 193 (2017): 70–79.

66 Larson, Heidi J., et al. "Measuring trust in vaccination: A systematic review." *Human Vaccines & Immunotherapeutics* 14.7 (2018): 1599–1609.

67 Baumgaertner, Bert, Juliet E. Carlisle, and Florian Justwan. "The influence of political ideology and trust on willingness to vaccinate." *PLOS One* 13.1 (2018): 1–13.

68 Badur, Selim, et al. "Vaccine confidence: The keys to restoring trust." *Human Vaccines & Immunotherapeutics* 16.5 (2020): 1007–1017.

69 Plohl, Nejc, and Bojan Musil. "Modeling compliance with COVID-19 prevention guidelines: The critical role of trust in science." *Psychology, Health & Medicine* 26.1 (2021): 1–12.

70 Peretti-Watel, Patrick, et al. "Vaccine hesitancy: Clarifying a theoretical framework for an ambiguous notion." *PLOS Currents* 7 (2015): 1–9.

71 Verger, Pierre, and Eve Dubé. "Restoring confidence in vaccines in the COVID-19 era." *Expert Review of Vaccines* 19.11 (2020): 991–993.

72 Dror, Amiel A., et al. "Vaccine hesitancy: The next challenge in the fight against COVID-19." *European Journal of Epidemiology* 35.8 (2020): 775–779; Majid, Umair, et al. "COVID-19 vaccine hesitancy and acceptance: A comprehensive scoping review of global literature." *Health Promotion International* 37.3 (2022): 1–12.

73 Thoresen, Siri, et al. "Trusting others during a pandemic: Investigating potential changes in generalized trust and its relationship with pandemic-related experiences and worry." *Frontiers in Psychology* 12 (2021): 1–9; Gambetta, Diego, and Davide Morisi. "COVID-19 infection induces higher trust in strangers." *Proceedings of the National Academy of Sciences* 119.32 (2022): 1–10.

people with either positive or negative intentions to get vaccinated.[74] The findings demonstrate that both negative and positive incentives have similar positive effects on individuals who express hesitancy about getting vaccinated or declare that they will not get vaccinated. Additionally, both positive and negative incentives have a crowding-out effect, but negative incentives create a larger crowding-out effect in individuals who express a preliminary intention to get vaccinated, in comparison to positive incentives.

Concerning following COVID-19 restrictions, a study conducted in Australia found that people who were resistant to following the rules were much less likely to comply with physical-distancing measures.[75] For individuals who are highly resistant and disengaged, police-initiated encounters that were considered procedurally unjust resulted in decreased compliance. Furthermore, highly disengaged individuals were less likely to follow guidelines if they were concerned about the ongoing loss of freedom after the pandemic ended. Without an understanding of the variations in compliance, it can be challenging to determine the appropriate motivation to employ at the right time.

CULTURE AND COVID-19

The varying success rates among jurisdictions in their COVID-19 response raised important questions about regional disparities. A significant contribution to this discourse emerged from Charron and colleagues' research,[76] which examined the relationship between excess mortality, societal trust, and political polarization across 153 European regions during the pandemic's initial wave. Their analysis provided valuable insights into regional variations in public health behavior adoption.

Their investigation revealed that the ideological stance and polarization of political parties correlated with increased mortality rates. This relationship manifested as parties often prioritized their core constituents' interests, such as business concerns, rather than fostering broader political consensus for implementing necessary but unpopular measures. The research aligned with numerous concurrent studies that highlighted the crucial role of mass polarization.[77] Notably, regions characterized by high political mistrust between government supporters and opponents consistently exhibited elevated levels of COVID-19-related excess mortality during the

74 Goren, Talia, Itai Beeri, and Dana R. Vashdi. "Framing policies to mobilize citizens' behavior during a crisis: Examining the effects of positive and negative vaccination incentivizing policies." *Regulation & Governance* 17.2 (2023): 570–591.

75 McCarthy, et al. "Policing COVID-19 physical distancing measures."

76 Charron, Nicholas, Victor Lapuente, and Andrés Rodriguez-Pose. "Uncooperative society, uncooperative politics or both? How trust, polarization and populism explain excess mortality for COVID-19 across European regions." *European Journal of Political Research* 62.3 (2020): 781–805.

77 Kerr, John, Costas Panagopoulos, and Sander Van Der Linden. "Political polarization on COVID-19 pandemic response in the United States." *Personality and Individual Differences* 179 (2021): 1–9.

pandemic's first wave. Not surprisingly, other studies show that countries with more liberal regimes and greater state capacity to respond generally fared worse during the pandemic compared to countries with less liberal regimes and lower incomes.[78]

THE COMPLIANCE OVERLOAD EFFECT

One notable dilemma faced by governments around the world is related to the question of how to create the best policy regarding wearing masks. Should we establish a basic and inclusive rule or provide individuals with more nuanced and informed options? If we want people to wear masks indoors, what practice is more likely to increase that likelihood: saying "Always wear a mask," or saying, "Wear masks only when you are indoors"? On the one hand, unambiguous rules are easier to understand and monitor, making them better for establishing social norms.[79] However, it is important to consider the legitimacy of the request; asking for too much may result in receiving nothing at all.

Elsewhere I have demonstrated that engineers in Silicon Valley, who believed that trade secret laws required them to do more than they thought reasonable (e.g., not using information they already possessed) were more likely to behave unethically, even outside their professional contexts.[80] The argument I developed was that if the law is seen as overly inclusive, it loses its legitimacy even among those who would support it.[81] In the context of COVID-19, if people are asked to obey the law and wear masks in public areas, they may comply. However, this may also lead to a decrease in trust in the legislators' decision-making abilities, ultimately eroding overall trust in the legal system. Research on compliance could benefit from integrating these lessons into a variety of other research contexts.

THE IMPORTANCE OF EFFICACY AND VULNERABILITY

Trust encompasses both confidence in the effectiveness of specific measures and faith in institutional legitimacy, with the former being more closely tied to intrinsic motivation. Studies across multiple countries show that perceived effectiveness of COVID-19 policies was the key factor in compliance.[82] People's belief in their ability

78 Besely, Tim. "Trust, resilience, and effectiveness of government." *LSE Economics* (December 2020). www.lse.ac.uk/Events/Events-Assets/PDF/2020/03-MT/Tim-Besley-PP.pdf.

79 E.g., Posner, Eric A. "Standards, rules, and social norms." *Harvard Journal of Law & Public Policy* 21 (1997): 101–118.

80 Feldman, Yuval. "The expressive function of trade secret law: Legality, cost, intrinsic motivation, and consensus." *Journal of Empirical Legal Studies* 6.1 (2009): 177–212.

81 Feldman, Yuval. "Experimental approach to the study of normative failures: Divulging of trade secrets by Silicon Valley employees." *University of Illinois Journal of Law, Technology & Policy* 1 (2003): 105–108.

82 Jørgensen, et al. "Compliance without fear."

to impact pandemic outcomes significantly influenced their behavior,[83] though self-reported compliance data may show reporting biases not found in econometric studies. Ganesh Iyer and colleagues highlighted that people's belief in the efficacy of preventive measures was the strongest motivator for compliance.[84] Sarah Kreps suggested that belief in the efficacy of vaccination was more important than financial incentives in encouraging vaccination uptake.[85]

The pandemic's limited enforcement capacity highlighted questions about what drives safety guideline adherence. While some research demonstrates that incentives influence vaccination decisions,[86] other studies found that understanding vaccine efficacy was more crucial.[87] US-based research supported this, showing health concerns and beliefs as primary motivators.[88]

Vlaev and colleagues propose using behavioral economics insights – like loss aversion and hyperbolic discounting – to improve health policy design.[89] A large study of 8,317 individuals found that belief in health precaution efficacy predicted voluntary compliance behaviors. Another study of 26,000 citizens across 8 Western countries during the first COVID-19 wave revealed that while fear of disease predicted self-protective behavior, self-efficacy had significant impact, especially among those perceiving lower threat levels. Notably, interpersonal and institutional trust did not improve compliance.[90]

SOFTER RHETORIC, GENDER, AND COMPLIANCE

To some extent, the interplay between intrinsic and extrinsic motivation is related to some of the intriguing discussions prevalent during the COVID-19 era. For example, it appears from a brief review of the literature that women leaders were less likely than their male counterparts to use war-like rhetoric.[91] Moreover, some studies have shown that women leaders were more likely than male leaders to prioritize minimizing human suffering, to adopt a more caretaking-orientated approach.[92]

83 Martela, Frank, et al. "Motivating voluntary compliance to behavioral restrictions: Self-determination theory-based checklist of principles for COVID-19 and other emergency communications." *European Review of Social Psychology* 32.2 (2021): 305–347.

84 See: Iyer, Nandur, and Soberman. "Vaccine hesitancy and monetary incentives."

85 Kreps, et al. "Public attitudes toward COVID-19 vaccination," 73.

86 Saban, et al. "Issues surrounding incentives and penalties for COVID-19 vaccination," 106763.

87 Clark, et al. "Predictors of COVID-19 voluntary compliance behaviors."

88 Kreps et al. "Public attitudes toward COVID-19 vaccination," 73.

89 Vlaev, et al. "Changing health behaviors using financial incentives."

90 Jørgensen, Frederik Juhl, et al. *Lockdown evaluations during the first wave of the COVID-19 pandemic.* Aarhus University Press, 2020.

91 Dada, Sara, et al. "Words matter: Political and gender analysis of speeches made by heads of government during the COVID-19 pandemic." *BMJ Global Health* 6.1 (2021): 1–12.

92 Luoto, Severi, and Marco Antonio Correa Varella. "Pandemic leadership: Sex differences and their evolutionary–developmental origins." *Frontiers in Psychology* 12 (2021): 1–23. www.frontiersin.org/

NON-COVID-19 INTRINSIC MOTIVATION STUDIES

Several studies in recent years have focused on using nudge interventions to promote healthier dietary choices. Tamara Bucher and her colleagues showed that by altering the order or placement of food products, it is possible to have a significant impact on consumers' food choices.[93] In a similar vein, the efficacy of nudge interventions in improving children's dietary habits within the home was explored by Kate Lycett and her team.[94] Their findings showed that 83 percent of the interventions were successful in increasing vegetable consumption and reducing the choice of unhealthy portion sizes. Furthermore, the study revealed that nudges were more effective among older children and adolescents. Numerous other studies have also explored the impact of nudging on food choices and nutrition. Arno and Thomas performed a systematic review of nudge strategies and discovered that these tactics effectively boosted the selection of healthy food options by an average of 15.3 percent.[95] These findings suggest that nudge interventions have the potential to positively influence public health by encouraging healthier dietary choices, although further research is needed to address the limitations identified in the current body of knowledge.

SELF-EFFICACY AS INTRINSIC MOTIVATION

As mentioned, self-efficacy – people's belief in their ability to successfully take protective actions – appears to be a critical factor in health compliance, enabling individuals to act on their intrinsic motivation. Self-efficacy refers to an individual's belief in their ability to execute behaviors necessary to reach specific goals and is a significant predictor of COVID-19 voluntary compliance behavior.[96] We can observe that higher self-efficacy can reduce stress related to COVID-19 and positively correlates with adolescents' protective behaviors.[97] Higher self-efficacy is also related to increased adoption and frequency of taking preventive measures.[98]

journals/psychology/articles/10.3389/fpsyg.2021.633862/full. See also other directions in research on this topic: World Health Organization. "Closing the leadership gap: Gender equity and leadership in the global health and care workforce." Policy action paper (June 2021). https://iris.who.int/bitstream/handle/10665/341636/9789240025905-eng.pdf.

93 Bucher, Tamara, et al. "Nudging consumers towards healthier choices: A systematic review of positional influences on food choice." *British Journal of Nutrition* 115.12 (2016): 2252–2263.

94 Lycett, Kate, et al. "'Nudge' interventions for improving children's dietary behaviors in the home: A systematic review." *Obesity Medicine* 7 (2017): 21–33.

95 Arno, Anneliese, and Steve Thomas. "The efficacy of nudge theory strategies in influencing adult dietary behaviour: A systematic review and meta-analysis." *BMC Public Health* 16 (2016): 1–11.

96 Meyer, Natanya, et al. "Biting the bullet: When self-efficacy mediates the stressful effects of COVID-19 beliefs." *PLOS One* 17.1 (2022): 1–16.

97 Meyer, et al. "Biting the bullet," e0263022; Fathian-Dastgerdi, et al. "Factors associated with preventive behaviors of COVID-19 among adolescents."

98 Ozdemir, et al. "Adoption of preventive behavior strategies and public perceptions about COVID-19 in Singapore," 579.

Morality and Social Norms

Regarding the impact of moral values on compliance with COVID-19 regulations, studies conducted in Switzerland revealed that individuals with lower care for intrinsic social and moral factors were more likely to be noncompliant.[99] In contrast, a different study of young participants (college students) found that acceptance of preventive measures was not linked to personal characteristics. Instead, it was related to how highly participants prioritized health concerns.[100]

In another study, the significance of social norms was found to be crucial in the context of COVID-19,[101] particularly regarding the acceptability of prioritizing health over other interests. Social norms rather than individual behavior played a crucial role in promoting public health acceptance.[102]

CONCLUSION

The COVID-19 pandemic has provided valuable insights into public health compliance strategies. While research reveals complex factors influencing individual behavior, the inconsistent findings present a key challenge for voluntary compliance approaches. This uncertainty makes it difficult for regulators to confidently shift toward trust-based policies, as the evidence about their effectiveness remains mixed. Although extrinsic motivators such as rewards and punishments have demonstrated some success, particularly in boosting vaccination rates, the significance of intrinsic motivation cannot be disregarded, at least not in the COVID context.

Empirical evidence demonstrated that compliance with COVID-19 guidelines was primarily driven by three intrinsic factors: belief in the effectiveness of preventive measures, institutional trust, and sense of social responsibility. The magnitude of these intrinsic motivators' impact proved notably higher in the COVID-19 context compared to environmental and tax compliance scenarios examined in Chapters 9 and 10.

Moreover, while belief in scientific evidence emerged as a particularly strong predictor of compliance, regulators faced significant constraints in their available extrinsic enforcement mechanisms during the pandemic. The limitations of

99 Nivette, Amy, et al. "Non-compliance with COVID-19-related public health measures among young adults in Switzerland: Insights from a longitudinal cohort study." *Social Science & Medicine* 268 (2021): 1–9.

100 Zhu, Nan, Judith G. Smetana, and Lei Chang. "Acceptance of society-level and individual-level preventive measures during the COVID-19 pandemic among college students in three societies." *Journal of Cross-Cultural Psychology* 52.7 (2021): 606–621.

101 Kittel, Bernhard, Fabian Kalleitner, and David W. Schiestl. "Peers for the fearless: Social norms facilitate preventive behavior when individuals perceive low COVID-19 health risks." *PLOS One* 16.12 (2021): 1–20.

102 Zhu, Smetana, and Chang. "Acceptance of society-level and individual-level preventive measures during the COVID-19 pandemic."

mandates and coercive measures, especially in liberal democracies, suggest that public health officials should balance targeted incentives with trust building, education, and appeals to collective responsibility. Moreover, the variations in reactions among various demographic groups and cultures indicate that policies designed for everyone are unlikely to be successful. Future public health strategies need to be adaptable, culturally sensitive, and designed in a way that motivates both intrinsic and extrinsic factors, with a particular emphasis on enhancing self-efficacy and social norms that promote healthy behaviors. The COVID-19 pandemic has provided us with valuable insights that can help us tackle future public health challenges and improve our society's resilience.

9

Voluntary Tax Compliance

INTRODUCTION

One of the areas in which the relative efficacy of voluntary compliance and monitoring has been extensively studied is that of taxation.[1] Taxation serves as a central example in compliance studies for several reasons. It presents a universal opportunity to examine unethical behavior, as every citizen faces tax-related decisions that could involve evasion at various levels. This makes taxation particularly valuable for studying compliance behavior, as it provides a natural context where individuals must choose between full compliance and various degrees of evasion.[2] This level of unethicality does not exist in other less ordinary contexts, where citizens do not have the capacity not to comply even if they wanted to do so. Throughout history, governments have faced the challenging task of increasing compliance with tax laws to maximize their tax income.[3] Widespread tax evasion raises the costs of tax collection because it requires more resources to detect and stop noncompliance. Moreover, tax evasion distorts the distribution of the tax burden, creating inequality and unfairness in that taxpayers who abide by the rules bear a disproportionately higher financial burden.[4]

1 For a discussion and evidence on the challenge of making a tax system fully successful without information and monitoring, see Dwenger, Nadja, et al. "Extrinsic and intrinsic motivations for tax compliance: Evidence from a field experiment in Germany." *American Economic Journal: Economic Policy* 8.3 (2016): 203–232; Batrancea, Larissa, et al. "Trust and power as determinants of tax compliance across 44 nations." *Journal of Economic Psychology* 74 (2019): 1–15; Ioan, Batrancea, et al. "An empirical investigation on determinants of sustainable economic growth. Lessons from Central and Eastern European countries." *Journal of Risk and Financial Management* 13.7 (2020): 1–25; Hartmann, Andre Julian, Martin Mueller, and Erich Kirchler. *Tax compliance: Research methods and decision processes*. Springer International Publishing, 2020; Kogler, Christoph, et al. "Trust and power as determinants of tax compliance: Testing the assumptions of the slippery slope framework in Austria, Hungary, Romania and Russia." *Journal of Economic Psychology* 34 (2013): 169–180; Alm, James. "What motivates tax compliance?" *Journal of Economic Surveys* 33.2 (2019): 353–388.

2 Andreoni, James, Brian Erard, and Jonathan Feinstein. "Tax compliance." *Journal of Economic Literature* 36.2 (1998): 818–860.

3 Andreoni, Erard, and Feinstein. "Tax compliance."

4 Slemrod, Joel. "Tax compliance and enforcement." *Journal of Economic Literature* 57.4 (2019): 904–954.

This chapter presents a comprehensive overview of research on tax compliance, with a particular emphasis on the complex relationship between intrinsic motivation, extrinsic factors, and government policies aimed at promoting tax payment. Among other issues, it explores the concept of tax morale – the intrinsic motivation to pay taxes – and its relationship to actual compliance behavior. These studies reveal a nuanced relationship between interventions aimed at improving tax morale and compliance outcomes. They suggest that the effectiveness of these interventions varies depending on the context, including factors such as cultural norms, current levels of compliance, and the wording used in the appeals.

Tax compliance not only presents a common dilemma for ordinary citizens but also poses unique challenges compared to other areas of regulatory compliance. First, the primary dilemma in taxation seems to be related to honesty, which is not the case in most environmental or COVID-related behavior. Second, taxes usually require less emphasis on compliance expectations or encouraging behavioral changes compared to environmental issues. This is because tax compliance is more of a bureaucratic requirement than compliance with other kinds of regulations, which require deliberate conduct. Third, tax compliance represents a context in which the dilemma can be viewed as a zero-sum game, where every dollar paid in taxes is taken away from the individual.[5] In contrast to tax compliance, environmental behavior, which is the focus of Chapter 10, present a different set of challenges and motivations. Whether it's purchasing an electric car, opting for green energy, or supporting circular economy products, these actions are often voluntary and can be driven by a mix of personal values, social norms, and economic incentives. Unlike mandatory tax payments, individuals have more choice in these environmental decisions and the benefits are often more tangible and immediate to the individual and their community.

From a governmental perspective, ensuring high compliance rates is essential. This underscores the importance of monitoring and applying research on trust-building strategies. Trust between government and citizens works reciprocally – when governments implement policies that enhance citizen trust, whether in taxation or other domains, the effects often extend beyond the policy's immediate scope, creating broader improvements in state–citizen relationships.[6] For example, policies that improve transparency, ensure consistent enforcement, or provide clear explanations for regulations may increase trust, even if that wasn't their primary goal. The key is that when citizens perceive the government as effective, fair, and responsive, trust tends to grow, regardless of whether the policies were specifically crafted with trust building in mind.

[5] Erard, Brian, and Jonathan S. Feinstein. "Honesty and evasion in the tax compliance game." *RAND Journal of Economics* 25.1 (1994): 1–19.

[6] Swaner, Rachel. "Trust matters: Enhancing government legitimacy through participatory budgeting." *New Political Science* 39.1 (2017): 95–108.

This chapter's review also highlights the crucial role of trust in the government and how it affects tax compliance. Research consistently shows that when people have higher levels of trust in government and institutions, they are generally more willing to pay taxes.[7] In addition, this chapter examines the effectiveness of different regulatory approaches, ranging from coercive measures to more cooperative strategies. It also examines the potential of utilizing behavioral interventions, or "nudges," to enhance tax compliance. Finally, it explores the cultural and cross-national differences in attitudes and behaviors related to tax compliance. This will highlight the significance of taking local contexts into account when developing tax compliance strategies.

Many questions remain unanswered regarding the most effective government strategies for encouraging tax compliance. As will be developed throughout the chapter, we will try to answer questions such as what is the conclusion that can be drawn from studies that focus on different framings of texts sent to people? What can be learned from the research on procedural justice and taxation? How significant is the impact? What can be learned from the various studies focusing on ethical nudges, such as requiring signatures at the beginning of tax forms,[8] as well as various pledges that might reduce the need for states to monitor people's ethical behavior?[9] As in Chapter 8, the focus of much of the discussion here will focus on trying to identify the best practices for improving compliance and what can be generalized from them to other contexts.

WHAT IS TAX COMPLIANCE?

An interesting example comes from an Indian study by Anil Kumar Jain on tax evasion, tax avoidance, and the black economy in India, as well as the impact of policies on these issues.[10] The research examined the underlying causes and consequences of evasion and avoidance and proposed measures to address these issues. The study also presented information about the quantity of offenders and the corresponding penalties they received.

Scott Dyreng and colleagues examined corporate tax avoidance over time using a measure called "the long-run cash effective" tax rate.[11] The study investigated to

7 Feld, Lars P., and Bruno S. Frey. "Trust breeds trust: How taxpayers are treated." *Economics of Governance* 3 (2002): 87–99.

8 Shu, Lisa L., et al. "Signing at the beginning makes ethics salient and decreases dishonest self-reports in comparison to signing at the end." *Proceedings of the National Academy of Sciences of the United States of America* 109.38 (2012): 15197–15200.

9 Pe'er, Eyal, and Yuval Feldman. "Honesty pledges for the behaviorally-based regulation of dishonesty." *Journal of European Public Policy* 28.5 (2021): 761–781.

10 Jain, Anil Kumar. "Tax avoidance and tax evasion: The Indian case." *Modern Asian Studies* 21.2 (1987): 233–255.

11 Dyreng, Scott D., Michelle Hanlon, and Edward L. Maydew. "Long-run corporate tax avoidance." *The Accounting Review* 83.1 (2008): 61–82, at 62.

what extent companies could reduce their tax burden over ten years. It also evaluated the reliability of annual tax rates as a predictor of long-term tax avoidance. After analyzing a sample of 2,077 firms, the researchers found that although the average tax rate was 30 percent, the effective tax rate amounted to 20 percent. Moreover, their findings indicate that annual tax rates do not necessarily predict a company's long-term tax avoidance behavior. However, firms that manage to maintain low effective tax rates can do so for extended periods. This study is valuable for its analysis of long-term corporate tax avoidance and its measurement of tax rates and effective tax rates, which are crucial in examining these issues.

Lei Guangyong and colleagues examined how the cultural diversity across Chinese cities where corporations operate influences organizations' tax avoidance behavior.[12] The researchers found that companies located in culturally diverse cities participated in less tax avoidance compared to companies located in more homogeneous cities. The impact of this effect was more significant in cases where companies had strong managerial incentives and when cities experienced higher levels of migration and even more so when companies were under internal or external monitoring. This study is valuable for its introduction of cultural diversity as a factor in the analysis of tax avoidance, which appears to be a relatively unexplored topic in the literature.

Finally, Keith Stavely conducted a study comparing the effectiveness of coercive policies versus service and value-based policies in minimizing tax evasion.[13] The research concluded that policies focusing on service and value were more effective, likely because they have the potential to foster trust between citizens and the government. The study's findings suggest that governments should prioritize building trust, improving service quality, and emphasizing the societal advantages of tax contributions to increase voluntary compliance and decrease tax evasion.

MONITORING, AUDITS, AND TAX COMPLIANCE

The presence of audit mechanisms in regulatory frameworks could undermine claims about regulators' genuine trust in regulated entities. Even in cooperative regulatory programs, the ongoing threat of audits suggests that compliance behavior may not be purely voluntary, but rather shaped by the prospect of verification and potential enforcement. Indeed, tax policy audits serve as a cornerstone of fiscal policy and tax administration, functioning as a critical deterrence mechanism in promoting tax compliance.[14] These systematic examinations of taxpayers' financial

[12] Lei, Guangyong, et al. "Cultural diversity and corporate tax avoidance: Evidence from Chinese private enterprises." *Journal of Business Ethics* 176 (2022): 357–379.

[13] Snavely, Keith. "Governmental policies to reduce tax evasion: Coerced behavior versus services and values development." *Policy Sciences* 23.1 (1990): 57–72. https://doi.org/10.1007/s10551-020-04683-2.

[14] For more elaboration see, for example, Allingham, Michael G., and Agnar Sandmo. "Income tax evasion: A theoretical analysis." *Journal of Public Economics* 1.3–4 (1972): 323–338; Alm. "What motivates tax compliance?"

records and declarations operate on multiple levels within the broader framework of tax enforcement, simultaneously verifying reporting accuracy, detecting potential fraud, and encouraging broader compliance through deterrence.

The implementation of tax audits encompasses various methodologies across a spectrum of scrutiny. At one end, auditors may conduct targeted reviews of specific line items or transactions. At the other end, they may perform comprehensive examinations of an entity's complete financial portfolio, including detailed analyses of supporting documentation, transaction histories, and accounting methodologies. Modern tax authorities have enhanced their audit efficiency through sophisticated risk assessment algorithms and advanced data analytics. These tools help identify returns exhibiting characteristics associated with higher probabilities of noncompliance or significant discrepancies, allowing for more strategic allocation of limited auditing resources.[15]

This strategic deployment of audit resources serves dual purposes. First, it increases the effectiveness of actual audit procedures by focusing examinations on returns most likely to yield significant adjustments or uncover noncompliance. Second, and perhaps more importantly, it amplifies the deterrent effect of audits across the broader taxpayer population. When taxpayers understand that sophisticated methods may detect noncompliance, they are more likely to file accurate returns, even if their actual probability of being audited remains relatively low.

The development of cooperative compliance programs in various jurisdictions has further evolved the role of audits. Under these programs, taxpayers who demonstrate robust internal controls and transparent reporting may qualify for reduced audit intensity or real-time issue resolution. For instance, the Netherlands' horizontal monitoring program and Australia's justified trust initiative represent innovative approaches where past compliance behavior influences future audit likelihood and intensity.

Empirical research consistently demonstrates the effectiveness of tax audits in promoting compliance. Studies across multiple jurisdictions show that both direct enforcement through completed audits and indirect deterrence through perceived audit risk significantly influence taxpayer behavior.[16] However, research also indicates that the relationship between audit probability and compliance is not linear, suggesting the importance of maintaining a sophisticated and adaptable audit strategy.[17]

[15] Atayah, Osama F., and Muneer M. Alshater. "Audit and tax in the context of emerging technologies: A retrospective analysis, current trends, and future opportunities." *International Journal of Digital Accounting Research* 21 (2021): 95–128.

[16] Kasper, Matthias, and James Alm. "Audits, audit effectiveness, and post-audit tax compliance." *Journal of Economic Behavior & Organization* 195 (2022): 87–102.

[17] Bentley, Kathleen A., Thomas C. Omer, and Nathan Y. Sharp. "Business strategy, financial reporting irregularities, and audit effort." *Contemporary Accounting Research* 30.2 (2013): 780–817.

Research indicates that audits, when done properly, can be a useful tool for increasing compliance. A recent study examined the impact of operational tax audits on self-employed US taxpayers and found significant effects on future compliance.[18] The study revealed that audits led to increased reported income in subsequent years. Overall, audited taxpayers reported 15 percent higher taxable income in the years following the audit. However, the effects varied based on the audit outcome:

1. Taxpayers who received additional tax assessments (i.e., were found to have underpaid) subsequently reported 64 percent higher income in the following year and this effect persisted, with a 44 percent increase still evident three years later.
2. Conversely, taxpayers who underwent audits but received no additional assessments (i.e., were found to be compliant) subsequently reported 15 percent lower income in the following year, with this effect increasing to a 21 percent reduction after three years.

These findings suggest that audit experiences significantly influence future tax-reporting behavior, but in different ways depending on the audit outcome. Moreover, the study implies that improving the targeting of audits toward noncompliant taxpayers could potentially increase both immediate audit revenue and future tax collections.

Interestingly, in some studies,[19] oversight by tax authorities has not been shown to affect compliance. A novel field experiment on tax compliance specifically focused on newly founded firms to examine the effect of tax authorities' supervision on timely tax payments. It is interesting to note that the results do not demonstrate a positive effect of close supervision on tax compliance.[20]

Monitoring and Trust in Tax Compliance

An increasing number of studies show that monitoring alone is not sufficient to ensure tax compliance. The field of taxation has become a leading area in which the relative efficacy of voluntary compliance versus strict monitoring and high sanctions has been widely and deeply studied.[21] We argue that any suggested association between audits and instrumental tax motivation ignores much of what we know about the importance

[18] Beer, Sebastian, et al. "Do audits deter or provoke future tax noncompliance? Evidence on self-employed taxpayers." *CESifo Economic Studies* 66.3 (2020): 248–264.

[19] Tax oversight might be seen as a more preventive approach.

[20] Gangl, Katharina, et al. "Effects of supervision on tax compliance: Evidence from a field experiment in Austria." *Economics Letters* 123.3 (2014): 378–382.

[21] See: Dwenger, et al. "Extrinsic and intrinsic motivations for tax compliance"; Andrighetto, Giulia, et al. "Are some countries more honest than others? Evidence from a tax compliance experiment in Sweden and Italy." *Frontiers in Psychology* 7 (2016): 1–8.

of other mechanisms in tax compliance.[22] In many countries, noncoercive initiatives have been proposed to obtain public cooperation. These approaches have some clear advantages, in terms of quality of compliance and enforcement costs, over coercive tax collection methods that rely on the exercise of state power.[23]

Behavioral tax compliance scholars, such as Erich Kirchler and Michael Wenzel,[24] have conducted considerable research in the field and have observed two competing forces: the power of authorities versus trust in authorities. The common discovery of many studies in that tradition is that when people perceive tax authorities as trustworthy, they are more likely to comply voluntarily with tax requirements, whereas if people perceive tax authorities as powerful, compliance tends to be coerced. This approach holds value, as power can discourage unwanted behavior through monitoring and sanctions, whereas trust can encourage cooperation and self-motivation.

Building on our earlier discussion, linking perceived trustworthiness to intrinsic compliance requires a more nuanced approach that combines both behavioral insights and institutional factors. First, based on research on conditional cooperation, we can demonstrate how people's willingness to pay taxes can increase when they know that the tax authorities are collecting taxes from other tax evaders.[25] Second, a meta-analysis examining the effectiveness of deterrence has shown that higher levels of trust can enhance the authorities' ability to deter individuals.[26] Third, most of the studies in this field overlook factors that we developed in previous sections. These include understanding the heterogeneity of the effect (i.e., identifying which segment of the population reacts to a particular regulatory approach), determining its durability and sustainability on taxpayers' behaviors in the years that follow, and evaluating its broader effects, such as how taxpayers will behave in other contexts.[27]

22 Kemper, Nathan, et al. "The effects of honesty oath and consequentiality in choice experiments." Paper presented at Agricultural and Applied Economics Association Annual Meeting (2016).

23 Muehlbacher, Stephan, Erich Kirchler, and Herbert Schwarzenberger. "Voluntary versus enforced tax compliance: Empirical evidence for the 'slippery slope' framework." *European Journal of Law and Economics* 32 (2011): 89–97.

24 Kirchler, E. *The economic psychology of tax behaviour*. Cambridge University Press, 2007; Kirchler, Erich, Christoph Kogler, and Stephan Muehlbacher. "Cooperative tax compliance: From deterrence to deference." *Current Directions in Psychological Science* 23.2 (2014): 87–92; Wenzel, Michael. "An analysis of norm processes in tax compliance." *Journal of Economic Psychology* 25.2 (2004): 213–228.

25 Frey, Bruno S., and Benno Torgler. "Tax morale and conditional cooperation." *Journal of Comparative Economics* 35.1 (2007): 136–159.

26 Balliet, Daniel, and Paul A. M. Van Lange. "Trust, conflict, and cooperation: A meta-analysis." *Psychological Bulletin* 139.5 (2013): 1090–1112.

27 "2020 global forum annual report: Tax transparency and exchange of information in time of COVID-19 (OECD)." www.oecd.org/en/publications/2020/04/global-forum-on-transparency-and-exchange-of-information-for-tax-purposes-switzerland-2020-second-round_0a70b055.html; Rogers, Daniel T. *Environmental compliance and sustainability: Global challenges and perspectives*. CRC Press, 2019. https://doi.org/10.1201/9780429400667.

ENFORCEMENT, POWER, AND TAX COMPLIANCE MOTIVATIONS

Tax studies have shown that the use of what is known as "high power," meaning stricter enforcement measures, can result in a decline in compliance.[28] Various approaches have been found to enhance tax compliance, including the use of financial and nonfinancial aids. These include appealing to an individual's morality, guilt, or sympathy.[29] It has also been found that political ideology can affect how people perceive the use of coercive measures and tax compliance.[30] To encourage tax compliance, tax authorities in different countries have implemented behaviorally based tax compliance programs (nudges, reminders, framing of letters, changing defaults, and so on)[31] to prime social norms and promote fairness.[32] This study, as well as many others, demonstrate that there is a relationship between people's tax motivation and factors beyond financial considerations, such as social norms and morality, that contribute to the overall perception.[33] Indeed, many countries have made changes to how tax authorities regulate the behavior of their citizens. For example, countries in Europe have been deploying cooperative strategies such as "enhanced relationships," "horizontal monitoring," and "fair-play initiatives."[34]

COERCION VERSUS TRUST IN TAX COMPLIANCE

Research on tax compliance reveals complex relationships between power, trust, and compliance behavior. According to Hofmann and colleagues' study, while coercive power alone affected reason-based trust and intended tax compliance, it didn't reduce implicit trust in tax authorities when combined with legitimate power.[35]

[28] Batrancea, et al. "Trust and power as determinants of tax compliance across 44 nations"; Kaplanoglou, Georgia, and Vassilis T. Rapanos. "Why do people evade taxes? New experimental evidence from Greece." *Journal of Behavioral and Experimental Economics* 56 (2015): 21–32; Pukeliene, Violeta, and Austeja Kažemekaityte. "Tax behaviour: Assessment of tax compliance in European Union countries." *Ekonomika* 95.2 (2016): 30–56.

[29] Alm. "What motivates tax compliance?"

[30] Lozza, Edoardo, et al. "The relationship between political ideology and attitudes toward tax compliance: The case of Italian taxpayers." *Journal of Social and Political Psychology* 1.1 (2013): 51–73.

[31] Hofmann, Eva, Erik Hoelzl, and Erich Kirchler. "Preconditions of voluntary tax compliance: Knowledge and evaluation of taxation, norms, fairness, and motivation to cooperate." *Zeitschrift für Psychologie/Journal of Psychology* 216.4 (2008): 209–217.

[32] John, Peter, and Toby Blume. "How best to nudge taxpayers? The impact of message simplification and descriptive social norms on payment rates in a central London local authority." *Journal of Behavioral Public Administration* 1.1 (2018): 1–11.

[33] Trivedi, Viswanath Umashanker, Mohamed Shehata, and Stuart Mestelman. "Attitudes, incentives, and tax compliance." *Canadian Tax Journal* 53 (2005): 29–61.

[34] Kirchler, Erich. "Strengthening tax compliance by balancing authorities' power and trustworthiness." No. 2019-03. WU International Taxation Research Paper Series (2019).

[35] Hofmann, Eva, et al. "Enhancing tax compliance through coercive and legitimate power of tax authorities by concurrently diminishing or facilitating trust in tax authorities." *Law & Policy* 36.3 (2014): 290–313.

A contrasting study in Greece by Kaplanoglou and Rapanos found that trust increased voluntary compliance, while power increased enforced compliance.[36] Notably, in high-trust situations, power had no impact on voluntary compliance. However, when trust was low, high power actually decreased voluntary compliance levels.

Other research by Matthias Kasper and colleagues suggests a link between trust, power, and intentions to comply in a real-world setting.[37] Their findings indicate that media reports on tax issues address issues of trust and power and that both factors have an impact on the intended level of tax compliance. In a comprehensive literature review, Kirchler and colleagues explored intrinsic and extrinsic factors affecting tax compliance, including fines, audit probabilities, tax rates, knowledge, attitudes, norms, and fairness.[38]

The review explores the power and trust dimensions, referencing these factors throughout. Kirchler also found that ideology played a role in tax compliance. Left-leaning taxpayers expressed higher levels of voluntary cooperation and showed resistance to the coercive power of authorities. In contrast, right-leaning taxpayers demonstrated higher levels of enforced tax compliance and were more averse to tax evasion, showing increased trust in authorities and institutions.[39] Moreover, this trust is strongly correlated with individuals' perceptions of tax justice.[40]

INTEGRATING COMPETING TAX ENFORCEMENT APPROACHES

Research in this area has found that coercive power by tax authorities typically triggers negative reactions, while trust fosters positive compliance outcomes. Studies by Kirchler and his coauthors demonstrate that effectively combining trust-building measures with appropriate power dynamics can significantly reduce noncompliant behavior, leading to more sustainable compliance strategies. Understanding tax compliance requires examining both regulatory design and enforcement approaches. Kirchler's extensive research comparing various regulatory and enforcement methods has significantly shaped this field.[41] While his work initially focused on enforcement strategies through coercive and legitimate power, later collaborations

36 Kaplanoglou and Rapanos. "Why do people evade taxes?"

37 Kasper, Matthias, Christoph Kogler, and Erich Kirchler. "Tax policy and the news: An empirical analysis of taxpayers' perceptions of tax-related media coverage and its impact on tax compliance." *Journal of Behavioral and Experimental Economics* 54 (2015): 58–63.

38 Kirchler, Erich, Erik Hoelzl, and Ingrid Wahl. "Enforced versus voluntary tax compliance: The 'slippery slope' framework." *Journal of Economic Psychology* 29.2 (2008): 210–225.

39 Lozza, et al. "The relationship between political ideology and attitudes toward tax compliance."

40 Güzel, Sonnur Aktaş, Gökhan Özer, and Murat Özcan. "The effect of the variables of tax justice perception and trust in government on tax compliance: The case of Turkey." *Journal of Behavioral and Experimental Economics* 78 (2019): 80–86.

41 Kirchler, Hoelzl, and Wahl. "Enforced versus voluntary tax compliance."

expanded to explore the theoretical interaction between power and trust.[42] This research revealed that effective compliance strategies must balance enforcement mechanisms with trust-building approaches.

The broader literature on tax compliance demonstrates how different factors influence cooperative behavior. For instance, Lars Feld and Bruno Frey emphasize that treating taxpayers fairly and thoughtfully enhances compliance.[43] Additionally, studies have shown that public social sanctioning plays a crucial role in promoting cooperation in public good scenarios.[44]

This research on cooperation and tax compliance has revealed important insights about why people cooperate in social dilemmas, particularly focusing on sanctioning mechanisms and the nature of different compliance challenges. These findings contribute to our understanding of how regulatory design can effectively promote voluntary compliance while maintaining necessary enforcement measures.[45]

TRANSPARENCY AND VOLUNTARY TAX COMPLIANCE

Transparency serves as a crucial mechanism for fostering taxpayer trust. Tax policy research indicates that promoting transparency, directing tax revenues toward social expenditures, and maintaining stable tax rates are fundamental strategies for building citizen trust in governmental institutions.[46] These trust-building measures can potentially reduce both tax avoidance and evasion, particularly among individual taxpayers.[47]

Corporate tax compliance presents distinct challenges that stem from different motivational factors than those affecting individual taxpayers.[48] Moreover, country-specific factors significantly influence tax compliance rates, requiring

42 Gangl, Katharina, Eva Hofmann, and Erich Kirchler. "Tax authorities' interaction with taxpayers: A conception of compliance in social dilemmas by power and trust." *New Ideas in Psychology* 37 (2015): 13–23.

43 Feld, Lars P., and Bruno S. Frey. "Tax compliance as the result of a psychological tax contract: The role of incentives and responsive regulation." *Law & Policy* 29.1 (2007): 102–120.

44 Kroll, Stephan, Todd L. Cherry, and Jason F. Shogren. "Voting, punishment, and public goods." *Economic Inquiry* 45.3 (2007): 557–570.

45 Molenmaker, Welmer E., Erik W. de Kwaadsteniet, and Eric van Dijk. "On the willingness to costly reward cooperation and punish non-cooperation: The moderating role of type of social dilemma." *Organizational Behavior and Human Decision Processes* 125.2 (2014): 175–183.

46 Prichard, Wilson, et al. "Innovations in tax compliance: Conceptual framework." World Bank Policy Research Working Paper 9032 (2019).

47 Slemrod. "Tax compliance and enforcement."

48 Tax avoidance involves legally minimizing one's tax liability by taking advantage of existing loopholes or incentives in the tax code, while tax evasion is the illegal nonpayment or underpayment of taxes, often through deliberate misreporting or concealment of income; a classic example of tax avoidance is contributing to a tax-deferred retirement account to reduce current taxable income, whereas hiding cash earnings from a business and not reporting them on a tax return is a typical instance of tax evasion. Stiglitz, Joseph E. "The general theory of tax avoidance." *National Tax Journal* 38.3 (1985): 325–337.

careful consideration of national contexts. The identification and analysis of these factors, while methodologically challenging, remains essential for understanding how cultural and sociological variables impact compliance behaviors across different jurisdictions.

Does Tax Morale Substantially Contribute to Tax Compliance?

Since the 1960s, substantial attention has been focused on investigating "tax morale"[49] – the intrinsic motivation to pay taxes – as a crucial determinant of compliance.[50] Numerous studies support the idea that higher levels of tax morale led to enhanced tax compliance.[51] However, a considerable amount of this evidence is based on self-reported intentions to comply rather than actual compliance behaviors.

Despite the presumed importance of tax morale in reducing tax evasion and the shadow economy,[52] Žiga Puklavec and colleagues found little consensus on its definition and measurement.[53] Their systematic literature review reveals a wide range of definitions, from narrow concepts of intrinsic motivation to broad interpretations encompassing various nonpecuniary factors. It also demonstrates how intrinsic motivation was rarely measured as a separate concept, with some confusion between intrinsic motivation, tax morale, and morality. Operationalizations vary greatly, with the most common being a single question about the justifiability of tax cheating. This heterogeneity in definitions and measurements creates a misalignment between conceptualization and operationalization, highlighting the need for a unified definition and improved measurement instruments to better capture the psychology of tax morale.

Although some studies suggest that subjective norms are associated with actual tax evasion, further research is needed to establish a definitive link between these

49 The existence of a parallel debate around moral suasion, as a regulatory strategy in tax and other domains, should be noted. Moral suasion has faced significant scrutiny from both empirical and philosophical perspectives. Torgler's 2004 Swiss field experiment revealed the limited practical impact of moral suasion in tax compliance, while Bardach raised fundamental philosophical concerns about its validity as a regulatory approach. These studies suggest the need for careful consideration when employing moral suasion as a policy tool. Torgler, Benno. "Moral suasion: An alternative tax policy strategy? Evidence from a controlled field experiment in Switzerland." *Economics of Governance* 5.3 (2004): 235–253; Bardach, Eugene. "Moral suasion and taxpayer compliance." *Law & Policy* 11.1 (1989): 49–69.

50 Horodnic, Ioana Alexandra. "Tax morale and institutional theory: A systematic review." *International Journal of Sociology and Social Policy* 38.9–10 (2018): 868–886.

51 E.g., Torgler, Benno, and Friedrich Schneider. "The impact of tax morale and institutional quality on the shadow economy." *Journal of Economic Psychology* 30.2 (2009): 228–245.

52 Cummings, Ronald G., et al. "Tax morale affects tax compliance: Evidence from surveys and an artefactual field experiment." *Journal of Economic Behavior & Organization* 70.3 (2009): 447–457.

53 Puklavec, Žiga, et al. "Unobscuring the concept of tax morale." Working paper, 2024 (on file with author).

two factors, given that other studies have proved less conclusive.[54] In general, the complex interplay between tax morale and tax compliance behavior is shaped by a range of contextual factors, resulting in diverse outcomes.[55]

Jonathan Slater and colleagues conducted a combined mega-meta-analysis of the association between tax morale and actual tax behavior.[56] This research could shed light on the intention–behavior gap, enabling researchers and policymakers to comprehend tax morale's influence on tax compliance. In another study on tax morale, the classical causality was reversed and the effect of tax dilemmas on tax morale was examined, rather than the usual approach of examining the effect of tax morale on tax dilemmas.[57] The study's simulation placed young adults with limited experience in taxation in a situation where their attitudes toward taxes could be observed and where their attitudes influenced their decisions. Although the use of a simulation may have its drawbacks, it has allowed researchers to analyze how participants responded to, experienced, and observed these dilemmas. The study found that such tax dilemmas reduced both tax morale and compliance.

Scholz and Lubell's influential study examined how the 1986 Tax Reform Act impacted Americans' trust in government.[58] Analyzing responses from 292 participants, they found a direct relationship between tax changes and trust levels: Individuals who experienced tax decreases developed greater trust in the state, while those facing tax increases showed diminished trust. These findings demonstrated how tax policy changes can significantly affect citizens' trust in government institutions.

Along those lines, Antonios Koumpias and colleagues conducted a study to examine the factors that can enhance a population's tax morale.[59] They analyzed data from World Values Surveys collected from ninety-two countries between 1981 and 2014. According to this comprehensive study, governments can establish trust with citizens most effectively by improving the efficiency of agencies and programs that are output-based, as these are the government entities that citizens interact with most frequently. Instead of examining the correlation between citizen trust in the government and tax compliance, this study focused on how governments can increase trust to attain this goal. Therefore, it could serve as a foundational piece of research, as

[54] Wenzel. "An analysis of norm processes in tax compliance."

[55] Azmi, Deena Azriana Wan Mohd, and Seri Ayu Masuri Md Daud. "Reconceptualizing tax compliance behavior: A theoretical matrix approach." *Accounting and Finance Research* 13.1 (2024): 1–67.

[56] Slater, Jonathan, et al. "The role of tax morale on actual tax compliance: A meta-analytical review." Working paper, 2024 (on file with author).

[57] Deglaire, Emmanuelle, Peter Daly, and Fabrice Le Lec. "Exposure to tax dilemmas deteriorate individuals' self-declared tax morale." *Economics of Governance* 22 (2021): 363–397.

[58] Scholz, John T., and Mark Lubell. "Adaptive political attitudes: Duty, trust, and fear as monitors of tax policy." *American Journal of Political Science* 42.3 (1998): 903–920. https://doi.org/10.2307/2991734.

[59] Koumpias, Antonios M., Gabriel Leonardo, and Jorge Martinez-Vazquez. "Trust in government institutions and tax morale." *European Journal of Public Finance* 77.2 (2020): 117–140. https://doi.org/10.1628/fa-2021-0006.

any discussion on this topic would likely begin with analyzing the methods used to establish trust between the government and its citizens. Further evidence supporting the importance of tax morale and conditional cooperation with tax requirements is presented in a study drawing on survey data from thirty countries in Western and Eastern Europe. This study reports a strong correlation between perceived levels of tax evasion and tax morale.[60]

Importance of Tax Morale and Intrinsic Compliance Motivation

In an important field study on the effect of extrinsic motivation on compliance motivation, Nadja Dwenger and colleagues examined the interplay of intrinsic and extrinsic motivations related to tax compliance, which are based on incentives and deterrence measures.[61] They focused on the local church tax system in Germany,[62] which traditionally lacked deterrence mechanisms, relying on intrinsic motivation to encourage compliance. Through their additional analysis of tax obligations and payment records, they found that people have a strong intrinsic motivation to comply with tax laws, which may be linked to a sense of duty and responsibility. Most importantly in the context of this book, their findings show that there is no crowding out of intrinsic motivation when economic incentives are introduced. In a different context, Ronald Cummings and colleagues have also suggested that enforcement efforts alone cannot explain all aspects of tax compliance.[63] Using multiple methods, including surveys, existing data, and experiments, they arrived at their conclusions regarding the limits of enforcement after reviewing various factors, such as fairness and attitudes toward the tax authorities and cultures.[64]

Indeed, since the early 2000s, extensive empirical research has been conducted on the determinants of tax compliance and their correlation with tax morale as the alternative explanation for tax compliance.[65] Several studies have examined the effectiveness of different measures aimed at improving tax compliance, especially through messages that promote tax morale. However, this research has yielded nuanced and sometimes conflicting results. For example, Michael Hallsworth and colleagues conducted large-scale natural field experiments involving over 200,000 UK taxpayers.

60 Frey and Torgler. "Tax morale and conditional cooperation."

61 See: Dwenger, et al. "Extrinsic and intrinsic motivations for tax compliance."

62 In Germany and few other European countries, church tax is collected by the state tax authorities on behalf of the religious communities.

63 Cummings, Ronald G., et al. "Effects of tax morale on tax compliance: Experimental and survey evidence." CREMA Working Paper, No. 2005-29 (2006).

64 Marandu, Edward E., Christian J. Mbekomize, and Alexander N. Ifezue. "Determinants of tax compliance: A review of factors and conceptualizations." *International Journal of Economics and Finance* 7.9 (2015): 207–218.

65 Luttmer, Erzo F. P., and Monica Singhal. "Tax morale." *Journal of Economic Perspectives* 28.4 (2014): 149–168.

They found that social norm messages emphasizing widespread compliance can significantly increase timely tax payments.[66]

Similarly, Kristina Bott and colleagues conducted a randomized field experiment with 15,000 Norwegian taxpayers considered likely to have misreported foreign income. According to their findings, moral appeals emphasizing the societal benefits of tax contributions positively influenced compliance among certain taxpayer groups.[67] However, the impact of tax morale interventions on compliance is not consistently positive. Jan-Emmanuel De Neve and his team conducted a comprehensive study that examined the tax records of Belgian taxpayers over a couple of years. They concluded that simplification and deterrence messages were highly effective. However, appeals to tax morale were not only ineffective but, in some cases, were even counterproductive.[68] The varying outcomes indicate that the effectiveness of interventions aimed at improving tax morale may be dependent on the context, including cultural norms, existing compliance levels, and how the moral appeal is presented.

MOTIVATIONAL POSTURES THEORY AND TAX COMPLIANCE

In contrast to Kirchler's view, which appears more dichotomous, Valerie Braithwaite presented a more nuanced perspective on what it means to collaborate with the tax authority. This nuanced approach makes the challenge even more complex for tax authorities interested in enhancing intrinsic motivation to comply. She argues that those who resist most vocally, challenge tax authority decisions, and are openly critical of the institution, are not necessarily more noncompliant as a group than taxpayers who engage with the tax system in other ways.[69] Furthermore, younger people were found to be less compliant in attitude and behavior than older people. However, in Australia, high tax compliance is attributed to its taxpaying culture rather than to its youth culture.[70] Research shows that higher perceived deterrence reduces tax evasion, while it was also found that individuals displaying dismissive defiance – a response that can vary with deterrence levels – are more likely to evade taxes.[71] In addition, a study was conducted to examine the impact of motivation

66 Hallsworth, Michael, et al. "The behavioralist as tax collector: Using natural field experiments to enhance tax compliance." *Journal of Public Economics* 148 (2017): 14–31.

67 Bott, Kristina M., et al. "You've got mail: A randomized field experiment on tax evasion." *Management Science* 66.7 (2020): 2801–2819.

68 De Neve, Jan-Emmanuel, et al. "How to improve tax compliance? Evidence from population-wide experiments in Belgium." *Journal of Political Economy* 129.5 (2021): 1425–1463.

69 Braithwaite, Valerie. "Dancing with tax authorities: Motivational postures and non-compliant actions." *Taxing Democracy* 3 (2003): 15–39.

70 Braithwaite, Valerie, and Monika Reinhart. "The taxpayers' charter: Does the Australian Tax Office comply and who benefits?" Centre of Tax System Integrity report (2000).

71 Braithwaite, Valerie, and Monika Reinhart. "Deterrence, coping styles and defiance." *FinanzArchiv/Public Finance Analysis* 69.4 (2013): 439–468.

in postures, tax audit strategies, and peer-reporting behavior through experimental studies. The study demonstrates that the strategy of tax audits and peer-reporting behavior affect decisions regarding tax compliance strategies.[72] Some results show that enforcement tools have led to the opposite behavior than was sought. This suggests that punishing offenders with maximum penalties is not an effective way to encourage compliance with regulations.[73]

BEHAVIORAL INTERVENTIONS AND TAX COMPLIANCE

The complexity of the factors that influence tax compliance, as discussed earlier in this chapter, can be observed through the inconsistent outcomes of behavioral public policy studies that aim to examine how to encourage people to pay their taxes through various forms of nudges. Research by John Peter and Toby Blume regarding nudges and tax compliance has shown that nudges can enhance tax compliance and public administration by improving messages and thereby increasing revenue.[74] Their study used factorial designs to examine the effectiveness of simplification and social norms in promoting local tax compliance in central London. It finds that simplification led to a 4 percent increase in payments among a specific group of taxpayers, but the social norm approach did not have the intended impact in a larger sample, possibly because of the diverse characteristics of the target population and the wording of the norm. In addition, a meta-analysis based on forty-four randomized controlled trials found that simple reminders increase compliance probability by 10.8 percent compared to baseline levels. Nondeterrence nudges targeting tax morale show a 16.4 percent improvement, while deterrence-based interventions prove most effective, enhancing compliance by 23.6 percent.[75]

An additional paper used reminders to promote tax compliance in a nationwide randomized controlled trial in Guatemala. Focusing on alternative messaging aimed at reminding people about tax compliance, this study demonstrated the effectiveness of deterrence messages on social norms and morality factors in promoting tax compliance.[76] The trial involved variations in the letters sent to individuals and firms who did not pay their income tax for the 2013 tax year. The most effective

72 Puspitasari, Elen, and Wahyu Meiranto. Motivational postures in tax compliance decisions: An experimental study, *International Journal of Business, Economics and Law* 5.1 (2014): 100–110.

73 Sabri, Bibi Khairani Mohamed, et al. "Measures in curbing poor compliance to building control regulation among renovated terrace houses." *International Journal of Law in the Built Environment* 9.3 (2017): 256–271.

74 John and Blume. "How best to nudge taxpayers?"

75 Antinyan, Armenak, and Zareh Asatryan. "Nudging for tax compliance: A meta-analysis." *The Economic Journal* 135.668 (2024): 1033–1068.

76 Kettle, Stewart, et al. "Behavioral interventions in tax compliance: Evidence from Guatemala." World Bank Policy Research Working Paper 7690 (2016). See also Chirico, Michael, et al. "An experimental evaluation of notification strategies to increase property tax compliance: Free-riding in the city of brotherly love." *Tax Policy and the Economy* 30.1 (2016): 129–161.

treatments included a message that discouraged nondeclaration by framing it as a deliberate choice, designed to overcome status quo bias. Another effective approach was a social norms message that referenced the 64.5 percent of taxpayers who had already paid this tax, thus encouraging people to conform to the status quo. Most importantly, the effects were persistent and remained at a twelve-month follow-up.

Another paper of great interest drawing on a similar methodology demonstrated the difference between moral and detection (i.e., deterrence) letters sent to taxpayers in Norway.[77] A study comparing tax compliance letters found that moral appeals were more effective at increasing payment amounts from existing taxpayers, while deterrence messages better motivated nonpayers to make some payment. Notably, deterrence messages showed more lasting effects on compliance behavior.

MESSAGE EFFECTS ON TAX COMPLIANCE

It is not surprising that when analyzing the effects of different messages on tax compliance, we can see that the taxpayers' ability to avoid paying taxes is the factor that moderates the magnitude of the manipulation effect.[78] This might be seen as a chilling effect on the perceived importance of intrinsic motivation in ensuring compliance. However, numerous studies demonstrate the significance of fairness in this context. For example, a study of Australian taxpayers revealed significant differences between self-employed individuals and other taxpayers in their perceptions of fairness and experiences with the tax system.[79] Similarly, Wenzel has conducted a line of studies indicating that fairness-oriented letters were more likely to increase compliance.[80]

An additional study has examined the different policies that can be used by the state to minimize tax evasion. It also assesses the effectiveness of coercive policies versus service and value-based policies.[81] This study has found that value-based policies are more effective. Three correlational studies conducted with over 500 US residents focused on the prosocial aspects of taxation as a motivator for tax compliance. The studies found that when citizens are aware of the benefits of their taxes, they are more willing to pay higher taxes and even find more satisfaction in doing so.[82]

77 Bott, et al. "You've got mail."

78 Slemrod, Joel, Marsha Blumenthal, and Charles Christian. "Taxpayer response to an increased probability of audit: Evidence from a controlled experiment in Minnesota." *Journal of Public Economics* 79.3 (2001): 455–483.

79 Ahmed, Eliza, and Valerie Braithwaite. "Understanding small business taxpayers: Issues of deterrence, tax morale, fairness and work practice." *International Small Business Journal* 23.5 (2005): 539–568.

80 Wenzel, Michael. "A letter from the tax office: Compliance effects of informational and interpersonal justice." *Social Justice Research* 19 (2006): 345–364.

81 Snavely. "Governmental policies to reduce tax evasion."

82 Thornton, Emily M., et al. "Prosocial perceptions of taxation predict support for taxes." *PLOS One* 14.11 (2019): 1–12.

Furthermore, these studies indicate that people who trust their government tend to do so because they are convinced that the taxes they pay are being used for socially beneficial purposes.

These findings provide support for the idea that when governments try to show citizens how their taxes are being used, citizens are more likely to trust the state. Thus, even when numerous studies demonstrate that fairness contributes to tax compliance, its importance may be challenged if two conditions are met:[83] First, if fairness alone cannot ensure compliance, and second, if its effect size is marginal compared to other factors such as the ability to evade. This challenge becomes especially relevant if emphasizing fairness hinders the effectiveness of other regulatory methods. Thus, while this area of tax compliance has been studied extensively, especially by behavioral scholars interested in compliance, it is not clear that a gold standard has been established for the best approach to framing a letter's message.

TAX MORALE, RECIPROCITY, AND SELF-INTEREST

In light of the tension between fairness and self-interest in predicting and ensuring tax compliance, reciprocity emerges as an important motivation. It combines aspects of both fairness and self-interest, potentially bridging the gap between these competing factors.[84] Indeed, in tax context, research on reciprocity suggests that there may be limits to tax morale being solely based on moral attitudes.[85] This challenges the idea that tax morale is completely separate from self-interest. The impact of reciprocity was examined in an experimental study by Matias Giaccobasso and colleagues.[86] This study, examining property tax protests as a measure of tax morale, explored how information about the usage of tax money affects tax morale, highlighting the complex nature of individual preferences that are driven by self-interest. When households learned that a larger portion of their taxes was allocated to public schools, their reactions varied:

1. Households *with* children in public schools became less likely to protest, suggesting an increase in tax morale.
2. Households *without* children in public schools became more likely to protest, indicating a decrease in tax morale.

[83] Hartner, Martina, et al. "Procedural fairness and tax compliance." *Economic Analysis and Policy* 38.1 (2008): 137–152.

[84] Fehr, Ernst, and Klaus M. Schmidt. "The economics of fairness, reciprocity and altruism: Experimental evidence and new theories." *Handbook of the Economics of Giving, Altruism and Reciprocity* 1 (2006): 615–691.

[85] Doerrenberg, Philipp, and Andreas Peichl. "Tax morale and the role of social norms and reciprocity: Evidence from a randomized survey experiment." (2018). https://papers.ssrn.com/sol3/papers.cfm?abstract_id=3237993.

[86] Giaccobasso, Matias, et al. "Where do my tax dollars go? Tax morale effects of perceived government spending." No. w29789. National Bureau of Economic Research, 2022.

The interaction effect indicated that a 10 percentage point *increase* in the perceived school funding share led to a 3.7 percentage point *decrease* in tax appeals from households with children. The same increase resulted in a 2.8 percentage point increase in appeals from households without children. These findings underscore how individuals' perceptions of government spending can significantly influence tax morale. The impact varies depending on personal circumstances and perceived benefits from such spending. However, the research also reveals that the effect sizes are relatively small. This raises a crucial policy question: Given our discussion in Chapter 5 on the perils of voluntary compliance, is investing in intrinsic motivations cost-effective?

GOVERNMENT SUPPORT AND TAX COMPLIANCE

In the same tradition, Yair Listokin and David Schizer have written an important paper on factors related to intrinsic motivation to tax compliance in which they examine the relationship between taxpayer support of government spending and the efficiency of the tax system.[87] The authors argue that taxpayers are more inclined to support government spending when they perceive that the tax system to operating efficiently. They suggest, therefore, that a more efficient tax system can lead to greater taxpayer compliance and reduced tax evasion. This study presents empirical evidence to support these claims, drawing on data from surveys and experiments.

CULTURE AND TRUST: TAX COMPLIANCE AND TAX EVASION

The landscape of tax regulation becomes even more complex when we consider studies demonstrating how a country's culture affects the efficacy of various regulatory approaches. This cultural dimension allows us to examine how different countries can rely on their citizens' cooperation to varying degrees. Research in this area has taken two main approaches: comparative perspectives across multiple countries and in-depth case studies of individual nations. Overall, many of these studies have found that trust, especially institutional trust, is positively correlated with a higher willingness to pay taxes.[88] In some contexts, this correlation between institutional trust and willingness to pay taxes has been related to people's perceptions of certain programs; in other contexts, it has been associated with the general culture in each country. An example, related to people's perception of certain programs, is a study by Antonios Koumpias and colleagues exploring factors that increase a population's tax morale.[89] After examining data from the

[87] Listokin, Yair, and David M. Schizer. "I like to pay taxes: Taxpayer support for government spending and the efficiency of the tax system." *Tax Law Review* 66 (2012): 179–216.
[88] Batrancea, et al. "Trust and power as determinants of tax compliance across 44 nations."
[89] Koumpias, Leonardo, and Martinez-Vazquez. "Trust in government institutions and tax morale."

World Values Surveys in ninety-two countries, the results suggest that governments can effectively build trust in their citizens by creating more efficient output-based agencies and programs. The second type of situation, which is related to cultural differences, has been examined in a series of case studies on both developing and developed countries. For example, Gustavo Flores-Macías found that, in Mexico, implementing mechanisms for civil society oversight and earmarking taxes for specific programs increased public support for taxation.[90] The study also analyzed the effects of these measures by considering factors such as trust in government, perception of the public good, and income.

Numerous studies conducted mostly in developing countries have demonstrated the significance of trust in tax compliance. For example, Peggy Jimenez and Govind Iyer have explored the influence of social and personal norms on tax compliance, finding that these norms both affect and are affected by trust in government, as well as by other factors.[91] Abel Kinyondo and Mwoya Byaro studied the connection between citizens' trust in government and their willingness to pay taxes in Tanzania.[92] They found that low trust, largely caused by failures in public services, led to a reduced willingness to pay taxes. In their study of the effects of various types of trust on willingness to pay more taxes for welfare in South Korea and Taiwan, Eunyoung Nam and Myungsook Woo found that, in South Korea, having trust in the government led to a higher willingness to pay taxes for welfare specifically.[93]

Analyzing tax culture in Russian society, Irina Ogorodnikova and colleagues focused on tax morality, tax literacy, and tax behavior, concluding that institutional trust is a crucial factor in shaping tax culture.[94] Moreover, the study of Georgia Kaplanoglou and Vassilis Rapanos analyzed the failures of the Greek tax system, which ultimately led to a recession, and attributed them to several factors, including low institutional trust.[95] Marcel Bergman's study comparing taxes and social policies in Chile and Argentina emphasized the crucial role of trust in government as a

[90] Flores-Macías, Gustavo A. "Building support for taxation in developing countries: Experimental evidence from Mexico." *World Development* 105 (2018): 13–24.

[91] Jimenez, Peggy, and Govind S. Iyer. "Tax compliance in a social setting: The influence of social norms, trust in government, and perceived fairness on taxpayer compliance." *Advances in Accounting* 34 (2016): 17–26.

[92] Kinyondo, Abel, and Mwoya Byaro. "Does citizen's trust in government increase willingness to pay taxes in Tanzania? A case study of Mtwara, Lindi and Dar es Salaam regions." *African Journal of Economic Review* 7.1 (2019): 176–187.

[93] Nam, Eunyoung, and Myungsook Woo. "Who is willing to pay more taxes for welfare? Focusing on the effects of diverse types of trust in South Korea and Taiwan." *Development and Society* 44.2 (2015): 319–343.

[94] Ogorodnikova, Irina Ivanovna, et al. "Tax culture and trust." *Comparative Sociology* 19.3 (2020): 363–387.

[95] Kaplanoglou, Georgia, and Vassilis T. Rapanos. "Tax and trust: The fiscal crisis in Greece." *South European Society and Politics* 18.3 (2013): 283–304.

factor influencing tax compliance.[96] His study found that citizens with higher levels of trust were more willing to pay taxes.

An earlier study by Feld and Frey focused on efforts to improve the relationship between tax compliance and tax evasion and suggested that promoting compliance is an effective strategy to combat evasion.[97] The researchers also analyzed the interaction between tax authorities and taxpayers, emphasizing the significance of this relationship in determining taxpayers' compliance with tax laws.

SUMMARY AND CONCLUSION

This chapter has utilized tax compliance as a lens through which to examine the broader concepts of voluntary compliance and intrinsic motivation. The extensive body of research on tax compliance provides a rich case study for understanding how individuals' internal drives interact with external factors and governmental policies.

These studies collectively underscore the critical role of trust and positive relationships between citizens and their governments in promoting tax compliance. By prioritizing trust building and fostering cooperative interactions with taxpayers, governments can more effectively encourage compliance and reduce tax evasion. These insights provide valuable guidance for policymakers in designing tax strategies that cultivate a more collaborative and compliant taxpaying environment, moving beyond traditional enforcement-based approaches to more nuanced, trust-centered policies.

By analyzing the concept of tax morale and its relationship to actual compliance behavior, we have gained insights into the nature of intrinsic motivation in a regulatory context. Research has explored various interventions to foster voluntary tax compliance, including social norm messaging and moral appeals.[98] These approaches reveal complex dynamics when compared to traditional command and control methods. Notably, conventional enforcement strategies often overlook the importance of intrinsic motivation and voluntary compliance. Significantly, the predictive power of tax morale proved limited across many studies reviewed in this analysis. This relatively weak correlation between tax morale and actual tax behavior is further corroborated by our ongoing meta-analysis in collaboration with Slater, mentioned earlier in the chapter. While these findings do not negate the value of investing in tax morale, they underscore the importance of maintaining a critical perspective when considering intrinsically motivated compliance as an alternative to traditional tax enforcement mechanisms.

96 Bergman, Marcelo. "Who pays for social policy? A study on taxes and trust." *Journal of Social Policy* 31.2 (2002): 289–305.

97 Feld and Frey. "Trust breeds trust."

98 Blumenthal, Marsha, Charles Christian, and Joel Slemrod. "Do normative appeals affect tax compliance? Evidence from a controlled experiment in Minnesota." *National Tax Journal* 54.1 (2001): 125–138.

As shown throughout this book regarding voluntary compliance, research on tax compliance presents mixed results. It remains unclear which approaches work best, how effective softer enforcement tools are, or what combinations of regulatory tools yield optimal results. This chapter shows that what drives people to comply with rules isn't simple. While internal factors like tax morale matter, their effectiveness depends on cultural norms, existing compliance rates, and how interventions are presented. Trust in government emerges as particularly important – when people trust institutions, they're more likely to comply willingly with regulations.

Looking ahead, we need longer term studies to understand how voluntary compliance holds up over time. We should also examine how different approaches work together – for instance, how enforcement measures might complement trust-building efforts. This could help create systems that encourage willing compliance while still preventing abuse. Chapter 10 will explore how these insights from tax compliance apply to environmental regulation and other areas.

10

Voluntary Environmental Compliance

INTRODUCTION

The previous chapter examined tax compliance, an area where legal obligations are clearly defined – taxpayers are only required to pay taxes on taxable income. Therefore, voluntary compliance primarily depends on how individuals' perceptions of enforcement and monitoring influence their willingness to meet these established obligations. In contrast, environmental compliance presents a greater challenge, as many behaviors that impact the environment are entirely voluntary choices – such as whether to fly, use public transportation, or choose plant-based meat alternatives.

Indeed, this chapter on environmental regulation seeks to enhance our comprehension of behavioral changes that cannot be solely enforced by law. For example, shifting to an electric vehicle or adopting green energy sources involves more extensive changes in behavior than does other compliance behavior, and coercion or imposing a duty may not be applicable in certain circumstances. This gives rise to several questions. What are the barriers to change in different countries? How will the different regulatory instruments affect the public views regarding alternative energy resources? Does public participation increase or decrease the public's willingness to switch to alternative energy resources? Do individuals and groups/collectives respond differently to efforts to change behavior regarding solar panels, electric cars, or other alternative energy sources? Does the choice of regulatory instrument vary depending on the target audience? Who should oversee the attempt to change the behavior of the public – the government or private firms? In the context of environmental issues, our comparison between countries will consider not only differences in motivation but also in the barriers each country faces. We will examine behavioral barriers such as resistance to change or free-riding, legal barriers like bureaucracy, economic barriers, and cultural barriers like community values and autonomy.

THE RISE OF NEW REGULATORY APPROACHES

Overreliance on command-and-control regulation can be behaviorally damaging, particularly in environmental contexts. There is often a significant gap between simply satisfying regulatory thresholds and adopting innovative and technological modifications, which are often more useful in improving corporate environmental behavior.[1]

In other words, many of the behavioral changes we are interested in cannot be effectively addressed through a traditional command-and-control regulatory system. This is because the behaviors in question, such as flying to a business meeting, while potentially environmentally harmful, is not in itself illegal or universally undesirable. Unlike clear-cut violations such as tax evasion or disregarding mask mandates during the COVID-19 pandemic, these behaviors exist in a gray area where prohibition is neither feasible nor desirable. Instead, they require more nuanced approaches to encourage positive change. We suggest here that more flexible regulations, such as market-based instruments, may be more effective in encouraging environmental compliance, along with technological innovation.

The field of environmental regulation is considered one of the most advanced regulatory areas, with various innovative regulatory options having been examined extensively and studied empirically.[2] Several noncoercive approaches have been implemented in the field of environmental regulation, with less stringent types of regulatory measures being evaluated and compared.[3] For example, voluntary sustainability standards (VSS) are commonly used in environmental contexts as private, market-based regulatory instruments to address sustainability issues in global value chains. Depoorter and Marx's study of VSS institutional design reveals that these standards employ three main mechanisms to foster compliance: enforcement, market incentives, and capacity building.[4] Their analysis shows that while enforcement is consistently used across VSS, there is significant variation in the use of market incentives and capacity-building mechanisms, reflecting differences in VSS approaches to generating compliance.

Overall, as the studies reviewed in this chapter demonstrate, there are many that show the advantages of trust-based regulation (including commitments, intrinsic motivation, and various nudges). However, for the most part, the effect sizes demonstrated in these studies are limited. Even more importantly, the lack of consistency in the effect of intrinsic motivation makes the ability to rely on such mechanisms quite limited. The purpose of this chapter is to analyze the data collected in this field and determine to what extent promoting behavioral change, without relying

1 Bergquist, Ann-Kristin, et al. "Command-and-control revisited: Environmental compliance and technological change in Swedish industry 1970–1990." *Ecological Economics* 85 (2013): 6–19.

2 Fiorino, Daniel J. *The new environmental regulation*. MIT Press, 2006; Percival, Robert V., et al. "Environmental regulation." *Law, Science, and Policy* 4 (2003): 1–60.

3 Black, Julia, and Robert Baldwin. "Really responsive risk-based regulation." *Law & Policy* 32.2 (2010): 181–213.

4 Depoorter, Charline, and Axel Marx. "Fostering compliance with voluntary sustainability standards through institutional design: An analytic framework and empirical application." *Regulation & Governance* 18.4 (2024): 1132–1152.

solely on coercion, is feasible. It will examine the best practices regarding both corporate environmental compliances,[5] and individual environmental behavior, such as recycling norms.[6]

WHAT MAKES ENVIRONMENTAL REGULATION DIFFERENT

The prevalence of compliance among individuals is less significant in environmental situations compared to scenarios such as pandemic response, where widespread adherence is essential for effectiveness. Moreover, environmental policy objectives are often less precisely defined than those in domains such as taxation, which complicates regulatory efforts. Environmental behaviors usually involve daily choices instead of sporadic actions, making them more pervasive in individuals' lives. The field also deals with challenges related to trusting scientific evidence, which is similar to what was experienced during the COVID-19 pandemic, discussed in Chapter 8. In addition, environmental policies are often politically controversial, dividing people along different ideological lines, although recent mega-studies have shed light on some areas of consensus. Moreover, conflicting identities at community

5 A meta-analysis of studies showed that nonbinding statements had a significant, even if limited, impact in encouraging companies that signed on to protect the environment. Lokhorst, Anne Marike, et al. "Commitment and behavior change: A meta-analysis and critical review of commitment-making strategies in environmental research." *Environment and Behavior* 45.1 (2013): 3–34. Also see Flankova, Svetlana, et al. "A meta-analysis of the effectiveness of voluntary environmental programs." *Academy of Management Proceedings* 1 (2018): 1–4. A study that surveyed the top 100 corporations in China showed that institutional regulation had a negative impact on green technology innovation, while self-regulation had a positive effect on it. See Li, Dayuan, Fei Tang, and Lu Zhang. "Differential effects of voluntary environmental programs and mandatory regulations on corporate green innovation." *Natural Hazards* 103 (2020): 3437–3456.

6 Knowledge about recycling and social pressure have been found to be two factors that greatly influence recycling behavior among students. Environmental concerns, conservation behavior, and behavioral experience also correlate with recycling participation. For more, see: Clay, Sean. "Increasing university recycling: Factors influencing recycling behaviour among students at Leeds University." *Earth and Environment* 1 (2005): 186–228. Findings show that a more reliable collection service, more evidence that the funds generated were being used for neighborhood improvement, and a better information system about the environmental program would increase and sustain residents' voluntary separation of waste. See Hernández, Orlando, Barbara Rawlins, and Reva Schwartz. "Voluntary recycling in Quito: Factors associated with participation in a pilot programme." *Environment and Urbanization* 11.2 (1999): 145–160. When employees feel supported by their organization, they become more committed and satisfied and are willing to engage in OCBE (organizational citizenship behavior for the environment). Whereas a direct effect is reported for employee commitment to the organization, findings indicate that perceived organizational support and job satisfaction have an indirect effect on OCBE. See Paillé, Pascal, and Olivier Boiral. "Pro-environmental behavior at work: Construct validity and determinants." *Journal of Environmental Psychology* 36 (2013): 118–128. Transformational leadership directly and indirectly affects employees' voluntary pro-environmental behavior. See Robertson, Jennifer L., and Erica Carleton. "Uncovering how and when environmental leadership affects employees' voluntary pro-environmental behavior." *Journal of Leadership & Organizational Studies* 25.2 (2018): 197–210.

and state levels, as observed in countries like France and Israel, can complicate environmental compliance.[7] Finally, motivating pro-environmental behavior can be complex due to the dichotomy between local and global environmental harm, immediate and tangible impacts versus long term and global consequences. The multifaceted nature of environmental regulation highlights the need for nuanced, context-specific approaches that promote voluntary compliance. This is especially important since multiple factors contribute to environmental regulation.

The unique regulatory strategies employed in environmental contexts, as distinct from other cases examined in this book, can be illustrated through a key study on recycling regulation. Wesley Schultz investigated the impact of feedback on community curbside-recycling behaviors. The research involved 120 households and provided valuable insights into how feedback mechanisms can influence recycling participation.[8]

In the study, participants were divided into five household groups to test different recycling interventions: One received only a basic recycling request, another got personalized feedback with their request, a third received community-level feedback alongside the request, a fourth was given general recycling information with their request, and the fifth served as a control group with no intervention.

Analysis showed that only the groups receiving either individual or neighborhood feedback demonstrated meaningful increases in recycling behavior compared to initial levels. The other approaches failed to produce significant changes. These findings indicate that while feedback plays a role in changing behavior, it may be most effective when combined with social norms rather than used in isolation.[9]

WHY INTRINSIC MOTIVATION MATTERS FOR ENVIRONMENT

Personal values and beliefs have been found to strongly predict pro-environmental behavior, resulting in more consistent and long-lasting adherence to environmental policies, according to Linda Steg and Charles Vlek.[10] In a 2019 meta-analysis, Alexander Maki and colleagues demonstrated that interventions aimed at increasing intrinsic motivation were more effective in producing positive spillover effects,

[7] Berkebile-Weinberg, Michael, et al. "The differential impact of climate interventions along the political divide in 60 countries." *Nature Communications* 15.1 (2024): 1–12.

[8] Schultz, P. Wesley. "Changing behavior with normative feedback interventions: A field experiment on curbside recycling." *Basic and Applied Social Psychology* 21.1 (1999): 25–36.

[9] Liu, Yuwei, et al. "Integrating norm activation model and theory of planned behavior to understand sustainable transport behavior: Evidence from China." *International Journal of Environmental Research and Public Health* 14.12 (2017): 1–16.

[10] Steg, Linda, and Charles Vlek. "Encouraging pro-environmental behaviour: An integrative review and research agenda." *Journal of Environmental Psychology* 29.3 (2009): 309–317.

thereby influencing other environmental behaviors beyond the targeted action.[11] This study analyzed 293 tests of spillover from 76 published and unpublished studies, providing robust evidence for the effectiveness of intrinsic motivation in promoting sustainable behaviors.

Similarly, Julia Steinhorst and Christian A. Klöckner found that interventions based on intrinsic motivation tended to have more enduring impacts on promoting environmental compliance.[12] This study examined the effects of different types of information framing on pro-environmental behavior and intrinsic motivation, supporting the idea that targeting intrinsic motivation can lead to more lasting behavioral changes.

Nonetheless, here too, there are other conflicting studies, where the relationship between intrinsic motivation and external interventions can be counterproductive or at the least dependent on the level of intrinsic motivation of the regulated entities. For example, Maoliang Ling and Ling Xu cautioned that external interventions, such as financial incentives or regulations, might, in some contexts, diminish people's intrinsic motivation to comply with environmental regulations.[13] This could ultimately result in policies being less effective over time. This study by Ling and Xu examines the potential "crowding-out" effect of external incentives on intrinsic motivation for pro-environmental behavior. Their work contributes to the ongoing debate about the most effective ways to promote sustainable behaviors and environmental compliance.

It should be noted that recent research has challenged some assumptions about the role of political ideology in environmental attitudes. Vlasceanu and colleagues conducted a large-scale study of 59,440 participants across 63 countries,[14] evaluating 11 expert-crowdsourced interventions focused on four climate mitigation outcomes: climate beliefs, policy support, information-sharing intention, and participation in a tree-planting task. The findings revealed that these interventions had modest and varied effects, with their effectiveness largely limited to individuals who were not climate skeptics. Moreover, some interventions actually decreased participation in the tree-planting task. These results suggest that the impact of behavioral climate interventions depends heavily on both the target audience and the specific behavior being encouraged. Similarly, other studies on compliance have emphasized the significance of aspects such as ability and societal expectations in influencing

11 Maki, Alexander, et al. "Meta-analysis of pro-environmental behaviour spillover." *Nature Sustainability* 2.4 (2019): 307–315.

12 Steinhorst, Julia, and Christian A. Klöckner. "Effects of monetary versus environmental information framing: Implications for long-term pro-environmental behavior and intrinsic motivation." *Environment and Behavior* 50.9 (2018): 997–1031.

13 Ling, Maoliang, and Lin Xu. "How and when financial incentives crowd out pro-environmental motivation: A longitudinal quasi-experimental study." *Journal of Environmental Psychology* 78 (2021): 1–10.

14 Vlasceanu, Madalina, et al. "Addressing climate change with behavioral science: A global intervention tournament in 63 countries." *Science Advances* 10.6 (2024): 1–19.

environmental conduct.[15] This suggests that an approach that considers various factors, both intrinsic and extrinsic, might be required to ensure the effective design and implementation of environmental policies.

THE BEHAVIORAL CHALLENGE OF ENVIRONMENTAL REGULATION

As mentioned in the introduction to this chapter, what distinguishes environmental behavior from most other regulatory domains is the requirement for individuals to internalize, be aware, willing to pay the price, and know what actions to take, among other factors. Simply providing instructions on what to do will only have a limited impact on an individual's environmental behavior, such as on their recycling habits.

Indeed, the threat of environmental damage poses numerous challenges to the health and future of individuals, communities, and the planet.[16] It also provides an opportunity to examine the different voluntary compliance behaviors exhibited by individuals. Another significant challenge related to the environment is the difficulty people face in adopting certain behaviors into their daily lives, leading to what we have termed "affective voluntary compliance." The environment shapes virtually every aspect of daily behavior, from basic energy consumption and recycling to broader lifestyle choices in transportation, consumption, dining, travel, and leisure activities. These choices reflect a growing awareness of environmental impact, as seen in trends like the circular economy and reduced use of disposable items.

THE POWER OF INTRINSIC ENVIRONMENTAL MOTIVATION

One of the unique characteristics of environmental compliance is that there is a wide variation in the levels of commitment to different environmental challenges. This variation can result in situations where individuals are committed to certain values but are not as dedicated to others. The following comparison between local and global harm provides a good example. Some people may be more dedicated to protecting the water in their area as it affects the health of their children or themselves, but they may be far less concerned about carbon emissions to the atmosphere.[17] Another distinct challenge in environmental behavior pertains to the feeling of remoteness that individuals experience when confronted with scenarios

[15] Ernst, Julie, Nathaniel Blood, and Thomas Beery. "Environmental action and student environmental leaders: Exploring the influence of environmental attitudes, locus of control, and sense of personal responsibility." *Environmental Education Research* 23.2 (2017): 149–175.

[16] Kasperson, Jeanne X., and Roger E. Kasperson. *Global environmental risk*. Routledge, 2013.

[17] White, Rob. "Global harms and the natural environment." In *The Palgrave handbook of social harm*, edited by P. Davies, P. Leighton, and T. Wyatt, Palgrave Macmillan, 2021: 89–114. https://doi.org/10.1007/978-3-030-72408-5_5.

in which people's behavior is not classified as a typical social dilemma. This is particularly evident when the type of environmental harm described is local, occurring at the municipal or state level, such as water or air pollution, as opposed to situations where the harm is global, such as global warming. In the following, we will explore whether communities can collaborate to address a local threat. We will examine how each of the described harms could affect interactions with various regulatory interventions.

IDENTIFYING EFFECTIVE REGULATORY INTERVENTIONS

As observed in the introduction of this chapter, the environmental area presents a unique blend of behaviors that cannot be legally bound, such as transportation and purchasing, with those that can be legally regulated, such as recycling and the use of specific chemicals.[18]

Van de Ven and colleagues researched effective environmental policies in the EU and how altering various behavioral patterns can contribute to reducing greenhouse gas emissions.[19] They categorized potential changes in behavior into three groups: food consumption, transportation, and household practices. Each group showed varying degrees of potential to reduce emissions.[20] They found that behavioral changes hold the potential to reduce emissions by 14 percent–40 percent in the EU, depending on the type and extent of behavior adopted. The authors pointed out that a vegan diet could contribute to reducing emissions by 5.4 percent to 8 percent.

Seth Wynes and Kimberly Nicholas,[21] as well as Kate Lacroix,[22] have identified several effective choices for reducing emissions in developed countries. These include limiting childbirth, avoiding car usage, refraining from air travel, and adopting plant-based diets. In 2009, Thomas Dietz and his colleagues analyzed seventeen different household and transportation behaviors and discovered that these actions could result in a 20 percent decrease in household emissions and a 7.4 percent reduction in overall US emissions.[23]

[18] Some of the literature review in this section is based on a report we submitted to the Israeli Democracy Institute in 2023 (www.idi.org.il/books/54536).

[19] Van de Ven, Dirk-Jan, Mikel González-Eguino, and Iñaki Arto. "The potential of behavioural change for climate change mitigation: A case study for the European Union." *Mitigation and Adaptation Strategies for Global Change* 23 (2018): 853–886.

[20] Van de Ven, González-Eguino, and Arto. "The potential of behavioural change for climate change mitigation."

[21] Wynes, Seth, and Kimberly A. Nicholas. "The climate mitigation gap: Education and government recommendations miss the most effective individual actions." *Environmental Research Letters* 12.7 (2017): 1–10.

[22] Lacroix, Karine. "Comparing the relative mitigation potential of individual pro-environmental behaviors." *Journal of Cleaner Production* 195 (2018): 1398–1407.

[23] Dietz, Thomas, et al. "Household actions can provide a behavioral wedge to rapidly reduce US carbon emissions." *Proceedings of the National Academy of Sciences* 106.44 (2009): 18452–18456.

BEHAVIORAL BARRIERS TO ENVIRONMENTAL CHANGE

Having identified the main factors that appear to influence people's decisions in the previous section, we will conduct experimental surveys to determine how various barriers impact their decision-making. We will compare how the same problem is presented to the public and attempt to establish a causal link between the obstacles and people's intention to behave a certain way. This may involve manipulating factors such as trustworthiness, level of cooperation with others, cost, level of uncertainty, rationale provided for the change, or moral and ecological considerations, all while keeping in mind solidarity with future generations and economic implications.

In his 2011 review, Robert Gifford's analysis identifies seven key psychological barriers to environmental action.[24] Among these, cognitive constraints – including limited awareness and outdated beliefs about environmental practices – prevent people from recognizing the urgency of climate issues. Disengagement represents another significant challenge, particularly because the climate crisis's effects are often delayed and people feel overwhelmed by information overload.[25] This disengagement can reduce attention and perceived urgency, worsening the impact of cognitive limitations.

Uncertainty about climate crisis causes often leads people to prioritize immediate personal interests over long-term environmental concerns. This uncertainty, combined with overoptimism, can create a false sense of security that discourages action. Additionally, people's perception of their behavioral control (locus of control) significantly influences their willingness to adopt eco-friendly behaviors. When individuals feel they lack resources or doubt the impact of their efforts against a global crisis, they're less likely to act.

CHANGING PUBLIC ATTITUDES TOWARD THE ENVIRONMENT

A key aim of this book is to examine and classify what we know about noncoercive regulations' effectiveness in changing both behaviors and underlying factors like attitudes and intrinsic motivation. In the context of environmental challenges, trust in science is of utmost importance, drawing parallels to the global response to the COVID-19 pandemic. The immediate and visible consequences of COVID-19, such as people getting seriously ill or dying, acted as a powerful catalyst for people to change their behavior and follow scientific recommendations. Nevertheless, there

[24] Gifford, Robert. "The dragons of inaction: Psychological barriers that limit climate change mitigation and adaptation." *American Psychologist* 66.4 (2011): 290–302.

[25] Uba, Chijioke Dike, and Andreas Chatzidakis. "Understanding engagement and disengagement from pro-environmental behaviour: The role of neutralization and affirmation techniques in maintaining persistence in and desistance from car use." *Transportation Research Part A: Policy and Practice* 94 (2016): 278–294.

are clear differences between the environmental context and other domains, such as tax compliance, where conduct is chiefly influenced by the conviction in the scientific principles related to the matter at hand. In contrast, environmental damage is often not as easily visible or tangible, making it difficult to generate public trust and action. Many environmental concerns, such as climate change, air pollution, and the depletion of natural resources, occur slowly over time and may not be immediately noticeable to the human eye. The absence of immediate, visible consequences can create a gap between the scientific evidence and the public's ethical commitment and willingness to engage in pro-environmental behaviors.[26]

To effectively promote trust in science within the environmental context, it is essential to employ strategies that account for the unique challenges and opportunities trust in science presents.[27] This may involve investing in public education campaigns that clearly communicate the scientific evidence behind environmental issues, while also highlighting the tangible benefits of pro-environmental behaviors.[28] Furthermore, building alliances between scientific institutions, local governments, and community organizations can help narrow the divide between scientific knowledge and public action, fostering a supportive environment that encourages trust and engagement.[29]

Additionally, highlighting the advantages of pro-environmental behavior, including enhanced public health, economic savings, and improved quality of life, can assist individuals and communities in realizing the immediate and long-term benefits of relying on science and taking action. Although building trust in science within the environmental context poses its challenges, it also provides valuable opportunities for driving community-based change and creating a broader impact.[30] By identifying and addressing specific aspects and utilizing strategies that appeal to the public and encourage collective action, it is possible to foster greater trust in science and motivate individuals and communities to collaborate toward a more sustainable future.

CULTURAL VARIATION IN ENVIRONMENTAL BEHAVIOR

Throughout the previous chapters, culture has been examined as an intrinsic factor that shapes people's views and behaviors independently of a country's formal legal

26 Rees, Jonas H., Sabine Klug, and Sebastian Bamberg. "Guilty conscience: Motivating pro-environmental behavior by inducing negative moral emotions." *Climatic Change* 130 (2015): 439–452.

27 Brewer, Paul R., and Barbara L. Ley. "Whose science do you believe? Explaining trust in sources of scientific information about the environment." *Science Communication* 35.1 (2013): 115–137.

28 Cvitanovic, Christopher, et al. "Strategies for building and managing 'trust' to enable knowledge exchange at the interface of environmental science and policy." *Environmental Science & Policy* 123 (2021): 179–189.

29 Lacey, Justine, et al. "Understanding and managing trust at the climate science–policy interface." *Nature Climate Change* 8.1 (2018): 22–28.

30 Gurău, Călin, and Léo-Paul Dana. "Environmentally-driven community entrepreneurship: Mapping the link between natural environment, local community and entrepreneurship." *Technological Forecasting and Social Change* 129 (2018): 221–231.

framework. Culture has been identified as a factor related to environmental concern, with collectivism associated with greater care for the environment.[31] Cultural values can influence the ethical evaluation of sustainable consumption, making consumers more likely to align their beliefs with their behavioral intentions.[32]

An interesting environmental report on voluntary compliance suggested the potential advantages of comparing voluntary compliance methods.[33] Although many of the countries reviewed in the report rely primarily on monitoring sanctions, some have taken softer approaches to encourage the public to play a more active role in environmental compliance. For example, the report finds that in Singapore, although it has a centralized governance system, streamlining responsibilities has been shown to improve efficiency and effectiveness. An environmental mobile application encourages the public to spot and report violations. Singapore's experience indicates that companies can maintain effective compliance without extensive monitoring from external sources.

Another recent study conducted in Mexico has identified several factors that contribute to improved environmental compliance.[34] These factors include internal management practices, the implementation of norms across all employees, regulatory pressure (such as inspections), public scrutiny, and the size of the company (which was discussed earlier). Studies examining environmental compliance in Europe have highlighted the importance of establishing institutionalized mechanisms for societal monitoring and enforcement at the national level.[35] In the context of promoting environmental compliance in Italy and Greece, nonstate actors, such as environmental nongovernmental organizations and industry associations, have been shown to have played a significant role in raising public awareness about environmental issues and advocating for more stringent environmental regulations.[36]

Research from China reveals a key limitation in corporate environmental compliance: Companies tend to prioritize short-term pollution reduction measures over long-term environmental improvements that require significant investment.[37] This

[31] Kalamas, Maria, Mark Cleveland, and Michel Laroche. "Pro-environmental behaviors for thee but not for me: Green giants, green gods, and external environmental locus of control." *Journal of Business Research* 67.2 (2014): 12–22.

[32] Sharma, Rajat, and Mithileshwar Jha. "Values influencing sustainable consumption behaviour: Exploring the contextual relationship." *Journal of Business Research* 76 (2017): 77–88.

[33] United Nations Environment Programme. "Environmental rule of law: First global report." (2019). www.unep.org/resources/assessment/environmental-rule-law-first-global-report

[34] Dasgupta, Susmita, Hemamala Hettige, and David Wheeler. "What improves environmental compliance? Evidence from Mexican industry." *Journal of Environmental Economics and Management* 39.1 (2000): 39–66.

[35] Bergquist, et al. "Command-and-control revisited."

[36] Koutalakis, Charalampos. "Environmental compliance in Italy and Greece: The role of non-state actors." *Environmental Politics* 13. 4 (2004): 754–774.

[37] Zhou, Yankun, and Hongtao Shen. "Supervision of environmental enforcement and corporate environmental performance: Evidence of quasi-natural experiment from talks on environmental protection." *Nankai Business Review International* 10.1 (2019): 42–66.

is also the case in some parts of Europe, where the effectiveness of criminal sanctions in environmental regulation has been studied and found to be inadequate in deterring harmful actions due to the limited enforcement mechanisms in place.[38]

Evidence for the need to adopt a more nuanced, responsive, and sensitive approach to environmental regulation has come from an interesting study in China.[39] The study aimed to understand how the moral aspect of the law, rather than incentives, has influenced behaviors such as water and electricity conservation and the protection of animals and plants. They have also found that laws have varying effects on people depending on their level of intrinsic motivation. According to the study, the effectiveness of regulations is determined not only by morality or by intrinsic factors, but also by the degree of enforcement. Effective implementation of laws and regulations increases their credibility, which makes it easier for the public to trust and be encouraged.

Even more surprising were the consistent findings that countries with high levels of trust in government, such as Sweden, Switzerland, and Norway, have been successful in reducing pollution through taxation measures. Conversely, in countries with high levels of distrust and corruption, energy producers are unwilling to pay the carbon tax and continue to emit increasing amounts of greenhouse gases.[40]

Regarding the subjects covered in the other chapters, when trying to comprehend the probability of compliance occurring without coercion, we must consider culture. Culture plays a crucial role in almost any compliance study, particularly when intrinsic motivation is viewed as a major factor in explaining compliance.[41]

Cross-cultural heterogeneity refers to the diversity and variations in behaviors, norms, and values across different cultures. Varying cultural backgrounds influence compliance behaviors and can affect the design and implementation of effective regulatory policies across different societies.[42]

Notably, in the field of recycling, differences in recycling rates across the world could signify the impact of cultural and social norms on environmental care. A global recycling rates report highlights significant differences between countries.[43]

[38] Faure, Michael, and Katarina Svatikova. "Enforcement of environmental law in the Flemish region." *European Energy and Environmental Law Review* 19.2 (2010): 60–79.

[39] Chen, Jielin, et al. "How does new environmental law affect public environmental protection activities in China? Evidence from structural equation model analysis on legal cognition." *Science of the Total Environment* 714 (2020): 1–14.

[40] Fairbrother, Malcolm, Ingemar Johansson Sevä, and Joakim Kulin. "Political trust and the relationship between climate change beliefs and support for fossil fuel taxes: Evidence from a survey of 23 European countries." *Global Environmental Change* 59 (2019): 1–15.

[41] McCarty, John A., and L. J. Shrum. "The influence of individualism, collectivism, and locus of control on environmental beliefs and behavior." *Journal of Public Policy & Marketing* 20.1 (2001): 93–104.

[42] Cronert, Axel. "When the paper tiger bites: Evidence of compliance with unenforced regulation among employers in Sweden." *Regulation & Governance* 16.4 (2022): 1141–1159.

[43] "Global recycling league table: Phase one report: Prepared March–April 2024." www.tomra.com/-/media/project/tomra/tomra/about-tomra/documentation/global-recycling-league-table-phase-1-report.pdf.

For example, Germany, Wales, and Singapore have the highest recycling rates in the world, whereas France, Hong Kong, and the United States have the lowest scores.

Vivian Tam and her colleagues conducted a study in Australia to explore the attitudes of practitioners in the construction industry toward recycling.[44] They discovered that, overall, practitioners held positive attitudes toward recycling. However, despite their favorable views, their actual recycling behavior was not as strong as anticipated. It also did not align with their attitudes about recycling when coercive measures were absent.[45]

Studies conducted in both England and Sweden have revealed the various factors that impact household-recycling rates and attitudes. A survey conducted in Exeter, England, revealed that several factors, such as the perceived value of recycling, the availability of curbside-recycling programs, environmental values, social norms, peer influence, personal experiences, and perceived benefits and challenges, play a significant role in shaping individuals' recycling behaviors.[46] Another study conducted in England showcased the achievements of the authorities' recycling program in generating public satisfaction and participation. However, the study also emphasized the necessity for enhancing public involvement to increase recycling rates overall.[47]

Research in Sweden has demonstrated that household-recycling behaviors are shaped by both economic and moral motivations.[48] Households are more likely to recycle when they believe their actions contribute to environmental improvements and when they observe others in their community recycling.[49] Infrastructure plays a crucial role – particularly in multifamily dwellings, where convenient collection systems lead to higher participation rates. Interestingly, while moral norms significantly explain differences in recycling rates between households, their influence tends to diminish when collection infrastructure improves and recycling becomes more accessible.

A study conducted in the Borough of Burnley, England, revealed that the household-recycling rate is only half of the national average, which is 12 percent.

44 Tam, Vivian W. Y., and Chi Ming Tam. "A review on the viable technology for construction waste recycling." *Resources, Conservation and Recycling* 47.3 (2006): 209–221.

45 Tam, Vivian W. Y., et al. "Practitioners recycling attitude and behaviour in the Australian construction industry." *Sustainability* 10.4 (2018): 1–23.

46 Barr, Stewart, Nicholas J. Ford, and Andrew W. Gilg. "Attitudes towards recycling household waste in Exeter, Devon: Quantitative and qualitative approaches." *Local Environment* 8.4 (2003): 407–421.

47 Williams, Ian D., and J. Kelly. "Green waste collection and the public's recycling behaviour in the Borough of Wyre, England." *Resources, Conservation and Recycling* 38.2 (2003): 139–159.

48 Specifically, convenience matters in the sense that property-close collection in multifamily dwelling houses leads to higher collection rates. The strength of moral (self-enforced) norms explains a large part of the variation across households, but the importance of such norms in driving recycling efforts partly diminishes if improved collection infrastructure makes it easier for households to recycle.

49 Hage, Olle, Patrik Söderholm, and Christer Berglund. "Norms and economic motivation in household recycling: Empirical evidence from Sweden." *Resources, Conservation and Recycling* 53.3 (2009): 155–165.

The study found that recycling is more commonly practiced by older and more affluent individuals, whereas younger households tend to have lower rates of recycling participation. Factors such as the availability of storage space and time also influence household-recycling rates, with the widespread terraced housing posing a challenge to achieving high recycling rates.[50] These studies demonstrate that household-recycling behaviors arise from multiple interacting factors. The Swedish research specifically showed how personal moral attitudes and economic incentives affect participation, while convenience of collection systems proved crucial in multifamily housing. Social norms manifest through the positive influence of observing others' recycling efforts and infrastructure accessibility can moderate the impact of moral motivations. Understanding this complex interplay of factors is essential for policymakers and local authorities to design effective strategies that both increase participation rates and improve the quality of recycling programs.

VOLUNTARY CORPORATE ENVIRONMENTAL BEHAVIOR

A study by Mousami Prasad and Trupti Mishra,[51] focusing on CO_2 emissions in India, highlights the need for industries to take responsibility for bringing about meaningful change. The study focuses on the impact of voluntary compliance and reveals that only 33 percent of the sampled firms in the Indian iron and steel sector comply with the International Organization for Standardization 14001 regulations. Empirical research, considering simultaneous factors and various company characteristics, suggests a noteworthy positive correlation between voluntary compliance and improved environmental performance. Therefore, the study suggests that voluntary compliance can be used as an additional policy tool to encourage low-carbon growth in industries. Another study in that same topic investigates the relationship between environmental compliance and firm performance in China.[52] Based on a survey of firms, the authors found that companies that comply with environmental regulations tend to perform better financially, as seen through higher returns on assets and increased sales growth. The study also shows that larger firms and those with more foreign ownership tend to have better environmental performance.

[50] Martin, Michael, Ian David Williams, and Michael Clark. "Social, cultural and structural influences on household waste recycling: A case study." *Resources, Conservation and Recycling* 48.4 (2006): 357–395.

[51] Prasad, Mousami, and Trupti Mishra. "Low-carbon growth for Indian iron and steel sector: Exploring the role of voluntary environmental compliance." *Energy Policy* 100 (2017): 41–50.

[52] Yang, Xi, and Yang Yao. "Environmental compliance and firm performance: Evidence from China." *Oxford Bulletin of Economics and Statistics* 74.3 (2012): 397–424.

Incentives in Environmental Behavior

One of the most common and widely studied regulatory tools in literature is incentives.[53] In the context of environmental behavior, incentives are widely used across all domains related to the environment, such as energy, transportation, food consumption, and purchasing habits. As discussed in earlier chapters, the relationship between incentives and voluntary compliance is complex – while individuals aren't forced to behave in certain ways, the opportunity to earn bonuses creates external motivation rather than purely intrinsic compliance.

The effectiveness of incentives varies significantly by context. For example, plastic bag fees work not just through pricing mechanisms but also by raising awareness.[54] When consumers must actively choose to pay for plastic bags rather than receiving them by default, they're more likely to switch to reusable alternatives. This decision often becomes habitual, influencing behavior even before cost considerations come into play.

A detailed study of transportation behavior at the University of Michigan illustrates the nuanced role of different types of incentives.[55] The study examined efforts to encourage ridesharing among university employees through various incentives, including parking discounts for carpoolers, car rental options for those leaving vehicles off campus, safety-related passenger information, coordination agreements, designated pickup parking lots, and partner-finding meetings. A 2012 follow-up survey to an earlier 2009 study revealed that employees still traveled alone 80 percent of the time, with shared trips accounting for only 8.3 percent of travel. Significantly, the research found that nonfinancial incentives focused on improving travel comfort and coordination procedures had greater impact on increasing shared trips compared to financial incentives, which showed minimal effect. The availability of information and coordination tools proved particularly valuable in promoting carpooling behavior.

An interesting observation that emerges from many of the studies is that incentives cannot always be translated directly into a simple price function.[56] For example, travel costs were more important than other benefits. Benefits related to driving and parking time were also found to be very helpful. Another example of nontraditional environmental incentives can be observed in payments for environmental services,[57] an innovative approach to conservation increasingly used in both developed and developing countries.

53 Stern, Paul C. "Information, incentives, and pro environmental consumer behavior." *Journal of Consumer Policy* 22.4 (1999): 461–478.

54 Senturk, Gulsah, and Devrim Dumludag. "An evaluation of the effect of plastic bag fee on consumer behavior: Case of Turkey." *Waste Management* 120 (2021): 748–754.

55 Kaplowitz, Stan A., and Arthur Slabosky. "Trying to increase carpooling at a major US university: A survey and an intervention." *Sustainability: The Journal of Record* 11.2 (2018): 74–80.

56 Javid, Muhammad Ashraf, et al. "Travelers' attitudes toward carpooling in Lahore: Motives and constraints." *Journal of Modern Transportation* 25 (2017): 268–278.

57 Wunder, Sven, Stefanie Engel, and Stefano Pagiola. "Taking stock: A comparative analysis of payments for environmental services programs in developed and developing countries." *Ecological Economics* 65.4 (2008): 834–852.

In addition, a comprehensive meta-analysis on the efficacy of incentives in environmental contexts summarized and compared the effects of incentives across many relevant domains.[58] The paper's overall conclusion is that incentives can be a valuable tool in promoting pro-environmental behaviors by contributing to sustained behavior change. The effectiveness of incentives varies by context and behavior type – for instance, noncash rewards prove more effective for promoting travel behavior changes, while cash rewards work better for encouraging recycling. The authors also found that incentive effectiveness depends significantly on the specific behavior being targeted. However, since this is a meta-analysis of existing studies, they acknowledge potential gaps in understanding, as some behaviors may have been easier to study than others. This research suggests that successful incentive programs need carefully calibrated distribution schedules tailored to specific environmental behaviors.

Negative versus Positive Incentives

In addition to the previously mentioned influence of incentives, it is evident that incentives impact not only through their price mechanism but also through their effect on various behavioral dimensions. This encourages individuals to comply with environmental regulations. The idea is not merely that, as most behavioral analyses suggest, people are less rational, but rather that consistently leading people to behave in a certain way requires a deeper understanding of how incentives shape their motivations for that behavior.

A paper examining the effect of changes in waste removal fees on recycling rates and waste production indicates that waste collection fees, which vary according to bin size, create economic incentives for households.[59] While higher prices have a limited impact on reducing nonrecyclable waste, they positively influence recycling rates. To improve waste management, it is important to consider both economic incentives and disposal options, with a focus on aligning pricing structures with environmental goals.

A New York experiment using quantity-based waste pricing demonstrated the significance of the accessible location of recycling bins in providing market incentives for waste.[60] The research examined individual recycling behavior and compliance with recycling laws, including legislative measures such as random trash inspections

[58] Maki, Alexander, et al. "Paying people to protect the environment: A meta-analysis of financial incentive interventions to promote pro-environmental behaviors." *Journal of Environmental Psychology* 47 (2016): 242–255.

[59] Hong, Seonghoon, and Richard M. Adams. "Household responses to price incentives for recycling: Some further evidence." *Land Economics* 75.4 (1999): 505–514. https://doi.org/10.2307/3147062.

[60] Reschovsky, James D., and Sarah E. Stone. "Market incentives to encourage household waste recycling: Paying for what you throw away." In *The economics of residential solid waste management*, edited by Thomas C. Kinnaman, Routledge, 2017: 233–252.

and weight limits on garbage bags that had been in place since the program's initiation in 1990. The findings reveal that recycling behavior is primarily driven by demographic factors – households with married residents and higher levels of education tend to have higher recycling rates. Physical factors like house size, waste storage capacity, and proximity to recycling centers also significantly influence recycling behavior. Notably, these demographic and structural factors appear more influential than financial incentives alone – the study suggests that implementing a waste-pricing policy in isolation may not significantly impact recycling rates. Instead, effective recycling programs are better achieved through a combination of legislation and convenient sidewalk waste collection systems that address these demographic and structural realities.

The Plastic Bag Tax Debate

An outstanding example of using incentives in an environmental context can be seen in the implementation of a plastic bag tax.[61] This tool is especially prevalent in the field of environmental regulation, with many approaches proposed to modify people's environmental behavior. In November 2016, the Chicago City Council repealed its ban on disposable plastic bags and replaced it with a seven-cent tax on disposable paper and plastic bags, effective February 1, 2017.[62] The City of Chicago collaborated with the behavioral design lab ideas, along with researchers from New York University and the University of Chicago Energy & Environment Lab, to conduct a joint study that tracked bag usage at major grocery chains in Chicago and surrounding suburbs before and after the implementation of the tax. Preliminary results from Chicago's bag tax study show significant changes in consumer behavior. After implementation, disposable bag usage dropped from over two bags per shopping trip to approximately one bag – a 40 percent reduction. Additionally, the percentage of customers using disposable bags decreased dramatically, falling from over 80 percent to less than 50 percent of shoppers. Notably, these financial incentives appear to foster habit formation, leading consumers to internalize more sustainable practices even beyond immediate cost considerations.

Public Perception of Environmental Regulatory Interventions

Beyond measuring the direct effects of environmental regulatory interventions, it is crucial to understand how public perceptions and responses to different approaches mediate their potential for fostering internalized behavioral change. Public attitudes

61 Homonoff, Tatiana A. "Can small incentives have large effects? The impact of taxes versus bonuses on disposable bag use." *American Economic Journal: Economic Policy* 10.4 (2018): 177–210.

62 Results are taken from: "The effects of the Chicago bag tax on disposable bag use." ideas42, November 2017. The report can be found on the ideas42 website at the following link: www.ideas42.org/wp-content/uploads/2018/09/Bag_Tax_Paper_final.pdf.

and willingness to cooperate significantly influence the effectiveness of various legal tools, including taxes, subsidies, and behavioral incentives. Several barriers can affect participation in environmental programs: uncertainty aversion, price-based procrastination, status quo bias, lack of trust in government or community members, and residential mobility concerns. Understanding these psychological, economic, and cultural factors is essential for designing effective environmental regulations.

Thus, the environmental phase introduces unique elements that set it apart from ethical, COVID-related, or tax-focused considerations. These factors require changes in behavior, even in areas unrelated to legal regulations. For example, transitioning to an electric car or adopting green energy requires a more extensive range of behavior modifications, where compulsion may not always be practical. This reality raises questions about the barriers to change in various countries. Understanding how various regulatory instruments impact public perceptions of alternative energy resources and whether public participation enhances or diminishes willingness to adopt these alternatives is crucial.

LACK OF CONSISTENCY IN ENVIRONMENTAL STUDIES

Our meta-analysis aims to elucidate the complex mechanisms underlying the relationship between regulatory approaches and internal motivations for environmental compliance. Specifically, we examine how different levels of trust embedded in regulatory tools affect individuals' intrinsic motivation to engage in environmentally friendly behaviors. By clarifying these interactions, we aim to contribute to the design of more effective and nuanced environmental policy frameworks.[63] Climate change and environmental degradation are critical global concerns that present challenges for regulators and policymakers. It is essential to have effective mitigation and adaptation strategies to tackle these challenges. However, their success is heavily dependent on public collaboration.[64] Governments frequently introduce external measures to strengthen compliance with environmental policies. The effectiveness of these interventions in influencing actual environmental compliance behavior has been the subject of extensive research.[65] However, there has been limited analysis of how such interventions impact pro-environmental motivation systematically. It is conceivable

[63] Slater, J., et al. "A meta-analysis of crowding effects on pro-environmental motivation." Working paper, 2024 (on file with author).

[64] Bryner, Gary. "Cooperative instruments and policy making: Assessing public participation in US environmental regulation." *European Environment* 11.1 (2001): 49–60.

[65] Some examples for meta analyses and systematic reviews are: Alt, Marius, et al. "Synergies of interventions to promote pro-environmental behaviors: A meta-analysis of experimental studies." *Global Environmental Change* 84 (2024): 1–13; Fontecha, John E., et al. "Scientists wanted? A literature review on incentive programs that promote pro-environmental consumer behavior: Energy, waste, and water." *Socio-Economic Planning Sciences* 82 (2022): 1–18; Osbaldiston, Richard, and John Paul Schott. "Environmental sustainability and behavioral science: Meta-analysis of pro-environmental behavior experiments." *Environment and Behavior* 44.2 (2012): 257–299; Świątkowski, Wojciech, et al.

that while external interventions might enhance behavioral adherence to pro-environmental policies, they could simultaneously undermine internal motivations. This potential backlash may lead to the "crowding out" of intrinsic incentives, which could create a long-term negative effect and result in noncompliance in the future.[66]

Corporations' versus Individuals' Environmental Compliance

It has been shown that incentives have the potential to improve environmental outcomes and provide economic benefits to stakeholders in the corporate context.[67] The effectiveness of these programs relies on their design, implementation, and monitoring. Further research has also supported the notion that there is a difference in the effectiveness of regulatory interventions based on the identity of the recipient, whether corporations or individuals.[68] For example, findings indicate that corporations may be more responsive to penalties than individuals. This is partially related to the famous s- versus i-frame paper,[69] where there is some criticism on the over focus on behavioral change by individuals.

The Importance of Corporation Size

Studies on corporate environmental compliance have shown that company size and social norms significantly influence compliance levels. Research indicates that larger companies tend to demonstrate better environmental behavior, with their compliance being particularly shaped by social norms and professional networks.[70] Similarly, with respect to voluntary environmental behavior,[71] a study focusing on large hotels revealed that larger corporations with greater resources were more likely to engage in pro-environment behaviors not mandated by law.

Research by Esty and Porter demonstrates that the structure of environmental regulations significantly influences a country's compliance rates.[72] Their analysis

"Interventions promoting pro-environmental behaviors in children: A meta-analysis and a research agenda." *Journal of Environmental Psychology* 96 (2024): 1–15.

66 Ling and Xu. "How and when financial incentives crowd out pro-environmental motivation."

67 Khanna, Madhu, and William Rose Q. Anton. "Corporate environmental management: Regulatory and market-based incentives." *Land Economics* 78.4 (2002): 539–558.

68 Chrun, Elizabeth, Nives Dolšak, and Aseem Prakash. "Corporate environmentalism: Motivations and mechanisms." *Annual Review of Environment and Resources* 41.1 (2016): 341–362.

69 Chater, Nick, and George Loewenstein. "The i-frame and the s-frame: How focusing on individual-level solutions has led behavioral public policy astray." *Behavioral and Brain Sciences* 46 (2023): 1–26.

70 Dasgupta, Hettige, and Wheeler. "What improves environmental compliance?"

71 Rivera, Jorge. "Institutional pressures and voluntary environmental behavior in developing countries: Evidence from the Costa Rican hotel industry." *Society and Natural Resources* 17.9 (2004): 779–797.

72 Esty, Daniel C., and Michael E. Porter. "Ranking national environmental regulation and performance: A leading indicator of future competitiveness?" The Global Competitiveness Report 2002 (2001): 78–100.

reveals substantial variations across nations – the Netherlands and Austria rank highest in environmental regulatory quality, followed by Denmark, while countries like Italy, Israel, and Greece rank lower. Two key factors emerge as crucial for compliance: information availability and enforcement by environmentally focused private sector entities. Building on these findings, additional comparative research has identified several factors that facilitate regulatory effectiveness.[73] Specifically, compliance monitoring becomes more manageable when there are fewer actors involved and when activities are concentrated in a small geographic area. Other significant factors influencing compliance include the economic value of the regulated activity, a nation's monitoring and regulatory capacity, and the organizational structure of the regulated activities.

Information vs. Incentives: Environmental Change

The literature has recognized the unique challenge of regulating individual behavior. Based on extensive reviews of various regulatory approaches, it is generally believed that information campaigns and the implementation of social norms are most effective in changing individuals' attitudes toward the environment.[74] This tendency can also be observed in people's attitudes toward electricity consumption and car purchasing. Research suggests that information campaigns promoting the adoption and proper operation of electrical vehicles can make a significant impact on individuals.[75] However, the measurement of the scope of these changes is still lacking.

In the context of corporate pollution, regulatory tools such as fines, taxes, and liabilities have proven quite effective.[76] However, when applied to individual behavior, the evidence is mixed and depends on various contextual factors. Interestingly, attitudes toward the environment did not appear to be highly predictive of financial decisions.[77] While individuals with strong pro-environmental attitudes were found to be more likely to engage in pro-environmental behavior, the connection between attitudes and actions proved weak. Research has indicated that personality traits, particularly "locus of control" – the perceived level of control people believe they have over the situation – can significantly influence an individual's sense of

73 Weiss, Edith Brown, and Harold Karan Jacobson, eds. *Engaging countries: Strengthening compliance with international environmental accords*. MIT Press, 2000.

74 Yamin, Paulius, et al. "Using social norms to change behavior and increase sustainability in the real world: A systematic review of the literature." *Sustainability* 11.20 (2019): 1–41.

75 Wang, Shanyong, et al. "Policy implications for promoting the adoption of electric vehicles: Do consumer's knowledge, perceived risk and financial incentive policy matter?" *Transportation Research Part A: Policy and Practice* 117 (2018): 58–69.

76 Faure, Michael. "Effectiveness of environmental law: What does the evidence tell us?" *William & Mary Environmental Law and Policy Review* 36 (2011): 293–336.

77 Walczak, Damian, et al. "Attitudes and behaviors regarding environmental protection in the financial decisions of individual consumers." *Energies* 14.7 (2021): 1–13.

self-efficacy and willingness to engage in pro-environmental behavior.[78] Studies have also found that altruistic and environmental attitudes, combined with financial capacity (higher income and fewer household members), reliably predict pro-environmental behavior, such as participation in green electricity programs.[79]

SUMMARY AND CONCLUSION

In this chapter we focused on the third case study on environmental regulation, focusing on the distinctive challenges and methods involved in promoting compliance with environmental standards and encouraging positive changes in behavior. Compared to other areas of regulation, promoting environmentally responsible behavior often involves encouraging individuals and organizations to adopt specific values, stay mindful of their environmental impacts, and willingly bear costs, even when there are no legal mandates in place. Environmental behavior differs from tax compliance, discussed in Chapter 9 in a crucial way: While tax behavior simply involves following specific rules, environmental changes require broader shifts in consumption patterns and lifestyle choices. The chapter examines different regulatory tools, such as command-and-control methods, market-based mechanisms, and voluntary programs, and it highlights a recent trend toward more adaptable and inventive regulatory strategies.

We have attempted to synthesize research on the various intrinsic and extrinsic factors that influence both environmental compliance and pro-environmental behavior in different contexts. It explores how incentives, information campaigns, social norms, and cultural variations all play a crucial role in shaping people's environmental attitudes and actions. It also compares the compliance patterns of individuals and corporations when it comes to environmental policies. Moreover, the chapter examines the diverse cultural outlooks concerning environmental regulation. It emphasizes how distinct elements such as the level of faith in government, economic conditions, and cultural values can impact the triumph of environmental policies and programs in varying countries.

Future research should focus on further enhancing our comprehension of voluntary compliance and environmental regulation. Specifically, there is, first, a need to conduct longitudinal studies on the long-term effects of voluntary programs, as numerous studies have already assessed their short-term impacts. Future studies should monitor participating organizations and individuals for extended periods to

78 Cleveland, Mark, Maria Kalamas, and Michel Laroche. "Shades of green: Linking environmental locus of control and pro-environmental behaviors." *Journal of Consumer Marketing* 22.4 (2005): 198–212.

79 Kollmuss, Anja, and Julian Agyeman. "Mind the gap: Why do people act environmentally and what are the barriers to pro-environmental behavior?" *Environmental Education Research* 8.3 (2002): 239–260.

determine whether voluntary compliance results in lasting changes in behavior and improvements in the environment. Second, additional research is needed to fully comprehend the psychological and cognitive factors that affect decision-making related to the environment, both at an individual and organizational level. This involves exploring how the motivational aspects discussed thus far can be utilized to create voluntary compliance programs and regulatory interventions that are more efficient. Third, there is a need for more extensive cross-cultural studies to comprehend the influence of cultural factors on voluntary compliance and the efficacy of diverse regulatory strategies in different countries and regions. This research should aim to develop culturally sensitive frameworks for environmental regulation. Finally, although this research primarily focused on individual behavior, future research should investigate the correlation between voluntary environmental initiatives, corporate performance, and market dynamics. This includes investigating how consumer preferences, investor behavior, and competitive pressures influence corporate decisions to engage in voluntary environmental compliance. One of the challenges of promoting voluntary compliance is that governments may struggle to assess whether people are behaving voluntarily without jeopardizing the voluntary nature of the behavior. Consequently, we need better methods to measure and assess the environmental impact of voluntary compliance programs. We need to create advanced indicators and metrics that can effectively measure all the environmental impacts and benefits.

As discussed earlier, voluntary compliance cannot be achieved solely by relying on intrinsic motivation. Therefore, further research should investigate how mandatory regulations and voluntary initiatives can be effectively combined and work together in order to attain environmental objectives. This entails studying the potential for hybrid regulatory methods that combine the benefits of both mandatory and voluntary mechanisms. Addressing these research areas would help scholars and policymakers gain a better understanding of the interaction between environmental regulation and voluntary compliance, which will lead to more effective and sustainable environmental governance strategies.

11

Conclusion

Reimagining Regulation in the Voluntary Era

INTRODUCTION

Throughout the first ten chapters of the book, we have explored voluntary compliance from various perspectives. Beyond clarifying its meaning, this book has examined its potential benefits for regulatory policy, emphasizing the importance of understanding when and how governments can trust citizens to comply voluntarily with laws and regulations and what regulatory approaches might achieve this goal.

The book began with an overview of voluntary compliance, addressing its definitions, potential advantages, and challenges. We examined how it intersects with concepts such as trust, legitimacy, and social norms, establishing a foundation for understanding the factors that influence compliance behavior. Many foundational concepts – such as voluntariness, intrinsic compliance motivation, coercion, and trust-based regulation – remain inadequately defined despite their central role in modern discussions on regulation and compliance. We outline the potential benefits of effective voluntary compliance in terms of compliance quality, sustainability, and positive societal spillover effects.

Building on this foundation, the book examined the behavioral aspects of voluntary compliance, focusing primarily on the interaction between intrinsic and extrinsic compliance motivations. We analyzed how moral, social, and economic factors affect compliance and how various regulatory approaches can influence individuals' compliance motivation.

This discussion led to a critical analysis of how external interventions, particularly regulatory frameworks, can potentially "crowd out" individuals' intrinsic compliance motivation, thereby undermining the very voluntary compliance these interventions aim to foster. We explored various trust-based regulatory approaches as alternatives to traditional command-and-control methods, investigating strategies such as responsive regulation, nudges, and trust-based regulation while acknowledging their limitations.

We also highlighted significant gaps in empirical knowledge regarding voluntary compliance, noting inconsistencies and small effect sizes in existing studies. Existing research on voluntary compliance often suffers from significant methodological limitations, particularly a lack of external validity. Many studies rely on narrow convenience samples or highly specific contextual settings, which impede researchers' ability to draw robust, generalizable conclusions about voluntary compliance's effectiveness across diverse regulatory domains and populations. This evidentiary uncertainty creates substantial challenges for regulators attempting to identify optimal intervention strategies. Without comprehensive, cross-cultural empirical evidence demonstrating which regulatory approaches reliably generate voluntary compliance, policymakers frequently retreat to traditional coercive methods. Although these regulators may recognize the potential advantages of more nuanced, cooperative approaches, the perceived risks of experimental strategies lead them to default to familiar enforcement mechanisms, potentially undermining the very compliance objectives they seek to achieve. In earlier chapters, we established that intrinsic motivation's predictive power remains ambiguous and contingent upon various factors, limiting its reliability as a standalone indicator. Moreover, the efficacy of trust-based regulation in fostering trust remains uncertain, with some scholars suggesting it may prove to be counterproductive.

We have also clarified the complexities of the crowding-out effect, which presents significant challenges when integrating trust-based approaches with monitoring-based strategies. Our analysis reveals that both intrinsic and extrinsic motivations encompass multiple subtypes and aspects, making the crowding-out process highly unpredictable.

Examining the risks and limitations of relying on voluntary compliance, we identified key challenges, including varying compliance motivations across populations and the potential exploitation by noncompliant actors, including state entities attempting to influence public attitudes rather than just behaviors. These challenges make a regulatory framework without monitoring infeasible, while raising the question of how to harness the benefits of trust – specifically, the valuable sense of trustworthiness individuals feel – without compromising public safety or disrupting societal expectations of enforcement.

We also examined the role of culture in shaping compliance behavior, exploring how cultural factors such as trust, social cohesion, and attitudes toward authority vary across societies, influencing the effectiveness of voluntary compliance initiatives. Cultural variation serves two important functions in regulatory design: it helps shape culturally sensitive regulatory approaches and fosters discussions on designing regulatory systems that account for cultural differences. Similarly, we analyzed the role of technology in facilitating or hindering voluntary compliance, particularly its impact on monitoring, enforcement, and trust in regulatory systems (Chapter 7).

The practical application of these concepts was demonstrated through an analysis of public health policies, with a particular focus on lessons learned from the

COVID-19 pandemic (Chapter 8). More specifically, we compared the trust-based approaches with command-and-control strategies in different countries, specifically examining compliance behavior related to mask wearing and vaccinations. This practical focus extended to tax policy in Chapter 9, where we explored tax moral, fairness perceptions, and trust in government. We weighed the effectiveness of these factors in the context of the effectiveness of audits and deterrence and considered the impact on tax compliance.

Continuing the practical focus, we examined environmental regulation in Chapter 10, exploring how intrinsic motivation, social norms, and regulatory approaches intersect to influence pro-environmental behaviors. Each regulatory domain presents a unique set of contextual parameters that fundamentally shape the potential for voluntary compliance.

These parameters include critical factors such as the visibility of specific behaviors, the social consequences of misconduct, and the community's collective response to regulatory expectations. By analyzing these nuanced dimensions, we can better understand the complex mechanisms that enable or constrain voluntary compliance across different regulatory contexts.

The varying visibility of behaviors – from highly observable actions to more private practices – profoundly impacts individuals' willingness to comply. Similarly, the social dynamics surrounding potential misconduct, including peer judgment, community sanctions, and reputational risks, play a crucial role in motivating cooperative behavior.

This approach allows for a more sophisticated understanding of voluntary compliance, moving beyond simplistic models of enforcement to appreciate the intricate interplay between individual psychology, social context, and regulatory design.

Overall, voluntary compliance – particularly intrinsically motivated compliance – has shown mixed results across various regulatory contexts. Many studies demonstrate the small effect size of factors related to intrinsic motivation and attitudes in predicting actual behavior.[1] Additionally, these factors are highly influenced by cultural differences.[2] The small effect sizes and inconsistencies in the relationship between intrinsic motivation and compliance limit the government's ability to rely solely on voluntary mechanisms to *ensure* compliance. However, understanding voluntary compliance helps researchers and policymakers assess how different regulatory strategies perform in broader contexts. That being said, we need to develop a new model of responsive regulation that draws on empirical evidence, incorporates

1 E.g., Berkebile-Weinberg, Michael, et al. "The differential impact of climate interventions along the political divide in 60 countries." *Nature Communications* 15.1 (2024): 1–12.

2 Morren, Meike, and Amir Grinstein. "Explaining environmental behavior across borders: A meta-analysis." *Journal of Environmental Psychology* 47 (2016): 91–106 (showing that attitudes are predictive in more individualistic countries).

behavioral public policy insights, recognizes national differences, and focuses on specific target behaviors.

By integrating the multifaceted strands of analysis discussed earlier, we gain a more nuanced understanding of the intricate interplay of factors that influence the achievement and sustainability of voluntary compliance across diverse domains. This comprehensive examination has facilitated the development of a framework for identifying the most effective regulatory tools to foster compliance and promote cooperation without relying on problematic methods, such as attitude manipulation (Chapter 5) or excessive technological prediction (Chapter 7).

This work has explored the intricate relationship between national context, institutions, and the potential efficacy of trust-based regulation across different countries, considering their unique ethical frameworks.[3] While substantial research exists on cross-national differences, traditionally speaking the scholarship has focused on singular dimensions such as honesty or trust, rather than the nuanced variations in voluntary compliance. As a result, the predictive power of compliance based on honesty, cooperation, or trust is inherently limited. Furthermore, a democratic state should strive to cultivate willing obedience among its citizenry, or at least foster a sense of trustworthiness, while maintaining necessary monitoring mechanisms. This dual approach, however, creates a complex dynamic regarding the wisdom of adopting trust-based regulation.

The evaluation of trust-based regulation demands a nuanced approach that carefully weighs potential benefits against inherent costs. As argued in the book, this necessitates a context-specific regulatory policy that acknowledges both the advantages of trust-based systems and the practical complexities of governance and compliance.

From a normative perspective, critical examination of persuasion strategies is essential. The law's diversity and distributional impact raise significant concerns, particularly regarding the potential vulnerability of less educated and privileged populations to preference manipulation through persuasion campaigns.

When assessing regulatory interventions, scholars must consider not merely immediate behavioral changes, but the long-term impact on public trust. Research suggests that individuals who feel trusted by the state tend to become more cooperative over time, indicating that interventions should be evaluated based on their capacity to build sustainable trust relationships.[4]

[3] Cook, Karen S., Russell Hardin, and Margaret Levi. *Cooperation without trust?* Russell Sage Foundation, 2005. Very recently, a new study has challenged the traditional view that mistrust undermines compliance and has actually found the reverse effect: that mistrust by the state decreased opportunism and increased compliance. See: Mendoza, Juan P., and Jacco L. Wielhouwer. "Compliance under distrust: Do people comply less when they feel distrusted?" *Journal of Public Administration Research and Theory* 47 (2024): 103–116.

[4] Tov, William, and Ed Diener. "The well-being of nations: Linking together trust, cooperation, and democracy." In *The science of well-being: The collected works of Ed Diener*, edited by Ed Diener, Springer Netherlands, 2009: 155–173.

The potential benefits of voluntary compliance extend far beyond immediate regulatory contexts. By fostering long-term cooperative commitment among even a portion of the population, states can generate significant positive externalities.[5] These may include improved regulatory effectiveness, enhanced public safety, more innovative compliance methods, more efficient resource allocation, and increased transparency in industry practices.

However, as explored in Chapters 5 and 8–10, determining the ideal trust level between government and public requires a delicate balance. While internal, sustainable change through trust is desirable, the risks of over-trusting must be carefully considered. Regulators must design governance strategies that promote voluntary compliance while maintaining essential safeguards.

For instance, excessive trust in an industry can potentially compromise public safety, even while seemingly improving government–industry relationships. The challenge lies in creating a nuanced approach that balances trust and oversight.[6]

Trust-Based Regulation: Three Levels

Throughout this book, we have examined the advantages of shifting from command-and-control approaches to more trust-based and intrinsically motivated regulatory mechanisms at three levels.

Our analysis of voluntary compliance unfolded across three critical levels of examination:

At the societal level, we investigated the transformative potential of voluntary compliance on social trust. This approach explores how reducing punitive enforcement might reshape social solidarity and cohesion, examining the broader societal implications of a more cooperative regulatory paradigm. The analysis considers how fundamental shifts in enforcement strategies could recalibrate the social contract between citizens and the state.

At the institutional level, we scrutinized how trust-based regulatory strategies might fundamentally alter the legitimacy of government institutions. This dimension probes the dynamic reconfiguration of public perceptions toward regulatory bodies, tracing how the relationship between regulators and regulated entities might evolve over time. We examined the delicate balance between institutional authority and public trust, exploring how more collaborative approaches could potentially reconstruct institutional credibility.

At the individual level, we delved into how emphasizing intrinsic motivation could reshape individual compliance behaviors across different regulatory domains.

5 In a work in progress with Liran Maimoni and Tami Kricheli Katz on the spillover effects of autonomy-based regulatory effects on lab participants who played a series of games, such as the dictator game and trust games.

6 Maman, Libby, Yuval Feldman, and David Levi-Faur. "Varieties of regulatory regimes and their effect on citizens' trust in firms." *Journal of European Public Policy* 30.12 (2023): 2807–2831.

This analysis extended beyond mere rule following to explore the potential for "beyond-compliance" behaviors – actions that demonstrate internalized commitment rather than superficial adherence. We critically examined the challenges and opportunities inherent in cultivating genuine intrinsic motivation, investigating the psychological mechanisms that transform external regulatory pressures into internally driven ethical conduct.

By examining voluntary compliance through these interconnected levels – societal, institutional, and individual – we offer a comprehensive framework for understanding the complex dynamics of regulatory behavior and cooperation.

We can also distinguish between short-term and long-term impacts of voluntary compliance at each of these levels. The short-term effect focuses on whether trust-based mechanisms can genuinely improve immediate compliance.[7] The long-term effect, however, is more complex, as it encompasses the broader impact of trust-based regulation on individual, social, and institutional factors such as reciprocity, solidarity, legitimacy, and social capital when observed over an extended period of time.

Drawing on the insights from previous chapters, we assess the potential advantages and disadvantages of voluntary compliance. This analysis provides a nuanced perspective on the circumstances in which voluntary compliance approaches are most effective and where traditional command-and-control methods may still be necessary. However, we argue that more studies are needed to determine the future of regulatory policy and the balance between trust-based and coercive approaches to governance.

The book explored the various factors that contribute to this regulatory dilemma at multiple levels and discusses the ethical considerations that must guide decision-making. It also examines the techniques used to compare and assess the costs of relying on voluntary compliance versus command-and-control strategies and the risks of errors associated with them. The main objective is to create a detailed plan for evaluating the effectiveness of voluntary compliance in various cultural and contextual settings.

This evaluation becomes particularly crucial when considering behavioral public policy approaches. While research suggests that morality can be a more effective means of achieving compliance than other approaches, significant questions remain about the reliability and scope of voluntary compliance.[8] For example, while a moral nudge may elicit a positive response from 20 percent of the population, there is still uncertainty about how long their contributions will last and how the remaining 80 percent will react. Will they experience crowding-out effects or simply disregard the nudge?

7 Tyler, Tom R., and Yuen J. Huo. *Trust in the law: Encouraging public cooperation with the police and courts*. Russell Sage Foundation, 2002.

8 E.g., Thurman, Quint C., Craig St John, and Lisa Riggs. "Neutralization and tax evasion: How effective would a moral appeal be in improving compliance to tax laws?" *Law & Policy* 6.3 (1984): 309–327.

REVISITING VOLUNTARINESS AS A MULTIDIMENSIONAL CONSTRUCT

Building upon the framework introduced in Chapter 2, we conceptualize voluntary compliance as a nuanced continuum rather than a simplistic binary construct. This multidimensional approach reveals the intricate dynamics of compliance behavior through a complex interplay of factors.

The perceived level of coercion serves as a critical dimension, spanning from overt mandates to subtle nudges, fundamentally shaping an individual's willingness to comply. Equally important is the role of intrinsic motivation – the internal psychological drivers rooted in personal values and social norms that determine the depth and authenticity of compliance. The clarity of behavioral instructions significantly influences compliance, as the precision and comprehensibility of regulatory expectations directly impact an individual's ability to adhere to regulations.

Moreover, an individual's contextual understanding and interpretation of compliance requirements mediate their response, reflecting the complex interplay between cognitive processing and regulatory expectations. The relative salience of these factors in an individual's decision-making calculus can vary dramatically across different regulatory domains and personal contexts.

By disaggregating compliance into these nuanced dimensions, researchers and policymakers can develop more sophisticated, context-sensitive approaches to understanding and fostering voluntary cooperation. This framework acknowledges the complex psychological and social mechanisms that underlie regulatory behavior, moving beyond simplistic models of compliance and revealing the subtle dynamics that shape human response to regulatory expectations.[9]

Such a multidimensional approach facilitates a more detailed analysis of compliance behaviors, which enables policymakers and researchers to develop regulatory strategies that are better suited to specific situations. These strategies can balance the benefits of voluntary compliance with the need for more directive approaches when necessary.

Moreover, we believe that the field is facing definitional inconsistencies across different disciplines, which are hindering interdisciplinary research efforts. The interpretation of voluntariness frequently differs between psychological, economic, and legal frameworks, which create obstacles in consolidating research findings into one unified body of knowledge.

VOLUNTARY COMPLIANCE AND HETEROGENEITY

As discussed in Chapter 5, the critical challenge lies in understanding the prevalence of conditional cooperators. The success of policies dependent on voluntary compliance hinges on the number of individuals willing to cooperate without

9 Aranson, Peter H. "Theories of economic regulation: From clarity to confusion." *Journal of Law & Politics* 6 (1989): 247–286.

coercion, a dynamic that is inherently unstable. The widespread presence of conditional cooperators introduces significant complexity, as these individuals modulate their compliance levels based on their observations and expectations of others' behaviors. Research by Fischbacher, Gächter, and Fehr suggests that approximately half of participants in public goods experiments can be classified as conditional cooperators, demonstrating their tendency to adjust contributions based on group behavior. This heterogeneity and conditionality pose challenges for policymakers in predicting the outcomes of voluntary compliance initiatives. The resulting uncertainty limits the scope and importance of voluntary compliance projects, especially in areas where noncompliance carries significant costs.

Designing effective policies becomes exceedingly difficult without accurate knowledge of how cooperators, noncooperators, and conditional cooperators are distributed in each population. As noted, there is a significant risk posed by the potential for cascading effects, where noncompliance among a critical mass of conditional cooperators can lead to widespread defection.[10] Furthermore, the composition of these groups may differ across various regulatory domains and cultural contexts, which makes it difficult to generalize. This heterogeneity demands sophisticated models and empirical research to better understand how voluntary compliance operates in diverse populations. Only through such nuanced understanding can policymakers develop more robust and flexible regulatory strategies. This research is particularly crucial because without the ability to distinguish between individuals and their propensity for voluntary compliance, the approach of "trusting the public" may be significantly limited in both its effectiveness and real-world application.

JURISPRUDENTIAL RELEVANCY OF VOLUNTARY COMPLIANCE AND INTERNALIZATION

This book primarily examines voluntary compliance through a behavioral lens rather than a jurisprudential one. While an entire book could have been dedicated to the jurisprudential perspective on voluntary compliance, exploring the costs and benefits for democratic governments in trusting their citizens and discussing the advantages of internalization, we chose to focus mainly on behavioral factors.

That being said, we could not conclude this book without acknowledging the rich body of legal philosophy on this topic. Numerous legal philosophers have extensively debated the implications of voluntary compliance with the law and internal motivations for adhering to it. This discussion highlights a fundamental tension between advocating for virtue through law and safeguarding individual rights and freedoms.

10 Lederman, Leandra. "The interplay between norms and enforcement in tax compliance." *Ohio State Law Journal* 64 (2003): 1453–1514.

First and foremost, it is important to note that even as far back as Aristotle, there has been an emphasis on the significance of individuals who embrace virtues through the processes of internalization. According to studies conducted by scholars who have studied Aristotle, such as Nancy Sherman and Julia Annas,[11] it is believed that virtues are acquired mainly through habit and practice, rather than through deliberative knowledge of what is the right thing to do as some of the more modern research we reviewed suggests. Aristotle famously talked about the importance of repetition in developing virtuous habits, insisting that virtues are formed by repeatedly performing virtuous actions until they become second nature.[12] Drawing from Aristotelian philosophy, we can reconsider the role of habit formation in compliance. While contemporary approaches often view habit formation techniques (such as those studied by Milkman and others)[13] as inferior to moral or science-based compliance, an Aristotelian perspective might suggest that for certain practices, habit formation could be normatively permissible – and even beneficial – in guiding more people toward "virtuous" behavior.

More contemporary legal philosophers have stated that the law should actively shape citizens' characters and promote moral values, a perspective rooted in the classical philosophies of philosophers such as Plato and Aquinas.[14] However, implementing this approach faces significant challenges in contemporary, diverse societies, where critics often assert that imposing moral values through the legal system can result in the suppression of minority views and infringe individual liberties.[15] Another related and important discussion is the distinction between morality in the public and private spheres which further complicates this issue. Famously, H. L. A. Hart argued that the law should focus only on actions that directly harm others and not on private moral choices.[16] In contrast, Patrick Devlin contended that the law should uphold public shared morality in order to preserve social cohesion.[17]

Other contemporary legal thinkers have sought to navigate these tensions by proposing more nuanced approaches. For example, John Rawls supported the political notion of justice that could be embraced by people with diverse moral views, seeking to strike a balance between encouraging shared values and upholding moral pluralism.[18] In contrast, Lon L. Fuller emphasized the

11 Sherman, Nancy. *The fabric of character: Aristotle's theory of virtue*. Clarendon Press, 1989; Annas, Julia. *Intelligent virtue*. Oxford University Press, 2011.

12 Jimenez, Marta. "Aristotle on becoming virtuous by doing virtuous actions." *Phronesis* 61.1 (2016): 3–32.

13 Milkman, Katherine L., et al. "Megastudies improve the impact of applied behavioural science." *Nature* 600.7889 (2021): 478–483.

14 Plato. *The republic*, translated by Benjamin Jowett. The Internet Classics Archive, classics.mit.edu/Plato/republic.html.

15 Hart, H. L. A. *Law, liberty, and morality*. Stanford University Press, 1963.

16 Hart, H.L.A. *The concept of law*. Oxford University Press, 1961.

17 Devlin, Patrick. *The enforcement of morals*. Oxford University Press, 1965.

18 Rawls, John. *A theory of justice*. Belknap Press of Harvard University Press, 1971.

importance of creating a stable and predictable legal framework, rather than enforcing a particular moral code.[19] In that regard, attempting to promote noncoerced widely shared intrinsic compliance motivation offers numerous potential benefits to such stability. Indeed, as discussed in the first chapters of the book, internally motivated compliance has the potential to lower enforcement and litigation expenses, increase the credibility of the justice system, and encourage greater participation from the public.[20]

The concerns raised in Chapter 5 about the risks of voluntary compliance resonate with Hart's cautionary view about using the law to change people's intrinsic moral beliefs. Just as Hart warned against using law to enforce morality, we should be cautious about regulatory systems that aim to fundamentally alter citizens' internal value systems rather than focusing on external behavior. This connects to the broader philosophical debate about the appropriate boundaries between state power and individual moral autonomy, mentioned in the previous paragraph.

In contrast, paradigms such as Oliver Wendell Holmes Jr.'s "bad man" theory of law, present a contrasting viewpoint, suggesting that the law should be understood primarily in terms of its consequences for those seeking to avoid punishment, implying that internalized motivations are less relevant than practical outcomes.[21]

The question of whether a state benefits from its citizens internalizing their motivations for complying with the law has been a subject of significant debate among legal theorists.[22] Many scholars argue that a legal system in which citizens comply due to internalized motivations rather than fear of punishment could lead to more stable and efficient legal institutions.[23]

Nevertheless, critics argue that emphasizing internalized motivations may be too idealistic and impractical, especially in pluralistic societies. This is because it may prove challenging to promote a widespread internalization of legal motivations due to diverse moral and cultural perspectives, especially as countries become less and less homogenous.[24] The debate also raises questions regarding the appropriate role of the state in shaping citizens' motivations, with some arguing that actively promoting the internalization of legal norms could infringe on individual autonomy and lead to state paternalism.[25]

19 Fuller, Lon L. *The morality of law*. Yale University Press, 1964.

20 Tyler and Huo. *Trust in the law*; Sunstein, Cass R. "On the expressive function of law." *University of Pennsylvania Law Review* 144.5 (1996): 2021–2053.

21 Holmes, Oliver Wendell. "The path of the law." *Harvard Law Review* 10 (1897): 467–468.

22 Tyler, Tom R. *Why people obey the law*. Princeton University Press, 1990.

23 Cooter, Robert. "Do good laws make good citizens? An economic analysis of internalized norms." *Virginia Law Review* 86 (2000): 1577–1602.

24 Kymlicka, Will. *Multicultural citizenship: A liberal theory of minority rights*. Oxford University Press, 1996.

25 Dworkin, Gerald. "Paternalism." *The Monist* 56.1 (1972): 64–84.

CAN WE RELY ON PEOPLE'S INTRINSIC MOTIVATION?

In Chapter 5, which focused on the perils of voluntary compliance, we have discussed many of the challenges associated with relying on people's intrinsic motivation to comply. We argued that the use of intrinsic motivation to encourage voluntary compliance poses a significant challenge because of the complex psychological mechanisms that affect human behavior. While intrinsic motivation is typically considered a vital predictor of cooperative behavior, recent research indicates that individuals may not always have accurate insight into their motivations or, even more so, may lack objective perceptions of the meaning of their actions. Various cognitive biases, particularly self-deception and motivated reasoning, affect the reliability of people's ability to use intrinsic motivation, which is free of these ethical biases and hence socially beneficial.[26]

Self-deception is a process through which individuals convince themselves of a desired reality, even when evidence suggests otherwise. This can cause people to believe that they are acting in alignment with their true values when in reality they are not.[27] This phenomenon poses a particular problem in the context of voluntary compliance, as individuals may justify noncompliant behavior while still holding onto the belief that they are abiding by their moral standards. Motivated reasoning further complicates compliance issues by causing individuals to selectively process information.[28] This selective processing often leads people to support conclusions that align with their personal desires, rather than what may be socially beneficial or in line with the states' preferences. As a result, individuals may justify noncompliance or misinterpret regulations in ways that serve their interests.[29] In the context of regulatory compliance, bias can cause people to interpret ambiguous situations in a way that justifies noncompliance while still maintaining their self-image as law-abiding citizens.

The implications of these psychological processes on regulatory policy are significant. It is hence highly likely that despite possessing strong intrinsic motivation to comply with regulations, individuals may be influenced by self-interest, high personal costs, or other external factors that can lead to noncompliant behavior without the individual fully recognizing or acknowledging this shift.[30] This disparity between perceived and actual motivations raises serious concerns about the reliability

[26] See Feldman, Yuval. *The law of good people: Challenging states' ability to regulate human behavior*. Cambridge University Press, 2018, at chapters 1–2, for a discussion of the relevancy of self-deception to compliance.

[27] Tenbrunsel, Ann E., and David M. Messick. "Ethical fading: The role of self-deception in unethical behavior." *Social Justice Research* 17 (2004): 223–236.

[28] Ditto, Peter H., David A. Pizarro, and David Tannenbaum. "Motivated moral reasoning." *Psychology of Learning and Motivation* 50 (2009): 307–338.

[29] Kunda, Ziva. "The case for motivated reasoning." *Psychological Bulletin* 108.3 (1990): 480–498.

[30] Feldman, Yuval, and Yotam Kaplan. "Behavioral ethics as compliance." *Bar Ilan University Faculty of Law Research Paper* 19–18 (2019).

of self-regulation, especially under conditions of limited monitoring, and the extent to which policymakers can trust the public to consistently engage in voluntary compliance over time.[31] Due to the lack of robust empirical evidence on the long-term sustainability of intrinsically motivated compliance in the face of conflicting interests, there is a risk that policies overly reliant on voluntary compliance may ultimately prove ineffective or even counterproductive.

TOWARD A DIFFERENTIATED VOLUNTARY COMPLIANCE

To encourage voluntary compliance, policymakers must consider various complex factors that go beyond conventional regulatory measures. The advantages of using legitimacy to promote compliance over morality have been increasingly recognized, as legitimacy tends to generate more sustainable and widespread adherence to rules. This shift demands a focus on procedural justice and transparent governance in order to establish public trust in regulatory institutions.[32]

Innovative legislation and advancements in monitoring technology provide promising approaches for improving regulatory strategies. Policymakers can gather empirical evidence on the effectiveness of various approaches to voluntary compliance by carrying out temporary or geographically restricted regulatory experiments. At the same time, advanced technologies are facilitating more refined and less intrusive monitoring methods that could potentially mitigate the adverse effects of surveillance on intrinsic motivation.[33]

These technological developments have particular relevance for implementing the concept of "watchful trust," despite its methodological limitations, in regulatory regimes – an approach that balances trust-based and control-based strategies.[34] This strategy involves maintaining a foundation of trust in regulated entities while implementing specific monitoring mechanisms. For example, the Internal Revenue Service's Compliance Assurance Process allows large corporate taxpayers to resolve tax issues in real time through enhanced transparency, rather than through aggressive post-filing audits. However, finding the proper balance between trust and monitoring presents a significant challenge. Excessive monitoring may undermine the trust it intends to validate, while policymakers must balance the aim of optimal regulatory performance with the need to maintain public trust and legitimacy.[35]

31 Bazerman, Max H., and Ann E. Tenbrunsel. *Blind spots: Why we fail to do what's right and what to do about it*. Princeton University Press, 2011.

32 Tyler, Tom R. *Why people obey the law*. Princeton University Press, 2006.

33 Andrejevic, Mark. *iSpy: Surveillance and power in the interactive era*. University Press of Kansas, 2007.

34 Verhoest, Koen, et al. "How trust matters for the performance and legitimacy of regulatory regimes: The differential impact of watchful trust and good-faith trust." *Regulation & Governance* 19.1 (2025): 3–20.

35 Six, Frédérique. "Trust in regulatory relations: How new insights from trust research improve regulation theory." *Public Management Review* 15.2 (2013): 163–185.

To encourage voluntary compliance, a comprehensive understanding of how various motivational factors, cultural contexts, and specific regulated behaviors interact with each other is crucial. Considering the intricacy of human motivation and the varied regulatory challenges, it is improbable that a uniform solution will prove effective. Instead, policymakers should strive for a balanced approach that integrates insights from behavioral science, legal theory, and empirical research to develop regulatory frameworks that are both effective and perceived as legitimate by the public.[36]

FRAMEWORK FOR DECIDING ON VOLUNTARY COMPLIANCE EFFICACY

Taxonomy of Contexts Where Voluntary Compliance Benefits Exceed Its Risks

To evaluate the effectiveness of voluntary compliance under different legal doctrines, it is important to understand that not all regulatory situations require the same amount of public cooperation or intrinsic motivation. One can develop a taxonomy of legal doctrines by considering factors such as the ease of enforcement, the significance of compliance quality, and the visibility of the regulated behavior. This framework allows for a more nuanced approach to regulatory strategies, acknowledging that in some cases, traditional command-and-control measures may be more appropriate and effective than relying on voluntary compliance. For instance, in high-risk industries such as nuclear power or hazardous waste management, where the potential consequences of noncompliance are severe and immediate; in situations involving persistent violators who have shown unwillingness to cooperate; or in emergencies requiring swift and uniform action across an entire sector, there is no point in attempting to achieve voluntary compliance and command and control will be the preferred option.[37]

Additionally, when behaviors are closely monitored, there may be less of a need to rely on voluntary compliance with regulations. In such cases, the threat of being caught and facing punishment can act as an effective deterrent, which could decrease the necessity of promoting intrinsic motivation among the general population. This approach might be particularly effective in contexts such as public littering or adherence to building codes, where violations are readily apparent.[38]

36 Feldman, Yuval, and Orly Lobel. "Behavioral trade-offs: Beyond the land of nudges spans the world of law and psychology." In *Handbook of behavioral economics and the law*, edited by Eyal Zamir and Doron Teichman, Oxford University Press, 2014: 301–331.

37 Van Rooij, Benjamin, and Adam Fine. "Toxic corporate culture: Assessing organizational processes of deviancy." *Administrative Sciences* 8.3 (2018): 1–38.

38 Etienne, Julien. "Compliance theory: A goal framing approach." *Law & Policy* 33.3 (2011): 305–333.

It is also important to consider situations where monitoring does not have a major impact on reducing intrinsic motivation. This is commonly seen in contexts where behavior is less personal or relationship-driven, such as corporate financial reporting or industrial emissions control. In such situations, implementing a combination of monitoring techniques and encouraging voluntary compliance could prove to be the most effective approach. This is because the presence of oversight is less likely to diminish individuals' sense of moral obligation.[39]

Developing and utilizing comprehensive taxonomies is crucial for policymakers when designing effective regulatory strategies. Although voluntary compliance and intrinsic motivation can be useful in certain situations, they may not be universally applicable or efficient. Policymakers can enhance resource allocation and minimize societal costs by customizing regulatory approaches to fit the unique features of each legal doctrine, thereby increasing compliance to the maximum extent possible.[40]

Regulatory effectiveness hinges on strategic decision-making that carefully evaluates multiple contextual variables. The framework delineates ten critical factors for selecting between voluntary compliance and command-and-control approaches, recognizing that regulatory strategies are not universally applicable but must be tailored to specific institutional and behavioral contexts.

Key determinants (detailed in Figure 11.1) include enforcement feasibility, compliance quality potential, behavioral visibility, and community-specific characteristics. Critical analytical dimensions encompass over-trust risks, enforcement resource allocation, and compliance sensitivity. Regulatory strategies must differentiate between domains: Personal relationship-driven contexts may benefit from flexible approaches, while high-stakes environments like food safety require rigorous monitoring.

The optimal regulatory strategy emerges through a comprehensive assessment of contextual nuances, including potential positive externalities, normative alignment, and cooperative potential without extensive surveillance. This approach demands a sophisticated understanding of institutional design, behavioral economics, and regulatory responsiveness.

Proportion of Compliers vs. Quality of Compliance

A critical question asked by policymakers and regulators is whether to prioritize increasing the number of compliers or improving the quality of compliance among

[39] Feldman and Lobel. "Behavioral trade-offs."

[40] Blanc, Florentin. *From chasing violations to managing risks: Origins, challenges and evolutions in regulatory inspections*. Edward Elgar Publishing, 2018; Farrow, Katherine, Gilles Grolleau, and Lisette Ibanez. "Social norms and pro-environmental behavior: A review of the evidence." *Ecological Economics* 140 (2017): 1–13; Coglianese, Cary, and David Lazer. "Management-based regulation: Prescribing private management to achieve public goals." *Law & Society Review* 37.4 (2003): 691–730.

FIGURE 11.1 A framework for assessing when to pursue voluntary compliance.
Note: The flowchart was influenced by the concepts developed by Christine Parker.[41]

existing compliers. Simply put: Is it more beneficial to have a larger number of people complying at a basic level, or fewer people complying based on intrinsic motivation or in a voluntary way, more thoroughly and effectively?

[41] Parker, Christine. "Self-regulation and the not-for-profit sector." Legal Studies Research Paper No. 372, Melbourne Law School, University of Melbourne (2019). https://papers.ssrn.com/sol3/papers.cfm?abstract_id=1337278.

In the context of regulatory compliance, we can draw an insightful parallel to concepts from behavioral economics, particularly the notions of extensive and intensive margins.[42] The extensive margin in compliance refers to the number of individuals adhering to regulations – essentially, how many people are complying. This is akin to a company increasing its workforce or adding more shifts. On the other hand, the intensive margin relates to the quality or depth of compliance – how well people are complying. This is comparable to enhancing worker productivity through better training or technology.

Regulators must carefully consider which margin to prioritize based on their specific objectives. For instance, in public health emergencies like pandemics, the extensive margin may be crucial – achieving widespread basic compliance with mask wearing might be more important than perfect adherence by fewer individuals. Conversely, in domains like financial regulation or industrial safety, the intensive margin often takes precedence – thorough compliance by key actors can be more valuable than superficial adherence by many.

Furthermore, these margins may interact in complex ways. High-quality compliance by visible actors might inspire broader adoption (expanding the extensive margin), while widespread basic compliance could gradually deepen as norms become established. The optimal balance likely depends on the specific context, risk profile, and goals of the regulatory framework, but understanding this distinction enables policymakers to craft more nuanced, tailored, and effective compliance strategies

TRUST VS. LEGITIMACY VS. MORALITY: COMPLIANCE EFFECTS

Throughout this book, we have presented a distinct approach that deviates from conventional methods for cultivating trust among individuals. Chapter 7 specifically examines how technology can help build trust while minimizing the potential impact of monitoring on people's behavior. However, our focus has been on the concept of intrinsic motivation and understanding the factors that drive interpersonal and institutional trust.

Although morality plays an important role in promoting compliance among certain individuals, our conclusions regarding cooperation and trust remain somewhat pessimistic. The establishment of trust requires a sufficient number of people willing to cooperate, yet a crucial issue lies in ensuring that cooperation actually occurs, particularly when faced with the problem of conditional cooperation. In this dynamic, an individual's willingness to cooperate is heavily influenced by

42 Gilpatric, Scott M., Christian A. Vossler, and Michael McKee. "Regulatory enforcement with competitive endogenous audit mechanisms." *RAND Journal of Economics* 42.2 (2011): 292–312. This paper discusses how different audit mechanisms can affect compliance behavior, touching on both extensive (frequency of audits) and intensive (depth of audits) margins.

the actions of others, creating an unstable environment. When there are many uncooperative individuals present, it can trigger a breakdown in cooperation, causing even those who were initially willing to cooperate to alter their behavior. Consequently, while some individuals may be intrinsically motivated to cooperate, they often find themselves outnumbered by others who ultimately exhibit different behaviors.

As discussed in *The Law of Good People*,[43] the concept of morality is a double-edged sword. People can interpret it in a way that aligns with their own self-interest and prior beliefs. It could also be influenced by shifts in people's political views about what is considered moral. In contrast, focusing on legitimacy and trust involves examining the procedural and institutional factors that influence intrinsic motivation, which is associated with legitimacy. Therefore, it appears that prioritizing institutional factors pertaining to trust and legitimacy is more effective in encouraging voluntary compliance than investing most efforts in persuading the public about the morality of the law. In that regard, one can expect that trust and legitimacy are less likely to be affected by self-interpretation than morality, though these factors are still shown to be politicized, especially in polarized countries. Nevertheless, while trust and legitimacy may offer greater resistance to individual interpretation compared to morality, they alone cannot guarantee stable compliance.[44]

These conclusions suggest that although it may be possible to trust individuals in certain situations, it is ultimately necessary to supplement this approach with other methods that are less prone to self-serving interpretations. In order to promote trust effectively, we need to make an effort to comprehend how different motivations can work together. This involves encouraging individuals by appealing to their sense of reason and understanding the most effective ways to motivate them. Although personalization has advanced significantly, it remains difficult to predict who will internalize this message. Therefore, a combined approach is essential. This, to some degree, summarizes the key insight of this book.

The "Watchful Trust" Paradigm

One of the greatest challenges in transitioning from command-and-control to trust-based regulation and focusing on intrinsic motivation is the ability to successfully integrate both regulatory approaches without them causing harm to one another. If policymakers did not have to worry about negative interactions between extrinsic and intrinsic measures, they would not need to choose between different regulatory and enforcement methods. They could use all of them simultaneously.

43 Feldman. The law of good people, 173.

44 Feldman. *The law of good people*, 173.

In Chapter 3 of the book, we discussed the crowding-out effect of a sanction-based approach, which poses a significant challenge to using monitoring and sanctions alongside more intrinsic methods. The research discussed in Chapter 4 by Koen Verhoest and colleagues proposes an important approach that seeks to reconcile these strategies. Their paper examines the crucial role of trust in regulatory regimes and its impact on performance and legitimacy. Their research utilizes cross-country survey data to measure trust and distrust among different actors (citizens, businesses, and stakeholders), providing valuable insights into how these relationships affect regulatory outcomes.

Verhoest and colleagues argue that constant suspicion and negative expectations toward other parties create mutual distrust and a zero-sum mentality, hampering the development of shared norms and values. This undermines system legitimacy, as regime actors struggle to accept procedures when they deeply distrust core regulatory actors. However, when regime actors maintain balanced trust – neither excessive suspicion nor blind faith – they're more likely to accept regulatory processes and decisions. This balanced approach supports legitimacy while preserving necessary oversight.

Ensuring Effective Voluntary Compliance through a Hybrid Extrinsic–Intrinsic Approach

Based on this analysis, the focus should be less on whether something is intrinsic or extrinsic, but rather on finding the right combinations between the two. Given that it is difficult to identify a single motivation that will be effective, and that personalization is also challenging, we may need to consider a different approach. For example, morality may be more effective than reasoning as a sole predictor of compliance, but when it needs to be combined with deterrence, reasoning may be more effective than morality. Given the significant role of heterogeneity, doctrinal context, and self-serving biases in shaping behavior, we challenge the notion that intrinsic motivation can operate effectively in the absence of external enforcement. Policymakers, when selecting the best regulatory tool to promote internal change, must consider which approach is least likely to be undermined by necessary extrinsic measures. This consideration is crucial for *ensuring effective* voluntary compliance.

For example, Kirchler and colleagues proposed the "slippery slope" framework in the context of taxes. They argue that understanding both the power and trust in authorities is crucial for understanding enforced and voluntary compliance and that it is impossible to focus only on one of them.[45] This paradigm could be seen as an important demonstration for a combined extrinsic–intrinsic regulatory approach.

[45] Kogler, Christoph, Stephan Muehlbacher, and Erich Kirchler. "Testing the 'slippery slope framework' among self-employed taxpayers." *Economics of Governance* 16 (2015): 125–142.

WHAT CAN STATES LEARN FROM RELIGION REGARDING INTERNALIZATION?

When considering examples of how populations can voluntarily internalize and follow rules, religion often comes to mind as a prime illustration. There are clearly limited enforcement mechanisms in place to ensure that believers follow the rules, while all religions emphasize the importance of adhering to rules when people are intrinsically motivated to do so, often viewing those who demonstrate higher levels of compliance are true believers.[46]

At least anecdotally, religious Jews demonstrate remarkable behavioral control by abstaining from technology, including phones, during the Sabbath.[47] Furthermore, even observant Jewish smokers who struggle to go without cigarettes for an hour maintain this restriction. Similarly, while most dietary interventions fail long term,[48] observant Jews, as do observant Muslims, consistently avoid certain foods throughout their lives.[49] These examples suggest that internalized religious restrictions can effectively modify addictive behaviors, even without external enforcement or reputation consequences, as these activities could theoretically be done in private.

Thus, in the context of religion and behavioral change, this can provide valuable insights into how states can encourage citizens to internalize certain values, which could inform ways to increase voluntary compliance with regulations. Throughout history, religious institutions have played a crucial role in developing intrinsic motivation through diverse methods, successfully encouraging adherents to internalize and act upon shared values and norms. These approaches can serve as valuable lessons for state institutions seeking to internalize values.[50]

Religious teachings often emphasize the importance of moral values, such as compassion and honesty, which can become deeply ingrained in individuals' motivational structures.[51] Religion can also provide a framework for finding meaning in life, giving people a sense of purpose that guides their actions and motivations.[52]

[46] Kagan, Robert A., Neil Gunningham, and Dorothy Thornton. "Fear, duty, and regulatory compliance: Lessons from three research projects." In *Explaining compliance: Business responses to regulation*, edited by Christine Parker and Vibeke Lehmann Nielsen, Edward Elgar Publishing, 2011: 37–58.

[47] Dein, Simon, and Kate M. Loewenthal. "The mental health benefits and costs of Sabbath observance among Orthodox Jews." *Journal of Religion and Health* 52 (2013): 1382–1390.

[48] Stroebe, Wolfgang, et al. "Why most dieters fail but some succeed: A goal conflict model of eating behavior." In *The goal conflict model of eating behavior*, edited by Wolfgang Stroebe, Routledge, 2017: 181–238.

[49] Regenstein, Joe M., Muhammad M. Chaudry, and Carrie E. Regenstein. "The kosher and halal food laws." *Comprehensive Reviews in Food Science and Food Safety* 2.3 (2003): 111–127.

[50] Flor, Douglas L., and Nancy Flanagan Knapp. "Transmission and transaction: Predicting adolescents' internalization of parental religious values." *Journal of Family Psychology* 15.4 (2001): 627–645.

[51] Allport, Gordon W., and J. Michael Ross. "Personal religious orientation and prejudice." *Journal of Personality and Social Psychology* 5.4 (1967): 432–443.

[52] Park, Crystal L. "Religion as a meaning-making framework in coping with life stress." *Journal of Social Issues* 61.4 (2005): 707–729.

These insights suggest that states could potentially encourage the internalization of values by defining clear moral frameworks and fostering a shared sense of purpose among citizens.

However, the use of religious approaches to promote voluntary compliance is limited in its effectiveness. This is due to religious institutions often rely on creating a sense of community to reinforce shared values and motivations, which may be challenging for states to replicate on a large scale.[53] Furthermore, studies on the concept of gods who punish suggest that fear of punishment, rather than purely intrinsic motivation, may play a significant role in religious compliance.[54] This raises questions about whether internalizing value is sustainable and authentic.

Like religious institutions, each state has the means to affect intrinsic motivation. For example, education is essential in shaping values and beliefs,[55] while public discourse has the power to frame issues and influence public opinion. Laws and policies can create incentives that indirectly affect intrinsic motivation.[56] However, the effectiveness of these state-driven approaches in changing deeply held beliefs and values remains uncertain.[57]

The long-term sustainability of changes in intrinsic motivation, whether brought about by religion or the state, is a key area of uncertainty.[58] Although it has been demonstrated both behaviorally and philosophically that religious practices, such as repetition and habit formation, can influence behavior in the long run, it is uncertain how well states can replicate these processes. Moreover, the extent to which people genuinely internalize religious teachings and state policies, as opposed to simply superficially adopting them, remains a subject of debate.[59] As states explore the potential of learning from religious practices in order to promote the internalization of values, they must also navigate the complexities and limitations that come with adapting these strategies to the unique context of civic life and governance. The challenge is to balance the potential benefits of promoting

[53] Graham, Jesse, and Jonathan Haidt. "Beyond beliefs: Religions bind individuals into moral communities." *Personality and Social Psychology Review* 14.1 (2010): 140–150.

[54] Johnson, Dominic, and Oliver Krüger. "The good of wrath: Supernatural punishment and the evolution of cooperation." *Political Theology* 5.2 (2004): 159–176. For a more comprehensive analysis of this effect see: Johnson, Dominic. *God is watching you: How the fear of God makes us human*. Oxford University Press, 2015.

[55] Dee, Thomas S. "Are there civic returns to education?" *Journal of Public Economics* 88.9–10 (2004): 1697–1720.

[56] Frey, Bruno S. *Not just for the money: An economic theory of personal motivation*. Edward Elgar Publishing, 1997.

[57] Maio, Gregory R., et al. "Ideologies, values, attitudes, and behavior." In *Handbook of social psychology*, edited by John Delamater, Springer, 2006: 283–308.

[58] Wrzesniewski, Amy, et al. "Multiple types of motives don't multiply the motivation of West Point cadets." *Proceedings of the National Academy of Sciences* 111.30 (2014): 10990–10995.

[59] Kirkpatrick, Lee A., and Ralph W. Hood Jr. "Intrinsic–extrinsic religious orientation: The boon or bane of contemporary psychology of religion?" *Journal for the Scientific Study of Religion* 29 (1990): 442–462.

intrinsic motivation with the practical limitations and ethical concerns of governmental intervention in individual values and beliefs.

COMMUNITY VERSUS STATE GOVERNANCE

Community-based governance provides several advantages to promoting voluntary compliance and intrinsic motivation compared to state government. In close-knit communities, monitoring mechanisms tend to be more effective due to the frequent and intimate interactions among members.[60] For example, reputation plays a critical role in these settings, as individuals are motivated to maintain a positive image among their peers, leading to increased compliance with community norms.[61] In community settings, people's true character and intentions are more transparent, making it difficult for individuals to conceal their true nature from neighbors who observe their daily behaviors.[62] This visibility can lead to a stronger and more internalized commitment to community values and regulations, as people are more likely to internalize and act upon these norms when they know they are being observed by those with whom they with interact regularly.[63] Furthermore, community settings create a sense of personal connection and foster a sense of belonging that can motivate individuals to perform their civic duties more diligently than they might for a distant state authority that has little knowledge of their personal circumstances.[64] Adopting a localized approach to governance can enable regulatory authorities to tap into deeper wells of motivation by leveraging social ties and local knowledge to encourage compliance. This is often more effective than centralized state governance, which often struggles to achieve similar results.[65]

PERCEIVED VS. ACTUAL TRUST BY THE STATE

While we have raised doubts about the government's ability to rely solely on intrinsic motivation and voluntary compliance, especially in areas where the factors discussed here are prevalent, it's important to recognize the nuanced approach required in effective governance. The lack of high and stable intrinsic motivation in certain contexts necessitates a more complex strategy than simple reliance on voluntary compliance.[66]

[60] Ostrom, Elinor. *Governing the commons: The evolution of institutions for collective action*. Cambridge University Press, 1990.

[61] Posner, Eric A. *Law and social norms*. Harvard University Press, 2000.

[62] Ellickson, Robert C. *Order without law: How neighbors settle disputes*. Harvard University Press, 1991.

[63] Putnam, Robert D. *Bowling alone: The collapse and revival of American community*. Simon Schuster, 2000.

[64] Scott, James C. *Seeing like a state: How certain schemes to improve the human condition have failed*. Yale University Press, 1998.

[65] Ostrom, Elinor. *Understanding institutional diversity*. Princeton University Press, 2005.

[66] Cooter, Robert. "Law and unified social theory." *Journal of Law and Society* 22.1 (1995): 50–67.

However, there are significant advantages to fostering an environment where people, especially those who have demonstrated trustworthiness, feel trusted by the state. This sense of trust can lead to increased cooperation, improved civic engagement, and a stronger social contract between citizens and government. Therefore, there is a strategic advantage for the state in creating the impression of trust, even if the actual level of trust needs to be carefully managed due to practical constraints.

It's crucial to note that this approach is not about deceiving the public, as such deception is likely to be counterproductive and erode public trust in the long term. Instead, the suggestion is similar to Dan Cohen's acoustic separation approach,[67] which explores ways in which the state can emphasize to the public that they are being trusted and demonstrate how compliance with rules and regulations generates meaningful benefits for both individual citizens and society at large.

In this context, monitoring systems, especially those utilizing advanced technologies, should be less conspicuous than traditional methods like publicly announced speed cameras. The goal is to reduce the feeling among citizens that they are under constant surveillance, which can be detrimental to the sense of trustworthiness and autonomy. This doesn't mean eliminating necessary oversight, but rather designing and implementing it in ways that are less intrusive and more respectful of citizens' privacy and dignity.

The integration of technological monitoring with a differentiated approach to trust-based regulation, as developed in Chapter 7, presents a promising avenue for enhancing societal cohesion and governance efficiency. By leveraging past behavioral data to identify trustworthy individuals, states can foster a positive reinforcement cycle where those deemed reliable are made to feel trusted, thereby encouraging continued beneficial behaviors without imposing additional risks on the public. This targeted approach, when implemented with careful consideration of cross-cultural effects as explored in Chapter 6, has the potential to elevate overall trust levels within a country, promoting solidarity among citizens.

However, the success of such a system hinges on its precise application – trusting the right segments of the population in appropriate contexts while minimizing potential costs and risks. Misplaced trust could backfire, leading to public perception of regulatory incompetence and a subsequent decline in trust-based governance. Therefore, the implementation of this approach demands a delicate balance: maintaining the myriad benefits of increased trust while carefully managing associated risks. This necessitates robust mechanisms for transparency, accountability, and dynamic reassessment of trust status, as well as safeguards against potential abuse. Moreover, the cultural adaptability discussed in Chapter 6, and comprehensive public education, are crucial for the system's effectiveness and acceptance. By thoughtfully navigating these challenges and building upon the technological

[67] Dan-Cohen, Meir. "Decision rules and conduct rules: On acoustic separation in criminal law." *Harvard Law Review* 97.3 (1984): 625–677.

mentoring concepts outlined in Chapter 7, states can harness the power of trust to enhance social harmony and governmental efficiency, ultimately creating a more cohesive and productive society.

By striking this balance – emphasizing trust while maintaining necessary oversight – the state can potentially achieve better compliance outcomes. This approach recognizes the complexity of human motivation and seeks to leverage both intrinsic and extrinsic factors to encourage lawful behavior and civic responsibility.

CONCLUDING REMARKS

This exploration of voluntary compliance reveals a nuanced landscape where trust-based regulation offers profound yet context-specific benefits. While voluntary compliance promises significant advantages – reduced enforcement costs, enhanced social cohesion, and increased governance legitimacy – its effectiveness varies considerably across contexts. Rather than viewing voluntary compliance as a universal solution, policymakers must adopt a more sophisticated, differentiated approach that recognizes the multidimensional nature of compliance behavior.

Intrinsic motivation undoubtedly plays a crucial role in fostering voluntary compliance, but the evidence suggests its limitations for ensuring consistent compliance across heterogeneous populations. The challenge lies in nurturing intrinsic motivation while acknowledging that it cannot be the sole foundation of regulatory policy. The persistent tension between individual autonomy and collective welfare, combined with the reality of conditional cooperators and free riders, necessitates complementary approaches that balance trust with appropriate oversight.

When evaluating voluntary compliance strategies, we must transcend narrow, immediate metrics and consider their broader impacts across multiple dimensions. The true value of voluntary compliance emerges when we examine its long-term effects on social trust, institutional legitimacy, and cultural norms – outcomes that conventional cost-benefit analyses often fail to capture. Regulatory approaches that successfully build relationships between citizens and government may generate positive externalities that extend far beyond their immediate regulatory contexts, creating virtuous cycles of cooperation that enhance governance across domains.

The challenge of heterogeneity in compliance motivations presents a significant obstacle, yet also offers an opportunity for more personalized regulatory approaches. By developing frameworks that recognize differences across individuals, contexts, and regulatory domains, policymakers can create more adaptive systems that enhance voluntary compliance while maintaining necessary safeguards. Technological advances offer promising avenues for this differentiated approach, potentially enabling less intrusive monitoring that preserves the benefits of trust while mitigating its risks.

Our research consistently suggests that legitimacy-based approaches may prove more effective and sustainable than those grounded primarily in moral appeals. By emphasizing procedural fairness, transparency, and institutional trustworthiness, regulators can foster compliance motivations that transcend ideological divisions and personal moral frameworks, creating more stable foundations for voluntary compliance.

Community-based governance models offer valuable insights for enhancing voluntary compliance, particularly in creating environments where social norms reinforce cooperative behavior. The success of local governance in fostering compliance suggests that regulatory approaches that leverage existing social connections and shared identities may achieve greater success than top-down state mechanisms alone. This insight points toward hybrid regulatory systems that integrate state oversight with community-based governance.

Rather than treating regulatory tools as isolated interventions, policymakers should conceptualize them as integrated systems where different approaches complement and reinforce one another. Experimental legislation combined with machine-learning techniques offers promising avenues for developing these integrated approaches, allowing regulators to systematically explore different combinations of regulatory tools while learning from their interactions.

The path forward lies not in choosing between trust and verification, but in developing sophisticated regulatory ecosystems that balance these approaches appropriately across contexts. By acknowledging the complexity of human motivation, the importance of institutional design, and the value of cultural context, we can develop regulatory frameworks that harness the benefits of voluntary compliance while protecting against its potential pitfalls. This balanced approach promises more effective, efficient, and equitable regulatory outcomes – building societies where cooperation flourishes not despite regulation, but because of it.

FUTURE RESEARCH

Building on our analysis of voluntary compliance, future research must address specific knowledge gaps through methodological rigor and interdisciplinary approaches. The modest effect sizes and inconsistent findings surrounding intrinsic motivation necessitate a more structured research agenda focused on measurable outcomes and contextual variables.

A primary research need is the development of standardized measurement instruments for voluntary compliance. Current methodological inconsistencies create validity concerns and limit cross-study comparisons. Researchers should establish operational definitions and validated scales that distinguish between different forms of voluntary compliance (noncoerced versus intrinsically motivated) and capture both behavioral and attitudinal dimensions of compliance.

Future research should move beyond evaluating isolated interventions to examine regulatory tools as integrated systems. Factorial experimental designs would be particularly valuable, as they allow researchers to systematically test various combinations of trust-based and verification-based elements across different regulatory contexts. Such designs would not only measure immediate compliance outcomes but also capture secondary effects on trust, legitimacy, and social capital. This approach would reveal important interaction effects between regulatory strategies and contextual factors that current single-intervention studies often miss.

The temporal dimension of voluntary compliance remains underexplored. Longitudinal panel studies tracking compliance behaviors and motivations over extended periods would provide critical data on the sustainability of trust-based regulatory effects and potential adaptation processes. These studies should incorporate measures of cultural shift and institutional trust to determine whether short-term behavioral changes translate into lasting normative change.

Advanced computational approaches offer promising avenues for addressing complex research challenges in voluntary compliance. Large language models (LLMs) could analyze vast regulatory corpora across jurisdictions to identify patterns in regulatory language, implementation approaches, and compliance outcomes. These models could help researchers understand the nuanced relationships between regulatory framing, cultural context, and compliance behavior, potentially revealing insights that traditional analytical approaches might miss. LLMs could also be employed to analyze qualitative data from interviews and focus groups with regulators and regulated entities, extracting themes related to trust, motivation, and compliance that might otherwise remain obscured.

Data-driven decision support systems represent another frontier in voluntary compliance research. By analyzing comprehensive datasets from regulatory documents, including ex ante impact assessments and post-implementation reviews, researchers can develop predictive models that evaluate intervention effectiveness based on factors such as compliance costs, social control mechanisms, institutional trust, and cultural norms. Such tools could help regulators move beyond binary choices to more nuanced, context-sensitive regulatory approaches.

Cross-cultural research requires particular methodological attention. Comparative studies should employ measurement invariance testing to ensure that instruments capture the same constructs across cultural contexts. Multilevel modeling techniques can account for cultural variations while identifying universal principles of voluntary compliance. Machine-learning algorithms trained on structured datasets from diverse regulatory environments could identify which approaches transfer successfully across cultures and which require significant adaptation to local contexts.

Translational research requires systematic documentation of regulatory implementation processes. Researchers should partner with regulatory agencies to develop standardized protocols for monitoring implementation fidelity, measuring compliance outcomes across multiple dimensions (extent, quality, sustainability), and assessing unintended consequences. These partnerships would generate practical knowledge while establishing evidence-based frameworks for regulatory decision-making.

By addressing these specific research priorities, scholars can develop a more robust empirical foundation for understanding when, how, and why voluntary compliance approaches succeed or fail. This knowledge would enable policymakers to make more informed decisions about regulatory design, balancing the potential benefits of trust-based approaches with appropriate safeguards against exploitation and noncompliance. Ultimately, this balanced approach may help bridge the gap between ideal regulatory theory and practical implementation, creating more effective and sustainable governance systems that benefit both states and their citizens.

Index

For EU product safety concerns, contact us at Calle de José Abascal, 56–1°,
28003 Madrid, Spain or eugpsr@cambridge.org.

www.ingramcontent.com/pod-product-compliance
Ingram Content Group UK Ltd.
Pitfield, Milton Keynes, MK11 3LW, UK
UKHW022139240226
468380UK00018B/375
* 9 7 8 1 0 0 9 0 6 0 9 4 3 *